Handedness and Brain Asymmetry

In this follow up to the influential *Left, Right, Hand and Brain* (1985) Marian Annett draws on a working lifetime of research to help provide answers to crucial questions. Central to her argument is the Right Shift Theory – her original and innovative contribution to the field that seeks to explain the relationships between left- and right-handedness and left- and right-brain specialisation. The theory proposes that handedness in humans and our nonhuman primate relations depends on chance but that chance is weighted towards right-handedness in most people by an agent of right-hemisphere disadvantage. It argues for the existence of a single gene for right shift (RS +) that evolved in humans to aid the growth of speech in the left hemisphere of the brain.

The Right Shift Theory has possible implications for a wide range of questions about human abilities and disabilities, including verbal and nonverbal intelligence, educational progress and dyslexia, spatial reasoning, sporting skills, and mental illness. It continues to be at the cutting edge of research, solving problems and generating new avenues of investigation – most recently the surprising idea that a mutant RS + gene might be involved in the causes of schizophrenia and autism.

Handedness and Brain Asymmetry will make fascinating reading for students and researchers in psychology and neurology, educationalists, and anyone with a keen interest in why people have different talents and weaknesses.

Marian Annett studied psychology at Bedford College and the Institute of Psychiatry in the University of London. Early work as a clinical psychologist was followed by research and teaching in several universities.

Handedness and Brain Asymmetry

The Right Shift Theory

Marian Annett

First published 2002 by Psychology Press
27 Church Road, Hove, East Sussex BN3 2FA

Simultaneously published in the USA and Canada
by Taylor & Francis Inc,
29 West 35th Street, New York, NY 10001

Psychology Press is a part of the Taylor & Francis Group

Typeset in 10/12pt Goudy by Graphicraft Limited, Hong Kong
Printed and bound in Great Britain by Biddles Ltd, Guildford and
King's Lynn
Cover design by Leigh Hurlock

British Library Cataloguing in Publication Data
A catalogue record for this book is available from the British Library

Library of Congress Cataloging-in-Publication Data
A catalog record for this book is available from the Library of Congress

ISBN 1-84169-104-6

To all my family

Contents

Preface

This book began many years ago as a revision of *Left, Right, Hand and Brain: The Right Shift Theory* (Annett, 1985a). Progress was slow because of ongoing research and because at several stages, new discoveries halted the writing entirely. Very little now remains of the original text, hence the new title.

The 1985 book was written in two main parts. The first part was a review of the literature, independent of my own theory, outlining what I took to be the chief problems that needed to be addressed. The second part was an exposition of the right shift (RS) theory and the solutions it offered to these problems. The present book does not have space for a comprehensive review of the literature because there is so much to say about the RS theory itself. The first chapter outlines the puzzles the RS theory sought to solve. Further exposition of other theories is deferred to chapter 16, when contrasts can be made with the RS theory, as explained in previous chapters.

The RS theory of 1985 remains unchanged in all essentials but it has been greatly strengthened by subsequent discoveries. Some recent developments were quite unanticipated in 1985, including the application to eye-dominance in families, and the predictability of combinations of asymmetries (hand and eye, writing and throwing, handedness and planum temporale). It was especially surprising to discover a possible application to schizophrenia and autism.

Between the introduction and conclusion, the book falls into four main sections. Chapters 2–5 describe the fundamentals of the research and theoretical analyses of the 1960s and 1970s on which the RS theory is based. Chapters 6–9 describe further developments as new problems were investigated in the light of the model and findings. The basic question was how do people vary for asymmetries of hand and brain. Chapters 10–14 tackle the critical question of the implications of the theory for individual differences. The RS theory led to new ideas about differences for speech, literacy, cognitive and motor skills. Most unexpectedly, it offered a hypothesis as to the causes of schizophrenia and autism. The RS story is told in chapters 2–14 without the distractions of alternative viewpoints. Chapters 15–16 describe independent replications and challenges, both to the specifics of research findings and to theoretical positions. The final chapter (17) summarises the main points of the RS analysis and looks at further questions about mechanisms and evolutionary origins.

The reader should start with the last chapter, if it is wished to begin with an overview.

My indebtedness to many people over these 40 years research is too great to be acknowledged in full. The work began at the Warneford and Park Hospitals, Oxford, in collaboration with Dr. Christopher Ounsted. It continued at the Universities of Sheffield, Aberdeen, Hull, The Open University, Lanchester Polytechnic (now Coventry University) and the University of Leicester. I am grateful for the facilities for research offered at all of these institutions. Thanks must be given to J.P.N. Phillips who drew my attention to the technique of association analysis, and to M.J. Norman who wrote the computer program for this analysis, in the heroic days of programming in the 1960s. More recent help with computer programming was kindly given by John Thompson and James Annett. John Annett suggested and helped to design the peg board for the assessment of hemiplegic children and subsequently collaborated in studies of hand skill in normal participants.

I am grateful to the geneticists who responded to my queries, especially Dr. C. Blank, Dr. Charles Smith and Professor Alec Jeffreys. Correspondence over several years with the late James Shields was a highly valued source of information and advice. T.P. Hutchinson and John Wilkin assisted with aspects of genetic analysis. Raphael Gillett answered many statistical and methodological queries. Any errors of application are, of course, my own.

I am indebted to teachers who permitted me to examine their pupils, to successive cohorts of psychology undergraduates who tested each other in laboratory classes, and to families who responded to my media appeals and welcomed me into their homes. The study of children with hemiplegia depended on the collaboration of Dr. R.J. Pugh and his fellow consultant paediatricians. I am grateful to Mrs. Beve Hornsby for inviting me to study pupils attending her remedial clinics for dyslexics. The late Dr. Freda Newcombe kindly allowed me access to the British World War Two Head Injury Archive. Information on the handedness of tennis players was given to me by the late C.M. Jones, and on cricketers by Norman Harris. My indebtedness to William Demarest for sending me a copy of his Ph.D. thesis is evident in chapter 15. I thank John Ashworth for drawing many of the Figures.

I am grateful to research asssistants Patrick Hudson, Ann Turner, Diana Kilshaw, Adrian Davis, Margaret Manning, Elizabeth Eglinton and Pamela Smythe. John, Lucy and James Annett often acted as unofficial research assistants, to accompany me on family visits.

Financial support is gratefully acknowledged for research grants from The Medical Research Council, The Spastics Society, The Social Science Research Council, the research fund of Coventry University and the Wellcome Trust. My final thanks must be to the patience and support of my husband, John Annett, and all my family.

Illustrations

Figures

Tables

Part I

Introduction

1 The puzzle of handedness and cerebral speech

This book is about *differences* between humans for handedness and for brain asymmetry. It has been known at least since the time that Galen was a surgeon to the gladiators in Rome that each side of the body is controlled by the opposite side of the brain. It was not until the mid 19th century that Paul Broca proposed his famous rule, "On parle avec l'hémisphère gauche" (Broca, 1865). Broca had performed post mortem examinations on a number of patients who had lost their ability to speak but were able to understand speech. He found lesions in the left frontal lobe in all cases. A few years later, the Austrian neurologist Carl Wernicke described another type of speech disorder in which patients produced a stream of fluent speech that was incomprehensible, and the patients themselves could not understand what was said to them. The cerebral lesion in these cases was in the region of the superior gyrus of the temporal lobe, again on the left side. Figure 1.1 illustrates some key features of the human cerebral cortex and the regions now known as Broca's and Wernicke's areas. Disorders of language may be associated with lesions over a wide area of the left cerebral hemisphere, with varying patterns of loss of function.

The left cerebral hemisphere was called "dominant" by neurologists when it was realised that for most people it is the side that controls both speech and the preferred hand, the right. By contrast, the right hemisphere seemed to have no major function and was termed "minor" or "non-dominant". The only disorders that were clearly linked to lesions of the right hemisphere and not the left were forgetting how to get dressed (dressing apraxia) and curious disorders of awareness of the left side of space, left-sided neglect (Brain, 1941). One of the main pursuits of modern neuropsychology has been to show that the right hemisphere has its own special functions, albeit ones not dependent on language. The split-brain operations of the 1960s confirmed that there is a pattern of cerebral specialisation, present in most people, the left brain for speech and language and the right brain for certain types of nonverbal functions. The latter include skills that cannot be put into words easily, such as recognising faces, understanding spatial relationships and interpreting non-speech sounds. The nature of cerebral specialisation continues to be explored, as will be considered further throughout the text. As a starting point, the term "cerebral dominance" (CD) will be used to refer to "the cerebral hemisphere that serves propositional speech", that is, the ability to express ideas in spoken words.

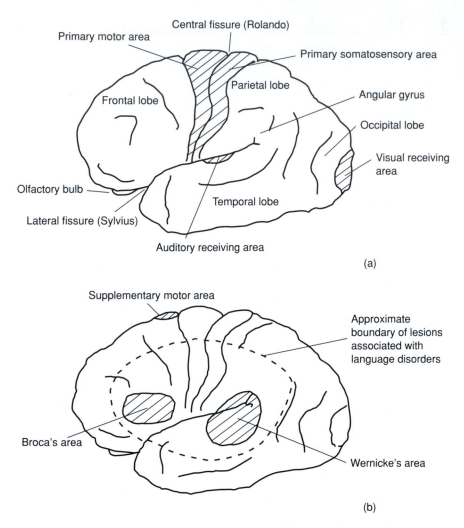

Figure 1.1 (a) Human cerebral cortex, lateral view; (b) language associated cortex.

What has been greatly underestimated in accounts of brain specialisation, in both popular and scientific literature, is the extent to which people *differ* for these key asymmetries of hand and brain. We know that some people are left-handed and also that some people have CD on the right side. Do the two atypical asymmetries go together? They do not. What rules govern their association? This question was of particular interest to some of the founders of modern neuropsychology (Hécaen and Piercy, 1956; Luria, 1970; Zangwill, 1960). The question became unfashionable as researchers sought for more detailed and universal specifications of left brain versus right brain functions. The puzzle of the relationship between handedness and cerebral dominance is the focus of the research described in this book. The puzzle leads to other questions about human evolution, genetics, brain and nervous system, skill, intelligence and mental illness. The purpose of this book is to outline my findings and conclusions to date.

My research on relationships between hand and brain asymmetries began some 40 years ago. It is a continuing detective inquiry that has followed certain principles. The first principle was to practise systematic doubt because the literature was already vast before the explosion of research since the 1960s. It seemed to me that there was more myth than fact, more speculation than evidence, in what was written about handedness. I saw my task as to strip away the many layers of opinion and surmise, to discover the key facts. As in an archaeological dig, I aimed to discover the bare bones from which a secure reconstruction could then be attempted. However, speculative theories continued to grow at a great rate, like the dragon's teeth that turned into warriors faster than they could be slain. Even worse, elements of my own theory became embedded in new theories in ways that glossed over key points. This led to inaccurate accounts of my theory in the literature. In order to understand the right shift (RS) theory, it is necessary to follow each step of the detective trail, as explained in the sequence of chapters of this book. A new map must be drawn. A few changes to the old map will not do. However, for readers who prefer to read their detective stories knowing the solution to the mystery, the last chapter summarises the key facts and assumptions.

The second related principle of the detective inquiry was that my theory must rest on evidence that was highly reliable. Each stage of the argument depends on empirical research, the chief findings tested by replication before they were accepted. At each critical stage for the theory, there was some mathematical regularity. This was often surprising, but led to new and productive ways of looking at the data. The building blocks of the RS theory are tied together through reliable quantitative relationships. It was the quantitative analyses that revealed links between the evidence from neurology to genetics, from genetics to ability, and from neuropsychology to mental illness. To one commentator (Michel, 1995), the theory is reminiscent of Dr. Pangloss, Voltaire's optimistic philosopher. This would be true if the theory were just a hopeful story. On the contrary, the theory was discovered through empirical research and analysis over many years. It was because the *numbers fitted* that the theory seemed to me logically necessary, not just a plausible tale. For readers who are maths aversive, numbers will be relegated to appendices when possible. It is important to understand, however, that the theory is supported by quantitative analyses that agree with its predictions.

The mutual interplay of theory and data in the advance of knowledge is an interesting topic for the philosophy of science. It touches on the present work in several ways. I have collected empirical data on as large a scale as feasible, not just for the sake of counting, but because I believed that handedness needed investigation as a feature of human biology, using samples representative of the population. Because the atypical patterns of interest are relatively infrequent, samples must be large to make reliable estimates of frequencies. The empirical data gathering was guided by specific questions. To those who suppose that theoretical pre-conceptions might have biased the research process, I would point out that the most interesting outcomes were often the most surprising. It is the "happy surprises" or "aha!" experiences that make scientific research worthwhile. The RS theory rewarded me with several. Popper (1963) pointed out that no scientific theory is ever "proven" because it might yet be bettered by a more comprehensive theory. However, a sense of scientific progress depends on finding puzzle pieces that seem to drop into place. The new or improved picture is a pleasant surprise but does it make sense in the light of the pieces assembled before? Do previous assumptions need reappraisal? What does the new puzzle edge suggest about the next pieces to look for? The RS theory has been fruitful because it suggested how some old puzzles could be solved and then led to new questions that gave further happy discoveries in their turn, sometimes many years later. The RS story depends on a dialectic interplay between new findings and developing theory. It was not dreamt up in a single act of creative imagination.

A major change in the scientific picture is what Kuhn (1970) called a paradigm shift. The RS theory leads to a new way of looking at handedness and cerebral dominance. Its main innovation, the idea that chance plays a key role in the determination of asymmetry, is now commonplace in theories of handedness. However, alternative theories use the chance postulate in ways that differ from the RS theory. Some try to assimilate it to more traditional paradigms, as will be considered in chapter 16. Psychologists face particular problems in their philosophy of science, partly due to the inherent difficulties of doing psychology scientifically, but also due to the statistical strait-jackets they have adopted as guarantees of scientific respectability. If a result is "statistically significant" at the 5% level, it is worth attention, otherwise not. The argument for statistical significance depends on the idea that the result should not have occurred "by chance" more frequently than 5 per 100 (or 1 in 20) times. The RS theory suggests that the effects that need to be investigated occur against a universal background of chance asymmetries. It is not surprising if effects are difficult to detect. Some reliable trends, such as the slightly greater frequency of left-handedness in males than females, or in dyslexics than non-dyslexics, are not likely to be statistically significant unless samples are very large. However, the direction of trends is often consistent over studies. The RS theory does not depend on a single test of statistical significance, but rather on a body of interrelated evidence that suggests a new way of approaching questions about hand and brain asymmetry. Reports of "failures" of the RS theory are considered in chapter 15.

HANDEDNESS AND CEREBRAL DOMINANCE AS A PROBLEM IN NEUROLOGY

The rule that humans tend to depend on the left cerebral hemisphere for the control of speech was probably discovered by a French country physician, Marc

Dax, but it was not recognised by neurologists until its formulation by Broca (Critchley, 1970). Modern brain imaging techniques show that both hemispheres are activated during speech, but the left typically more extensively than the right (Frackowiak, 1994). Most treatments of cerebral specialisation assume that the left hemisphere speech rule is so general that exceptions can be safely ignored. Or if there is some doubt, it is considered sufficient to restrict research samples to right-handers, often males only, in the belief that unwanted variability will be avoided. This view is almost certainly mistaken. The natural variability of the general population is greatly under-estimated.

How were exceptions to the classic rule regarded by neurologists? There is some dispute about Broca's own views. Eling (1984) describes Broca's original paper as discussing the existence of exceptions for speech laterality, just as there are exceptions to the rule of right-handedness, and warning the reader not assume that the two exceptions go together, "Because it seems to me absolutely not necessary that the motoric part and the intellectual part of each of the hemispheres are solidary to one another" (Broca, 1865, p. 386). Harris (1991) argued that the balance of Broca's later writings on this point suggests that he inclined to the mirror-reversal or opposite rule, that left-handedness would go with right-brainedness as right-handedness goes with left-brainedness. Whatever Broca actually believed, and in spite of many publications on "exceptions" to the opposite rule, the belief that hand and brain asymmetry "ought to go together" is so compelling that it continues to dominate accounts of handedness and brain asymmetry. It was asserted recently by the medical correspondent of *The Times* newspaper.

The search for rules of association between speech side and handedness depends on exceptions, people with disorders of speech (dysphasias) following right-sided brain lesions and left-handers with unilateral cerebral lesions of the speech areas in either hemisphere, with or without dysphasia. Cases of interest are infrequent in the experience of any one clinician, but many individual case reports were published in the medical literature. Goodglass and Quadfasel (1954) found 110 cases of left-handers with unilateral lesions of the speech areas described in the literature, and added 13 cases of their own. The speech hemisphere was the left in 53% and the right in 47%. They concluded that, "the tendency for language to centre predominantly in the left hemisphere is in large measure independent of handedness" (p. 531).

There are several difficulties about evidence drawn from cases in the literature. Reports are more likely to be published if cases are deemed interesting, so there is a danger of selection bias. Unusual cerebral laterality may be missed by clinicians in the same way that infrequent and unexpected signals are often missed. There was an important problem due to prejudices against the use of the left-hand for writing, eating and other "visible" actions. Until about the mid 20th century these pressures were severe. Neurologists were aware that most left-handers had been forced to use the right-hand, and had become what they termed "shifted sinistrals". Hence, neurologists searched for *any evidence of left-handed tendencies* in the patient and relatives. It was not realised that such a

Table 1.1 Hypotheses for the cerebral speech of left-handers

Right	Classic contralateral rule
Left	Goodglass and Quadfasel (1954)
	Penfield and Roberts (1959)
Either	Bingley (1958)
	Chesher (1936)
	Humphrey and Zangwill (1952)
Both	Conrad (1949)
	Hécaen and Piercy (1956)
Some combination of the above	Roberts (1969)
	Zangwill (1960)

search will reveal some evidence of non-right-handedness in about half of the population (see chapter 2). Thus, neurologists came to believe that right CD does not occur in right-handers, but only in left-handers. On the contrary, the RS analysis led to the very surprising idea that people with right CD should include more right- than left-handers (see chapter 4).

What theories were proposed as to the speech laterality of left-handers? There are five logically possible alternatives, right, left, either, both or some combination of these, listed in Table 1.1, along with their proponents. The classic "opposite" rule (speech in the right hemisphere contralateral to the preferred left-hand) will not do because, as shown by Goodglass and Quadfasel above, left CD is at least as frequent as right CD in left-handers. If the speech hemisphere is independent of handedness, then left CD should be as prevalent in left-handers as in right-handers, but this is not true. Penfield and Roberts (1959) supported the "left for everyone" rule because they found very few cases of right CD (1.5%) among their series of patients undergoing elective brain surgery for the treatment of epilepsy. However, they disregarded several cases of brief speech disturbance that they attributed to "articulation" problems only. The "either hemisphere" rule was suggested by Chesher (1936) for people with mixed-hand preference; definite left-handers were expected to follow the contralateral rule. Bingley (1958) supported the "either" rule for all left-handers. In his own sample there were approximately equal numbers with left and right CD, as in the literature. The "both" rule, or the "bilateral speech" hypothesis, seems to have been prompted by a report that speech disorder was more frequent in left-handers (38%) than right-handers (26%) among German World War Two (WW2) head injury cases (Conrad, 1949). Speech disorders were also considered more often transient in left-handers. The bilateral speech hypothesis was strengthened by a report that left-handers were more likely than right-handers to experience speech disorders during epileptic auras (warnings of attack) independently of the hemisphere affected (Hécaen and Piercy, 1956). Finally, a combination of these theories acknowledges that left-handers may have right or left or bilateral speech, in proportions unknown.

How can progress be made on this question? Oliver Zangwill (1967) realised that the problem should be studied as one of human biology, in samples representative of the general population, not *ad hoc* collections of clinical cases. What was needed was a series of cases with strictly unilateral brain lesions, studied for speech disorder and for handedness, but drawn from the population in such a way that inclusion in the series was independent of handedness or lesion side. (Of course patients with brain injuries are not representative of the general population *after* their injury, a point that worried some of my students, but they were representative *before* their head injury, in consecutive series of stroke patients seen in a neurology service, or service personnel with war wounds.) Five series that met these criteria of impartial selection were found. The combined data confirmed that handedness and speech laterality are not independent. The left hemisphere rule for all will not do because left-handers are more likely to have right CD than right-handers. However, right-sided speech was not the norm for left-handers. Details of the five series will be considered in chapter 4 because their further analysis was of great importance for the development of the RS theory. For the present, we should note an important problem for research that incidences of left-handedness in the several series differed markedly. This raises the fundamental question of how reliable data can be collected on a characteristic that is measured in different ways by different investigators.

The evidence as to speech laterality above depended mainly on clinical inference and post mortem studies. Direct assessments of speech laterality in living patients were first made by stimulating the exposed cortex with a brief electrical pulse during operations for the relief of epilepsy at the Montreal Neurological Institute (Penfield and Roberts, 1959). Before removing tissue thought to be causing the epilepsy, surgeons needed to ensure that it was not critical for speech. A technique for assessing the speech side *before* operation involved injecting a sedative into a carotid artery (Wada, 1949, cited by Rasmussen and Milner, 1975). The artery on each side was injected in different sessions. The Wada procedure impairs cerebral function for a short time so that the patient is unable to talk for a few minutes after an injection to the speech side, whereas an injection on the non-speech side disrupts speech very little. Patients in Montreal considered doubtful as to speech laterality, either because of handedness or psychological test findings, were given the Wada test.

Rasmussen and Milner (1975) summarised the findings for 262 patients in whom there was no evidence of early brain damage that might have affected speech laterality. These data, shown in Table 1.2, have been widely regarded as

Table 1.2 Speech laterality and handedness in 262 patients without clinical evidence of early damage to the left cerebral hemisphere: based on Rasmussen and Milner, 1975

Handedness	No. of cases	Speech side (%)		
		Left	Bilateral	Right
Right	140	96	0	4
Left or mixed	122	70	15	15

giving definitive findings for handedness and speech side. Among 140 right-handers, there were 96% with left cerebral dominance (CD) and 4% with right CD. None were described as bilateral. Among 122 left-handers there were 70% left-sided, 15% bilateral and 15% right-sided cases. Bilateral speech occurred but it certainly was not the norm for left-handers. For the majority of left-handers (70%) the speech side was the left. Later reports of similar data from Montreal give a similar pattern of findings, but added some right-handers with bilateral speech (Loring, Meador, Lee et al., 1990; Ratcliff, Dila, Taylor et al., 1980). Thus all types of speech laterality may occur in both right- and left-handers. The patients at Montreal had epilepsies of several years duration, and further, they were more likely to be tested if they were suspected of having atypical CD. They were not representative of the general population nor even of the clinic population from which they were drawn. It will be shown later (chapter 4) that the findings of Rasmussen and Milner fit predictions of the RS theory very well for certain classifications of right- and left-handedness, but they do not describe the population as a whole.

THE EVOLUTION AND HISTORY OF HANDEDNESS

An account of the evolution of human handedness must explain three key facts. First, that the distribution of handedness in the population today, a majority of right-handers and a minority of left-handers is characteristic of all human groups. No tribe or society is known that does not include a majority of right-handers. None has been found with a majority of left-handers. Estimates of the size of the left-handed minority vary between cultures and between generations within cultures but there are no societies where left-handedness is unknown (Perelle and Ehrman, 1994).

The second main point for theories of evolution is that left and right-hand preferences occur throughout the primates. Primates are the branch of the evolutionary tree that includes humans along with apes, monkeys and prosimians. Manipulative hands are a primate characteristic and the human hand resembles that of other primates except that the thumb is relatively larger and better adapted for the precision grip (as in holding fine implements like needles and pencils). Left and right paw preferences occur in cats, mice, rats and other animals. Discussions of human handedness often imply that the chief puzzle is what causes left-handedness but this is mistaken. Left-handedness is part of our primate heritage. Chimpanzees in captivity (Finch, 1941), in the wild (Marchant and McGrew, 1996), and gorillas in captivity (Annett and Annett, 1991) and in the wild (Byrne and Byrne, 1991) include some with strong left-hand preferences, some with strong right-hand preferences and a majority with mixed hand use. The puzzle about humans is not the presence of left-handers, but that there are more than 50% right-handers.

The third question about evolution, how long have humans included a majority of right-handers, cannot be answered with any certainty. A bias to right-handedness may have been present since the earliest hominids, such as *Australopithecus africanus* (Dart, 1925). These were creatures with the human characteristic of fully upright walking, but brains not much larger than a modern chimpanzee. Dart (1949) suggested that crushed baboon skulls found with remains of australopithecines, about 3.5 million years old, could have suffered wounds from implements wielded in the right-hand. The inference must be regarded as tentative, of course. Archaeologists have examined stone tools for evidence as to the handedness of the flint-knappers that made them. Several have concluded that right-handedness was the rule and left-handedness the exception in prehistoric workmen (Keeley, 1977; Toth, 1985; Wilson, 1891).

The earliest written references to handedness in western culture occur in the Bible. The King James version of the book of Judges, Chapter 20, verses 15–16 reads, "And the children of Benjamin were numbered at that time out of the cities twenty and six thousand men that drew sword, beside the inhabitants of Gibeah, which numbered seven hundred chosen men. Among all this people there were seven hundred chosen men left-handed; every one could sling stones at an hairbreadth, and not miss." These left-handers (2.6% of the army) were not necessarily all the left-handers present, and of course there might have been some right-handed slingers. The passage is interesting because it describes a small group of left-handers, noted for a high level of manual skill. The handedness of modern sports-people, in tennis, baseball and cricket, will be considered in chapter 12.

The Egyptians decorated their tombs with scenes representing the life of the deceased, and these were often prepared long before death. Dennis (1958) examined the hands used in unimanual actions and found 14/225 (6.2%) instances where it was the left. Coren and Porac (1977) surveyed more than 12,000 works of art for representations of hand preference, dating from before 3000 B.C. to the present, grouped in 16 periods. Incidences of dextral hand use were consistent over this time span (mean 92.6%, range 86–98%). Analyses for seven geographical areas, including Europe, Asia, Africa and America, were also consistent. If these pictorial representations reflect actual hand use as observed by the artist, then about 7% have been sinistral for as long as man has drawn the human form. The evidence is consistent with the present distribution of handedness. There are no reasons to believe there was a time when left-handers were either missing or predominant.

THE EVOLUTION OF CEREBRAL ASYMMETRY FOR SPEECH

The brain asymmetry of chief interest in this book is the functional difference between the right and left hemispheres for the control of speech. There are two important distinctions that must be made, first the distinction between speech and language, and second the distinction between the capacity for speech itself and left cerebral specialisation for speech. Languages are systems for communication through symbols. Speech is a unique vehicle for symbolic communication that evolved in humans, but not in other primates. But there are other vehicles of symbolic communication, as in sign languages for the deaf and musical notation, that do not depend on speech. Any large-brained primate would be likely to develop language but what is very special to humans is that they can *talk*. Speech is a human species universal. It develops in every individual unless grossly handicapped or reared in isolation. However, left CD for speech is not universal like speech itself. It is subject to natural variation. The chief question for this book is why humans vary for speech laterality.

Human speech does not have any true precursor in the primate world. Chimpanzees and other primates make characteristic calls but these depend on different parts of the brain from those involved in human speech. Attempts to teach chimpanzees to produce speech sounds have failed, even with extensive training and rearing alongside a human infant. The failure of chimpanzees to imitate human speech, although they are excellent mimics in other respects, is probably due to physical differences in the structure of the vocal tract and the brain. With regard to the vocal tract, human babies and chimpanzees of all ages can drink and breathe at the same time, because the larynx is positioned high in the throat. The larynx descends as humans grow until we are liable to choke if we talk and eat at the same time (Lieberman, 1998). Charles Darwin pondered the reason for this change to the vocal tract because it is a highly dangerous arrangement, a significant cause of death. The fact that the human vocal tract has evolved in ways that carry serious risk to human health is an indication of the importance of vocalisation for humans as a species. The RS theory suggests that cerebral specialisation is another aid to the development of speech that is also bought at a significant cost to human health. It will be argued that cerebral speech laterality varies in modern humans because the mechanism inducing the typical left-sided asymmetry is also dangerous. The risks are too great to allow unlimited spread in the population. The agent of normal brain asymmetry might be associated with cognitive deficits and even risk of psychosis.

In contrast to the sharp distinction for speech between humans and the higher apes (chimpanzees, gorillas and orang-utans), there is no clear distinction for *language*. Languages use symbols with arbitrary relations with their referents. For example, an apple can be represented by a spoken word, a written word, a configuration of the hands in sign language, an arbitrary shape on a computer key or a hieroglyph. Attempts to teach apes to speak failed, but they have been taught to use the hand gestures of sign language, and to communicate with humans via computer keys. The question whether apes can acquire true language is a matter of controversy (Deacon, 1997; Fouts and Mills, 1997; Terrace, Petitto, Sanders et al., 1979). My own view is that apes are capable of the lower levels of symbolic communication, such as acquired by a human child around 2 years of age. From this, I infer that a large brained primate on the hominid line of evolution would almost certainly have developed a true language, simple at first, but growing in complexity in the course of human evolution. Human language is a marvellous instrument, of course, but what is unique for humans is the use of speech as its chief medium.

Having stressed the difference between humans and other primates in the use of speech as a method of communication, there is an important feature that might have presaged human speech. Recordings from neurons in the brains of monkeys, in areas that are probably analogous to Broca's area in humans, have found some that respond when the animal is making certain movements but also when it *sees another animal or the experimenter making a similar action* (Rizzolatti and Arbib, 1998). The gesture made by the self or another is monitored by the same neural system, in so-called "mirror" neurons. Humans undergoing functional magnetic resonance imaging were asked to imagine observing someone moving the fingers of the right-hand (Binkofski, Amunts, Stephan et al., 2000). Activation was observed in the area numbered 44 by Brodman, part of Broca's region. Thus the adaptation of Broca's area to serve speech gestures in the human brain might have been built upon a foundation that served communication by manual or other physical gestures.

Similarly, parts of Wernicke's area, at the junction of the parietal and temporal cortex, believed to be associated with understanding the meanings of words may have a wider role in communication. Gallagher, Happé, Brunswick et al. (2000) investigated by functional neural imaging the brain regions involved in understanding cartoons and stories that required appraisals of actions and intentions ("theory of mind" awareness). In addition to the expected activation of prefrontal cortex, there was also increased activity at the temporal parietal junction of both hemispheres. They suggest that these regions might be sensitive to stimuli that signal intentions or intentional activity. That is, the posterior brain regions long associated with decoding language might also decode the nonverbal signals that are critical for understanding the behaviour of others.

The idea that gestures are fundamental for speech was intrinsic to the revised motor theory of speech perception (Liberman and Mattingley, 1985). A biologically distinct module was proposed, specialised to detect the intended vocal gestures of the speaker. Distinctions between phonetic categories depend on the gestures required to produce them, such that speech production and perception are tightly linked. The special and unique role of Broca's and Wernicke's areas for human vocalisation would confer the advantage of communication at a distance without the need for visual interaction.

The clearest nonhuman analogue of functional asymmetry for speech occurs in songbirds such as canaries and chaffinches. Bird-song is a powerful means of communicating at a distance to attract mates and to warn off intruders, often in visually obscure environments. Nottebohm (1970) reported that cutting the nerves to the syrinx, the avian vocal organ, had different effects between the sides. Lesions on the right were followed by the loss of a few elements of song, whereas lesions on the left led to a severe disruption of almost all elements. Other asymmetries in the brains of chicks are related to the early learning known as imprinting (Horn, Rose and Bateson, 1973). Mammals that developed vocal systems of communication are those that re-adapted for life in water, the whales, dolphins and manatees (the mermaids of lost sailors). Whales have structural asymmetries of the skull, the majority showing a leftward bias to the blowhole

Ness, 1967). There is also evidence for behavioural asymmetries in whales for
~ding and movement (Clapham, Leimkuhler, Gray et al., 1995). Asymmetries
he natural world will be considered in chapter 3.

~e functional asymmetries for speech related to physical asymmetries in the
ı brain? Certain areas of the brain tend to be not fully symmetrical, as will
sidered in chapter 8. A question for evolutionary theories is whether
~ysical asymmetries occur in other primates and how early they are seen
in human fossils.

THE GENETICS OF HANDEDNESS

Sir George Humphry wrote in 1861, "I am driven, therefore, to the rather nice
distinction, that, though the superiority [of the right-hand] is acquired, the
tendency to acquire the superiority is natural [i.e. hereditary]" (cited by Merrell,
1957, p. 325). Jordan (1911) was the first to suggest that left-handedness might
depend on a recessive gene, following the classic rules deduced by Gregor Mendel.
Jordan's data on the handedness of students and their relatives did not quite fit
the model but he believed they could be reconciled with the theory, "by the aid
of the suggested hypotheses of degrees of intensity of bias, and mild dominant
and intense recessive strains of left-handedness" (Jordan, 1914, p. 79). In other
words, left-handedness might be a Mendelian recessive character if "fudge"
factors are invoked to blur the rules. Several subsequent theories of handedness
are variations on the theme of the dominant/recessive gene pair, alleles R for
right and L for left, with differing interpretations of the "fudge" factors.

Table 1.3 summarises the findings of four studies of handedness in students
and their relatives, three published in the first half of the 20th century (Chamberlain, 1928; Ramaley, 1913; Rife, 1940), and my first major study of students,
whose parents must have attended school before 1940 (Annett, 1973a). These
were all the large samples available for fitting to my RS genetic model (Annett,
1978b). In all of the studies, the proportion of left-handed children was more
than twice as high in L × R families than R × R families. In adoptive families
this was not true (Carter-Saltzman, 1980), suggesting that the association in
biological families might be genetic. The critical test for the recessive gene

Table 1.3 Percentage left-handed children in three types of family

	Parents' handedness		
	Right × Right	Left × Right	Left × Left
Ramaley (1913)	12.2	32.3	85.7
Chamberlain (1928)	4.3	11.4	28.0
Rife (1940)	7.6	19.5	54.5
Annett (1973a)	9.7	21.0	20.0

theory depends on L × L families, where the classic model requires *all* of the children to be left-handed. On the contrary, right-handed children occurred in these families in every study. In the four studies of Table 1.3 combined there were 48 children in L × L families and 20 (41.7%) were left-handed. Chamberlain (1928) found 24 additional L × L families contacted through newspapers, whose 75 children included 39 (52.0%) left-handers. Similarly, Annett (1973a) found 64 additional L × L families with 35% left-handed children. In 17 of my families both parents were *consistent left-handers* (using the left-hand for all the 12 actions of my questionnaire). Forty-four percent of their children were left-handed. Thus, there can be no doubt that families of L × L parents include many right-handed children, even when left preference is strong in both parents. The classic model of left handedness as a recessive gene will not do.

The four studies illustrate again the problem for research mentioned above, the difference between studies for frequency of left-handedness. Incidences ranged from 3.5 to 8.0% for parents and from 4.8 to 15.7% for children. However, in spite of these superficial differences, a remarkable consistency was found when Trankell (1955) estimated the frequency of the hypothesised recessive gene. Trankell argued that the L allele was imperfectly penetrant in recessive homozygotes. That is, some natural left-handers fail to express their left-handedness. Algebraic equations were used to estimate the frequency of the recessive gene, within each type of family. The nine estimates (three types of family in each of three studies) were all in the range 0.39–0.44 (where 1 represents the whole gene pool). The means for each of the three studies were 0.40 for Chamberlain, 0.41 for Rife and 0.43 for Ramaley, a remarkable agreement in spite of the differences for incidences of left-handedness. The consistency must imply an underlying regularity in the transmission of handedness in families. I assumed from the start that a successful genetic theory of handedness must be able to account for all of these data. Some theories (Klar, 1996; Levy and Nagylaki, 1972) have been fitted to one data set only, that of Rife. The estimates of gene frequency that Trankell derived for Rife were similar to those for Chamberlain and Ramaley. All are consistent with the estimate derived by the RS theory, from an entirely different line of reasoning (in chapter 4).

Another variation of the classic genetic model suggested that a gene for left-handedness might not be fully recessive but partly expressed in heterozygotes (RL genotypes). Ramaley (1913, p. 735) suggested that, "Possibly some heterozygous . . . persons may easily learn to use the left-hand." Expressed in this way, heterozygote variability becomes another "fudge" factor. Rife (1950) tried to account for identical twins pairs that include one right- and one left-hander through heterozygote variability. The idea was that one twin expressed the R allele and one twin expressed the L. However, no mechanism is known that could produce such an effect. Even more problematic is that it would have to occur in DZ twins as often as in MZ twins. Annett (1964) suggested heterozygote variability might explain the fact that the majority of so-called "left-handers" actually have mixed-hand preferences, using the right-hand for some actions and the left for others. This was different from Rife's idea because both alleles were expressed in the same individual. If cerebral dominance for speech were also variable in heterozygotes, there would be scope for all the combinations of hand and brain laterality actually observed. This theory was wrong but it represented an important stage in the development of the RS theory.

The occurrence of RL pairs of monozygotic (MZ) twins is often taken to be a grave difficulty for genetic theories of handedness because MZ twins carry identical genes. Non-identical (dizygotic or DZ) twins have, on average, half their genes in common. If handedness were fully determined genetically, then MZ twin pairs should be identical for handedness. If there were a strong genetic influence, MZ twins should be more alike than DZ twins. Neither is true. The chances that a pair of twins will differ for handedness are about the same for MZ and DZ pairs (Collins, 1970). This last observation also discounts mirror imaging as a major factor in the handedness of MZ twins. The puzzle of twin handedness has led many to reject the possibility of a genetic influence on handedness. This is a mistake, but a mistake that can be rectified by the RS theory. There is an observation that strongly supports the theory of genetic influence, even in twins. Rife (1950) showed that RL twin pairs were more likely to have another left-hander in the family than RR twin pairs. Whatever the effect of twin birth itself, left-handedness in twins is associated with the presence of other left-handed relatives.

Another problem for genetic theories is that searches for genes for paw preferences in mice and rats proved entirely negative. It is clear that in these species, paw preferences are strong, but not inherited. If this is true of mice and rats, is it also true of humans? There are several reasons for believing that there is a genetic influence on human handedness. Fingerprints are inherited and laid down early in foetal life. There are small but statistically significant differences between right- and left-handers in the distribution of certain patterns (Rife, 1955, 1978). Eye preferences are unlikely to be influenced by specific training but they are correlated with hand preferences. Eye preferences are correlated between relatives and eye dominance in families will be shown to fit predictions of the RS genetic model (chapter 7). Anatomical asymmetries of the skull and the brain differ not only between right-handers and left-handers but also between left-handers who do and do not have left-handed relatives (LeMay, 1977). All of this evidence confirms that asymmetries of hand and brain are related, have a biological foundation, and are influenced by some inherited factor.

IS HANDEDNESS ACQUIRED THROUGH LEARNING?

There is an important sense in which handedness must be learned, in the same way that a native language must be learned. Nature makes the infant disposed to attend to speech sounds and to try to imitate them. The disposition to speak is inherited but the language spoken depends on experience. Similarly, there may be a disposition to use one hand for actions demanding skill, using tools, slinging stones, flaking flints, throwing, sewing or writing, but skill in these actions is acquired through practice. That culture makes a difference to the expression of handedness cannot be doubted because there are marked differences between cultures and also between generations within the same culture in the prevalence of left-hand use. The strongest pressures to use the right-hand in eating are probably exerted by cultures where it is the practice for individuals to take food from a common bowl. The right-hand must be reserved for "clean" and the left for "unclean" functions. Less than 1% of Japanese schoolchildren used the left-hand for eating or writing but for throwing, cutting with scissors, striking a match and kicking a football, incidences of left preference were comparable to those of English children (Komai and Fukuoka, 1934). Changes within racial groups in different environments underline the role of culture. For example, Chinese children in Taiwan rarely use the left-hand for eating or writing but in the USA more often (Teng, Lee, Yang et al., 1976). A sample of parents and children in Hawaii is especially interesting because incidences of left-handed writing differed between parents of different ethnic origin (Japanese versus European) but not between their children, presumably because social sanctions against left-handedness had eased among Japanese families living in Hawaii (Ashton, 1982).

A difference between the generations, more left-handers among children than parents, has been found in every study of family handedness. The causes of the generation difference need careful scrutiny. The argument that the age difference is due to differential longevity between left- and right-handers will be shown to be false (chapter 6). An important factor in the generation difference is the change of cultural attitudes to left-handedness in Western societies during the 20th century. A conviction that everyone should write with the right-hand was highly prevalent in Western society until about the time of WW2. Pitiful accounts of the cruel methods that were employed to force right-hand use were sent to me by parents whenever I sought information about handedness in families through the media. Cyril Burt (1937), London's first educational psychologist, reported 3–4% left-writing in schools in his earliest samples, around WW1. A questionnaire study of Londoners attending a dental hospital in the 1970s found about 10% left-handed writers among younger respondents (15–44 years) but only about 3% in older respondents (55–64 years) who would have been at school when Burt visited (Fleminger, Dalton, and Standage, 1977). A questionnaire distributed with the *National Geographic Magazine* elicited over a million replies in the USA (Gilbert and Wysocki, 1992). There was a marked fall in incidence after 50 years of age. Similar trends were found in Australia (Brackenridge, 1981). However, to agree that the skills through which handedness is expressed are learned, and that handedness is influenced by culture, is not to argue that hand preference depends on learning alone.

It is often said that our "right-handed world" forces left-handers to adopt right-handedness. Some tools such as normal scissors are particularly difficult to use in the left-hand. Many actions taken for granted by right-handers present difficulties for left-handers, such as using a typical chequebook, or opening a five-barred gate from horseback. Perhaps many subtle actions train left-handers to adapt to the "right" way of doing things. Does it make sense to say that training causes hand preference? Among the older left-handers I have personally tested for preference and skill there were some who had been forced to write with the right-hand from starting school and continued to write with the right-hand, half a century later. For all other actions of my handedness questionnaire (see Figure 2.1) and for peg moving they remained strongly left-handed. The forced training of the right-hand for writing, and 50 years practice had not generalised to other actions, nor had the right-hand become more skilful than the left. Similarly, in the experience of pianists I have questioned, years of practising scales with both hands may not remove the superiority of the preferred hand, whether right or left. Provins and Glencross (1968) showed that trained typists could type as fast with the left-hand as the right, while novices were better with the right. Practice certainly allowed the left-hand to improve, but the similarity between the hands does not imply that the difference in skill has been removed; the right-hand might have typed even faster if not held back by the left.

In the search for causes of left-handedness, researchers have studied its earliest manifestations. Gesell and Ames (1947) studied the asymmetric position typically adopted by newborn infants when placed on their back, known as the tonic neck reflex. The head is typically turned to the right, with right arm and leg extended while the left arm is flexed. Follow-up studies some years later found that all right turning infants were right or mixed handed while about half of the left turning infants were left-handed. The orientation of the head during birth is also weakly related to handedness. Is handedness determined by position in the womb? Peterson (1934) delivered rats by caesarean section, noting from which horn of the uterus they were taken. There was no effect on paw preference. Ultrasound scanning of human foetuses has revealed thumb sucking in the womb. There is a very early asymmetry here because some 90% of such observations were for the right-hand (Hepper, Shahidullah and White, 1991). This lateral bias was evident from as early as 12 weeks of foetal growth. The cerebral cortex is barely developed at this time. A bias to the right-hand in humans seems to have a very early origin indeed.

DOES HANDEDNESS MATTER? ABILITIES, LITERACY AND PSYCHOSIS

Speculation that disorders of speech and reading might be due to anomalies of speech laterality began soon after the notion of cerebral dominance was first accepted. The question whether stuttering is caused by forced changes of the writing hand has been a matter for concern for almost a century, and remains one of the most frequent questions about handedness.

Questions about dyslexia remain highly controversial. Samuel T. Orton (1925, 1937), an American paediatric neurologist, was struck by the number of children with developmental language problems who were not consistently right-sided but showed varying degrees of "motor-intergrading", or mixed preferences. The idea that some children may have particular problems in learning to read is now widely accepted, but the relevance of handedness is generally discounted (Bishop, 1990a). For many teachers and educational psychologists (Burt, 1937; Crabtree, 1976) dyslexia is a myth. Among the very large number of slow readers and poor spellers in school, there seemed no ground for distinguishing a small select sub-group and giving them a probably pseudo-medical label. Some recent analysts agree with this assessment (Stanovich, 1994). The idea that dyslexics include a high proportion of non-right-handers has also been described as a myth (Satz and Fletcher, 1987). The RS theory has implications for these controversies (chapter 13).

Aside from questions of literacy, does left-handedness have particular associations with specific talents or weaknesses? It is more frequent among the mentally handicapped, but also among people with special skills including surgeons, sports-people and artists. The typical pattern of anatomical asymmetries has been found reduced in schizophrenics. These differences are relevant to one of the most interesting implications of the RS theory, that there could be a balanced polymorphism with heterozygote advantage (BP + HA) for the RS genetic locus. This implies that risks and benefits for different types of ability are part of an inter-locking pattern of advantages and costs associated with a gene for cerebral speech laterality that happens to influence handedness.

SUMMARY

The puzzle of handedness and brain asymmetry is that, although most people are right-handed and left brained for speech, exceptions for hand and brain do not go together. Left-handers are more often right brained than right-handers, but left-handers are also more often left than right brained. The rules that govern this pattern of association are the topic of this book.

My 40 years of research have sought to discover the bare bones of the problem, by stripping away unproven assumptions. I have used the analogies of an archaeological dig, and also a detective enquiry. My aim was to base a theory of relationships between hand and brain on facts of which I could be sure. Quantitative regularities underpinned the key assumptions at each stage of the process of research and theory building.

Relationships between hand and brain are, in the first place, a problem for neurology. All possible theories have been put forward for the brain laterality of left-handers, left, right, either, both or some combination of these. Much of the literature has depended on individual reports of cases taken to be exceptional. What is needed is systematic study of series of cases. The widely cited data from the Montreal Neurological Clinic, based on Wada testing, does not represent the general population.

Theories of the evolution and history of handedness must consider how individual differences for handedness are characteristic of all human groups, a majority right-handed and a minority left-handed in all modern populations. The same distribution has been present, as far as can be judged, in historic and prehistoric times also. Other primates, including our closest cousin, the chimpanzee, also have strong hand preferences, but without species bias to right-handedness. Comparisons between humans and apes for communication skills suggest that any large brained primate would be capable of language, using some medium or other. What is unique to humans is the use of speech. Only humans can talk.

There is evidence for a genetic influence on human handedness, but not on the paw preferences of rats or mice. Several versions of the theory that left-handedness in humans is due to a recessive gene have been proposed but none fits all the facts. Nevertheless, there is a remarkable consistency in estimates of the frequency of the supposed recessive gene, as derived by Trankell from several studies that differed for actual incidences in parents and in children. This suggests some underlying regularity of genetic influence on human handedness. A genetic theory must be able to account for the fact that MZ twins may differ for handedness, and in fact do so about as often as DZ twins.

Learning clearly influences handedness but this cannot be taken to mean that handedness is *solely* a matter of training. Cultural pressures against left-handed writing were strong in Western societies in the early part of the 20th century but have eased in later years. Influences on early development may play a role in the development of hand preferences, but evidence that 90% of foetuses thumb-sucking in the womb suck the right thumb shows there is some very early asymmetry involved.

The question of the implications of individual differences for handedness raises questions about relevance for learning to speak and to read. Are left-handers more frequent in certain talented groups, in arts and in sport? Is handedness and cerebral asymmetry of significance for mental disorders, including psychoses? These are among the questions addressed in this book.

Part II
The right shift theory

2 Human handedness

Discrete types or continuous varieties?

The scientific study of handedness must resolve many problems, but the first and most fundamental is the problem of frequency. A review of the literature by Hécaen and Ajuriaguerra (1964) found incidences of left-handedness ranging from some 1 to 40%. How can laws be discovered for something so inconsistent between studies? This chapter examines the classification of handedness. The proposed solution to the problem of inconsistent frequencies is the foundation of the RS theory. The argument is that left-handedness is not a "type" whose "essence" remains elusive. It is rather a characteristic that varies continuously between strong left and strong right, with several varieties of mixed-handedness in between. The variability is the essence that has to be described and explained. It is as if height were classified as "tall" or "short", but who was called tall or short differed for every investigator. If handedness varies continuously, like height, the problem is how to describe it in a way that will permit the construction of a reliable scale of measurement. Discrete types, right and left, are in common usage but nevertheless misleading.

WHY A LEFT VERSUS RIGHT TYPOLOGY WILL NOT DO

When asked whether they are right or left-handed, most people are prepared to describe themselves as one or other of these types on the basis of the hand preferred for some salient action. But which action should be the criterion? The writing hand may perhaps be used today in the UK or USA, but not for people who were at school before WW2 nor for people in other societies with strong prejudices against the use of the left-hand. In current western research, the few people not prepared to describe themselves as right or left-handed are often termed "ambidextrous" and then omitted from the sample or perhaps classified with left-handers. Ambidexterity means equal skill with both hands, as contrasted with the term "ambilevous" meaning equally unskilled with both hands (or described as having "two left hands"). As few people write with either hand equally well, few can be called truly ambidextrous. The term ambilevous is not in common use. The point here is that the right/left dichotomy is usually considered sufficient. My first discovery in handedness research, and my continuing experience, suggest that this view is mistaken because about one in three people are mixed-handers (not ambidexters), as explained below. This is one of the main reasons for inconsistent assessments of incidence. But before looking at mixed-handedness, it is useful to review other reasons for inconsistencies between estimates.

The causes of variability of most interest to researchers are genuine differences between groups. Recruits to military service in the United States were asked, "Are you (check one) [   ] right-handed [   ] left-handed?" There were 7.9% who checked "left" among 6040 men qualifying for service. Among 6119 *not qualifying* for service, presumably because of disabilities, there were 10.1% (Karpinos and Grossman, 1953). Gordon (1921) asked London schoolchildren to throw a blackboard duster and found 7.3% left throwers in normal schools but 18.2% in schools for mental defectives (learning disabled). A higher proportion of left-handers in those disqualified for military service and in the mentally handicapped might be due to early brain damage that caused a disability and also a shift of handedness from right to left (so called "pathological" left-handedness). *Some* left-handedness may be due to pathology but this does not imply, of course, that *all* left-handedness is due to pathology (see further on pathology in chapter 16). However, some pathologies could be associated with genuine differences of incidence between groups that are of interest to medical and other researchers.

A second source of variability of incidence is *who* is making the report, the individual or a relative. Undergraduates always report fewer left-handers among their parents than themselves. Porac and Coren (1979) asked high school students about their parents' handedness and then sent a questionnaire directly to the parents. There were 4.1% left-handed parents according to the students, but 9.1% according to the parents themselves. Another related threat to the reliability of report data is that inaccuracies are not independent of the handedness of the reporter. When students were asked to describe themselves very few mentioned handedness, but among those who did, almost all were left-handers (McGuire and McGuire, 1980). Left-handers are likely to report their parents' handedness more reliably than right-handers (Kang and Harris, 1996). Inaccurate report of the handedness of relatives is a problem for studies of handedness in families (Annett, 1999c, and chapter 7 here).

A third source of variability of incidences might arise through methods of data collection. Data may depend on either observation or questionnaire. The report of an observer who sees a participant (P) perform an action is likely to be more objective than P's response to a questionnaire. When questionnaires are distributed with a request for return later, returns are often less than 50%. Right-handers may be more likely to bin the forms than left-handers. If returns are not independent of handedness type, information will not reflect true incidences in the population.

A fourth reason for variable incidences is variable consistency of preference. When Ps are allowed to give more than a right versus left self-classification they may say, for example, "I write with the right (or left) hand but use the other hand for X, Y or Z." These are people with definite preferences for one hand for particular skilled actions, but the preferred hand differs between tasks. These are what I term "mixed" hand preferences. Mixed preferences are neglected in most of the literature. There are two main reasons for this neglect, the concept of the "shifted sinistral" and the concept of the "right-handed world". Researchers in medicine, education and psychology were aware of the strong prejudices against the use of the left-hand that influenced the expression of left-handedness until the latter half of the 20th century. They interpreted *any* left-hand preference as a sign of a shifted sinistral, a natural left-hander forced to use the right. A right-handed writer who used the left-hand for another action was likely to be classified as left-handed. Left-handed writers who prefer the right-hand for other actions were explained as adapting to the pressures of the right-handed world. Both concepts, the shifted sinistral and the right-handed world, led to the same conclusion, that people with combinations of left and right-hand preferences (mixed-handers in my terminology) were in fact left-handers. The incidence of left-handedness then depends on the diligence of the enquiry. The more questions asked, the more likely that left-hand preference will be uncovered and the higher the incidence recorded.

The question of the consistency versus inconsistency of hand preferences was of particular interest to Oliver Zangwill. One of his postgraduate students (Humphrey, 1951) showed that inconsistency is much more prevalent among left-handers than among right-handers. This difference has been rediscovered in the literature many times. But what is the cause of the inconsistency of left-handers? Is it due to the pressures of the right-handed world? Gillies, MacSweeney and Zangwill (1960) found some undergraduates who wrote with the left-hand but did *everything else right-handed*. If such an individual has not succumbed to sociocultural pressures with respect to writing, is it likely that these pressures will have caused right-handed throwing, tennis playing and so on? It was concluded that handedness is a graded characteristic, not a discrete one. This conclusion had been reached before. "Right-handedness and left-handedness are relative terms" (Burt, 1937, p. 270) and "Handedness . . . is nothing absolute; it is a question of degree" (Brain, 1945, p. 837). If this is true, how are the gradations of handedness to be described and how is the continuum to be quantified?

WHY LATERALITY QUOTIENTS WILL NOT DO AS MEASURES OF THE PREFERENCE CONTINUUM

Various methods of quantifying handedness questionnaires have been proposed. Crovitz and Zener (1962) asked Ps whether they preferred to use the right-hand always (score 1), right-hand mostly (2), either hand (3), left-hand mostly (4) or left always (5) for each of 14 actions. The Edinburgh Handedness Inventory (EHI) asked Ps to indicate preference by placing crosses (+) in columns labelled "right" and "left", two crosses for strong preference, one cross for mild preference for the corresponding hand, or a single cross in both columns to indicate either hand preference (Oldfield, 1971). This is a five-point scale, like that of Crovitz and Zener. A laterality quotient (LQ) was derived using the formula $(100 \times (R - L)/(R + L))$, where R and L refer to the number of crosses placed in the respective columns. The quotient ranges from −100 to +100, however many crosses are made. Geschwind suggested giving each of Oldfield's "+"s a score of 5, sometimes referred to as "Geschwind scores", but this merely adds a constant to the score distribution and gives no additional information.

Schemes such as these are widely used. How well do they measure handedness as a continuous variable? Peters and Durding (1978) correlated LQs with a measure of right minus left (R − L) hand tapping speed, and found a roughly linear relationship. This supports the argument that both types of handedness, for preference and skill, vary continuously. However, the LQ is a very crude instrument. It gives the same numerical value to actions that require different levels of skill, for example, writing and sweeping. Are these actions likely to be equivalent for handedness, or is this counting cabbages with kings? A second objection is that equal weight is given to directional responses (left versus right) and to estimates of the *strength* of preference (how easy to use the other hand). Opinions about the latter may have no objective validity. It will be shown below that "either" responses to questionnaires tend to be unreliable when checked against observed performance. Reports might depend more on an optimistic and extraverted attitude than genuine equality of hand use.

Bryden (1977) gave the EHI and Crovitz and Zener questionnaires to 1107 undergraduates at the University of Waterloo. Comparing responses to the same items on the two scales, he found that Ps were more likely to indicate strong preference when using numbers (1–5) than they were to put a double cross (+ +) in the columns for left or right. Some items were given "either" responses more often than not (holding a glass of water for drinking, or opening a box lid). There was evidence of automatic responding, without paying careful attention to questions that asked for the "other" hand, as explained further below. Females were more likely than males to claim they "always" rather than "usually" performed actions with one hand. These observations support the conclusion above that self-ratings of strength of preference should not be taken at face value.

After deriving an LQ, what use is normally made of it? Investigators generally divide the sample into right- versus left-handers, at any one of the many possible cut-off points. The basis for the classification is now obscure. For example, a score of 80+ would be obtained by a left-handed writer who preferred the right for all other actions and also a right-hander who merely indicated "either" hand preference for one action. It would be more transparent to use a specified criterion, such as "writing hand" or "any left-hand preference". In my view, "indices" and "quotients" of hand preference put a gloss on ignorance. They are pseudoscience because they assign numbers without objective referents and therefore obscure what they purport to describe. The claim of Briggs and Nebes (1975) to have "improved" my questionnaire (Figure 2.1) by adding a rating scale and deriving a laterality index is not one with which I agree. My approach led to a classification in subgroups, as explained below.

Handedness research

Name .... Age .... Sex ....
Were you one of twins, triplets at birth or were you single born? ....

Please indicate which hand you habitually use for each of the following activities by writing R (for right), L (for left), E (for either).*

Which hand do you use:
1. To write a letter legibly? ....
2. To throw a ball to hit a target? ....
3. To hold a racquet in tennis, squash or badminton? ....
4. To hold a match whilst striking it? ....
5. To cut with scissors? ....
6. To guide a thread through the eye of a needle (or guide needle on to thread)?
7. At the top of a broom while sweeping? ....
8. At the top of a shovel when moving sand? ....
9. To deal playing cards? ....
10. To hammer a nail into wood? ....
11. To hold a toothbrush while cleaning your teeth? ....
12. To unscrew the lid of a jar? ....

If you use the *right-hand for all of these actions*, are there any one-handed actions for which you use the *left-hand*? Please record them here ....
....

If you use the *left-hand for all of these actions*, are there any one-handed actions for which you use the *right-hand*? Please record them here ....
....

* This instruction was omitted in some versions with the intention of discouraging "E" responses.

Figure 2.1 The Annett Hand Preference Questionnaire: Annett, 1970a.

EVALUATING HAND PREFERENCE ITEMS: FACTORS, FREQUENCIES AND RELATIVE SKILL

If mixed hand preferences are not to be glossed over by laterality quotients, how are they to be evaluated? One way that psychologists have tried to simplify hand preference data is by the method of factor analysis. Items are correlated with each other and the correlations examined for the presence of "factors" common to several items. Bryden (1977) obtained three factors from the combined items of the EHI and Crovitz and Zener questionnaires. The first factor gave high loadings for writing, drawing, tennis racquet, and toothbrush, actions requiring considerable skill and ones for which a definite preference would be expected. A second factor loaded on items scored in the "other" direction, the hand that holds the bottle while opening it, the needle while threading it, or the potato being peeled. The reverse scoring was intended to make Ss consider their responses carefully (rather than responding automatically) but their strong association suggests that many students were not attentive enough to notice the reversal (mentioned above). Factor 3 depended mainly on three items, match, broom and box lid, two handed actions that right-handers often claim to do left-handed. Bryden concluded that there is only one main finding, a single dimension of hand preference. Similar conclusions were reached from other factor analyses (Porac, Coren, Steiger et al., 1980; White and Ashton, 1976).

Recent factor analyses have sought evidence for the idea that different factors for hand preference might arise because actions depend on different parts of the motor system. There are several neural pathways controlling limb movements (Brinkman and Kuypers, 1973, see Kolb and Whishaw, 1996 for review). An important distinction can be made between the pathways that govern movements of the proximal muscles required for gross movements of the arm, as in swinging an axe or a baseball bat, versus those governing the distal muscles of the fingers when using a precision grip in grasping a needle or pen. Healey, Liederman and Geschwind (1986) found a first factor that loaded on writing and drawing as expected and a third factor that loaded on axe and baseball bat. However, the latter accounted for a tiny proportion of the variance (2.4%) compared with the first factor (71.5%). Steenhuis and Bryden (1989) made a similar attempt to discriminate between types of items in a factor analysis. They found a factor for "picking up" small items, but this was not surprising as many "pick up" items were included in the questionnaire. It is a truism that the outcome of a factor analysis depends intimately on the input. Traditional factor analysis seeks to reduce the data, but there is a method that expands the data in order to seek meaningful differences, called "association analysis", as described below.

The AHPQ (Figure 2.1) has been the basis of my research on hand preference, by observation or report, since the late 1960s. One way to evaluate questionnaire items is to examine each one in relation to another variable, such as frequency in the population or association with R–L hand skill. Annett (1970a) described frequency data for 2321 young adults, students and service recruits, for written responses to the AHPQ, and also observed hand use for these actions and peg moving times for 283 students and teenage schoolchildren. By the 1990s, it was possible to assemble corresponding data for over 2000 participants, all observed performing the AHPQ actions, and most also tested for peg moving.

Table 2.1 shows the 12 actions ranked for frequency of "left" responses in the 1970 and the 1990 samples. The ranks are fairly consistent between both sets of data, in spite of the different decades of testing and the different methods of data collection. The most frequent "left" preferences were "dealing playing cards" (17% in both data) and "unscrewing the lid of a jar" (22% by observation and 17% by questionnaire). The least frequent in both was "cutting with scissors" (6.9% and 6.2% respectively). Most items changed rank by not more than one, and only two items changed by as much as two places. This close agreement between questionnaire and observation suggests that reports of left-hand prefer- ence are probably valid and reliable.

Table 2.2 gives the ranks for "either" (E) hand responses in the two sets of combined data. E responses were more frequent by questionnaire than observation for all actions except throwing. During observations E responses could be checked,

Table 2.1 AHPQ items ranked for percent "left" preference in two groups of combined samples: the 1970 sample assessed by questionnaire and the 1990 sample by observation

Rank by frequency	1970 (N = 2321)		1990 (N = 2064)	
	Q. item	%	Q. item	%
1	Cards	17.0	Jar	22.0
2	Jar	16.5	Cards	17.1
3	Shovel	13.5	Broom	15.9
4	Broom	13.5	Needle	15.5
5	Needle	13.1	Shovel	14.2
6	Write	10.6	Match	9.8
7	Match	10.0	Write	9.8
8	Throw	9.4	Throw	9.5
9	Hammer	9.2	Toothbrush	9.2
10	Toothbrush	8.1	Racquet	8.4
11	Racquet	8.1	Hammer	8.0
12	Scissors	6.2	Scissors	6.9

Table 2.2 AHPQ items ranked for percent "either" preference in two groups of combined samples: the 1970 sample assessed by questionnaire and the 1990 sample by observation

Rank by frequency	1970 (N = 2321)		1990 (N = 2064)	
	Q. item	%	Q. item	%
1	Jar	17.5	Jar	9.7
2	Broom	16.9	Broom	7.5
3	Shovel	11.9	Needle	5.2
4	Needle	9.7	Shovel	4.5
5	Match	8.7	Throw	4.3
6	Toothbrush	8.5	Match	3.7
7	Scissors	6.8	Toothbrush	3.1
8	Cards	3.3	Cards	2.5
9	Racquet	2.6	Hammer	2.3
10	Hammer	2.5	Racquet	1.9
11	Throw	1.3	Scissors	1.3
12	Write	0.3	Write	0.05

of course, by asking Ps to try again. Only if both hands continued to feel equally skilful was an E response recorded. Studies of questionnaire reliability by test versus retest found E responses less reliable than R or L responses (Annett, 1985a; McMeekan and Lishman, 1975).

Table 2.3 gives data for L–R hand time for peg moving. The peg moving task (described more fully in Appendix II) asked Ps to move 10 pegs from a starting

Table 2.3 AHPQ items ranked for L–R peg moving time (in ¹/₁₀s) in participants preferring the left-hand for that item: two groups of combined samples, all hand preferences assessed by observation (standard errors for 1990 means about 1.0)

Rank by L–R diff.	1970 (sample N = 283)		1990 (sample N = 2054)	
	Q. item	*L–R time*	*Q. item*	*L–R time*
1	Needle	2.1	Broom	0.9
2	Jar	1.8	Jar	0.5
3	Broom	1.0	Needle	0.2
4	Shovel	0.6	Shovel	−0.2
5	Cards	−1.1	Cards	−1.9
6	Throw	−4.3	Throw	−5.3
7	Racquet	−4.6	Racquet	−5.3
8	Match	−5.6	Match	−5.5
9	Toothbrush	−6.3	Toothbrush	−6.0
10	Write	−6.5	Scissors	−6.5
11	Scissors	−6.8	Write	−6.8
12	Hammer	−7.0	Hammer	−7.0

row to a finishing row, one at a time as fast as possible. There were three to five trials per hand, alternating the hands between trials. (The difference between the hands in skills is calculated here as L–R time per hand, because the left-hand is slower for most people. The difference is given in ¹/₁₀s, and negative differences imply that the left-hand is faster. For hand skill tasks involving hitting targets the subtraction is R − L because the right-hand hits more targets. For most purposes below it will be convenient to refer to differences between the hands in skill as R − L, implying that the right is more skilful in most people. Later, the measure R − L%, difference as a proportion of total time will be introduced.) The data in Table 2.3 shows the L–R peg moving time of people reporting left preference for hammer, and similarly for each other action considered separately. Table 2.3 shows the mean differences for the original 283 Ss of Annett (1970a) and for 2054 S in the 1990 combined samples. The items are ranked for size of difference in both samples. For 8 out of 12 items, the rank orders were identical. In both data sets, the item associated with the strongest bias to sinistral skill was "hammer" (mean −7.0 for both series, S.D. 8.3 for the larger 1990 series). Left-handed writing and cutting with scissors were close to hammer for skill asymmetry. Groups with left preferences for needle, jar, broom, shovel and cards were not strongly biased to either side (but all were much less dextral than the general mean, 7.1, S.D. 8.8).

These data confirm that hand preferences for different actions differ in frequency and also in associated relative skill. To give equal weight to these items in a laterality index would indeed be counting cabbages with kings. How should these degrees of preference be described and quantified? The analyses above looked at separate items. How do items combine to give patterns of preference?

MIXED-HANDEDNESS: THE BINOMIAL PROPORTIONS
OF RIGHT-, MIXED- AND LEFT-HANDERS

My first study of handedness was a brief enquiry by questionnaire, requesting information from parents on their epileptic children. I was surprised to find that about one-third of the children were described as mixed-handers (Annett, Lee and Ounsted, 1961). Was the high proportion special to epileptics? Every subsequent sample, drawn from cohorts of undergraduates or random samples of schoolchildren, has included some 25–35% mixed-handers. The samples date from the early 1960s in Aberdeen to the late 1990s in Leicester. Mixed hand preferences occur in many combinations. For example, Bishop (1990a, p. 69) described her own handedness as left for writing, eating with a spoon, combing hair and sewing, but right for holding a toothbrush, tennis racquet and scissors. It will be shown in the next section that patterns of mixed hand preference can be reliably ordered for R–L hand skill. But first, there are some points to make about the distribution of right-, mixed- and left-handedness.

At the start of my enquiries I knew that Humphrey (1951) had found left-handers often inconsistent, as mentioned above. Did that imply that all left-handers were really mixed-handers? I was assured by some psychologists that *all* left-handers were inconsistent because some actions *must* be performed with the right-hand, most notably cutting with scissors, because scissors are designed for use in the right-hand (the right-handed world explanation of mixed-handedness). My first research objective was to discover whether consistent left-handers exist (left preferent for scissors and all other actions of my questionnaire). If so, what are the relative proportions of the three types of handedness in the population, consistent left, mixed and consistent right?

Figure 2.2 shows the number of individuals performing from 0 to 12 actions with the left-hand, among 241 service recruits who completed the AHPQ in class. The distribution is J-shaped. The majority reported no left-hand preference (66.8% consistent right-handers), a few reported no right-hand preference (3.7% consistent left-handers) while the remainder performed from 1 to 11 actions with the left-hand (29.5% mixed-handers). Consistent left-handers were found in this and all subsequent samples, but they were always fewer than mixed left-handers. Porac and Coren (1981, p. 16), commenting on the J-shaped preference distribution, wrote, "Ambilaterality is relatively rare in preference distributions." What is shown in Figure 2.2 is not ambilaterality but mixed-handedness. True ambilaterality is indeed rare but mixed-handedness occurs in some 30% of the population.

To avoid confusion, some careful distinctions must be made about the basis of classification. Ambilateral means equal or indifferent preference for either hand, as explained above. But the preferences recorded in Figure 2.2 were not E ("either") responses but definite preferences for the left-hand. The last section showed that L and E responses occurred for all items. Should E responses be counted as evidence of non right-handedness? A decision on this point must depend on the discretion of the researcher. It was said at the start of this

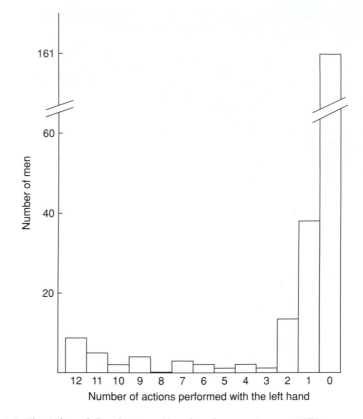

Figure 2.2 The J-shaped distribution of hand preference: Annett, 1972.

chapter that reported incidences of left-handedness range from some 1 to 40%. In my first student questionnaire samples, I found that if E responses were counted as evidence of left preference, left-handers would be well over 50%. It seemed to me that E responses diluted the meaning of left-handedness to an unacceptable extent. Thereafter, it was my practice to count as mixed-handers only people with definite preferences for each hand, some left and some right. (That is, combinations of R + E = consistent right; L + E = consistent left; R + L = mixed, with or without some E preferences. In the very rare case of 100% E responses, I would first wonder if the respondent was making a serious appraisal, but then probably put this very unusual individual with the other rare group, consistent left-handers. The decision is arbitrary, and must be made by the individual researcher.)

Although claims to equal skill with both hands must be treated with caution, it must be acknowledged that when hand use is observed, some people are unable to distinguish a preferred side even after trying the action a few times. The probability of this response is inversely proportional to the degree of practice and skill involved. Table 2.2 showed that the frequency of "E" responses was highest for unscrewing a jar lid and sweeping with a broom, and lowest for cutting with scissors and writing. E responses for writing were 3 per 1000 by questionnaire, but only 5 per 10,000 by observation. Children that I *observed* to change hand use for the same task, in a representative sample of 6- to 15-year-olds, were about 1 in 3 for placing buttons in a narrow necked bottle, but only 1 in 278 for drawing or cutting with scissors. This demonstrates the rarity of ambidexterity for pens and pencils but also shows that changes of hand use for some other tasks may be commonplace. Hence, my decision to ignore "E" responses, and to require definite combinations of right and left-hand preference as the criterion of mixed handedness.

Other researchers have noted these changes of response hand and introduced new terms to describe them. The terms "ambiguous" handedness (Soper and Satz, 1984) and "random" handedness (Bishop, 1990a) were used for changes of hand between trials of the same task. Such changes were suggested to be characteristic of learning disabled and autistic children. Ambiguous in this sense means the same as "either" hand in response to questionnaires. It would not be surprising if young children were uncertain which hand to use for unfamiliar and unpractised actions. Changes of this kind should not be regarded, in my view, as indicating "either", "mixed" or "ambiguous" preferences, but rather as examples of the preliminary trial and error required to "get the feel" of a new action. Reports of high incidences of bilateral or mixed preferences in young children may depend on such trial and error, rather than bilateral or mixed handed stages of development as suggested by Gesell and Ames (1947). Handedness must be learned in the sense that the actions to be performed must be learned, as argued in chapter 1. The hand that works best for a particular action must be discovered with use. Ambiguous or either hand use in disabled children is more likely to be due to slow learning than "abnormal" handedness.

The above discussion of various terms for "uncertain" hand preferences was necessary to explain some of the terms used in the literature, and to clarify my own classification of consistent right-, mixed- and consistent left-handedness. For my classification, what is the distribution in the population? Annett (1967, Table 1) summarised data for seven samples of children, undergraduates and recruits. The proportions of consistent left-handers ranged from 2.0 to 5.0%, mixed-handers from 25.1 to 37.0% and consistent right-handers from 58.4 to 71.5%. These findings confirmed that about two in three people are consistently right-handed. Among the one in three with some definite preference for the left-hand, most are mixed-handers. Because only 3–4% are consistently left-handed, it is also clear that most left-handed writers (about 9–11% in these samples) must also be mixed-handers. This analysis has an important contribution to make to the problem with which the chapter began, the variability of incidences. The range of incidences found in the literature might occur because some investigators classify as left-handed people who perform *all* actions with the left-hand (3%) and some who perform *any* action with the left-hand (around 35%), while others adopt any of the several possible criteria in between.

Annett (1964) suggested that mixed-handedness might be due to the joint expression of two alleles, one for left (L) and one for right (R) handedness. This version of the classic genetic model suggested that the L gene is not fully recessive but sometimes expressed in heterozygotes (RL genotypes). It was not suggested in 1964 that *all* heterozygotes should be mixed-handers (even if all mixed-handers were heterozygotes). It was a great surprise to find that the three types of handedness, right, mixed and left, occurred in binomial proportions. These are the proportions expected if there were indeed two alleles as hypothesised but that both were expressed in all heterozygotes (if RL genotype = mixed-hander). Binomial proportions will be important later, in understanding findings for twins, so it is useful to be clear that they imply a chance pairing of two independent variables. Suppose the frequency of the allele R was 0.8, and that of L 0.2, then a random pairing would be like putting two sets of 100 tokens, each with 80 marked R and 20 marked L into a bag, shaking them up and then drawing out two at a time; on average there would be 64 RR, 32 LR and 4 LL pairs. These resemble the distributions of consistent right-, mixed- and consistent left-handers respectively observed by Annett (1967). In all of the seven samples the distributions agreed with expectations for binomial proportions. This implies that there is a quantitative regularity in the data. What does it mean? If right-, mixed- and left-handedness depended on RR, RL and LL genotypes, then two consistently right-handed parents would have only right-handed children, and two consistently left-handed parents would have only left-handed children. At the time the binomial proportions were discovered, I knew this was not true (Annett, 1967). The genetic model was wrong, but the binomial distribution of the three types of handedness was a reliable feature of the data. Further, and even more puzzling, binomial proportions occurred in other species, to be described in chapter 3.

If one in three people are mixed-handers, and others show varying levels of indifferent preference, what is to be made of all this variability? There are three main alternatives. One is to attribute the variability to errors of measurement (McManus, 1985a). A second approach is to quantify the variability using a laterality index or quotient, rejected as flawed above. A third alternative is to investigate mixed-handedness further. Can meaningful distinctions be made between types of mixed-hander? Does the apparent variability conceal types that would be better described as right or left, or does it reflect true varieties, continuously distributed degrees of relative preference?

CLASSIFICATION OF HAND PREFERENCE BY ASSOCIATION ANALYSIS

Association analysis is a technique developed by botanists for analysing ecological patterns in the distribution of species (Williams and Lambert, 1959, 1960, 1961). The terrain to be investigated is divided systematically into plots, and the number of plants of each species is noted within each plot. It begins like a factor analysis, calculating the correlations between all possible pairs of species. The correlations are summed for each species and the species with the highest sum is taken to be the most informative. The plots are divided between those where this informative species is present versus absent. The calculations are repeated for each subdivision, to make an inverted branching tree. Whereas factor analysis tries to discover what is common to a set of individuals in order to reduce the diversity, association analysis looks for meaningful distinctions. Botanists studying the ecological relationships between plants and their environment found unexpected features such as hidden old railway tracks. If individuals are taken as analogous to plots and actions are analogous to species, association analysis might suggest meaningful distinctions between patterns of hand preference.

Association analyses were run for the total sample of 2321 young adults described for frequency of left responses in Table 2.1. The analyses were run in several ways and for different subgroups (groups classified for sex, generation and source of subjects) but the outcomes were substantially the same. Six items were highly correlated and at similar levels, writing, throwing, tennis racquet, striking a match, hammering and toothbrush. These six were designated "primary" actions. The other six items were also significantly related but had smaller summed correlations (scissors, needle, broom, shovel, dealing cards, unscrewing jar lid). The distinction resembles those described above between the first and later components of factor analyses.

Figure 2.3 shows the outcome of the association analysis represented as an inverted tree. Each branch gives the action used as a basis for the division and the percentages of the total sample involved. The letters A–J refer to the 12 actions of the AHPQ, capitals for right-hand and lower case for left-hand preferences. The first division distinguished 9.2% left-handed hammerers from 90.8% right-handed hammerers. The latter were then divided for writing; 1.94% right-handed hammerers wrote with the left-hand. The height of the division on the graph (the ordinate) depends on the largest chi square at each division (range 5–500, transformed to a logarithmic scale). Having made these major divisions for hammering and writing, the majority of subsequent divisions among right-handers depended on the bimanual actions: shovelling, striking a match, unscrewing the lid of a jar and sweeping. Among left-handed hammerers also subsequent divisions are mostly for the two handed actions, match, unscrewing a jar, sweeping and shovelling. There were divisions for throwing at several levels of the analysis among both right- and left-handers. This suggests some genuine independence between sidedness for throwing and these other actions. (Relations between writing and throwing will be considered further in chapter 9.) The bottom line of Figure 2.3 distinguished some 24 subgroups, each including a relatively small percentage of subjects, except at the extreme right, consistent right-handers (72%).

The association analysis did not reveal any major divisions, analogous to the botanists' old railway tracks, but it was interesting that hammering was more strongly correlated with other preferences than writing. Skilled control of the hands for hammering must have a long evolutionary history for man the toolmaker. Writing was invented, as far as we know, only a few thousand years

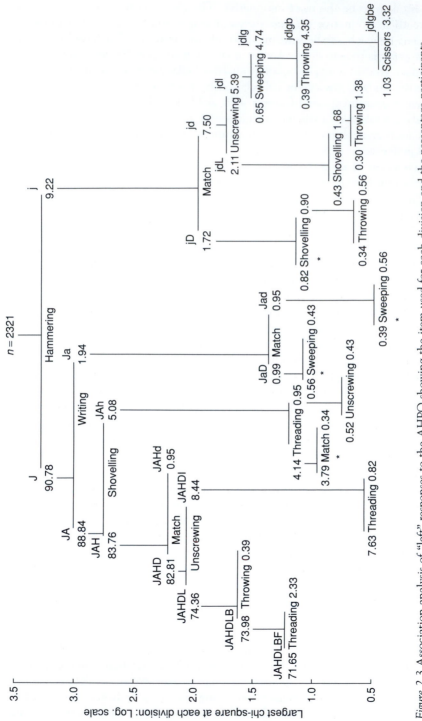

Figure 2.3 Association analysis of "left" responses to the AHPQ showing the item used for each division and the percentage participants in each subgroup: the letters A–J refer to items 1–12 of AHPQ respectively, upper case right and lower case left responses: Annett, 1970a. *Further subgroups involving less than five participants omitted.

ago. The strong association between hammering and other items, as well as its rank in Table 2.3, suggests that the need to make fast controlled movements with precisely specifiable outcomes is fundamental to hand skill and therefore hand preference (see also Annett, Annett, Hudson et al., 1979). Tasks such as sweeping, shovelling, opening box lids and drinking from a glass have more loosely specifiable outcomes than hammering and writing.

The main conclusion drawn from the association analysis was that there are many patterns of mixed-handedness but most with small numbers of cases. There was no evidence for types. The evidence was interpreted as reinforcing the conclusion of the previous researchers, cited above, that handedness is a continuous variable.

SUBGROUPS OF MIXED HAND PREFERENCE ORDERED FOR R–L TIME FOR PEG MOVING

How is a reliable *measurement scale* to be established for this continuous variable? What is required is some independent measure of lateral asymmetry. At the time of the association analysis, I had data for observed hand preference (for the 12 actions of the AHPQ) and for peg moving asymmetry for two samples in Hull. These were psychology students who had tested one another in laboratory practical classes, and a cohort of 12-year-old children tested by myself and assistants in a comprehensive school (LS sample). What could these data for hand preference and hand skill in the same subjects reveal about the relationship between these two variables? There were over 2000 subjects in the association analysis and only 283 with peg moving times, so there were insufficient data to test all the subgroups in Figure 2.3. I made top down binary divisions to create an inverted tree, following the association analysis as far as feasible. At each division of the sample, I tested the relevant pairs for difference for L–R peg moving time.

Figure 2.4 shows the classification and the statistical comparison at each division. The first division was made for writing and the difference between right writers (A) and left writers (a) for L–R peg moving was highly significant, as expected (p < 0.001). Although hammering was the most powerful discriminant, writing hand was judged more useful for a scheme of classification. The next decision on each side was between those who performed any of the other primary actions (throwing, racket, match, hammer and toothbrush) with the non-writing hand. There was a significant difference between left-writers (one-tailed) who did and did not perform other primary actions with the right-hand. The corresponding difference between right-handed writers was not statistically significant. The classification by primary actions was retained for right-handers, however, because the lack of significance could be due to chance factors in these small samples. (Later studies continued to find class 5 out of line and the subgroup scheme was revised as shown in Table 2.5 below.) Among left-handers who performed all primary actions with the left-hand, a further division was

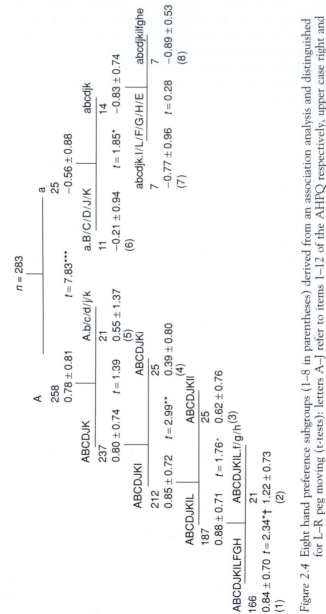

Figure 2.4 Eight hand preference subgroups (1–8 in parentheses) derived from an association analysis and distinguished for L–R peg moving (t-tests): letters A–J refer to items 1–12 of the AHPQ respectively, upper case right and lower case left responses: Annett, 1970a. *** p < 0.001; **p < 0.01; * p < 0.05 (one-tailed); †difference in the unpredicted direction.

made between those who were consistently sinistral versus those who performed a non-primary action with the right-hand. The L–R difference was small but in the expected direction.

Among right-handers performing all primary actions with the right-hand, further divisions depended on *findings for L–R peg moving asymmetry*. The largest difference was found between those who deal playing cards left (ABCDJKi) versus right-handed (ABCDJKI) (t = 2.99, d.f. 235, p < 0.01, 1-tail). The group of right-handed writers who deal playing cards left-handed (taking the card from the pack with the left-hand and placing on the table) was found to be of considerable interest in later analyses. It is important to be clear that this group was distinguished on the basis of an empirical examination of relative L–R hand skill.

Among the right-handed dealers, there was a difference (one-tailed) between those unscrewing the lid of a jar with the left-hand. Finally, a left-hand response to any of the three actions, needle threading (F), sweeping (G) and shovelling (H) produced a significant difference in the *opposite* direction to that expected. That is, subjects performing these actions left-handed were more *dextral* than the remaining subjects on the peg moving task. This analysis gave a total of eight subgroups, or hand preference classes. Classes 1 and 8 were consistently right and left-handed respectively, classes 6–7 were mixed left-handers and classes 2–5 mixed right-handers. Table 2.4 summarises the subgroup scheme in words and shows the percentages of males and females in each group in the combined samples available at that time, as described by Annett and Kilshaw (1983).

Figure 2.5 shows the L–R means for the eight hand preference groups just described, in the two Hull samples on which the original classification was based. Hand preferences and hand skills were related in a similar fashion in both samples. Both showed the trend to greater *dextrality* for class 2 than for

Table 2.4 The definition of eight classes of hand preference identified in Figure 2.4: percentages per class in combined main samples

Definition	Males (%) (N = 617)	Females (%) (N = 863)
1 Right (or R + E) for all actions	64.7	61.4
2 Left for any of needle, broom or spade	6.5	12.7
3 Left for jar and no others except above	7.6	6.9
4 Left for cards and no others except above	9.7	5.8
5 Right writing but left for any other primary action	4.1	4.4
6 Left writing but right for any other primary action	2.4	3.0
7 Left for all primary actions but right for any others	2.4	2.1
8 Left (or L + E) for all actions	2.6	3.6

Note
Primary actions are those most highly inter-correlated: writing, throwing, racquet, match, hammer and toothbrush (Annett, 1970a).

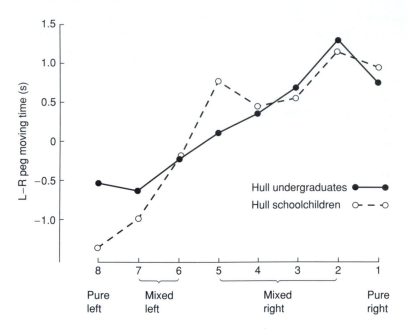

Figure 2.5 Hand preference subgroups with L–R peg moving time: two samples from Hull.

class 1. Class 5 took its "proper" place between classes 4 and 6 for the undergraduates, but not for the teenagers. A difference between classes 7 and 8 was clear for the children but not for the undergraduates. However, numbers were small in both samples. The important question was whether these findings would be repeated in another sample.

The reliability of the subgroup classification was tested a few years later when data were collected from 804 Open University (OU) students attending psychology summer schools (Annett, 1976). A practical class on laterality included the observation of hand use for the AHPQ and measures of peg moving time. Written instructions for the class were supplied by me but groups were run by summer school teachers at a number of locations. Observations and measurements were made by pairs of students taking turns as experimenter and participant. Students were asked to make a copy of their data, to be collected and sent to me. I checked the arithmetic, excluded those who reported any physical problem of the hands or arms, and classified the remainder in the eight preference groups defined above. Figure 2.6 shows the mean L–R peg moving times for subgroups in the OU sample along with the combined data of the two original Hull samples. The means were virtually identical for several subgroups. There was the same "bump" for class 5 in both. For the OU sample, class 2 was intermediate between 1 and 3 and class 8 was not more sinistral than 7. Apart from these small differences, the overall similarity between the Hull and OU samples confirmed that patterns of mixed hand preference are related to differences between

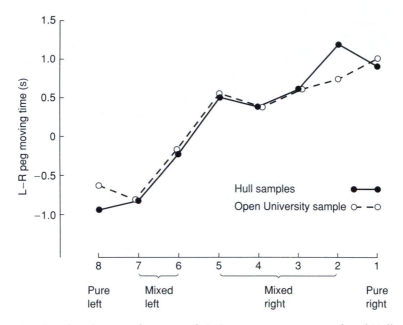

Figure 2.6 Hand preference subgroups with L–R peg moving time: combined Hull samples and Open University students.

the hands for peg moving skill in a reliable and systematic manner. It was astonishing for a psychologist to find such a close agreement between data for two large samples, collected years apart, especially when most of the measurements were by students. This demonstration of the reliability of the co-ordination of data for hand preference, as defined by the subgroup analysis, and R–L hand skill, as measured by peg moving time, is one of the quantitative foundations of the RS theory.

Inspection of Figure 2.6 reveals that subgroup 5 was out of line in the otherwise linear relationship between preference and skill. Further, the standard deviation was larger than for other classes suggesting that class 5 was more heterogeneous. Because my aim was to describe levels of hand preference that would be systematically ordered for R–L skill, relationships between skill and preference were re-examined in classes 3–5. All the data available at that time (from the combined samples of Annett and Kilshaw, 1983) were examined.

Table 2.5 lists the original hand preference classes (1–8) along with the Ns, L–R means and standard deviations. Class 5, right-writers with any left preference for other primary actions, was analysed further as shown. It can be seen that those who performed only *one* primary action left-handed and did *not* deal playing cards left-handed resembled the original class 3 for L–R time (6.9 and 7.0 respectively). Those performing one primary action left-handed but also

Table 2.5 Revision of the hand preference classes from 8 to 7, deleting class 5

Hand pref. class	N	L–R mean ($^1/_{10}$s)	S.D.	Revised classes	N	L–R mean	S.D.
1	929	9.5	7.3				
2	150	9.0	7.8				
3	107	7.0	6.8	3 + a i	142	7.0	7.3
4	110	3.7	7.4	4 + a ii or b iii	132	3.7	7.2
5	63	4.2	9.4				
6	41	−3.7	7.1				
7	33	−6.8	7.8				
8	47	−8.0	7.2				

	N	R–L mean	S.D.
a. One primary action only			
i not cards	35	6.9	8.6
ii plus cards	4	3.2	5.4
b. Any two primary actions			
iii	18	3.8	7.0

Notes

Combined main samples, omitting six reporting forced change to right-handed writing (Annett and Kilshaw, 1983).

Revised definitions of classes 3 and 4 (see also algorithm in Figure A.I.1): Class 3: Right-handed writers who perform any one primary action with the left-hand and/or unscrew the lid of a jar with the left-hand. Class 4: Right-handed writers who perform any two primary actions with the left-hand and/or deal playing cards with the left-hand.

dealing cards with the left-hand resembled the original class 4 (3.2 and 3.7 respectively). Class 5, when performing *two* primary actions left-handed resembled the original class 4 (3.8). Hence class 5 was removed from the revised scheme and its members re-assigned; those who performed *not more than one* other primary action left-handed and did not deal playing cards left-handed were reassigned to class 3 (along with the original class 3, unscrewing the lid of a jar left-handed). Those performing *two or more* primary actions with the left-hand were re-assigned to class 4 (along with others dealing playing cards left-handed). The redefined classes 3 and 4 are listed in Table 2.5. It can be seen that the Ns for both groups were substantial, that the standard deviations were similar to those of other groups, and that the means of classes 3 and 4 were about roughly symmetrical with 6 and 7 (to either side of 0).

Figure 2.7 graphs the L–R times of the revised classes for the combined samples just described, together with new data for further combined samples (Annett, 1992d, N = 888). The L–R means are virtually identical for several classes. The linear relationship between hand preference classes and hand skill asymmetry is clear, with the interesting exception of class 2. It will be recalled that class 2 was more dextral than class 1 in both of the original Hull samples

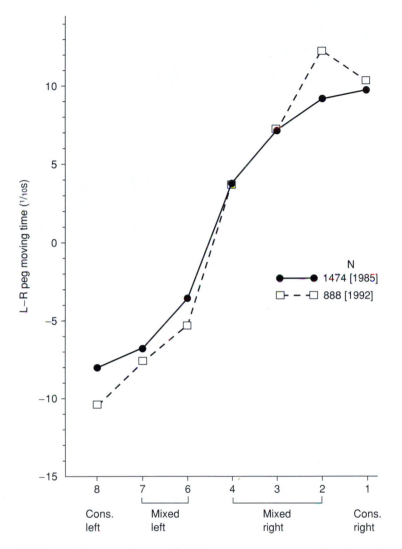

Figure 2.7 Hand preference classes with L–R peg moving time: combined samples of 1985 and new combined samples of 1992.

(Figure 2.5) but not in OU students (Figure 2.6). The re-appearance of this curious finding in new large combined data suggests that it must be taken seriously, even if not evident in every sample. The stronger dextrality of class 2 will be important later when considering findings for subgroup handedness and spatial ability.

The outcome of these analyses was a scheme that is represented as an inverted branching tree in Figure 2.8. An algorithm for deciding the hand preference class, given a set of AHPQ responses, is given in Appendix I. There is one

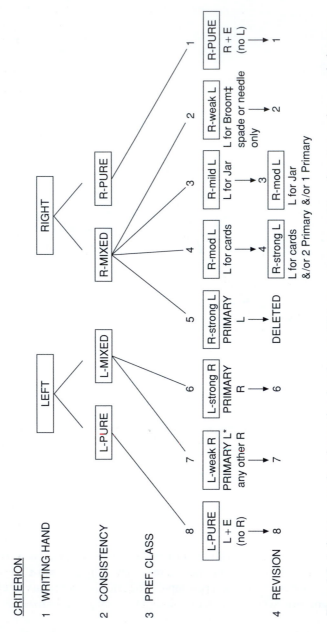

Figure 2.8 A decision tree for subgroup hand preference. *Primary actions are writing, throwing, racket, match, hammer, toothbrush; Non-primary are scissors, needle, broom, spade, dealing cards, unscrewing jar. ‡Classes to the left take precedence.

modification between Figure 2.8 and the algorithm, concerning "scissors". Scissors did not feature in the original decision tree because it seemed unnecessary. Left-writers who use scissors in the right-hand were catered for (class 7 if no primary action "right" and class 6 otherwise). Right-writers using scissors in the left-hand were expected to be non-existent (in the light of the fact that scissors are designed for use in the right-hand). In fact, some right-handers do use scissors in the left-hand. The algorithm places scissors for right-handers among the primary actions. The scheme now covers all logical possibilities, except for the very rare individual who claims to be "either" for everything. If such a case were *observed*, I would try to discover whether, on balance, there was a right or a left-hand preference for some main action, and classify as consistent right or consistent left accordingly. If by questionnaire, the decision would be arbitrary but probably consistent left.

The reader will see from the above account that the classification of varieties of mixed-hand preference depended on *empirical* comparisons for relative hand skill. The preference classes were defined so as to maximise L–R differences between adjacent groups. However, the standard deviations indicate considerable overlap between the groups. The groups are reliably ordered for relative hand skill, but not distinct in the sense of being discrete. No absolute divisions can be drawn. Previous studies of hand skill asymmetries in right- and left-handers have reported considerable overlap (Benton, 1962; Johnstone, Galin and Herron, 1979; Satz, Achenbach and Fennell, 1967). Non-significant differences between the groups have been interpreted as reason to doubt that there are strong relationships between preference and skill. However, the non-significant findings depended on relatively small groups of self-classified left- and right-handers, many of whom were likely to be mixed-handers. The apparently negative data of these studies is a problem only for "type" theories of handedness. It is not a problem if hand preference is expressed in many varieties, along the continuum of R–L skill. The elusive "essence" of handedness can be pinned down when degrees of preference are related to degrees of relative skill. But having reached this empirical description of the laterality continuum, does it have any practical value? Is it predictive of other lateral asymmetries?

SUBGROUP HAND PREFERENCE VALIDATED AGAINST OTHER ASYMMETRIES

The subgroups distinguished above were reliably ordered for R–L peg moving time in several samples. Is this due to some specific property of the peg moving task, or does the sequence apply more generally? Are the subgroups similarly ordered for measures of hand skill other than peg moving? I invested considerable effort in trying to find an alternative to the peg moving task that could be used for testing groups, such as classes of schoolchildren. Several pencil and paper tests of hand skill were given to children and to students, square marking, dotting or line drawing between circles and punching holes through targets printed on stiff paper. All of these tests produced distributions of R–L skill that tended to the bimodal, in contrast to the unimodal distribution for peg moving. This is not surprising because all of the group tests involved the control of a pen or pencil. However, all of the group tests could be used to derive relative asymmetry scores. When these were examined in hand preference subgroups, the sequences were identical with those for peg moving (Annett, 1992d, p. 592). This demonstrates that the handedness continuum, as defined by peg moving asymmetry, is relevant to other hand skill asymmetries also.

But does the scheme of classification have relevance beyond measures of hand preference and hand skill? It will be shown in later chapters that the subgroup scheme is indeed relevant to the description of other types of lateral asymmetry. Roughly linear relationships occur between subgroup order and frequency of left eye dominance, left foot preference and the probability of left-handed relatives. All of these are related to subgroup hand preference in ways expected if the subgroup classification does in fact represent a scale of measurement. That is, the classes give a reliable indication of degrees of relative bias to left and right along an underlying asymmetry continuum.

SUMMARY

This chapter examines a fundamental difficulty for research on handedness that reports of incidence vary from some 1 to 40%. Although the terms "left" and "right" are sufficient for ordinary discourse about handedness, they are insufficient for scientific study because there is no fixed and agreed definition of either term.

Differences for incidence between studies arise for several reasons. There may be genuine differences between groups, such as the learning disabled versus normal samples. There are differences between self-report and indirect report. Students are not always aware of the handedness of their parents or other relatives. Left-handers are more aware than right-handers. Assessments of handedness by observation differ from those by questionnaire. Surveys that request later return are likely to have poor return rates, and also incidences that differ from those from "captive" groups, such as students in class asked to return the forms immediately.

The chief reason for different incidences is that people differ in patterns of mixed hand preference and investigators vary in their classification of these patterns. Ambidexterity, meaning equal skill with either hand for writing is rare (about 3 per 1000 by questionnaire) but mixed-handedness, changes of hand preferred between different tasks is common (about 3 in 10). The importance of mixed-handedness has been obscured by two factors that distort the expression of left-handedness. The first is cultural pressure against the use of the left-hand through prejudice, and the second is physical pressure due to the design of tools and the "right-handed world". Both of these factors were taken to mean that any sign of left-hand preference was a sign of a "true" left-hander. Yet if any report of left or either hand preference for a 12-item questionnaire were taken as an indication, some 50% of the population would be called left-handed. Hence, different investigators are likely to set their criteria of sinistrality in different ways, and thus reach a variety of estimates.

The first step toward a scientific study of handedness is to recognise that it is not a discrete variable, right or left, but a continuous one that can be expressed at many levels between strong left and strong right. The second step is to establish incidences for identifiable groups, such as consistent left, consistent right and mixed handers. These three groups were found in the proportions expected if there were two alleles, R (right) and L (left) that combined at random to give LL, RL and RR genotypes, that were left, mixed and right respectively. However, this genetic model was not valid, so how did the binomial proportions arise? (The question is tackled in chapter 3.)

An analysis of patterns of mixed hand preference was made through an association analysis, a type of reverse factor analysis that looks for meaningful distinctions. The groups distinguished were examined for differences between the hands for peg moving skill (L–R skill). It was shown that responses to individual questionnaire items were stable between two large sets of combined data for "left" responses, "either" responses and for L–R skill. A search for patterns of preference that are ordered for L–R skill led to the identification of eight hand preference subgroups (later reduced to seven) that were reliably associated with differences for skill between samples. They are also relevant for later analyses in several chapters, for eye dominance, foot preference, proportion of left-handed relatives and certain measures of ability.

3 The right shift theory of handedness

Chance plus or minus right loading

This chapter shows how the right shift (RS) theory was founded on a comparison of handedness in humans versus nonhumans, in the light of the conclusion of the previous chapter that handedness can best be thought of as a continuum. The paper that first proposed the RS theory was called, "The distribution of manual asymmetry" (Annett, 1972). Several types of distribution were examined, preferences in humans and nonhumans, hand skill for peg moving and handedness in families. The analyses suggested that human handedness is similar to that of other primates and mammals in all but one key respect. The essentials of the argument are that asymmetries depend on accidental differences between the sides that arise during early growth in bilaterally symmetrical organisms. What is specific to humans is a factor that weights the accidental chances in favour of right-handedness. The presence of the RS factor (later RS + gene) does not specify right-handedness, but loads the dice in that direction.

ASYMMETRIES IN NATURE

There is a multitude of asymmetries in the universe of physical and living things (Gardner, 1967; Hegstrom and Kondepudi, 1990). Asymmetries occur at many levels from the spin of subatomic particles to that of heavenly spheres, the genome to human cerebral dominance. Does the spin of the earth on its axis affect the direction in which the bathwater drains in the southern versus northern hemispheres? There are many questions of this type that can be posed about asymmetries, and few certain answers. The basic molecules of life that carry the genetic code, deoxyribosenucleic acid (DNA) and ribosenucleic (RNA), take the form of a helix that normally turns to the right. Amino-acids, the building blocks of all proteins, are left-handed although right-handed forms can be constructed in the laboratory and presumably existed at one time (Mason, 1991). Pasteur discovered that certain crystals are right or left-handed. Solutions of right-handed crystals rotated polarised light in one direction and solutions of left-handed crystals rotated light in the opposite direction. Mixtures of right and left-handed crystals (racemic mixtures) did not rotate light. Most plants can be divided into mirror halves by a cut in more than one plane but the coil of tendrils of climbing plants is directional. The bindweed coils to the right and the honeysuckle to the left; "so doth the woodbine and sweet honeysuckle gently entwist", says Titania when embracing Bottom in *Midsummer Night's Dream*. The Narwhal grows a single tooth like a spear that may be 8 or 9 feet long with a counter-clockwise twist. The human umbilical cord may have a clockwise, counter-clockwise or alternating spiral. What relevance do these asymmetries have for human handedness and brain asymmetries? The answer is probably "none" but until they are understood we cannot be sure. It seems likely, however, that different levels of physical and biological asymmetry are independent (Bock and Marsh, 1991).

A pattern of asymmetries in the arrangement of the viscera is characteristic of vertebrates, including the heart and stomach to the left and the liver to the right. The development of these left–right asymmetries appears to depend in part on the beating of cilia that transport relevant substances over the embryo. Cilia clear substances from the respiratory tract, enable sperm to swim to the egg, and also transport substances within cells. Afzelius (1976) found that patients with an inherited disorder called Kartagener syndrome had immotile sperm and respiratory cilia, as well as about 50% situs inversus of the viscera. He predicted that the left–right orientation of the embryo might depend on ciliary function. The determinants of visceral asymmetries are under active investigation. Several genes are thought to be involved (Hyatt and Yost, 1998; Supp, Potter and Brueckner, 2000). The mechanisms involved in visceral asymmetries and in handedness are likely to be different, but they might follow similar rules. Layton (1976) proposed a theory for *situs inversus*, involving an *iv* gene, that has a strong resemblance to the RS theory for handedness (Annett, 1972). It was an example of two researchers reaching similar original theories independently at about the same time. Similarities and contrasts between the theory of the *iv* gene and the RS theory will be examined in chapter 16.

Evidence for what might be the earliest behavioural asymmetry has been found in the scars of trilobites, creatures that were very common some half a billion years ago but have been extinct since the Permian era. The healed scars on the carapace were more often located on the right side than the left. This suggests that either the predators or the trilobites moved asymmetrically (Babcock and Robison, 1989). The shells of the water snail *Limnae* typically coil to the right, but some are left-handed. The mechanism depends on genes that follow the classic rules of Mendelian inheritance, but they are expressed not directly on the offspring but through the cytoplasm of the mother (Boycott, Diver, Garstang et al., 1930; review in Weaver and Hedrick, 1992). The mouths of cichlid fish may open on the left or the right side, and the relative prevalence of the two varieties fluctuates in ways that are likely to be governed by selection for feeding success (Hori, 1993). Flounders are bilaterally symmetrical in early life like other fish but as adults they lie on the sea floor and one eye migrates over the top of the head so that both eyes look upward. There are some 500 species in several families. Some are right eyed species, others are left eyed species and some are racemic (asymmetrical in either direction). Investigations suggest that the directional asymmetry may be determined genetically in some species, but not in others (Policansky, 1982). There is an asymmetry in the midbrain nuclei of frogs (Morgan, 1977). Toads have been reported to strike with their tongue at other toads in their left visual field more often than in the right visual field (Robins, Lippolis, Bisazza et al., 1998). Crabs and lobsters may have one claw much larger than the other, and the larger claw may be on the right or the left (Govind, 1989; Vernberg and Costlow, 1966).

Reports that parrots are left footed for holding and manipulating food date back to the 17th century (Harris, 1989). Observations on 15 species of parrot appeared to support this view (Friedman and Davis, 1938) but according to re-analysis of these data by Rogers (Bradshaw and Rogers, 1993) six species were left footed, one species right footed, and eight were without particular bias. In another study of Australian parrots and cockatoos, eight out of nine species were left footed for manipulating food objects. Foot biases have been studied in goldfinches for manipulating doors and catches with a beak and a foot; all the birds preferred the right foot. Lateral asymmetries of perception, learning and memory are under investigation in the domestic chick (Andrew, 1997). Lateral asymmetries in birds at the species level are likely to have different evolutionary origins from those of humans but both could have been driven by similar pressure for vocal control in song and speech. Humans are the only primates that talk. Perhaps it was the complexity of the sounds produced by birds and humans for communication that required control by one side. This argument is supported by the evidence, mentioned in chapter 1, of behavioural asymmetries in the swimming and feeding of whales. These are mammals re-adapted to the sea, like dolphins and porpoises, that communicate in songs that travel over vast distances.

The asymmetries most relevant to human handedness are the hand preferences of nonhuman primates and the paw preferences of other mammals. The human hand is based on an ancient vertebrate plan for five digits. Primates (humans, apes, monkeys, lemurs and other prosimians) have hands capable of grasping branches and other objects, often with considerable manipulative skill. The hand preferences of higher apes (chimpanzee, gorilla and orang-utan) are of special interest because these are our closest cousins in the animal world. Small mammals, mice, rats and cats have been observed for paw laterality in various tasks, most involving reaches for food. Experiments using these animals have been designed to throw light on the causes of preference.

Finch (1941) observed 30 captive chimpanzees, each making 200 reaches for food in each of four situations. The number of right-hand reaches out of 800 per animal ranged more or less continuously between nil and 100%. It was symmetrical about 400 reaches, 15 animals or 50% to either side. Taking a criterion of 90% reaches with one hand, nine (30%) were left-handed and nine right-handed but 40% were inconsistent. Now there is a curious feature of these findings for chimpanzees and other species that was noted by Annett (1967). The proportions are consistent with a pair of alleles (R and L) that combined in pairs by chance, the pairs being associated with consistent right, mixed and consistent left-handedness in binomial proportions as described in chapter 2.

(For humans, alleles of frequencies R = 0.8 and L = 0.2 would give genotypes in the proportions RR 64, RL 32 and LL 4, per 100 population. For nonhumans, two alleles of equal frequency, 0.5 would give 25, 50 and 25% respectively.) It was pointed out earlier that the genetic model that suggested the possibility of binomial proportions is wrong, so these observations raise several questions. Are the findings reliable? Are they generally found in other species? Should animals with inconsistent preferences for a relatively simple task, reaching for food, be called "mixed-handers" like humans who change hand preference between tasks? What causes the binomial distribution if there are no genes "for" handedness?

With regard to reliability, Finch's findings for captive chimpanzees have been fully endorsed by field observations of 42 chimpanzees living in the Gombe National Park in Tanzania. Some 43 categories of limb movement were recorded over several months as the animals performed spontaneous activities. None of the chimpanzees were fully consistent for right or left-hand use. They were rather mixed handed over the several tasks. There was certainly no evidence of species bias to either side (Marchant and McGrew, 1996). Is this true of other apes? Annett and Annett (1991) observed 31 gorillas (lowland species) in European zoos, while they were feeding on several types of food in different situations, within their living space. Records were made of the hand used to pick up food and convey it to the mouth. Percentages of right-hand preference ranged from 12 to 83% in a continuous distribution as found by Finch for chimpanzees. Taking a division at 50% reaches, there were 16 left-handed and 15 right-handed animals. Byrne and Byrne (1991) observed 38 mountain gorillas in the wild in Rwanda, feeding on different types of food. Hand use was consistent in most individuals for most foods, but the hand preferred often differed between food types. That is, many animals were mixed handed in the sense of changing the hand preferred for manipulating different foods. Byrne and Byrne looked carefully for evidence of species bias to one hand and found none. A report that gorillas are right-handed for chest-beating displays (Schaller, 1963) probably has no bearing on hand preference for purposeful actions because it is an automatic behaviour. Byrne and Byrne point out that chest-beating bias was statistically significant for only one animal and that at least one animal used the left-hand first. Information on other apes is sparse but my observations of five orang-utans at Twycross Zoo, suggested a handedness distribution like that of chimpanzee and gorilla (Annett, 1985a, p. 171). Orangs being prepared for rehabilitation in the wild showed no group bias to either side for hand use when feeding (Rogers and Kaplan, 1996). Chivers (1974) watched a family of Siamangs (a type of gibbon, a lesser ape) in the wild over a period of 6 months and noted both left and right preferent animals. Bonobos, or pygmy chimpanzees (*Pan paniscus*), probably resemble the more common chimpanzee (*Pan troglodytes*) for handedness (De Vleeschouwer, Van Elsacker and Verheyen, 1995).

Several studies of monkeys agree with the findings for apes. Warren (1953) observed 84 rhesus monkeys picking up food from a tray, for 120 trials per animal. Twenty-three (27%) were right preferent and the same number left preferent for 90% or more reaches, while 45% were inconsistent. In 171 rhesus monkeys studied by Lehman (1978) the distribution of relative preference between the sides was clearly continuous. Taking a 90% criterion of consistency, my estimate from Lehman's Figure 1 is that 23% were right preferent, 24% left preferent and 53% inconsistent. Bonnet monkeys were classified by Brooker, Lehman, Heimbuch et al. (1981) for statistically significant bias to either side. The animals about equally divided between right- (33%), left- (31%) and mixed- (36%) handers.

Milner (1969) made an independent test of the binomial hypothesis (of Annett, 1967), using handedness data for 58 rhesus monkeys that had been trained to make tactile discriminations of shapes in the dark, including some animals previously described by Ettlinger and Moffett (1964). This analysis is of interest for several reasons. First, the animals were immature at the start of testing but were trained on two tasks, the first relatively easy (to discriminate a cylinder from a sphere) and the second rather difficult (to discriminate a C versus a C in mirror image). The number of animals with inconsistent preference fell steadily over the test series, from the first pre-criterion trials of task 1 (55% inconsistent) to the trained criterion trials of task 2 (21% inconsistent). This agrees with the argument that preferences are learned in particular situations, becoming stronger for one hand with practice. That is, consistency for a particular task increases with age and experience. The second point of interest is that the proportions of right, mixed and left animals fitted expectations for the binomial theorem for most of the analyses. There were fewer mixed-handers than 50% (as required to fit the binomial) in task 2, presumably because the animals had developed consistent preferences with practice, as said above. But with increasing consistency, similar proportions of animals became left-handed (43%) as right-handed (36%). Proportions were not binomial for another analysis, when preferences were classified over all trials, including the early trials of the naïve and immature animals. Here there were too many mixed-handers (69%). This last analysis shows that the majority of animals tried either hand at some point in the course of the experiments. However, when those initial trials are omitted, the classification based on all remaining trials was a virtually perfect fit to binomial expectations (24% R, 26% L, 50% M).

Five different tasks were examined for hand use in 81 immature and adult rhesus monkeys (Warren, Ablanalp and Warren, 1967). Did the monkeys prefer the same hand for all of the five tasks, or did preferences vary between tasks, as in mixed handed humans? A re-analysis of the Warren data by Passingham (1982) found some animals consistently right or left-handed but most preferred different hands for different tasks. This analysis confirms that monkeys may be mixed handed in the way defined above for humans. That is, they may have specific preferences for particular tasks, but prefer different hands for different tasks.

Cole (1955) observed 60 cats, each making 100 reaches for food. On a criterion of 75 or more reaches per paw, there were 20% right pawed, 38% left pawed and 42% ambi-pawed animals. The distribution does not differ significantly from predictions for 25%, 25% and 50% (chi square = 5.70, d.f. 2, n.s.). Collins (1969) studied paw preferences in mice as they reached into a feeding tube placed in the centre of a transparent panel. Fifty reaches were counted for some 850 mice. The distribution was U-shaped. Some animals had strong preferences for the left paw, others for the right paw and about half were spread over intermediate levels of preference. When animals were classified as consistent if they made not more than 5/50 entries with the "other" paw, right, mixed and left-paw preferences were 26, 44 and 30% respectively. These proportions resemble those described above for cats, monkeys and chimpanzees. All found some animals left preferent, some right preferent, but many animals without strong preference.

The causes of right versus left preference can be examined experimentally in rodents and other small mammals. The question whether paw preferences are inherited was thoroughly investigated for mice and for rats. Collins bred mice from R–R and L–L parents for three generations of selection and found 50% left-handed offspring in both breeding lines. Peterson (1934) bred 30 litters of rats from various combinations of right, left and ambidextrous parents. There was no discernible effect on the paw preference of offspring. These experiments conclusively rule out the hypothesis that paw preferences in rats and mice are genetically transmitted. Left and right paw preferences in these mammals are not caused by genes.

What else might cause preferences in nonhumans? Peterson tested various theories in experiments on rats, position in utero, origin of the carotid arteries, influence of the dominant eye, practice, and brain damage. There was only one specific associate of paw preference, the small part of the motor cortex directly responsible for each paw. The only experimental manipulation that changed preference depended on identifying the area of the brain that produced paw movement when electrically stimulated, and then destroying this area. Very small lesions of the brain that destroyed all of this area caused permanent changes of paw preference. If the area was not completely destroyed the animal might transfer back to its original preference after recovery from the operation. Destruction of 50% of the hemisphere outside this cortical area did not affect preference. These findings agree with clinical observations in humans that hand preferences are not changed by brain lesions unless there is an injury that gives a specific motor weakness to one side (Milner, 1974). The findings should be recalled when it is argued that human left-handedness might be due to non-specific, covert or minimal brain damage.

The relevance of learning has been investigated in experiments on the effects of age, specific training for one hand, and the pressures of right-handed versus left-handed worlds. The 81 rhesus monkeys described above for five tasks were observed over a 2-year period. No systematic changes occurred with increasing age. With regard to the development of preferences in individual monkeys, Warren (1977, pp. 164–165) pointed out that, "The initial performance of inexperienced monkeys is somewhat unstable, inconsistent and largely task specific [but] as monkeys become experienced . . . they develop skills and strong hand preferences for dealing with limited classes of manipulanda." This agrees with the argument above for the early trials of naïve monkeys, and for the interpretation of so-called "ambiguous" handedness in normal children (see chapter 2).

The development of paw preferences was investigated for eight tasks given to cats between the ages of 6 months to 1 year, some retested after 2 years (Warren, Ablanalp and Warren, 1967). Preferences were consistent, enduring and not affected by extensive early practice. Forcing cats to use the non-preferred paw in a specific situation increased the chances that the animal would use that paw in that situation, but did not generalise to other situations. Experimentally placed lesions in the sensorimotor area of the brain contralateral to the preferred side induced changes in paw preference, but not lesions elsewhere in the brain (Warren, Cornwell, Webster et al., 1972).

The effects of early experience were examined in mice reared in what Collins (1975) called right-handed or left-handed "worlds". The apparatus was modified by placing the feeding tube flush with a right (or left) wall such that it was difficult to reach into except with the corresponding hand. Young mice were given their first experience of reaching for food in a biased world, either right or left. Most animals conformed to the world bias and used the easier paw, but about 10% persisted in using the opposite paw. This experiment is often cited as support of the "right-handed world" hypothesis for human handedness because about 10% of people in western societies write with the left-hand. However, the next part of Collins' experiment, generally ignored by reviewers, was the critical test. The animals that had been reared in right or left-handed "worlds" were then placed in "worlds" of opposite handedness (that is, mice experienced for reaching into the tube flush against the right wall were tested with the tube flush against the left wall and vice versa). It was found that some animals adapted to the new arrangement easily, and others did not. The ones that adapted easily were those that had found it hard to adapt to their original biased world, whereas the ones that did not adapt to the new world had adapted easily to the old. These very important findings show that *preference predated the animals' first experience of reaching*. Paw preferences were not caused by training, although their expression was undoubtedly influenced by the environment.

If paw preferences in mice are not inherited or learned, what is the cause? Collins (1970) measured the grip strength of each front paw and showed that the mean strength of the preferred paw was significantly greater than that of the non-preferred paw. There is likely to be an asymmetry continuum as argued above for humans. Collins (1977, 1985, 1991) continued to investigate paw preferences in mice, looking for genes that might influence the *degree* of asymmetry. Although he was convinced that genes did not cause the direction of asymmetry, right or left, he looked for evidence that the strength of asymmetry is genetic and differs between the sexes. Strength of right-hand preference differs between the sexes in humans also (see Figure 3.2 below). The important conclusion to be drawn from Collins' work for the present purpose is that the *direction* of preference, left or right, is congenital (present at birth) but does not depend on genes. Paw preferences are present before the animal's first experience of reaching, and they are equally likely to be for the left or right sides. Preferences must depend, therefore, on accidental environmental influences on the development of each individual animal.

There are several important conclusions to be drawn from these studies of hand and paw preferences.

1. Right- and left-handedness occur as natural variants in all of these species; both can be presumed to occur as natural variants in humans also.
2. Both varieties of handedness can occur without genetic causation.
3. There are many levels of relative right and left-hand preference in non-humans, with the majority of animals showing mixed preferences. The distribution of right, mixed and left preferences in nonhumans fits the binomial theorem, just like the distribution for humans, although the actual proportions are different and although we know genes are not involved.
4. There are no directional biases to left or right-hand preference at the species level in chimpanzees or other nonhuman primate or small mammal tested for handedness.

These conclusions form a major part of the foundations of the RS theory. Is there any serious challenge to their validity? There was certainly no reason to doubt them in 1972. Since that time, many researchers have looked for evidence of species level asymmetries in nonhumans and some have claimed to find them (review by Bradshaw and Rogers, 1993). A major impetus to this research was given by three linguists, MacNeilage, Studdert-Kennedy and Lindblom (1987), who suggested that absence of species biases for handedness in nonhuman primates would imply that human left hemisphere specialisation arose *de novo* in human evolution. They argued that there was neglected evidence for handedness biases in other primates and that there might, therefore, be evolutionary precursors of human specialisations. Why should three linguists (in common with many others) believe that it is necessary to demonstrate evolutionary continuities for *handedness* when there are no continuities for *speech*? Although handedness and speech laterality in humans are associated in some way it is not known exactly how. The puzzle is the purpose of the present book. There are some implicit and perhaps false assumptions in the argument that species level asymmetries for handedness "ought to exist" in other primates.

McNeilage et al. argued that there are species biases to left-handedness in monkeys and other primates for simple reaching, but species biases to right-handedness for more complex manipulative activities. Further, they suggested that preferences would be influenced by postural constraints. The evidence offered for these speculations does not bear scrutiny, as I showed in open peer commentary associated with the McNeilage et al. paper (Annett, 1987b). Only two sets of findings were claimed to give statistically significant results. One was for rhesus monkeys tested in the laboratory of Ettlinger, including the data of Milner (1969) described above. The predicted trend (excess of left-handed reaching) was present only in the naïve animals during their first training trials, but not at any later stage (as shown above). However, it was data for that first stage that was combined with data from other reports from this research group. However, the other papers included at least some of the *same animals* so that a small group trend was probably amplified by double counting. The second statistically significant result depended on combined data for Japanese macaques when mixed handers were omitted. Overall there were 38% left, 29% right and 33% mixed preferent animals. Does this look like good evidence for species bias to left preference?

With regard to the argument for right preferences for manipulative actions, an experiment on gorillas manipulating a sliding panel in order to reach for food found the *left*-hand was used by seven out of eight animals, although there was no group bias for other tasks (Fagot and Vauclair, 1988). The predominance of left-hand use in this small group may be due to accidents of sampling or to factors specific to the test situation. Is it possible that species level preferences are present for skilled manipulations but not unskilled ones? Humans do not show handedness biases for self-touching movements in children (Brown, 1962; Ingram, 1975) nor adults (Dalby, Gibson, Grossi et al., 1980; Kimura, 1973a, 1973b). Marchant, McGrew and Eibl-Eibesfeldt (1995) looked at cinematic records of people in three traditional (non-literate) cultures and noted the hand used for actions where a preference could be scored. An overall bias to use the right-hand was clear for tools, but less marked for actions without tools. McGrew and Marchant (1997) reviewed the evidence on asymmetries in primates, distinguishing several possible levels of bias. They concluded, "that there is yet no compelling evidence that nonhuman primates are lateralized at the population level" (p. 226).

I believe it is fair to conclude that reports of species biases for hand preference in chimpanzees and other primates should be considered, in the light of the negative evidence above, as curious findings probably due to special factors in particular investigations. Apparent species biases may occur for many reasons. First, the reports are probably selected for publication because they are deemed to give "positive" results, while many others with "negative" results are not published. Second, accidents of sampling could produce a group of animals with a bias to one side, but one that would not be maintained when tested for replication in an independent group. It should be noted that when balls fall in a pinball machine (see Figure 3.9, below) a normal distribution is found *on average*, but not on every run. Third, asymmetries may also be a product of specific testing situations. I find no grounds in recent studies to revise the conclusion (Annett, 1972) that the distribution of handedness in primates arises by chance.

DISTRIBUTIONS OF HAND SKILL AND PREFERENCE
IN HUMANS

An anonymous referee of my paper on the binomial distribution of hand preference (Annett, 1967) asked how the findings might relate to the normal distribution of asymmetry for hand strength described by Woo and Pearson (1927). I confessed I had no idea. The hand strength data were collected at the suggestion of Francis Galton, a founder of British psychology and a cousin of Charles Darwin. Visitors to a health exhibition in London in 1884 were invited to press a dynanometer with each hand, and to take a test of visual acuity. Data collected from 6992 males, aged 6–81 years, remained in a cupboard at University College London for some 40 years before publication. Differences between the hands in strength took the form of a normal (Gaussian) curve with the mean at 3.34lb (S.D. 7.26lb) in favour of the right-hand. Age groups were compared to enquire whether dextrality and sinistrality change with age. About 65% were superior with the right-hand at all ages. Hand strength and visual acuity differences were not associated. Woo and Pearson concluded (p. 199), "Dextrality and sinistrality are not opposed alternatives, but quantities capable of taking values of continuous intensity and passing one into the other." This agrees perfectly with the argument for continuity in chapter 2. But how does the normal distribution of asymmetry for hand strength relate to the binomial distribution of hand preference?

In the late 1960s I began to collect data on hand skill for peg moving. The test is illustrated in Figure 3.1. The task was devised in order to assess the hand skills of children with hemiplegic cerebral palsy. I knew from experience as a clinical psychologist that very small children enjoy moving and placing pegs, sometimes when they refuse all other tasks. The peg task was a great success

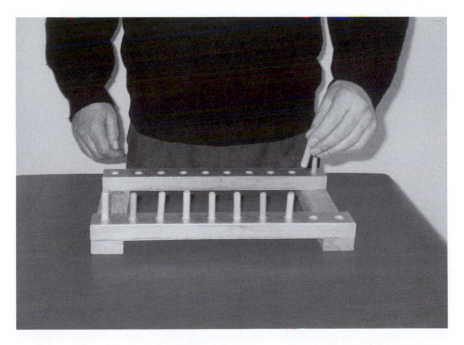

Figure 3.1 Peg moving task apparatus.

with the hemiplegic children who were almost always willing to try with the "bad" hand as well as with the "good" hand. I needed normative data in order to quantify the impairment of the handicapped children, so a random sample of children, 3–15 years, was tested in normal schools (Annett, 1970b). The peg moving task was also used in undergraduate practical classes, where students tested each other and entered the findings, along with observations of hand preference and other asymmetries, on data sheets that were given to me for checking and recording before return.

The task is to move the 10 pegs from the further row to the nearer row, one by one using one hand in each trial. Five trials are normally performed by each hand (three for small children) alternating the hands between trials. Time is recorded by stopwatch from touching the first peg to releasing the last in each row, discounting trials where pegs are dropped or there are other distractions. (Appendix II gives a description of the test, its administration and norms.) The aim was to discover how fast each hand performs on unspoiled trials. Feedback on the time taken is reported to the S on each trial, with encouragement to be faster next time. The intention is to make the task fun. Other investigators often report slower times than in my samples, perhaps because the task was not treated as a game in this way. The mean time is calculated for each hand, and then the difference between the hands. The test–retest reliability of asymmetry scores was shown to be good (Annett, Hudson and Turner, 1974).

Peg moving times can be examined for the absolute skill of each hand, and this changes with age, as will be shown in chapter 6. As a measure of asymmetry, it is the difference between the hands that is of interest. My early reports relied mainly on the raw difference (L–R time to an accuracy of $1/10$s). Later analyses calculated the difference as a proportion of total time taken, a value I refer to as "right minus left percent" (R–L% = ((L − R)/(R + L) × 100). (Note that when the measure of skill depends on time taken to perform a task such as peg moving, the subtraction must be L − R, because the left-hand takes longer. When the measure depends on targets hit, as in square marking, dotting or hole punching, the subtraction must be R − L because the right-hand hits more targets. Positive scores mean right-hand superiority and negative scores left-hand superiority. The term R − L skill, or R–L% skill, refers to the difference in skill between the sides, superior for the right in most people.)

From my first plots of L–R times in children and in undergraduates, it was clear that the distributions resembled a normal curve, like the Woo and Pearson data for hand strength. Figure 3.2 shows the distribution of L–R peg moving times in combined school and university samples, for 617 males and 863 females (Annett and Kilshaw, 1983). The distributions are continuous, roughly normal, and without natural division between right-handers and left-handers. The proportions of subjects at 0 or no difference between hands are about as expected for unimodal normal curves. The female distribution is slightly to the right of the male distribution everywhere except at the left-hand tail. There is no obvious sex difference among left-handers but among right-handers females are more strongly biased to dextrality than males. The distribution of differences for hand

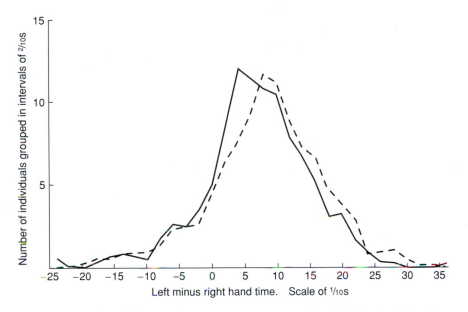

Figure 3.2 L–R hand difference for peg moving time in males (solid line) and females (dashed line): based on Annett and Kilshaw, 1983.

skill resembles that found earlier for hand strength. Both are very different from the J-shaped distribution of hand preference.

If right- and left-handers are part of a single normal distribution of R–L skill, where do the two sorts of handedness fall under the curve? Figure 3.3 shows the R–L% distribution for combined data from two later samples of undergraduates and teenage schoolchildren, total N = 1106 (Annett, 1992d). The location of 125 left-handers (for writing) is shown within the total distribution. The overall curve is unimodal and approximately normal, with mean just under 5%. The curve for left-handers is also unimodal and normal, with mean just above −5%. Left-handers tend to be to the left and right-handers to the right, but there is considerable overlap and no sharp division between the two hand preference groups.

Another sample of children collected by Annett and Turner (1974) included a large number of left-handers because the children were sampled in two ways, first a random sample (by birthday, to get a representative sample) and second, all the remaining left-handers in class (to get a complete sample of left-handers). The children were observed for hand use and then classified into four groups, pure left-, mixed left-, mixed right- and pure right-handers. L–R peg moving means, with bars representing standard deviations, are shown in Figure 3.4. The linear relationship between hand preference and relative hand skill is clear. The groups are overlapping, not discrete, but a strong relationship between preference and skill is indisputable. Overlap between groups of right- and left-handers for hand skill asymmetry may surprise those who expect handedness to be a discrete variable, but it is not surprising for a continuously graded characteristic.

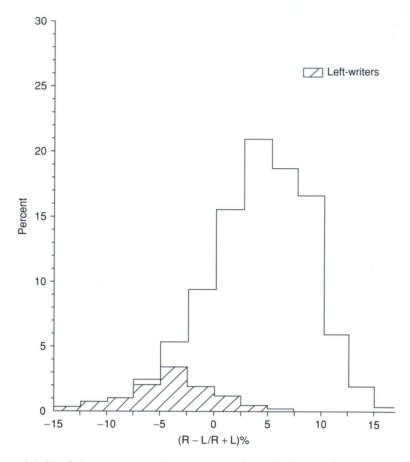

Figure 3.3 Handedness asymmetry for peg moving (R–L%) showing the total
   distribution and the distribution of left-writers.

Figure 3.5 shows the R–L% distribution of over 3000 Ss, my combined data
up to the early 1990s. There can be no doubt that it is a unimodal approximately normal curve. There is a small but statistically significant negative skew,
consistent with the presence of more people to the left than expected for a
single true, normal distribution.

PUZZLES ABOUT HANDEDNESS AND THEIR
RESOLUTION BY THE RIGHT SHIFT THEORY

By the early 1970s, my findings convinced me of four main facts.

1. The proportions of consistent left-, mixed- and consistent right-handers are
    about 4, 30 and 66% in human samples.

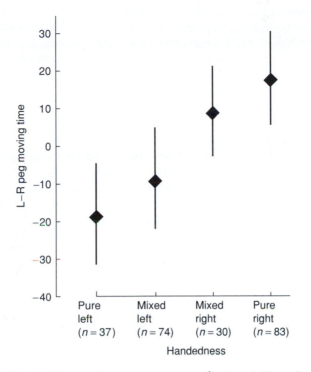

Figure 3.4 L–R hand difference for peg moving time (¹/₁₀s) in children classified for hand preference showing the mean and standard deviation: based on Annett and Turner, 1974.

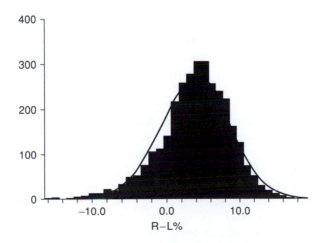

Figure 3.5 The distribution of handedness asymmetry for peg moving: R–L% in combined data for 3206 participants.

2.   In nonhuman primates and in other mammals investigated for paw prefer-
     ences the corresponding proportions are about 25, 50 and 25%.
3.   The distribution of R–L asymmetry for hand skill approximates a normal curve.
4.   Preference is related to skill, as expected if the strength of preference is a
     function of relative skill.

These facts present several puzzles. First, if hand preference depends on hand
skill why does the preference distribution take the form of a "J" or "U" and the
skill distribution the form of a normal curve (contrast Figures 2.2 and 3.2)?
Second, why do the proportions of left-, mixed- and right-handers in humans
and nonhumans both fit the binomial theorem, although the incidences are very
different? Third, how can the evidence for a genetic influence on human handedness be reconciled with the evidence that there is no genetic influence on the
direction of paw preferences in rats and mice? There was the further puzzle, of
course, as to the genetic mechanism in humans. The data fitted neither the
classic Mendelian pattern of dominant and recessive alleles nor the theory of
heterozygote variability (unless lack of fit is attributed to imperfect penetrance).

The geneticists I consulted at that time were not keen to discuss single gene
models but very enthusiastic about models of polygenic inheritance. Exciting
progress was being made in the investigation of diseases that might depend on
many genes of small effect (Falconer, 1965). Key features of the multigene
models had direct parallels with my analysis of handedness. First, the risk of
developing a disease was thought to vary along a continuous scale, low at one
extreme for people presumed to carry few of the relevant genes and high at the
other extreme for people presumed to carry many. Second, the distribution of
risk in the population as a whole takes the form of a normal curve. Those who
develop a clinically diagnosed disorder can be thought of as a certain proportion
under the "at risk" tail of the curve. Third, this proportion is not fixed but varies
with environmental and other circumstances. The number of people diagnosed
would depend on their readiness to seek medical help, the thoroughness of the
medical examination, and the criteria set for positive results in clinical tests.
The proportion ascertained as sick can be described as a threshold, or cut-off
point, under the normal curve. The threshold is not an absolute quantity. It is
rather defined empirically in terms of the *proportion of the population identified*
above or below it. Fourth, there may be differences between the sexes in liability to the disorder. Assuming a similar scale of risk in both sexes and a common
threshold for clinical symptoms, females as a group may be less likely to breakdown than males because they are protected by other factors associated with
female sex. Therefore, females who are affected can be assumed to be carrying a
high proportion of risk factors. In so far as the risk factors are genetic, the
relatives of affected females will be at greater risk than those of affected males,
as deduced by Carter (1961).

For handedness, the research reviewed above suggests that there is a continuous
scale of relative asymmetry, the distribution itself taking the form of a normal
curve. The classification of handedness is notoriously variable, but the variability

has a lot to do with self-classification, methods of enquiry and differing criteria between investigators. The threshold concept is especially attractive, because the association analysis had found several varieties or shades of mixed hand preferences. If the threshold of left-handedness may be drawn anywhere between consistent left- and consistent right-handedness, the large range of incidences reported in the literature could be explained. Further, there are sex differences such that females are less likely to be left-handed than males, but family studies suggested that left-handed mothers are more likely than left-handed fathers to have left-handed children.

If varieties of hand preference depend on a continuum of underlying skill, what do the proportions of left-, mixed- and right-handers tell us about the locations of the corresponding thresholds along the continuum? A table of the normal distribution function gives the percentage cut-off at each point along the baseline. (The table is given in every statistics textbook or set of mathematical tables. Readers with a table to hand may confirm that there are two main values listed, first, the distance from the mean, set at 0, along the baseline in units of the standard deviation, z, and second, the proportion under the curve below each unit of z, .500 or 50% at 0z, 69% at about 0.5z, 84% at 1.0z and so on.) Figure 3.6 shows a normal distribution with 100 letters, each representing 1% under the curve. The 25 L, 50 M, 25R, represent the hand preferences of nonhumans. The lines between the Ls and Ms, and between the Ms and Rs are the *thresholds* needed to divide left- from mixed- and mixed- from right-handers. Consider first the threshold between M and R. There are 75% of animals below this point, so looking up this value in the table of the normal distribution, we

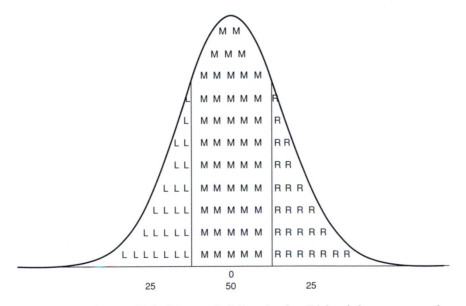

Figure 3.6 Incidences of left- (L), mixed- (M) and right- (R) handedness represented under the normal curve (each as 1%).

see that the threshold must be drawn at about .67z. The threshold between L and M must cut off 25% of animals; the normal curve table lists only one half of the distribution (50% and above) because the other half is necessarily a mirror image; we need the value (1 − .25 = .75) but expressed as a threshold *below* the mean, −.67z. The distance between the two thresholds, representing all of the mixed-handers, is 1.34z.

What are the corresponding thresholds for human hand preferences? The threshold between consistent left- and mixed-handers, the cut-off for 4% pure left-handers (1 − .04 = .96) is at −1.75z. The cut-off between mixed-handers and consistent right-handers must divide 34% non-right-handers (mixed plus left) from right-handers (1 − 0.34 = 0.66), a threshold at about −0.41z. The difference between the two thresholds is 1.34z. The distance along the hypothesised asymmetry continuum needed to represent the division between mixed and consistent handers is *the same for humans as for nonhumans!* This was the "Aha!" experience on which the RS theory was founded. The distributions look very different, but there is an underlying constancy. Figure 3.7 illustrates the human distribution superimposed on the nonhuman one and the match between thresholds. The distributions of hand preference in man and other species could be similar in all respects except that the human distribution is *shifted to the right* in comparison with that of other species. There is no substantial difference except the location of the mean, hence the name, "Right Shift Theory".

Why are both the human and nonhuman distributions of left, mixed and right preference in binomial proportions? It appears that when a normal curve is

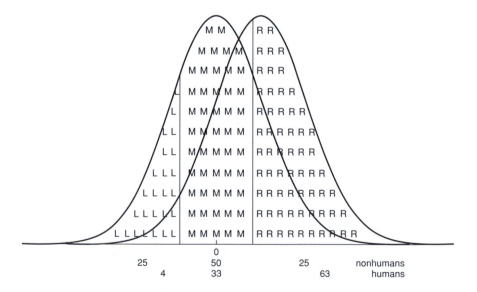

Figure 3.7 Incidences of left- (L), mixed- (M) and right- (R) handedness represented under the normal curve (each as 1%) showing the distributions expected for nonhuman primates and humans.

shifted a short distance to either side of the mean, retaining thresholds at the same position along the x-axis as required to give binomial distributions in the unbiased curve (25, 50, 25), the areas under the curve remain roughly binomial. This was a surprise to an eminent statistician I consulted about the phenomenon. The heterozygote variability hypothesis was inadequate as a genetic model, but it led to the discovery of binomial proportions for the three-way classification of handedness. The binomial proportions are not important in themselves, but they led to the discovery of this striking consistency between human and nonhuman asymmetry distributions.

It will be recalled that when the frequencies of various levels of hand preference are plotted they are J-shaped for humans and U-shaped for nonhumans. How do these fit under the normal distribution of L–R skill? Figures 3.8A and B

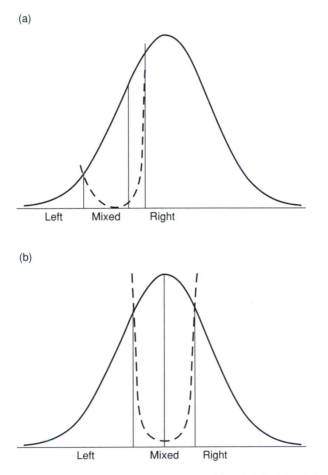

Figure 3.8 Relationships between hand preference and hand skill: (a) a J-shaped distribution of preference in humans, (b) a U-shaped distribution of preference in nonhumans.

illustrate the relationships. The upright extremes of the J and the U must be aligned with the thresholds because consistent handers do not vary for preference, although they do vary for skill. The variability in the preference distribution depends on the mixed-handers, 30% of humans and 50% of nonhumans, who fall between the two thresholds. The unimodal distribution of hand skill is closely related to the superficially bimodal distribution of preference. The uprights of the preference distributions do not imply bimodality but rather lack of discrimination between further levels of asymmetry. Bishop (1989) demonstrated by computer simulation that a J-shaped distribution of hand preference could be generated from a normal distribution of hand skill.

Figure 3.7 captured all the main features of the above analyses. To summarise:

1. There is a continuous distribution of asymmetry for strength and/or skill in all species having hand or paw preferences.
2. The distribution takes the form of a single unimodal approximately normal curve.
3. The likelihood of manifesting mixed preferences depends on a region of the continuum to either side of O or L = R. This region is of similar extent in the species of mammals so far classified for hand preference.
4. The mean of the L–R distribution in nonhumans is at L = R, and the mean for humans is to the right of L = R.
5. The distributions of left versus right, or left, mixed or right preferences differ between man and other species but in proportions that are directly predictable from areas under the normal curve and relatively stable thresholds of mixed-handedness.
6. There is no fundamental difference between humans and other species for handedness, except that the human distribution is displaced in a dextral direction from the symmetrical distribution of nonhumans.

WHAT DOES THE RS ANALYSIS IMPLY ABOUT THE CAUSES OF HANDEDNESS?

The analysis of handedness represented in Figure 3.7 solved some difficult problems but presented some new ones. There are two features to be explained, first the normal distribution that is common to several species, and second the shift to dextrality that is specific to humans. Normal distributions are likely to be the product of several factors, each having small effects and combining at random. Such factors could be genetic or nongenetic, or some combination of both. Genetic determinants of paw preferences in mice and rats were ruled out by the selective breeding experiments of Collins and Peterson described above. If genes are not needed to produce the normal distribution of asymmetry in nonhumans, why should they be needed for humans? This is not to say that polygenic inheritance in man is disproved, but it would not be a parsimonious hypothesis. (Polygenes will be considered further in chapter 5.) Collins' (1975) biased world experiments suggested that paw preferences are congenital but not genetic. What does this imply?

The left and right sides of bilaterally symmetrical organisms are set on their developmental paths at an early stage of division of the fertilised egg. The instructions for building the body may be identical for the two sides but the realisation of the recipe for making nerves and muscles may differ between the sides in subtle ways. A normal distribution of asymmetry could be the product of numerous small accidental differences between the development of the left and right sides of the body. The majority of animals would be fairly well balanced and therefore not inclined to favour strongly one side or the other. Such animals would be likely to develop mixed hand preferences for different actions, and occasionally true ambidexterity for the same action. Some animals would have constitutional biases favouring one side that promote more consistent hand preference for that side. These accidental differences probably occur mainly in the course of embryonic and foetal growth. In following up the implications of the RS theory, as described in the following chapters, I have found no reason to doubt that the normal distribution of asymmetry arises mainly through accidents of congenital development.

The second factor to be explained is the shift of the human distribution to the right. If RS occurs in all human societies, and none have been found biased to the left, the influence must be systematic and not accidental. Why is the shift always toward the right? Some might argue that the bias to the right is due to cultural transmission from our earliest cultural antecedents (Provins, 1997). However, this would imply the bias to the right-hand is learned, and that humans become more right-handed with age. Relative hand strength was found not to change between 6 and 81 years (Woo and Pearson, 1927). Studies of school samples have found no change of frequency for the writing hand with age (Annett, 1970b; Hardyck, Goldman and Petrinovich, 1975). Is the human bias to dextrality genetic? By distinguishing the shape of the distribution from its location, we can envisage two types of cause, non-genetic for the shape and genetic for the location. The evidence for a genetic influence on human handedness, not present in other species, might be explained if a genetic factor influenced the position of the distribution along the asymmetry continuum in humans, while the shape of the distribution was non-genetic and common to all relevant species. The expression of left-hand preference in humans is influenced by cultural influences that raise or lower the observed incidence for socially significant actions such as writing or eating. These differences can be represented as movements of the threshold of expression. Thresholds may be located more to the left or to the right, as pressures become stricter or more relaxed. There are no reasons to believe, on present evidence, that Oriental and Western samples differ for the basic distributions that underlie asymmetries, although their thresholds of expression differ strongly.

The above analysis implies three main "causes" in the recipe for human handedness. First, accidental asymmetries of congenital development that occur in all species; second, a weighting of the congenital chances toward dextrality in humans; third, culturally imposed enhancements of the dextral bias, as human groups put pressure on their members to conform to the majority. Left or right preferences are universal in primates and other mammals, and therefore need no further explanation in humans. What is special for humans is the raised probability of right-sided preference. Whereas the classic genetic models postulated two alleles with opposite coding, R versus L, the RS analysis needs only one directional influence, R but not L. From the beginning it was suggested that the outcome for preference would depend on the joint influence of two variables, chance plus shift. An individual carrying the RS factor may be left-handed, because chance biases to the left may be strong enough not to be outweighed by RS loading to the right. In the absence of RS, handedness would depend on the normal distribution alone as in nonhumans, giving approximately 25% left-handers, 50% mixed-handers and 25% right-handers. At the time the RS theory was formulated, I had AHPQ data on 47 children from families of two left-handed parents. The children included 23% pure left, 28% mixed and 49% pure right handers; 40% were left-handed writers. The proportion of pure left-handers was almost exactly as expected, and some five–six times higher than in general samples, but there were more pure right-handers and fewer mixed-handers than expected for a completely random distribution. The findings were consistent with the idea that some left-handed parents carry the RS factor, although many do not. Subsequent studies of personally visited families of L × L parents support this interpretation (Annett, 1974, 1983a, see chapter 5).

The important and original idea was that there could be a one-way directional bias to the right, present in some but not all humans, and no complementary bias to the left. The rightward bias is added to a universal random distribution. In the absence of RS, there are only random biases to either side. The key points may be illustrated with a device used by Galton to explain the normal distribution function, as shown in Figure 3.9(a). Small balls are dropped through the funnel at the top. They bounce against the pins as they fall into the slots below, some to the left, some to the right and most in the centre. For our purpose, we can think of the fertilised egg on its developmental journey as a pin-ball, buffeted by encounters with various hazards that produce random asymmetries in all bilaterally symmetrical organisms (mice and men). Figure 3.9(b) shows the same apparatus, but with a small deflector just below the funnel, that makes the ball begin its random fall a little to the right of the exit. The random buffeting proceeds exactly as before, but the final position of the balls has been weighted by a constant. The effect of the RS factor is to *add* a constant value to the chance probabilities. It does not replace them.

Annett (1978c) made the point in terms of loaded and unloaded dice. To give a simple illustration, suppose that handedness depended on the throw of a die, the numbers 1–3 meaning "left" and the numbers 4–6 meaning "right". There would be equal chances for left and right, three of each, analogous to our primate cousins. Suppose now that 2 points were added to every outcome. The numbers on the die would range from 3 to 8. Only one number would give left-handedness (number 3) but there would be five chances for right-handedness

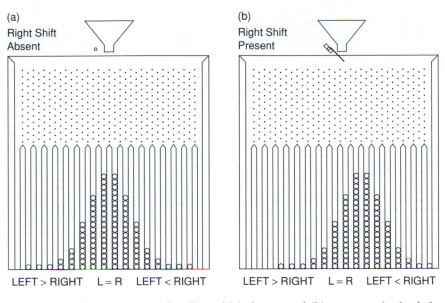

(a)
Right Shift
Absent

LEFT > RIGHT   L = R   LEFT < RIGHT

(b)
Right Shift
Present

LEFT > RIGHT   L = R   LEFT < RIGHT

Figure 3.9 A demonstration of the effect of (a) absence and (b) presence of right shift: based on a machine used by Galton to illustrate the normal distribution.

(numbers 4–8). The range of the continuum would be unchanged and the threshold or criterion would be the same also. The difference between humans and nonhumans would be a constant weight, added to the chance probabilities in people that carried the RS factor. This model is quite different from models that propose a directional bias for some and chance bias for others (Klar, 1996; Layton, 1976; McManus, 1985a), described in chapter 16. For the RS theory everyone lateralises by chance, but in the absence of the RS factor there is *only* chance. In its presence, there is chance plus something else. This formulation may sound more complicated but it follows directly from Figure 3.7. Clarity on this point is essential for understanding subsequent applications of the theory to cerebral dominance, genetics, twinning and other puzzles as described in the following chapters.

Finally, Annett (1972) considered the nature of the RS factor. It has the following qualities: (1) it is present in humans but no other primate, (2) it increases the strength/skill of the right side of the body, and (3) it is more effective in females than males. The hypothesis that must immediately leap to mind is that it is something to do with the human tendency to develop speech in the left cerebral hemisphere. No other primate has speech. Females are more biased to dextrality than males (see Figure 3.2) and they have advantages over males in the rate of speech acquisition. They are much less likely than males to suffer speech disorders and dyslexia. Some boost to the left hemisphere that makes it readier to serve speech, might also increase the motor skill of the right side of the body. Right brained or bilateral speech could arise in just the way suggested for handedness, accidental variation in the absence of the factor inducing left-brainedness. There must be some genes that man does not share with the rest of the animal kingdom, and what could be more probable than that they have a role in human speech? Since 1972, I have examined the implications of the theory and sought to test them empirically. The following chapters report this process and show ways in which the theory has been strengthened and enriched. There has been no reason to change the fundamentals of the analysis above.

SUMMARY

There are many asymmetries in the natural world and the causes are often not understood. It is likely that there are no direct links between the causes of asymmetries at different levels of analysis of the physical and living worlds. Left and right asymmetries may be governed by genes, or they may occur racemically (by accidental chance assortment). Visceral asymmetries appear to depend on several genes. For hand and paw preferences, there is a fundamental similarity between humans and other species in the presence of tendencies to develop strong preferences, right and left. There is also a fundamental discontinuity between humans and other species because only humans have a species bias to right-handedness. Paw preferences in mice are not genetic but they are congenital, present before the animals' first experience of reaching. Preferences may be presumed, therefore, to depend on accidental influences on the development of the two sides of the body.

The resolution of various puzzles about the incidences of left, mixed and right-hand preferences in humans and nonhumans, and puzzles about relationships between hand preference and hand skill depend on the assumption that preferences depend on a continuous, unimodal distribution of lateral asymmetry. The wide range of incidences of left-handedness reported in the literature depends on different methods of measurement and variable criteria that give different cut-off points or thresholds along the continuum. The human distribution resembles that of other mammals in all essential respects (shape, origin, and range likely to give mixed preferences) except that the human distribution is displaced along the L–R continuum in a dextral direction. The right shift of the human distribution is probably a by-product of a factor that induces speech representation in the left cerebral hemisphere. The left hemisphere speech-inducing RS factor could be inherited. The gene(s) involved would be "for" left hemisphere speech, not handedness. In the absence of the influence toward left hemisphere speech, cerebral asymmetry and handedness are likely to occur at random.

I talked about "fudge" factors in chapter 1, factors that make it impossible to formulate and test precise predictions. I have also talked about the search for the elusive "essence" of laterality. The right shift theory turns the problem on its head by asserting that the chief fact about handedness is its random variability.

There are no elusive *types* but random chances that occur afresh in each individual. The variability is a constant background against which trends associated with the human shift to the right have to be detected. The analysis shows why it is difficult to test theories about handedness because all predictions have to be expressed in terms of probabilities. There are no simple rules such as "all right-handers are . . ." or "no left-handers are . . ." because there are no distinct types. The task of working out the implications of the theory involves trying to work out just what proportions of so-called right- and left-handers should be left and right brained, have right or left-handed children, or suffer advantages and disadvantages of intellectual growth.

It was said in chapter 1 that the RS theory required a paradigm shift. The reason for this suggestion was that the theory requires us to think in terms of distributions, whereas all other theories in the literature continue to think of types. The foundation of the analysis is a continuous, unimodal distribution of relative asymmetry. The variable of interest for humans is not handedness, but the factor that displaces the handedness distribution in a dextral direction. It is a theory of an unknown factor that exerts a species specific influence upon human hand preferences.

4   A right shift factor for left cerebral dominance

The central puzzle addressed by the RS theory is the relationship between two lateral asymmetries, hand preference and speech hemisphere. The puzzle was outlined in chapter 1. It was shown that all of the logically possible answers to the question of the speech hemisphere of left-handers have been offered, right, left, either or both. Studies of patients with known speech hemisphere, diagnosed by the Wada test, revealed that left-handers may indeed have right or left or bilateral speech, but that right-handers may have all these speech lateralities also. If relationships between hand and brain are to be understood as a feature of human biology, their distribution must be studied in patients that are representative of the general population. However, when the distribution of speech laterality in right- and left-handers was examined in five large representative series the findings were very variable (Zangwill, 1967). My approach to this puzzle was to examine the five series in some detail so as to locate the source of the variability. As might be expected, in the light of the analysis in chapter 2 above, most of the variability was due to different classifications of left-handedness. Underlying these superficial differences were some important constant features. The constant values can be used to estimate parameters of the RS model. This chapter explains the RS solution to the puzzle of handedness and CD. It builds on the analyses of the previous two chapters, and provides the foundation for the genetic analyses to follow.

The examination of handedness in chapters 2 and 3 found that variable incidences occur everywhere. It was concluded that handedness is not a "type" but a continuous variable. Different incidences represent thresholds or cut-points along the baseline of a normal distribution of asymmetry. Answers to questions about handedness and CD depend, therefore, on the proportion of the population classified as left-handed. The most original and interesting feature of the RS analysis was a distinction between the asymmetry distribution itself, and its location. Handedness is not especially interesting because it depends in humans, as in other primates, on congenital accidents. What is distinctive about human handedness is that the chance distribution is displaced along the asymmetry continuum in a dextral direction. If the cause of this right shift (the RS factor) is an agent of left hemisphere advantage, that normally induces the left hemisphere to serve speech, what would this imply for relations between handedness and CD?

The first important implication would be that there is no direct relationship between hand and brain asymmetries. The overlap of the distributions (see Figure 3.7) shows that the dextral weighting does not carry everyone into the region of faster right than left-hand skill (to the right of 0). Handedness is *influenced by but not determined by* the RS factor. The relatively small dextral advantage does not outweigh a strong chance bias to the left-hand. Thus some people may carry the agent of typical left hemisphere CD, but still prefer the left-hand. But how does right CD arise? If some people carry the RS factor (RS +) and some do not (RS −), right CD could occur in the latter by chance. Cerebral asymmetries, like manual ones, might be caused by accidents of congenital development. The main alternative hypothesis is that everyone "ought to have" left CD. This would imply that right CD is pathological.

The assumption that atypical asymmetries are pathological runs through most of the literature. It relies on a "medical model" of deviance, that everyone who is different is aberrant in some respect (considered further in chapter 16). With regard to handedness, the pathology hypothesis involves several assumptions, that the natural primate causes of left- and right-handedness were lost in humans, that a specific cause of right preference became fixed as a human universal and that left-handedness was reintroduced in humans as a function of abnormal growth. The RS theory does not require this complex evolutionary scenario. Left-handedness is expected to occur by chance in humans as in other primates. But what of the pathology argument for cerebral dominance? If both speech and RS are new in humans in comparison with apes, it might seem reasonable to suggest that left CD is a human universal and right CD abnormal. Why should right CD be regarded as a natural variant? The main reason is that it is found in people with no evidence of abnormality. It was evident in cases of head injury sustained as war wounds, among service personnel who were the fittest section of the population before wounding. It occurs in stroke patients with no previous brain damage. Some right CD could occur as a result of pathologies of brain development, of course, but most of these are likely to belong to at risk clinical populations, such as the epileptic or learning disabled. The RS analysis suggests that right CD will occur by chance in people who lack the RS factor (RS −). Those carrying the factor (RS +) are all expected to develop left CD (given normal growth). These simple assumptions lead to specific predictions about relationships between handedness and CD. The question is whether the predictions are supported by evidence. (The genetic model in chapter 5 follows from the present analysis but, to anticipate, RS + can be taken to imply carriers of an RS + gene while RS − are non-gene-carriers.)

What would be expected for hand skill asymmetry in the RS + and RS − sections of the population? The distributions would be like those shown in Figure 3.7 except that the RS − proportion would be considerably smaller relative to the RS + proportion. Figure 4.1 represents my first surmise that the RS − proportion would be about 20% of the population, and the shift (distance between the means of RS + and RS −) about 1.5z. These guesses were useful for exploring the logical properties of the model. The logical consequences had to

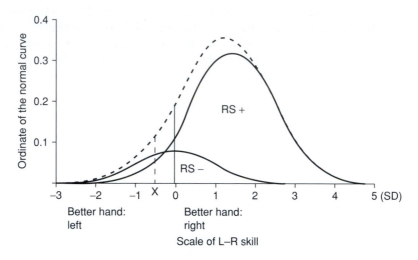

Figure 4.1 The distribution of L–R hand skill as hypothesised by Annett, 1975: the RS + proportion is 0.8 and the RS + mean is shifted 1.5 S.D. to the right of the mean of RS –: variances of RS + and RS – are equal: X is a possible threshold for sinistrality.

be investigated first, before ways of estimating the true values could be discovered. The sum of the two distributions, shown by the dashed line, gives the asymmetry distribution of the total population, roughly normal but with a negative skew. The line "X" gives a possible threshold for left-handedness, cutting off 10% at the left extreme. The interesting implications of the model depend on the overlap of the distributions. RS + are well represented to the left of X (left-handed carriers) while the majority of RS – are to the right of X (right-handed non-carriers).

What do these distributions imply for relationships between handedness and CD? Consider first the left-handers (to the left of X). If left CD occurs in all RS + and in half of RS –, then left CD must be more frequent than right CD among left-handers. With a stricter classification of left-handedness the threshold will move further to the left. The relative proportions of right CD among left-handers would rise and left CD fall, but never below 50%. As the threshold (X) moves rightward to match incidences of non-right-handedness, the proportion of right CD will fall in both handedness groups (because of the increasing predominance of RS + in both). The model explains very well what was known about relationships between cerebral speech and handedness, namely that right CD is more frequent in left-handers than right-handers, but that right CD is not the norm. The majority of left-handers have left CD, like most right-handers.

If the question of relationships is approached from the starting point of right CD, what is predicted as to the handedness of people with right CD? In the absence of the only systematic influence on asymmetries (the RS factor), all asymmetries occur by chance, independently for hands and hemisphere speech.

Right CD is expected to occur in 50% of people with RS – but their hand skill distribution will be the same as for RS – with left CD. The RS – distribution of R–L skill will be a normal curve with a mean at 0 or R = L. For an unbiased measure of hand skill, such as peg moving, there should be as many above the mean as below it for R–L differences. However, when the threshold of left-handedness is below 0, as drawn for X in Figure 4.1, *there should be more right-than left-handers among people with right CD*. This implication of the model was surprising and paradoxical. The predominant view in the neurological literature was that right CD is relatively infrequent and practically unknown among right-handers. The occasional case of a right-hander with right CD was explained as a "shifted" sinistral or perhaps a "stock-brained" (i.e. hereditary) left-hander. The idea that right-handers should be more frequent than left-handers among people with right CD was unprecedented. It was an original and counter-intuitive implication of the RS analysis. Was this apparent challenge to the RS theory well founded?

THE RS THEORY TESTED IN SERIES OF PATIENTS WITH UNILATERAL LESIONS AND DYSPHASIA

The British WW2 Head Injury study (Russell and Espir, 1961) was one of the five population representative series identified by Zangwill (1967). A new analysis of these data by Newcombe and Ratcliff (1973) appeared at the time I was working out the ideas above. This analysis found 27 cases of dysphasia following right unilateral lesions and of these 19 (70%) were right-handed. There were more right- than left-handers as predicted by the RS analysis. Another of the five series was of German WW2 head injuries (Conrad, 1949). Conrad described 18 right lesion dysphasics, of whom 11 (61%) were right-handed. Thus, both war wound series supported the counter-intuitive predictions of the RS theory. By contrast, Hécaen and Ajuriaguerra (1964) found no right-handers but 11 left-handers with dysphasia and right-sided lesions. Why should the findings for this clinic series differ from those of the war wound series? A systematic comparison of the five series was undertaken (Annett, 1975) as follows.

Table 4.1 lists the original data for numbers of left-handers with left and right-sided lesions, right-handers with left and right-sided lesions, and the numbers (percentages in parentheses) recorded as dysphasic (with symptoms of speech disorder). The first two series and the last are those mentioned above. The other two series were of surgical cases, for the relief of epilepsy at the Montreal Neurological Clinic (Penfield and Roberts, 1959) and for epilepsy and temporal lobe tumours in Sweden (Bingley, 1958). As noted above, the raw data were remarkable chiefly for their variability. What was the source of this variability?

My procedure was to compare the five series for each variable in turn (dysphasia, handedness and side of lesion) as shown in Table 4.2. All the series were large (Ns ranged from 214 to 767) giving ground for confidence in the power of the statistical comparisons (all by chi square). The percentages of cases

Table 4.1 Five samples of dysphasics classified for laterality of cerebral lesion and handedness

	Left-handed		Right-handed	
	Left lesion	*Right lesion*	*Left lesion*	*Right lesion*
Conrad (1949)				
N	19	18	338	249
Dysphasic	10 (52.6%)	7 (38.9%)	175 (51.8%)	11 (4.4%)
Newcombe and Ratcliff (1973)				
N	30	33	388	316
Dysphasic	11 (36.7%)	8 (24.8%)	218 (56.2%)	19 (6.0%)
Penfield and Roberts (1959)				
N	18	15	157	196
Dysphasic	13 (72.2%)	1 (6.7%)	115 (73.2%)	1 (0.5%)
Bingley (1958)				
N	4	10	101	99
Dysphasic	2 (50.0%)	3 (30.0%)	68 (67.3%)	1 (1.0%)
Hécaen and Ajuriaguerra (1964)				
N	37	22	163	130
Dysphasic	22 (59.5%)	11 (50.0%)	81 (49.7%)	0 (0.0%)

Note: Adapted from Zangwill (1967) by Annett (1975).

Table 4.2 Five samples compared for percentages of key variables

	Total (N)	*Dysphasic*	*Left-handed*	*Left-sided lesion*	*Dysphasia and right-sided lesion*
Conrad (1949)	624	32.5	5.9*	57.2	2.9
Newcombe and Ratcliff (1973)	767	33.4	8.2	54.5	3.5
Penfield and Roberts (1959)	386	33.7	8.5	45.3*	0.5*
Bingley (1958)	214	34.6	6.5	49.1	1.9
Hécaen and Ajuriaguerra (1964)	352	32.4	16.8*	56.8	3.1

Note
*p < 0.05 or less by chi-squared.

suffering dysphasia were consistent between the series, range 32.4–34.6%. The percentages having left-sided lesions were fairly consistent, 45.3–57.2%, and about as expected if trauma were equally likely on either side of the brain. However, the statistical comparison found that Penfield and Roberts recorded fewer left-sided cases than the other series. The number of dysphasics with right-sided lesions was also smaller for Penfield and Roberts than for the other series. The Penfield and Roberts cases were undergoing elective surgery, so it

Table 4.3 Five series compared for key variables in dysphasics only

	All dysphasics	Left-handed		Right lesion		Right-handers among right lesion cases	
	(N)	(N)	(%)	(N)	(%)	(N)	(%)
Conrad (1949)	203	17	8.4	18	8.9	11	61.1
Newcombe and Ratcliff (1973)	256	19	7.4	27	10.5	19	70.4
Penfield and Roberts (1959)	130	14	10.8	2	1.5*	1	50.0
Bingley (1958)	74	5	6.8	4	5.4	1	25.0
Hécaen and Ajuriaguerra (1964)	114	33	28.9*	11	9.6	0	0.0

*indicates $p < 0.01$ by chi-squared.

was not surprising that there were fewer left-sided cases than in non-elective series, nor was it surprising for such a series that there were few right lesion dysphasics. Inspection of Table 4.2 shows that the major difference between the five series was for left-handedness, with incidences ranging from 5.9 to 16.8%. Conrad had fewer and Hécaen and Ajuriaguerra more left-handers than the rest. Different incidences of left-handedness are perfectly legitimate (on a threshold model) but they are associated with different distributions for cerebral speech.

The count for each variable separately was repeated for dysphasics only, as shown in Table 4.3. The advantage of this analysis is that it is based on all cases with a lesion affecting the speech areas, a complete set of patients with lesions of the speech areas on *either* side. This new analysis showed the five series to be consistent in most respects. There were only two statistically significant differences. Penfield and Roberts had fewer cases of right CD than any other series, confirming the analysis above. Hécaen and Ajuriaguerra had many more left-handers (28.9%). For this series the incidence of left-handedness was 16.8% in the total sample but 29% among dysphasics (compare Tables 4.2 and 4.3). The difference implies that among non-dysphasics the incidence was 11%. Thus, the criteria of sinistrality *changed within the Hécaen sample*. It is easy to see how such a change might arise, as fuller inquiries were made of dysphasic patients and their relatives. In most of the present studies the frequency of left-handedness was somewhat higher among dysphasics than non-dysphasics. However, the absence of right-handers with right CD in the Hécaen sample depended on a very high incidence of left-handedness (about 29%). At this incidence the threshold would be well to the right of 0 (in Figure 4.1), in the region where there would be virtually no RS −. Hence this apparent exception to the rule that people with right CD should include more right- than left-handers (when the threshold is to the left of 0, as in Figure 4.1) turns out to be an exception that proves the rule. The finding fits the model very well because the threshold of left-handedness was moved to the region where no right CD is expected. It gives no reason to doubt that with a reasonably strict criterion of handedness, people with right CD are more often right than left-handed as predicted.

There was another influential study in Vienna by Gloning (Gloning, 1977; Gloning and Quatember, 1966) that also found no right handers with right CD. The data for over 700 patients included 19 patients suffering dysphasia associated with right unilateral lesions, but none were recorded as right-handed. Was this another instance of a very generous criterion of left-handedness? In the total series there were 8.2% left-handers, but among dysphasics 17.2%; this implied that only 2.3% of non-dysphasics were recorded as sinistral (Gloning and Quatember, 1966, Table 3). Clearly, there was a massive shift in criterion of left-handedness between dysphasics and non-dysphasics. As for the study of Hécaen and Ajuriaguerra, it can be inferred that the absence of right-handers with right hemisphere lesions and dysphasia was due to a very generous criterion of left-handedness in dysphasics. Thus two major predictions of the RS model about right CD were supported. First, when criteria of left-handedness are about as expected for left writing, the majority of people with right CD are right-handed. Second, when this is not true there has been a shift of threshold to a level consistent with non-right-handedness. This unravelling of the confusions about handedness and CD in the dysphasia literature depends on treating incidences as indicating thresholds along an asymmetry continuum.

The analyses above classified CD as a binary variable, as it was treated in the studies concerned. However, CD might not be a "type" variable but continuous like handedness. How is "bilateral" speech to be considered? Random cerebral asymmetry in the RS – might make some people symmetrical for cerebral speech, just as some are symmetrical for handedness (with ambidextrous and mixed preferences). The proportion classified as bilateral would differ with different methods of assessment and criteria. It would imply that *some* left-handers have bilateral speech, but *not all* as sometimes suggested. The idea that left-handers might be characterised by bilateral speech originated in reports that left-handers are more likely to suffer dysphasias than right-handers. However, it has been shown above that instead of an excess of dysphasics among left-handers, there might be an excess of people classified as left-handed among dysphasics. Tables 4.2 and 4.3 show that Conrad's total cohort of WW2 head injuries included 5.9% left-handers, but among those with dysphasia there were 8.4%. The shift in assessment criteria was small compared with the Hécaen and Gloning samples, but nevertheless present. Another study arguing for bilateral speech in left-handers examined incidences of speech disturbances occurring as an epileptic aura. The percentage of left-handers in the total series was high (23%), but in the group of paroxysmal dysphasics it was nearly twice as high (42%) (Hécaen and Piercy, 1956). Once again, it is evident that criteria of left-handedness were especially generous for dysphasics. These comparisons support the conclusion that cerebral bilaterality in left-handers has been over-estimated. The generalisation that all left handers have bilateral speech, prevalent in much of the literature, is almost certainly false. Bilateral speakers occur among both right- and left-handers, but in neither handedness group is it the norm (Kurthen,

Helmstaedter, Linke et al., 1994; Mateer and Dodrill, 1983; Strauss and Wada, 1983; Zatorre, 1989).

AN INDEPENDENT TEST OF THE MODEL IN PATIENTS OF KNOWN SPEECH HEMISPHERE

The laterality of cerebral speech was inferred above from the presence of unilateral brain lesions and the symptom dysphasia. Patients in Montreal with speech hemisphere diagnosed by the Wada technique were examined for an asymmetry of cerebral anatomy and for handedness (Ratcliff, Dila, Taylor et al., 1980). The cerebral asymmetry was for the angle of a posterior branch of the middle cerebral artery, as visualised on carotid angiograms that were given routinely before major brain surgery. The angle depends on the position of the lateral or Sylvian fissure, in the posterior speech areas of Wernicke (see Figure 1.1). Hochberg and LeMay (1975) found that the angle tended to be smaller on the left side. This was true in two-thirds of right-handers, but left-handers were unbiased to either side. The Montreal data could be examined for CD as well as for handedness.

Figure 4.2 shows my plot of the data for cerebral asymmetry in two distributions, one for patients with right-sided and bilateral speech (presumed RS −) and one for those with left CD (most RS + but some RS − by chance). Both

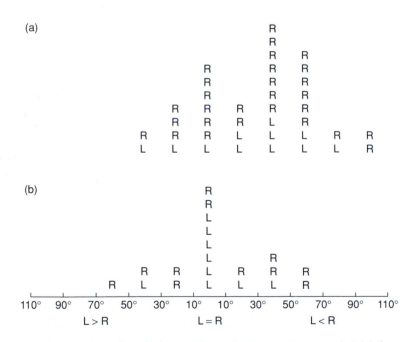

Figure 4.2 The distribution of Sylvian arch asymmetry in patients with (a) left, (b) right or bilateral cerebral speech and right- (R) or left- (L) handedness: redrawn from Ratcliff, Dila, Taylor et al., 1980.

distributions are continuous and roughly normal. For patients with typical left CD, the distribution is displaced to the right and 67% have the typical bias for cerebral anatomy. For patients with atypical CD, the distribution is not displaced to either side but centred on L = R. About as many were biased in the typical as the atypical direction. With regard to handedness, patients with atypical speech included 55% right-handers. This is about as expected by chance. It is also independent of the asymmetry of cerebral anatomy. These findings agree with predictions of the RS in every essential respect (except, of course, for the relative sizes of the RS – and RS + distributions, because this was not a population representative sample). No other theory predicted that an asymmetry of cerebral anatomy that has a characteristic bias in most people, would be distributed by chance in people with atypical CD, and that in the latter handedness would also be by chance, but with right handers slightly more frequent than left-handers. Asymmetries of cerebral anatomy will be considered further in chapter 8.

ATYPICAL CEREBRAL SPECIALISATION: HOW MANY PEOPLE HAVE IT?

The findings above give confidence that the model in Figure 4.1 captures essential relationships between handedness and cerebral dominance. The model solves the problem in principle, but can it be more precise? To make specific predictions for particular thresholds, we need good estimates of two key parameters, the relative sizes of the two distributions, and the extent of shift. Is it possible to estimate the parameters of the model from real data?

The relative sizes of the RS + and RS – distributions represent the relative proportions of carriers and non-carriers. If right hemisphere CD occurs only in the RS –, and at random within the RS –, then the RS – proportion is twice the percentage of people with right CD in the population. (For every case of right CD there must be a case of left CD, who is also RS –.) The estimate of RS – depends, therefore, on the estimate of right CD. The key question is *what proportion of the total population has right hemisphere speech, irrespective of handedness?* Previous researchers have asked about CD in right-handers and then in left-handers separately, as if these were two independent and clearly defined types. The difficulty is that they are not types and they are far from clearly defined (see chapters 2 and 3). The threshold model adjusts for different incidences of left-handedness by moving the cut-point (X) along the laterality continuum, but the relative proportions of RS – and right CD within left-handers differ between different thresholds (as X moves in Figure 4.1). What we need to know, is the absolute size of the RS – proportion, over the whole continuum.

Among the five series examined above, the elective surgery series of Penfield and Roberts differed from the others for percentage left-sided lesions (Table 4.2) and also for the percentage of dysphasics with right-sided lesions (Table 4.3). This series was omitted, therefore, from the following calculations. In the other four series, the percentage of dysphasics with right unilateral lesions ranged from 5.4 to 10.5%. Combining the data for the four series gave a total of 647 dysphasics. The cerebral lesion was right-sided in 60 (9.27%). Note that Hécaen and Ajuriaguerra, although differing from other series in the percentage of patients called left-handed, did not differ for the proportion of dysphasics with right-sided lesions (9.6%). These findings imply that just under 10% of the population have right CD. This proportion is generally met with astonishment because of an argument that proceeds something like this, "Right hemisphere speech is virtually non-existent in right-handers and it occurs in less than half of left-handers, therefore right CD is negligible." This argument is misleading because it was based on a rather vague consensus from studies that made very different classifications of handedness.

Is it true that nearly one in ten people has right CD? The importance of this question led me to seek checks on the evidence. One check was to undertake a personal re-count of the British WW2 Head Injury archive (by kind permission of the late Dr. Freda Newcombe). The main purpose of this re-examination was to assess the total proportion of dysphasics with right unilateral lesions, irre-spective of handedness (right, left, uncertain or unknown) for reasons explained above. A second purpose was to examine the duration of dysphasia as a function of handedness and side of lesion in order to assess whether transitory dysphasias are more frequent in left-handers (Subirana, 1958) or perhaps more transitory in people with right-sided lesions. My procedure was to select from the total archive (some 1000 cases) all those noted as having dysphasic symptoms on admission or discharge. From these were selected cases likely to have a unilat-eral lesion (omitting cases with midline or possibly bilateral lesions and also those with a missile track toward the side opposite the lesion). There were 217 cases of dysphasia judged to have unilateral lesions. Among these there were 20 (9.22%) whose lesion was on the right side. This result agreed very well with the estimate from the combined series above.

Individual case notes of the 217 dysphasics were then inspected for informa-tion on handedness, lesion side and duration of dysphasia. The findings are summarised in Table 4.4. The trend for left- and mixed-handers to have more

Table 4.4 Duration of dysphasia in relation to handedness and side of cerebral lesion

| | Duration of dysphasia (%) | | | |
| | Handedness | | Side of cerebral lesion | |
	Left + Mixed (N = 24)	Right (N = 182)	Right (N = 20)	Left (N = 195)
Hours or days	21	16	35	14
Weeks	29	27	25	30
Years	50	57	40	56
	Chi-square: ns		Chi-square: 6.16, d.f. = 2, p < 0.05	

transitory dysphasias than right-handers was not statistically significant. However, right lesion cases were less likely than left lesion cases to have persistent dysphasias (chi square = 6.16, d.f. 2, p < 0.05). Disorders of speech that recovered in hours or days were noted for 14% of left lesion but for 35% of right lesion cases and disorders lasting for years were recorded for 56% of left and 40% of right lesion cases. These findings suggest that one reason why dysphasias associated with right hemisphere lesions are relatively rare in the experience of neurologists is that they are more often transitory. The difference must not be exaggerated, however, since follow-up examinations of these cases for 20 or more years after injury found that persisting dysphasias from right-sided lesions were as disabling as those from left-sided ones (Newcombe, personal communication). If speech laterality occurs at random in the RS −, a normal distribution of asymmetry might be expected, some individuals strongly lateralised to the right or left, but some bilateral. Transitory dysphasia might be associated with bilateral representation, and faster recovery of speech for this reason. Another estimate of the frequency of atypical CD could be derived from the British WW2 series. Dysphasia occurred in 64 cases as part of the warning (aura) of an impending epileptic attack. Of these, 6 (9.37%) had lesions of the right hemisphere (Russell and Espir, 1961, Table 18).

Two independent surveys confirmed that the estimates of atypical cerebral speech laterality were not exaggerated. Both surveys were epidemiological, community based investigations of patients' symptoms and needs following stroke. Handedness and lesion laterality were noted but these were not the primary interest of the investigators. A survey in Bristol, UK, found 101 patients with dysphasia some 2–4 weeks after the stroke and 12 (11.9%) had right-sided lesions (Wade, Hewer, David et al., 1986). A survey of over 800 patients in the vicinity of Copenhagen found 326 new cases with dysphasias, of whom 30 (9.20%) had right-sided lesions (Pedersen, Jorgensen, Nakayama et al., 1995). These studies agree that right CD occurs in just over 9% of the general population.

The cerebral speech laterality of healthy people has been assessed by functional magnetic resonance imaging (Pujol, Delis, Losilla et al., 1999) and by transcranial doppler sonography (Knecht, Dräger, Deppe et al., 2000). These samples were not population representative because additional left-handers were recruited. Handedness was assessed by laterality indices. However, as far as can be judged, the findings were consistent with those of the aphasia and stroke studies.

The estimate of 9.27% right CD, derived from the four combined series above, was used in my further calculations. If these represent half of the RS −, then twice this proportion (18.54%) gives the percentage of RS − in the population. The second parameter that must be estimated is the difference between the means of the RS + and RS − distributions. Annett (1975) estimated this value from combined data for three of the representative series above (Conrad, Newcombe and Ratcliff, and Bingley) because these three did not differ significantly for any major variable. In order to estimate the extent of shift, we must assume that the threshold for left-handedness (X) is identical for the RS + and RS − subgroups, because both have been exposed to the same pressures on the expression of handedness. The percentages of left-handers in each group tell us how far the threshold is below the mean of each distribution (in z values of the normal curve). The difference between the two z values gives the difference between the two means. Because RS − is 0, by definition, the difference between the means estimates the extent of shift for the RS + distribution. The difference, estimated from all cases of dysphasia in the three series, was just under two standard deviations (1.9z). Another estimate based on data for persistent dysphasia (Annett, 1975, Table 8) was similar (1.7z).

These estimates were necessarily rough, but they served well enough as a starting point for explorations of the genetic implications of the model. To anticipate subsequent chapters, the model as derived here *works* in the sense that it proved highly fruitful in further investigations. The values of parameters derived above successfully predict handedness in families. This agreement between two major sets of data (for cerebral speech in clinical neurology and for handedness in families) is, to my mind, convincing support for the model. However, before moving on to the arguments for genetics, it is useful here to explain more fully the predictions of the model for relationships between handedness and cerebral dominance and to test these predictions against actual data. It is important to be confident that the present analyses do offer a solution to the problem of handedness and CD, because this is the pivotal point of the argument.

QUANTITATIVE PREDICTIONS FOR HANDEDNESS AND CEREBRAL DOMINANCE

My analysis of relationships between handedness and cerebral dominance in the five series above was published in 1975, but it had little impact on neurological and psychological thinking. Questions about relationships between handedness and brainedness continued to be asked for right-handers and left-handers separately. Investigators ignored the problem of different incidences of left-handedness between the studies, and different incidences between dysphasics and non-dysphasics within studies (Carter, Hohenegger and Satz, 1980; Kimura, 1993; Segalowitz and Bryden, 1983). In the early 1990s, a neurologist with particular interest in questions of atypical cerebral dominance, Michael P. Alexander (Alexander, Fischette and Fischer, 1989; Fischer, Alexander, Gabriel et al., 1991) wrote to ask me about the predictions of the RS theory. From our correspondence, a new method of explaining the neurological implications of the theory was developed. Alexander and Annett (1996) described 10 new cases of atypical CD and reviewed the literature on right-handers with right CD, in the light of the RS theory. Annett and Alexander (1996) made explicit the quantitative predictions of the model and tested these predictions against published series of cases.

Predictions for relationships between handedness and CD depend on the incidence of left-handedness, as said above. The incidence defines the threshold or cut-point along the asymmetry continuum that is required to map the particular incidence to the underlying asymmetry distributions. Annett and Alexander (1996) illustrated the model for two thresholds, 10% and 30%, to represent left-writers and non-right-handers respectively. In order to explain the model as concretely as possible, and to avoid the use of percentages and decimals, the reader was asked to imagine a set of 2000 cases of recent stroke, 1000 in the left and 1000 in the right hemisphere. It must be imagined that all of these cases had no previous brain lesion, but then suffered a cerebro-vascular accident (CVA) of sudden onset, affecting the speech areas of the brain (areas that would serve speech if speech were lateralised to the affected side).

Figure 4.3 shows the 2000 cases in a central star, the cases then split between 1000 with left CVA above and 1000 with right CVA below the star. Within each 1000, there is a division between 820 that carry the RS + factor and have typical left CD (top shaded rectangles) and 180 RS − (in white ovals, the 18.54% deduced for the population above but rounded down to a convenient whole number). For 10% left-handers, each 1000 cases include 100 left-handers and 900 right-handers. These are represented in the left and right quadrants of Figure 4.3 respectively. How many right- and left-handers are RS + and RS −? The best estimate that can be made (in the light of the genetic analyses to follow, and Appendix III) is that when 10% of the population is classified as left-handed, these 10 people per 100 include 4 RS + and 6 RS −. In our imaginary sample of 1000 left CVA there are 40 RS + left-handers and 780 RS + right-handers and 60 RS − left-handers and 120 RS − right-handers.

How many right-handers and how many left-handers are expected to suffer dysphasias from lesions of each side? The answers are found by examining each quadrant in turn. Among 900 *right-handers with left* CVA, in the top right quadrant of Figure 4.3, there are 780 with RS + who suffer standard aphasias. What is expected for the 120 RS − in whom cerebral lateralities occur at random? Consider two main regions involved in speech functions, posterior (W) and anterior (B) (for Wernicke's and Broca's area respectively). If each locates in either hemisphere by chance there are four possible combinations, each with 30 cases, RW–RB, RW–LB, LW–RB, LW–LB. When W and B are in the same hemisphere, patients would have standard aphasia for L–L cases but crossed non-aphasia for R–R (unexpected absence of aphasia). The other 60 cases would have the two aspects of speech function in different hemispheres. How would the resulting speech disorders appear during neurological examination? MPA suggested that the diagnosis is likely to depend on lesion site and size, as well as the thoroughness of the examination; small lesions associated with mild deficits may not be noticed, but large lesions associated with unexpectedly mild aphasia might be seen as atypical. There could be several types of unusual impairment that lead to interesting case studies. How these 60 cases might be classified is uncertain. MPA suggested that subtle speech disorders would be missed in about one half of the cases (so that 30 must be added to the crossed non-aphasics). The remainder would be divided between those classified as aphasic (15 added to the 30 accidental standard aphasics, giving 45 in all) and those recognised as anomalous (15 anomalous aphasics).

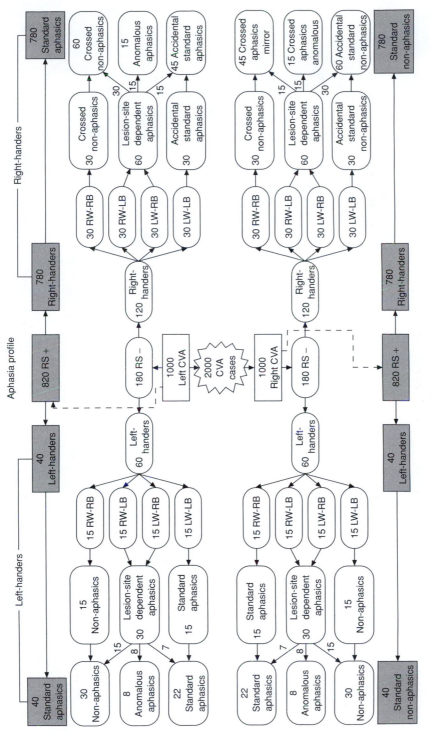

Figure 4.3 Predictions for aphasia in left-handers and right-handers when 10% of the population is classified left-handed: Annett and Alexander, 1996.

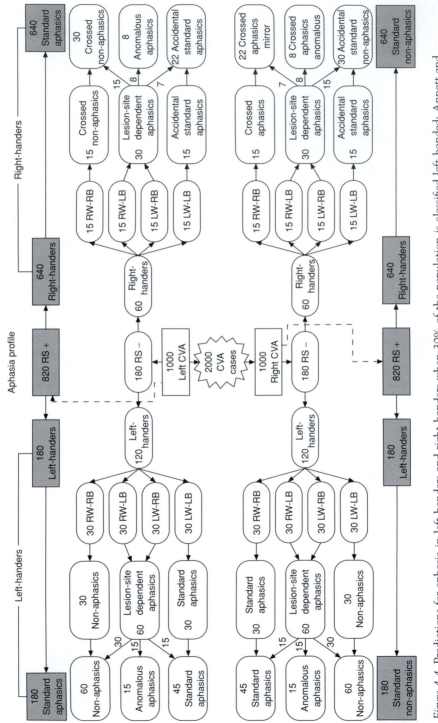

Figure 4.4 Predictions for aphasia in left-handers and right-handers when 30% of the population is classified left-handed: Annett and Alexander, 1996.

The lower right quadrant of Figure 4.3 shows the 900 *right-handers with right* CVA. There are 780 RS + and 120 RS − as above. The RS + are not aphasic. The 120 RS − have exactly the same types of cerebral laterality as just described for left CVA. The 30 cases with mild and subtle disorders that are missed must be added to the standard non-aphasics (60 in all). There are 45 cases likely to show standard aphasias (crossed mirror aphasics) and 15 will be crossed anomalous aphasics. In all, 6% of a representative population sample are likely to be right-handers with dysphasia and a right-sided lesion.

The predictions for left-handers are shown at the left side of Figure 4.3. These resemble those for right-handers in all respects except for the smaller numbers and the relatively larger proportion of RS − to RS +. The RS + left-handers with left CVA (top left quadrant) have standard aphasia and those with right CVA (bottom left quadrant) do not. The 60 RS − left-handers have the same accidental combinations of anterior and posterior speech lateralisations as right-handers. There are 30 non-aphasics, 22 standard aphasics and 8 anomalous cases among left CVA cases, and among right CVA cases also.

When the criterion of sinistrality is more generous and includes any tendencies to left preference (some 30% of the population), there are 300 non-right-handers to the left of Figure 4.4 and 700 right-handers to the right. The numbers of RS + and RS − are the same overall, but the numbers called "left" (or non-right) are raised to 180 RS + and 120 RS −. The same logic applies to the RS + and RS − in Figure 4.4, but the atypical cases form a smaller proportion of those called non-right-handers (30%) than for the left-handers (10%) in Figure 4.3. Classifying a large proportion of the population as non-right-handers dilutes the relative proportion of RS −. The number of RS − called non-right-handers on the 30% criterion is twice as large as for the 10% criterion (120 versus 60), but the number of RS + called left-handed is increased even more (180 versus 40). Hence the relative proportion of RS − at the "non-right" criterion (120/300 = 40%) is smaller than for the "left" criterion (60/100 = 60%). This illustrates the point made above, that predictions for cerebral speech differ not only between left- and right-handers, but also between different levels of incidence within handedness groups.

Table 4.5 summarises the predictions for aphasia in right-handers with left versus right brain lesions and similarly for left-handers, at the 10% and 30% levels of non-right-handedness. (Recall that all lesions are assumed to fall in the areas relevant for speech on either side.) At the 10% criterion, right-handers include 93.3% left brain and 6.7% right brain speakers, and left-handers 70% left brain and 30% right brain speakers. At the 30% criterion, the corresponding proportions are 95.6% and 4.3% for right-handers and 80% and 20% for non-right-handers. Annett and Alexander (1996, Tables 1 and 2) suggested how patients might be distributed for apraxias (typically associated with left-sided lesions) and configurational spatial deficits (typically associated with right-sided lesions) if these assort at random in RS − genotypes. These further possible implications of the model need to be followed up in new research. My purpose here is to show that the model for cerebral speech laterality and handedness predicts the findings for the following population representative samples.

Table 4.5 Summary of predictions for cerebral speech laterality in right- and left-handers at 10% and 30% levels of non-right-handedness

	10% criterion (Figure 4.3)	30% criterion (Figure 4.4)
Right-handers		
Left hemisphere speech	840/900 = 93.3%	670/700 = 95.7%
Right hemisphere speech	60/900 = 6.7%	30/700 = 4.3%
Left-handers		
Left hemisphere speech	70/100 = 70%	240/300 = 80%
Right hemisphere speech	30/100 = 30%	60/300 = 20%

Table 4.6 The distribution of dysphasics for lesion side and handedness in British World War Two head injury series (personal count by MA)

Lesion	Expected proportion	Expected (N)	Observed (N)	Chi-square
Right-handers				
Left	0.84	188.2	190	0.02
Right	0.06	13.4	13	0.01
Left-handers				
Left	0.07	15.7	14	0.18
Right	0.03	6.7	7	0.01
Total				0.22*

Note
*d.f. = 3, p > 0.50.

Table 4.6 summarises the predictions and findings of the British WW2 series, in cases where handedness was recorded, as counted by myself. Almost 10% were called left-handed or ambilateral. Previous accounts (Newcombe and Ratcliff, 1973; Russell and Espir, 1961) omitted ambilaterals and mixed-handers in order to exclude ambiguous cases, but the RS theory makes predictions for the population, so a *complete sample* is required, as far as possible. There were 224 dysphasics with information on handedness and strictly unilateral lesions. The numbers (and proportions) required are those for dysphasics in all 4 quadrants of Figure 4.3. (Because 50% of the hypothesised 2000 cases have dysphasias, there are 1000 dysphasics in all.) The analysis in Table 4.6 is based all dysphasics in the WW2 series. The predictions suggest that dysphasics should include 84% right-handers with left-sided lesions (780 + 15 + 45 = 840, see top right of Figure 4.3), 6% right-handers with right-sided lesions (45 + 15 = 60, bottom right), 7% left-handers with left-sided lesions (40 + 8 + 22 = 70, top left), and 3% left-handers with right-sided lesions (22 + 8 = 30, bottom left). Table 4.6 shows that the distribution of observed cases was virtually identical with that predicted (chi square = 0.22, d.f. 3, p > 0.50). (Note that a small chi square indicates excellent fit between prediction and observation.)

Table 4.7 Dysphasia in right- and left-handers with left and right hemisphere lesions: data of Hécaen and Ajuriaguerra, 1964

Lesion	Expected proportion	Expected (N)	Observed (N)	Chi-square
Right-handers				
Left	0.67	76.4	81	0.28
Right	0.03	3.4	0	3.42
Left-handers				
Left	0.24	27.4	22	1.05
Right	0.06	6.8	11	2.53
Total				7.28*

Note
*d.f. = 3, p > 0.05.

Table 4.7 examines the model against the data of Hécaen and Ajuriaguerra (1964). It will be recalled that 29% of dysphasics were classified as left-handed in this sample. Predictions must be tested for the 30% criterion in Figure 4.4. The proportions among dysphasics should be as follows; right-handers with left-sided lesions 67% (640 + 8 + 22 = 670), right-handers with right-sided lesions 3% (22 + 8 = 30), left-handers with left-sided lesions 24% (180 + 15 + 45 = 240), left-handers with right-sided lesions 6% (45 + 15 = 60). No right-handers were observed among dysphasics with right hemisphere lesions although three–four were expected, but there were eleven left-handers although only about seven were expected. However, the overall fit was acceptable in spite of the relatively poor match for right lesion cases.

Ludwig (1939) examined the records of German service personnel in WW1 for speech disorders in cases of *right-sided lesion* only. The sample represented a complete cohort of right lesion cases, as represented for the 1000 right-sided CVAs in the bottom halves of Figure 4.3 and 4.4. Because Ludwig did not include left lesion cases this study could not be included in Zangwill's compilation of representative series. Nevertheless, we can examine Ludwig's data in the light of our predictions for right-sided lesions. Ludwig described 979 right uni-lateral cases of whom 99 (10.1%) were classified as left-handed. Tests are made, therefore, for the 10% criterion of Figure 4.3. Table 4.8 lists the predictions, 84% right-handers without aphasia (780 + 60 = 840), 6% right-handers with aphasia (45 + 15 = 60), 7% left-handers without aphasia (40 + 30 = 70) and 3% left-handers with aphasia (22 + 8 = 30). The fit was excellent for left-handers. For right-handers, Ludwig described 10.2% as having a speech problem on initial examination but on follow-up some months later, the proportion with a persisting speech disorder was 3.2%. Figure 4.3 predicts 6%, midway between these initial and final estimates. Thus, for either the early or late assessment in Ludwig's series, the overall fit to predictions was poor.

How might this poor fit have arisen? It should be recalled that the Annett and Alexander predictions allowed for 30 lesion site dependent RS – dysphasics to be missed in routine neurological screening. If Ludwig's records were exceptionally

Table 4.8 Presence and absence of dysphasia in right- and left-handers with right hemisphere lesions: data of Ludwig, 1939

Dysphasia	Expected proportion	Expected (N)	Observed (N)	Chi-square
Right-handers				
Absent	0.84	822.4	780	2.18
Present	0.06	58.7	100	28.98
Left-handers				
Absent	0.07	68.5	72	0.18
Present	0.03	29.4	27	0.19
Total				31.53*

Note
*d.f. = 2, p < 0.01.

thorough and these cases were not missed, the proportion would be 9%. As a proportion of right-handers only, the incidence would be 90/900 or 10%. Ludwig's estimate of 10.2% is consistent, therefore, with a thorough assessment, such that no cases of speech disorder were missed on initial screening. Many of the speech disorders were transient, but this would be expected for lesion site dependent cases, if certain features of cerebral speech are represented in both hemispheres. In fact, only the 30 crossed aphasics with both W and B in the right hemisphere might have severe and persisting disabilities, consistent with the 3% observed. It is possible, therefore, that Ludwig's findings are an exceptionally good fit to the model. Further independent evidence is needed, of course, to test this interpretation.

The influential findings of Rasmussen and Milner (1975, see Table 1.1 here) cannot be examined in the same way as the series above because they were not population representative. Left- and right-handers were each selected from a wider sample. For 140 right-handers without evidence of early brain damage, there were 95.7% with left and 4.3% with right-sided speech. These proportions match exactly the predictions of the model for consistent right-handers when 30% of the population are called non-right-handers (see Table 4.5). They are as expected if right-handers were carefully selected to exclude all people with any sign of left-handedness. For 122 left-handers, there were 70.5% with left-sided speech and 29.5% with right or bilateral speech. These findings are very close to predictions for left-handers when 10% of the population are classified as sinistral (70:30%). This is as expected if left-handers were carefully selected for definite preferences for the left-hand. Thus, the findings of Rasmussen and Milner (1975) for handedness and speech laterality are fully consistent with the model, for some 70% of the population who are fully right-handed and for some 10% of the population who are definitely left-handed. The 20% of the population that are right mixed-handers is missing. The findings are not representative, therefore, of the population as a whole. In a representative sample at the 30% criterion, right CD would be expected in 4.3% of right-handers and 20% of non-right-handers. This prediction may be checked in future studies.

SUMMARY

Previous chapters suggested that what is distinctive about human handedness is not the shape of the distribution of asymmetry but its displacement in a dextral direction, along the laterality continuum. The key question is what is the right shift (RS) factor. Could it be an agent of left hemisphere advantage that normally induces left CD? The implications of this idea were examined in the light of the following assumptions: (1) most people carry the RS factor but a substantial minority do not, (2) the RS + develop left CD and have enhanced chances of right-handedness, (3) the RS − have no laterality biases so that they develop CD and handedness at random, and independently of each other. The implications of these hypotheses were examined in the light of expected distributions (in Figure 4.1) when the frequency of left-handedness is about 10%. Inspection of the overlapping distributions at the threshold of left-handedness (marked "X") showed that the model is consistent with what is known about relationships between handedness and CD, namely that the incidence of right CD is higher in left- than right-handers, but still less frequent in left-handers than left CD. The analysis led to a further surprising and apparently paradoxical prediction, that among people with right CD there should be more right- than left-handers.

This unexpected prediction gave a useful challenge to the theory. Tests of the prediction against data for representative samples of dysphasics found that the prediction was supported in two studies, both of the German and the British WW2 head injury series. Two clinic samples, by contrast, found no right-handers among dysphasics with right CD. An analysis of incidences of left-handedness in these series revealed that there were many more left-handers among dysphasics than non-dysphasics in these series. The threshold required to match the incidence of 29% left-handers in the dysphasics described by Hécaen was far to the right of that in Figure 4.1, such that all RS − were likely to be classified as "non-right-handers". This apparent variability between the five series described by Zangwill (1967) was shown to be mainly due to different classifications of handedness.

The variable of particular interest for the RS analysis was the proportion of the population with atypical CD, that is, in whole cohorts of patients, irrespective of handedness. Combined data for four series that were consistent in this respect gave an estimate of 9.27% right CD. Several checks were made on this estimate, from dysphasia studies and also from two independent community surveys of stroke patients. The evidence is consistent with an incidence of right CD in the population just below 10%.

This estimate of right CD could be used to estimate the proportion of RS − in the population (18.54%) and hence RS + (81.46%). These values, together with an estimate of extent of shift, also derived from the dysphasia series, allowed further exploration of the theory. A method of representing relationships between handedness and CD in the population was developed in collaboration with Michael P. Alexander (Alexander and Annett, 1996; Annett and Alexander, 1996). An imaginary sample of 2000 cases, 1000 with left CVA and

1000 with right CVA, all in the speech areas (if speech were located on the relevant side) was used to make the predictions as explicit as possible. Predictions were developed for 10% and for 30% levels of left- or non-right-handedness. Tests of predictions against data drawn from representative samples gave good fits in most cases. Ludwig's (1939) report of dysphasia in WW1 German head injury cases gave an exact fit for left-handers, but reports for right-handers in early and in late stages of recovery straddled the expected value. The apparent mismatch could be accommodated by the model very well if Ludwig's statistics are regarded as unusually thorough, while Annett and Alexander had assumed that a certain proportion of subtle cases would be missed. The overall conclusion is that the RS theory offers an excellent solution to the puzzle of the relationships between handedness and the laterality of cerebral dominance for speech.

5 The single gene theory of right shift

The discovery that a single gene might account for the RS factor, a gene that I called RS + (Annett, 1978b), was one of the greatest surprises of the RS story. For those who think theories are invented (out of the head of a thinker, or perhaps handed down as inspiration from sources on high) I would point out that this particular development of the RS theory depended on a research process that began some 17 years earlier. Some key steps in the process have been described already. To summarise briefly, my research in this field began with children who had unilateral epileptic foci, and the surprise that one-third of these children were mixed handed (Annett et al., 1961). Finding a similar proportion of mixed-handers in all subsequent samples, I suggested that uncertainties about relationships between handedness and cerebral dominance might be due to variability of hand preference and also variability of hemisphere speech, in this neglected subgroup of the population. My first genetic hypothesis (Annett, 1964) was that lateral asymmetries in mixed-handers might be due to variable expression in heterozygotes (RL genotypes, when R and L represented alleles for right- and left-handedness respectively). It was soon realised (1967) that this version of the classic genetic model could not be true when strictly interpreted (all heterozygotes mixed handed, and all mixed-handers heterozygote although, of course, variable penetrance could have rescued the model). Meanwhile, findings for hand preference and right minus left (R–L) peg moving skill suggested that both preference and skill are continuous variables, reliably related to each other. The binomial proportions of left-, mixed- and right-handedness, in all human samples that had been described in sufficient detail to be tested, and also in nonhuman samples although actual incidences were very different, raised some deep puzzles how these various phenomena could be related. The most difficult and pervasive problem, that incidences of left-handedness in the literature ranged from some 1 to 40%, was solvable if handedness was recognised to be a continuous variable that could be classified at any of a wide range of thresholds. The thresholds required to distinguish consistent left-, mixed- and consistent right-handers in humans, turned out to be identical with those required to distinguish these groups in nonhumans (when estimated at about 25, 50 and 25% under the curve of the normal distribution) if the human distribution was displaced to the right. Thus, it was possible to distinguish the shape of the distribution, continuous and unimodal in all species, and the location of the distribution, shifted to the right in humans only.

By the early 1970s I had collected considerable data on handedness in students and their families, some by report of the students themselves, and some from questionnaires sent to their homes, with requests for parents to complete their own questionnaires for the students to return to me. These findings were described in terms of the genetic analyses appropriate to threshold models and polygenic inheritance (Annett, 1973a, 1978a). Methods appropriate to multigene models were applied, not because of any conviction that handedness depended on many genes of small effect, but because it was this type of model that had led me to think of handedness as a threshold variable. At that stage I had rejected the classic single gene model and had no alternative to put in its place. Polygenic inheritance could not be ruled out. The question of interest to these models is whether there is significant heritability. That is, do probands, left-handed male and female students in my data, have more left-handed relatives than expected by chance? This was not clear in all analyses but significant heritability was typically found for mothers, and between females and their sisters, but more rarely for male relatives.

The new findings leading to the single gene theory depended on findings for handedness in children with two left-handed parents (Annett, 1974) and also the analysis of atypical cerebral dominance (as outlined in chapter 4). If CD could depend on a single gene, present in most people but absent in some, and if the frequency of this gene could be deduced from the proportion of atypical CD in the population, what would follow for handedness in families? The application to families was successful. The application to twins led to a new discovery, that the expression of the RS + gene is reduced in twins compared with the singleborn (singletons). The overall success of the single gene theory led to new questions about the genotype distribution. Could there be a genetic balanced polymorphism for the RS locus? This idea, considered in chapters 10–14, is one whose potential significance can hardly be overstated. The task of this chapter is to explain the arguments and early calculations for the single gene theory. Further developments of the genetic model, required to account for sex differences and possible additivity of expression for handedness (but not additivity for CD) will be described in chapter 7.

HANDEDNESS IN THE CHILDREN OF L × L FAMILIES

In the early 1970s I was in contact with several L × L families that had responded to appeals for information in local media. I sought permission to assess the laterality of all members of the family, by observing parents and children performing the 12 actions of the AHPQ and testing for peg moving skill. Some families visited the psychology department but most I visited at home, accompanied by a research assistant. With two pegboards we could test two members of the family in parallel, usually generating a healthy rivalry as to how fast everyone could be. The visits were in progress at the time the RS theory was formulated. When first plotting the R–L times of the children, I found that the number faster with the left-hand was the same as the number faster with the right-hand. This was a happy surprise that I rushed out to share with a research assistant. The finding was predictable, of course, if the children lacked bias to either side, but this clear early support for the theory was encouraging. As further families were visited the proportion of right-handed children rose slightly, but this was expected if some left-handed parents were RS + (see overlap in Figure 4.1). An important finding depended on a few parents who had histories of early problems that might have been sufficient to make them pathological left-handers. The eight children in these families were shifted to the right for peg moving, as are children in general samples. These findings (Annett, 1974) gave the first clear evidence that the presence or absence of the RS factor might be inherited, and that non-carriers have children without bias to either side for R–L hand skill.

The reliability of these observations needed checking in a second sample, again sought through the media. The findings for the second sample resembled those of the first so the two samples were combined to give a total of 115 children (Annett, 1983a). There were 34% left-handed writers, 26% right mixed-handers and only 40% consistent right-handers. Figure 5.1 shows the L–R peg moving distribution, a normal curve roughly symmetrical about 0. The hatching shows 20 children who had a parent judged to be a possible pathological left-hander because of a history of personal birth complications or abnormally slow right-hand time on the peg moving task and no close left-handed relative. Such a parent might be a carrier of the RS + gene. The 20 children of these families were significantly biased to the right (L–R mean = 8.0, S.E. 2.9) while the other 95 children were not significantly greater than 0 (L–R mean = 1.5, S.E. 1.5). All the children were reared by two left-handed parents so that experiences of handedness in the home were similar for the two groups. The findings support the argument that there is a genetic bias to dextrality. They complement the evidence from adoptive families of left-handed parents. Carter-Saltzman (1980) found that the biological children but not the adopted children of left-handed parents were more likely to be left-handed.

An interesting feature of the children in L × L families was the absence of difference between males and females for R–L hand skill, in contrast to general samples (see Figure 3.2). The observation is consistent with the idea that the stronger bias to dextrality in females is a function of stronger expression of the RS + factor, but as this factor is absent in most people in L × L families, the usual difference between the sexes is absent also.

A SINGLE ALLELE FOR LEFT HEMISPHERE ADVANTAGE

The idea that handedness might depend on a single genetic locus, a dominant allele for right- (R) and a recessive allele for left-handedness (L) has a long history, as outlined in chapter 1. Although breeding experiments in mice and rats were unambiguous that paw preferences are not inherited (chapter 3), there

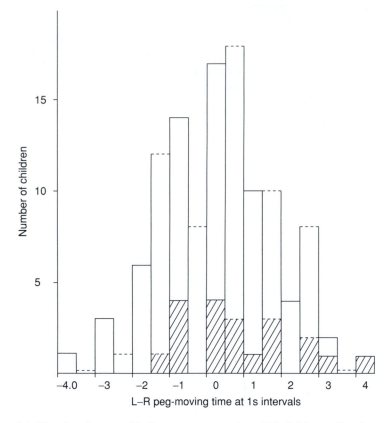

Figure 5.1 The distribution of L–R peg moving time in 115 children of L × L parents: males (solid line), females (dashed line) and 20 children of parents whose left-handedness was possibly pathological (hatched).

is evidence for a genetic influence on human handedness, but not one that follows the classic Mendelian rules for dominant and recessive alleles. The RS theory suggests a resolution to these inconsistencies by distinguishing the *shape* of laterality distribution (normal and accidental in all species) from its *location* (displaced rightwards in humans only). The shape might be non-genetic but the location inherited. If most humans inherit RS but some do not, then the distributions would approximate those suggested in Figure 4.1. It is important to be clear that both are *chance* distributions, the larger represents chance plus RS, and the smaller chance without RS. Whereas earlier genetic models, including Annett (1964), assumed that left-handedness would need a specific cause (an allele for L) the RS analysis made this redundant. The only genetic influence is toward dextrality. Right- and left-handedness do not need genetic determinants because they occur by chance.

My findings for family handedness were first examined in terms of the models appropriate for polygenic inheritance (Annett, 1973a, 1978a), as mentioned

Table 5.1 Correlations between relatives for L–R peg moving time in personally visited families: Annett, 1978a

Pairs of relatives		L × L Hull		R × R Bedford		R × L Coventry		All families		SE
		N	r	N	r	N	r	N	r	
Fathers	Sons	25	−.11	16	.03	26	.23	79	.08	.11
Fathers	Daughters	20	.13	19	−.12	21	−.44*	80	−.19	.11
Mothers	Sons	25	.22	20	−.02	29	−.11	86	.17	.11
Mothers	Daughters	20	−.07	24	−.18	24	.44*	88	.28*	.10
Brothers	Brothers	10	−.09	13	−.12	13	.79*	36	.21	.16
Sisters	Sisters	3	—	11	.13	5	—	24	−.01	.21
Brothers	Sisters	19	.13	29	−.45*	25	.07	74	.08	.12

Note
*p < 0.05.

above. The failure of attempts to breed mice and rats for paw preference made it unlikely that the shape of the distribution (the normal or Gaussian curve) was due to genes. If the curve was due to chance in other species, it could be due to chance in humans also. However, the question whether R–L asymmetries for hand skill in humans might be caused by polygenes needed to be tested. If R–L hand skill, as measured by my peg moving task, was influenced by multigene inheritance, then there should be correlations between relatives for R–L scores. My data from personally tested families included the L × L families described above, and also families with left-handed fathers or left-handed mothers (R × L) and some with both parents right-handed (R × R). These families were visited over several years and drawn mainly from three UK locations, Hull, Bedfordshire and Coventry. Each group of families could be examined for seven pairs of relatives, as shown in Table 5.1. Most of the correlations were trivial. They were as likely to be negative as positive, and the few that were statistically significant were not replicated in families from another location. I concluded that there was no evidence that the distribution of R–L hand skill was genetic. This allowed the question of inheritance to focus on the agent of shift, RS +.

It was argued in chapter 4 that the RS factor is not for handedness but rather for left hemisphere advantage. Some relative advantage for the left over the right hemisphere would be sufficient to add a constant value to the random chances for handedness, to load the dice in favour of the right. A constant value, present in most people, would have little effect on the *variability* of R–L skill and so it would have little influence, therefore, on the correlations described in Table 5.1. If the variability depended on many genes, the correlations should have detected their presence. A gene giving an advantage to the left hemisphere might have appeared in the course of human evolution and been selected because it facilitated the development of speech and language.

Lateralisation to one hemisphere would be likely to aid speech acquisition because it would avoid the slow and uncertain transmission of information between the hemisphere, via the corpus callosum. Young infants are effectively split-brained, because the corpus callosum is relatively late to develop full transmission efficiency (because of slow myelination of the neural tracts). All humans talk, unless severely deaf or otherwise disabled, so we are not looking for a gene that is essential for speech and language (certainly not Chomsky's language acquisition device). We are looking for a gene that aids a unique and complex learning process, how to produce the sounds of human speech. People vary in the speed and efficiency of speech acquisition, and some suffer speech disorders. The dysphasia literature (see chapter 4) suggests that there are natural individual differences for cerebral dominance. People with atypical CD can be presumed to lack an agent of left hemisphere advantage that is present in most people. The possible risks associated with atypical CD will be considered in relation to the balanced polymorphism hypothesis. For the present, the question is whether we can estimate the proportion of the population that lacks the hypothesised RS + gene. The best clue to this value is the proportion with right CD.

In chapter 4 the estimated proportion of the population with right CD was 9.27%, from 647 dysphasics drawn from four representative samples. The estimate was supported by several checks in other data. Twice this percentage (18.54%, or 0.1854 of the total population) can be assumed to lack the RS factor (because speech is hypothesised to lateralise by chance in the RS −). If there is a single genetic locus for RS, and if the RS + allele is dominant for left CD (that is, left CD in RS + + and RS + − genotypes) then we can infer that non-gene-carriers, RS − − genotypes, are 0.1854 of the population. The square root of this quantity (0.4306) gives the frequency of the RS − allele(s). (There could be one or several RS − alleles; they are presumed to be whatever ancient alleles were present before the RS + mutation.) The frequency of RS + is 1 − 0.4306, or 0.5694. A pair of alleles with these frequencies combine at random to give three genotypes in the following proportions:

$$RS + + = 0.3242 : RS + - = 0.4904 : RS - - = 0.1854$$

These estimates suggest that the three genotypes are all present in substantial numbers in the population. The highest frequency is the heterozygote, RS + −, with 49% when the maximum possible for a single locus is 50%. The genotype distribution leads on to questions about why these proportions might occur. Are they associated with costs and benefits of the RS + gene, as explored in chapters 10–14? The important point is that the proportions were deduced from data for dysphasia, data that is quite independent of studies of handedness in families. However, the estimate of frequency of the RS − gene (0.43) agrees with the estimate made by Trankell (1955) from family data for a recessive gene for left-handedness. For Trankell the relevant gene was L (for left) a recessive allele with imperfect penetrance. For the RS theory, the gene is recessive to RS + for left CD, but neutral for handedness. The hypothesis of imperfect penetrance is redundant.

The gene and genotype frequencies define the relative sizes of the RS + (RS + + and RS + −) and RS − (RS − −) distributions. My guess in Figure 4.1 was that the RS − proportion would be about 20% of the population. The estimate above is close, at 18.5%. A second parameter of the RS model is required, the extent of right shift of the RS + distribution. This was deduced from the findings for dysphasics also (in chapter 4) at just under 2 standard deviations (1.937z). Could these estimates of the gene frequency and shift predict findings for family handedness? My first calculations were as simple as possible, not least because they were performed by hand, genotypes matched to incidences of left-handedness by trial and error with the aid of a table of the normal curve, and all sums by desk calculator. (Each set of family data took about 2 hours to calculate, while today's computer runs are based on perfect matches and virtually instant.) No distinction was made for the sex of parents or sex of children, and the same shift for handedness was assumed for RS + + and RS + − genotypes. It is important to be clear that the RS gene was always regarded as "for" CD and dominant for left hemisphere speech. This was intrinsic to the method of calculating gene frequency. However, the influence of the gene on handedness could differ between RS + + and RS + − genotypes. Chapter 7 will examine predictions for an additive model for handedness when the sexes are treated separately. Here, I will outline the calculations of the simple dominant model for the non-technical reader, treating percentages as numbers per 1000, and rounding to avoid decimals. (A worked example using the data of Chamberlain, 1928, is reproduced in Appendix VIII, from Appendix IV of Annett, 1985a, in order to show the method of calculation of Annett, 1978b.)

The stages of calculation were as follows:

1. *Calculate the genotypes of right-handed parents and left-handed parents.* The genotype proportions deduced above imply that in the population as a whole, the numbers per 1000 are about RS + + 325, RS + − 490, and RS − − 185. Chamberlain (1928) found 3.56% left-handers in the parent generation, or 36 per 1000. How many of these would carry each genotype? For a dominant model, with shift just under 2z, the expected numbers for 36 left-handers are about RS + + 1, RS + − 1 and RS − − 34. Right-handed parents, therefore, are approximately RS + + 324, RS + − 489 and RS − − 151.

2. *Calculate the genotypes of children in R × R, L × R and L × L families.* For the above genotype frequencies for parents, the children that result from all possible combinations of parental genotypes must be calculated for each type of family. Because right-handed parents may carry any of the three genotypes there are nine possible combinations of genotypes in R × R families (+ + × + +, + + × + −, + + × − − etc., as set out in Appendix VIII). The offspring are distributed between the three genotypes according to the rules of random combination of alleles in pairs (+ + × + + = 100% + +; + + × + − = 50% + + and 50% + −; + + × − − = 100% + − and so on). The sums of the three genotypes represent the children in R × R families as proportions in the total population, but it is usual to work with the proportions

within each family type separately. The genotypes of the children are RS + + 347, RS + − 484, RS − − 169 (per 1000 in R × R families). (The calculations assume random mating, that handedness does not influence the choice of mate or the number of children. These are possible, of course, but must be ignored for the present purpose.)

Similar calculations must be made for R × L families and for L × R families, identical when the handedness of fathers is not distinguished from that of mothers. The sums can be performed once and then doubled. The genotypes for children are RS + + 21, RS + − 583 and RS − − 396 per 1000 in R × L families. For L × L families the expected distribution is RS + + 1, RS + − 69 and RS − − 930.

3. *Calculate the genotype proportions of right- and left-handers in the filial generation.* The frequency of left-handedness in children differs from that of parents in every family study, so the genotype distribution of the filial generation has to be worked out for the appropriate threshold. The children in Chamberlain's study (students, brothers and sisters) included 4.77% left-handers. For 48 left-handers per 1000 in the total population, the numbers in the three genotypes are about RS + + 2, RS + − 2 and RS − − 44. These numbers are associated with a threshold that gives about 0.4% of the RS + distribution and 24% of the RS − − distribution as left-handed.

If 0.4% (or 0.004) are called left-handed in gene-carriers, how many of the children in R × R families will be RS + + and RS + − left-handers? How many of the RS − − when multiplied by 0.24? Appendix VIII C shows that the total proportion of left-handers in R × R families should be 0.0438 or about 44 per 1000. Similar calculations are made for R × L and L × L families, giving proportions of 0.0973 (97 per 1000) and 0.2229 (223 per 1000) respectively.

4. *Compare the numbers of left-handers predicted in each family type with those observed.* Chamberlain's sample included 7225 children of R × R parents. At about 44 per 1000, there should be some 317 left-handers in this family type in this sample. The number recorded was 308, a remarkably good fit. The predicted numbers of left-handers for R × L and L × L families were 45 and 5.6 respectively and 53 and 7 were observed. The total chi square, calculated for observed and predicted left-handers, was small (chi square = 1.9574, d.f. 2, ns), indicating excellent agreement.

There were five sets of data available to me in 1978b (the samples of Ramaley, Chamberlain, Rife and my samples of students, from the University of Hull, and the Open University). My samples could be examined for a strict criterion, left-handed writing, or a more generous criterion, any left-hand preference in 12 actions or non-right-handedness. This gave seven tests of the fit of the model. All gave very good fits except the data of Ramaley, where there were more left-handed children in the families of left-handed parents than expected.

The 1978b calculations were re-done using a more efficient computer program, with the same parameters as before, but correcting minor errors, and including the chi-square tests of predictions for right-handers as well as left-handers within

Table 5.2 Family handedness studies cited by McManus, 1985a: comparison of fits for the McManus (MM) and right shift (RS) genetic models: Annett, 1996a

	N	% L		X^2	
		Parents	Children	MM model	RS model
Chamberlain (1928)	7714	3.6	4.8	1.88	2.20
Annett (1973a)	7477	4.1	10.6	0.40	1.57
Rife (1940)	2178	5.2	8.8	3.36	2.94
OU: Annett (1978b)	2000	5.5	8.5	1.74	3.96
Ramaley (1913)	1130	8.1	15.7	17.34*	9.53*
Leiber and Axelrod (1981)	2257	8.1	10.6	0.46	0.73
ICM1: McManus (1985a)	2213	10.1	15.2	2.91	3.37
Chaurasia and Goswami (cited McManus, 1985a)	1379	10.4	14.7	8.20*	3.19
McGee and Cozad (1980)	1586	18.2	24.2	13.67*	2.56
Total				49.96	30.05
Difference					19.91*

Note
*for d.f. = 2, p < 0.025.

families (Annett, 1996a). The five samples were reported together with findings for four later studies, as shown in Table 5.2. There was only one poor fit, for Ramaley as above. All other chi-squares were well below the level required for statistical significance. (For d.f. = 2, the value required for significance at the 5% level is 5.99; values below this level indicate good fit.)

Also shown in Table 5.2 are the values for the genetic model of McManus (1985a), labelled "MM". Details of this model will be described in chapter 16. Six of the nine studies fitted well to the McManus model, but three did not. The sum over all chi-squares was smaller for (in favour of) the RS than the MM model. The point of this comparison (in Annett, 1996a) was to show that although the RS model has been developed in certain ways to be explained in chapter 7, the original model with parameters deduced as described above was more successful than a supposed alternative theory. The critical point here is that McManus (1985a) estimated gene frequencies by maximum likelihood methods from the family data itself. That is, the McManus gene frequencies were selected to give the best fit to the data to be explained. The RS values were deduced from independent evidence, and then found to fit the family data. That is why the RS single gene theory was a surprising discovery, not an invention designed to do the job.

It was said above that two of my samples could be analysed for a strict criterion, left writing, but also a generous criterion, any preference for the left-hand in 12 actions. Fits were good at both levels. The predictions were very different at the two levels, but both fitted the observations at the corresponding level. This would not be possible if the underlying distributions were not stable, and the cut-points or thresholds for different incidences mapped to the underlying genotypes in a consistent manner. In one of my samples both parents and children had completed the AHPQ so both generations could be classified for the generous criterion. Whereas the strict criterion yields small numbers of children in a few L × L families, the generous classification found families of Non-right × Non-right parents that included 76 children. The predicted number of non-right children was 46 and 45 were observed. The total chi-square over all family types, and including tests for right- and for left-handers, was very small (chi-square = 0.58, d.f. 2, ns) indicating excellent fit.

A SINGLE GENE FOR RS IN TWIN PAIRS

The problems presented by twins to genetic theories of handedness were outlined in chapter 1. If handedness were fully genetic, then identical (MZ) twins should be identical for handedness. If there were a strong genetic influence, MZ pairs should be more alike than DZ pairs. Neither of these is true. In combined data reviewed by Collins (1970), the percentages of pairs with both twins right-handed (RR), one twin left-handed (RL) and both left-handed (LL) were 75, 23 and 2% for MZ pairs, and 78, 21 and 1% for DZ pairs respectively. Loehlin and Nichols (1976) described a new large sample of twins and found the corresponding proportions were 74, 24 and 2% for MZ and 78, 21 and 1% for DZ pairs, almost identical with those of Collins. Hence, we can be confident that these are reliable estimates of the handedness distribution of twins. It is important to notice that the distributions of MZ and DZ pairs are very similar. It is sometimes suggested that opposite handedness in MZ twin pairs (RL pairs) is caused by mirror-imaging. Mirror-imaging may occur occasionally when there is late division of the zygote, to give reversed asymmetries for the viscera and direction of hair-whorl at the crown of the head. However, mirror-imaging does not occur in DZ pairs, so it is unnecessary to suppose that it is major factor in MZ pairs for handedness.

Collins pointed out that not only were the distributions remarkably similar between MZ and DZ pairs, they were almost exactly as expected if the twins were assorted by chance. That is, they were as expected if right and left-handed twins were like black and white marbles, put in a bag, shaken up and taken out in twos at random (in binomial proportions, as explained in chapter 2). Rife (1950) noticed the binomial distribution of handedness in twin pairs and tried to account for this genetically, but there is no known mechanism by which this could occur (especially not for DZ pairs). Collins concluded that the mechanisms of human handedness must depend on chance, like those of mice. However, some genetic influence on handedness in twins was implied by Rife's observation that RL twins were more likely to have another left-hander in the family than RR twins.

These intriguing puzzles about handedness in twins are interpretable by the RS theory, for reasons that can be best understood by referring back to the distributions of Figure 4.1. The RS analysis distinguishes the non-genetic variability which is due to *chance* (the Gaussian curves) and the genetic variability for the location of the chance distribution (RS + or RS −). The shift acts like a mathematical constant that is added to every value in the chance distribution but does not affect its variability. Recall the analogy of the throw of a dice, with or without the addition of a constant "2" to each throw. The presence of the genetic factor (or RS + gene) adds a 2 to every value of the random throw. If a pair of MZ twins both carry the gene, 2 will be added to the throw for both. This makes both more likely to be right-handed, but there are still six possible outcomes for each individual and these are non-genetic. If MZ twins do not carry the gene, there will still be six chance outcomes for each twin. Collins was correct that the handedness of pairs of twins resembles that of pairs of marbles taken from a bag at random. The RS theory simply points out that the RS + gene puts more black (right) than white (left) marbles in the bag. There are more right- than left-handers among twins just as among singletons, both due to the influence of the RS + gene. The variability due to chance is very large in comparison with the small variability associated with the presence or absence of the RS + gene. MZ twins are identical for presence or absence of the RS + gene, whereas DZ twins are not, but enormous numbers of pairs are needed to demonstrated the difference statistically (see chapter 7). This same reasoning applies to handedness in pairs of siblings (Carlier, Beau, Marchland et al., 1994) and also to brain asymmetries in twins (Steinmetz, Herzog, Schlaug et al., 1995). Thus, the theory can explain the observations but does the model, as developed above for handedness in families, predict the distribution of twin pairs?

The application of the RS genetic model to twin pairs was first tested using the same parameters of the model (proportions and shift) as above. The frequency of left- or non-right-handedness determines the threshold, and the distribution of RR, RL and LL pairs is then predicted for each genotype and summed to find the expected totals for each sample. *The predictions did not fit the observations.* How could a genetic model that had worked so well for the family data not work for twins? It was soon found that twin distributions were predicted very well if a change was made to one parameter. This was that the extent of RS must be smaller in twins than in the singleborn. This implied that the expression of the RS + gene must be smaller in twins than the singleborn. They should have a slightly higher incidence of left-handedness.

The outcome for a shift of $1.0z$ (instead of $1.937z$ as above) is shown in Table 5.3, for the distribution of MZ pairs in the combined data collected by Zazzo (1960). There were 1210 MZ twins pairs with a total incidence of left-handedness of 16.2% (threshold at $-0.245z$). The fit was perfect. The calculations were repeated for Zazzo's collection of 1145 DZ pairs, where the frequency of left-handedness was 12.9% (threshold at $-0.4z$). Table 5.4 shows that the fit was almost perfect.

The need to change a parameter for twins compared with the singleborn has been argued to cast doubt on the RS theory (McManus, 1980a, 1985a; McManus

Table 5.3 Predicting handedness in MZ twin pairs: shift between RS + and RS − means is 1.0z: data of Zazzo, 1960, analysed by Annett, 1978b

Sinistral incidence			Threshold	Sinistral proportion
0.1616		RS + +, + −	−1.245z	0.1065
		RS − −	−0.245z	0.4032

MZ pairs	Frequency in population	RR	RL	LL twin pairs
RS + +, + −	0.8146	0.6503	0.1550	0.0092
RS − −	0.1854	0.0660	0.0892	0.0301
Sum		0.7163	0.2442	0.0393

		Test for 1210 MZ pairs			
Expected N	866.7	295.5	47.5	
Observed N	867	295	48	
Chi-square	0.0001	0.0002	0.0042	Sum = 0.0045

Table 5.4 Predicting handedness in DZ twin pairs: shift between RS + and RS − means is 1.0z: data of Zazzo, 1960, analysed by Annett, 1978b

Sinistral incidence			Threshold	Sinistral proportion
0.1288		RS +, + −	−1.40z	0.0808
		RS −	−0.40z	0.3446

DZ pairs	Frequency in population	RR	RL	LL twin pairs
RS + +, + − × + +, + −	0.7240	0.6117	0.1075	0.0047
RS + +, + − × − −	0.1811	0.1091	0.0669	0.0050
RS − − × − −	0.0949	0.0407	0.0428	0.0113
Sum		0.7616	0.2173	0.0210

		Test for 1145 DZ pairs			
Expected N	872.0	248.9	24.1	
Observed N	871	253	21	
Chi-square	0.0012	0.0689	0.0348	Sum = 0.1049

and Bryden, 1992). On the contrary, the parameter change has important positive implications for the theory in three respects. First, it led to the specific prediction that twins must be more often left-handed than the singleborn. For the dominant version of the model above, when 7% of singletons are left-handed, there should be about 13% among twins. (For an additive model and a 33% reduction of shift, considered in the chapter 7, the percentages would be 9% and 13% respectively.) It has been suggested before that twins are more often left-handed than singletons but the evidence was weak and controversial (McManus 1980a). Good evidence would require twins and singletons to be studied by exactly the same methods in the same research sample, for reasons discussed in Chapter 2. Rife (1940, 1950) assessed students and twins using standard criteria. He found about 9% of students and about 12% of twins were left-handed. Among my parents responding personally to the AHPQ there were about 4% left-handers among singletons but 11% among those reporting twin birth.

Clear and strong evidence that twins are more likely to be left-handed than singletons was found in a national survey of some 30,000 people answering a questionnaire on hearing disabilities (Davis and Annett, 1994). The questionnaire asked about sex, handedness and birth status. The findings will be considered more fully in chapter 6. The important point here is that overall percentages were 7.1% for the singletons and 11.7% for twins, close to the RS predictions above.

The second interesting point about the reduced shift in twins was that *the same reduction fitted the data for MZ as DZ twins*. This suggested that the reduction is not a function of the type of twin, but of twin birth itself. The rate of growth of twins is slowed in later foetal life, in order to accommodate two foetuses in the womb (Tanner, 1978) and this physical constraint applies, of course, to both MZ and DZ pairs. If the expression of the RS + gene depends on rate of growth in late foetal life, a similar reduction of RS would be expected in both types of twin pairs, and other multiple births. Chi, Dooling and Gilles (1977) found, in a study of foetal brain growth, that twins were delayed by 2 or 3 weeks in the appearance of cerebral convolutions in comparison with non-twins. The reduction of RS in twins suggests that the mechanisms through which the gene is expressed depend on factors associated with rate of cerebral growth. This could offer a unified explanation for differences associated with sex, low birth weight and pathologies of growth, as considered later.

The third point concerning the reduced expression of the RS + gene in twins is that the gene is hypothesised to facilitate the acquisition of speech. One of the best established findings of twin research is that twins tend to be slow to talk and to suffer delays in the growth of other language skills (Mittler, 1971). The explanation usually offered is that twins do not need to talk because they develop private means of communication with each other. This may or may not be true, but it could be only part of the story. Perhaps twins develop special methods of communication *because* the development of speech is delayed. The observation that twins are slower to talk than singletons, that males are slower to talk than females and that incidences of left-handedness are higher in twins and in males than females, would have a single explanation. All would be due to differences in relative maturity at birth, a factor that influences the expression of the RS + gene.

SUMMARY

A genetic influence on human but not nonhuman handedness can be explained if there is a non-genetic, chance distribution of R–L asymmetries in all species, and a single gene for left hemisphere advantage in most but not all humans that weights the chance asymmetries in favour of the right-hand. Children in L × L families are distributed for R–L skill as expected by chance without significant RS, consistent with the idea that most of the children lack the hypothesised RS + gene. However, left-handed parents likely to be pathologically sinistral have children who are biased to the right-hand, as expected if the RS + gene were present. These observations complement those for adopted children in the families of left-handed parents.

The gene frequency and extent of RS were inferred from findings for dysphasia, as analysed in chapter 4. The genetic model was then able to predict the numbers of left-handed children in families of R × R, L × R and L × L parents in five samples available in 1978. Two of these samples could be examined for strict as well as generous criteria (left-handed writing and non-right-handedness). Fits were good at both levels. The data of Ramaley (1913) gave the only poor fit to the model. Data for handedness in families published after 1978 also give excellent fits. A worked example of the genetic calculations is given in Appendix VIII.

The RS genetic model can also predict the distribution of handedness in twin pairs, both MZ and DZ, because the major part of the variability for handedness is due to non-genetic congenital accidents that affect every individual independently. The RS analysis required that the expression of the RS + gene is reduced in twins compared with singletons. This has three interesting implications. First, twins are more likely to be left-handed, by some 3–5% for left-handed writing. Second, expression of the RS + gene is likely to depend on the rate of foetal growth, because this growth is slowed in twins compared with the singleborn. Third, speech and language acquisition are slowed in twins, as found in studies of twin development. Whereas the change of one parameter for twins in the RS theory has been widely taken as a reason to doubt the theory, it is on the contrary a good example of how the RS analysis may lead to new and productive insights into previously controversial and unexplained findings.

Part III

Explorations in the light of the theory

6 Stability and change

Handedness with age, sex
and time

This chapter is about distinguishing what is constant and predictable about
handedness from what is superficial and changeable. What are the facts about
which we can be certain? Chapters 2 and 3 tackled the principal source of
uncertainty, the different incidences between studies. It was argued that
incidences reflect thresholds, or cut-off points, along an underlying asymmetry
continuum. The RS solution to the problem of relationships between asymmetries
of hand and brain depends on the assumption that people who do and do not
carry an agent promoting left hemisphere advantage differ for handedness only
in the *locations* of R–L distributions along the continuum. Handedness distributions in families and in pairs of twins are predictable on the assumption that the
RS factor is a single gene "for" left hemisphere advantage. Handedness itself
depends on chance, accidents of congenital development. This might seem to
imply that handedness will be unpredictable and therefore not accessible to
scientific study. On the contrary, the laws of chance are highly predictable,
provided the groups studied are of reasonable size and drawn without selection
biases. Small samples may differ through accidents of sampling, a problem for
the interpretation of findings in the laterality literature. In order to understand
the influence of the RS + gene, we need to discover what systematic influences
reliably affect the chance distribution of asymmetry.

The chief effect of the RS + gene on handedness is to displace a normal
distribution of asymmetry toward the right, thus increasing the relative skill of
the right-hand and raising the percentage of right-hand preference above
50% (the starting hypothesis of the RS theory). Human groups tend to
demand conformity, such that any biological bias towards dextrality is likely to
be exaggerated by cultural pressures. Pressures differ between societies and within
societies over time. Changes in prejudices against left-handedness during the
20th century in Western societies have led to the practical problem that studies
of relationships between preference and age may be confounded by changes due
to secular trends over time. Neglect of secular trends led to the mistaken idea
that left-handers have reduced longevity, as considered below.

The RS theory distinguishes the effects of biological and cultural biases by
suggesting that biology determines the frequency of the RS + gene and its effectiveness (the proportions and shift deduced in chapter 4) while culture influences

the threshold of expression. The threshold may be far to the left as in Japanese society where there are about 1% left-handers, or well to the right as in Western samples where some 30–40% may be called non-right-handers. The power of the threshold approach to solve the problems of chapters 4 and 5 depends on the stability of the underlying distributions of R–L hand skill. Variable incidences imply variable thresholds but there are stable underlying proportions. The RS analysis, as developed in chapter 3, depended on empirical evidence that levels of relative R–L hand skill are reliably related to levels of hand preference.

In order to investigate the stability or change of handedness with age, sex and time, we need to know whether these variables influence hand skill, preference or relationships between preference and skill. This chapter examines several questions about the growth and expression of skill and preference. The evidence depends on findings for preference and skill gathered over some 30 years. The main outcomes that need to be taken into account in subsequent chapters are first, that there is a reliable difference between the sexes. Females are more strongly biased to the right-hand than males. Second, the evidence points un-equivocally to the conclusion that the agent of RS is something that weakens the left-hand. The inference that the RS + gene is associated with a relative handicap to the right hemisphere and that this weakness is greater in females than males, is important for subsequent developments of the theory.

NORMATIVE STUDIES OF PEG MOVING TIME

How do the skills of the right and the left hands grow with age? Peg moving time was measured for three–five trials by each hand in several samples of schoolchildren and undergraduates from the 1960s to the 1990s. Annett (1970b) published norms based on a random sample of over 200 children, aged 3–15 years, drawn from eight schools in the City of Hull. These norms were based on means for each hand, smoothed by averaging over adjacent year groups. Combined data were described for several school and undergraduate samples, including all data available in the late 1970s (Annett and Kilshaw, 1983; Kilshaw and Annett, 1983). Annett (1992d) described further school and university samples for peg moving and other tests of hand skill. The present compilation includes samples collected up to 1991, age range 3–63 years. These data were examined with respect to age, sex and time (Annett, 1998a). Revised norms are given in Table A.II.1

Some general points about the samples should be noted. Children from 3 to 15 years of age were drawn from schools representative of the general population. There were no 16-year-olds because this is the last year of compulsory schooling in the UK and preparations for national scholastic examinations did not allow time for psychological research. From 18 years the samples depended on undergraduates and were not necessarily representative, therefore, of the general population. All of the higher education samples included some mature students but the majority of 25- to 63-year-olds were Open University (OU)

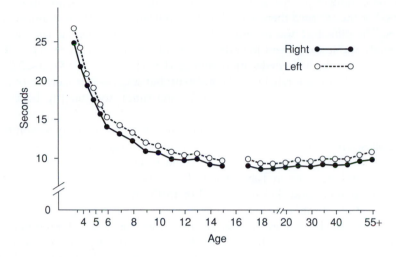

Figure 6.1 Right and left-hand peg moving time(s) with age.

students taking part in a summer school practical class in psychology. These data were collected in a similar way to that of most other undergraduates. That is, students tested each other in class exercises, timing each other for peg moving and observing hand use for the actions of the AHPQ, under supervision by trained assistants. Findings were recorded on data sheets that were collected for me. I checked the arithmetic and the preference classifications. Participants were excluded if there was a history of injury, arthritis or other physical problem that might have affected performance. Young children were included only if they were mature enough to follow the rule to move the pegs "as fast as you can", without play or other distraction in the course of a trial. The samples fall into two main groups, those collected between 1966 and 1975 (Annett and Kilshaw, 1983; Kilshaw and Annett, 1983) and between 1980 and 1991. The span of years allows us to ask whether there have been changes in handedness over this period of some 25 years.

Figure 6.1 shows the mean times taken to move ten pegs by each hand as a function of age. Age is plotted at 6-month intervals up to 6 years, at 1-year intervals from 6 to 19 years and in 5-year intervals from 20 to 55+ years. The smallest N is 15. Standard errors are not shown because for most groups they fall within the range of the symbols depicting the means. The graph shows that peg moving time falls rapidly during the nursery years and then at a decelerating rate until the late teens. Times were fastest for young adults and then slowed gradually with increasing age. (The story is identical if considered in terms of speed, or 1/time.) The growth curves for the left and right hands are parallel.

Do the sexes differ for time taken by each hand? For the *right-hand*, there was no significant sex difference. Females tended to be slightly faster than males up to about age 8 years but the sexes were similar thereafter. The slightly faster right-hand time of younger girls is consistent with their earlier maturation than males. For the *left-hand* there was a highly significant sex difference in favour of males. The difference was examined for the school and undergraduate samples separately and it was present in both, the school samples (F = 5.054, d.f. 1:1436, p = 0.025) and the higher education samples (F = 16.27, d.f. 1:1547, p < 0.001). The sex difference was reliable and consistent, but small as a proportion of total time taken (about 200 ms, or 2% of left-hand time), too small to be shown clearly in Figure 6.1.

The growth curves are not entirely smooth, due to accidents of sampling in age groups. The curves were smoothed by regression to give the best estimate of the time taken at each age. The smoothed mean times and standard deviations for each hand are given in Table A.II.1. These standards can be used as norms to assess whether hand skill is impaired or in the normal range, in individual cases or groups of interest.

The analyses above found similar growth curves for skill in both hands but the left a little slower than the right at all ages. Does the *difference* between the hands change with age? The *absolute* difference between the hands was larger for younger than for older Ss (see Figure 6.1) but the difference must be considered *relative to total time*. The difference that I term "right minus left percent" (R–L% = ((L − R)/(R + L)) × 100) is plotted by age in Figure 6.2. The youngest and oldest groups have been combined to include less than 5 years (N = 45) and 50 years plus (N = 70). There are three main points to be made about Figure 6.2. First, there were no systematic changes. The flat linear trend shows that *R–L asymmetry does not change with age*. Second, there was a highly significant sex difference (F = 19.805, d.f. 1:3171, p < 0.001). Mean asymmetry was greater for females (4.2%) than for males (3.4%). Third, although the trend is

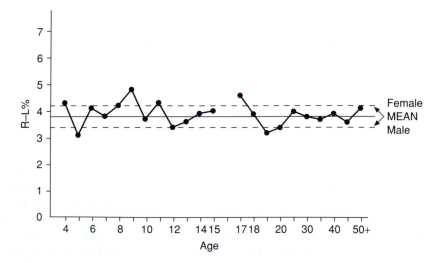

Figure 6.2 R–L difference between the hands (R–L%) with age, showing the means for males and for females.

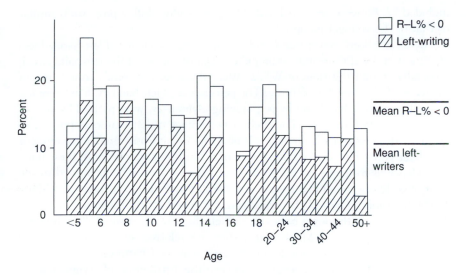

Figure 6.3 Two measures of handedness with age, left writing and left-hand faster than right for peg moving (R–L%).

horizontal the line is not straight. The zig-zags are due to accidents of sampling that occur when Ns are relatively small (as in some year groups). There were no consistent changes with age. This has the important implication that R–L hand skill asymmetry is constant, although actual times for each hand differ with age. It is reasonable to assume, therefore, that relationships between incidences, thresholds and the underlying asymmetry distributions are similar for different age groups.

These analyses of R–L% by age and sex suggest three important conclusions. First, asymmetry is stable with age. Second, it is larger in females than males. Third, the difference between the sexes depends on the left-hand tending to be slower in females than males. This last observation is important for arguments about gene mechanisms.

Do hand *preferences* change with age? Figure 6.3 shows the proportions of left-handers when handedness is defined in two ways, by the writing hand and by the hand faster for peg moving (R–L% < 0). In the total sample there were 16.1% faster with the left-hand and 10.8% left-writers. There were no significant trends over age for either measure of hand preference. Handedness was also classified in the seven classes or subgroups, defined in chapter 2. The subgroup mean was higher (more sinistral) in males than females, but there were no trends with age.

The oldest group (50+ years) is of particular interest because the OU students were assessed in 1974. This age group would have started school in the 1920s when pressures against left writing were strong. Only 2.9% were left-writers, fewer than in any of the other groups, but consistent with samples assessed at that time (Burt, 1937; Chamberlain, 1928) and with older Londoners assessed in the 1970s (Fleminger, Dalton and Standage, 1977). However, the 50+ group included 12.9% who were left-handed by peg moving skill, a proportion similar to that of the younger groups.

There have been secular trends toward increasing frequency of left-handedness over most of the 20th century as prejudices against the use of the left-hand eased, especially around the time of WW2. Were these secular trends continuing in the second half of the 20th century? The percentages of left-handers in my samples, defined by writing hand and by peg moving asymmetry, were plotted by year of testing from 1966 to 1991. The highest percentage of left-writers happened to occur in the first school sample of 1966 (14.3%) and no trends were evident over later years. The secular change was not continuing according to these data.

Evidence as to trends over a much longer time span can be examined in the light of skeletons found in a medieval graveyard in Yorkshire (Steele and Mays, 1995). The long bones of the arms were compared for 80 skeletons of adults. The proportion with longer bones on the left than the right was 16%, while 3% were equal. Steele and Mays argued that the relative lengths of the bones depend on use, the right side longer because it is used more often. Steele and Mays noted a remarkable agreement between the distribution of asymmetries of arm length and asymmetries of peg moving, as described by Annett and Kilshaw (1983). The present analyses confirm that 16% of my samples were faster with the left-hand for peg moving. The proportion recorded as equal depends, of course, on the sensitivity of the measuring instrument. For peg moving in the present samples a difference within 100ms was counted equal. This interval included 2.8% of my samples, like the 3% recorded by Steele and Mays. These striking similarities suggest that distributions of R–L asymmetry may have been stable for centuries, not only for the years covered by the present samples.

ARE LEFT-HANDERS AT RISK OF EARLIER MORTALITY?

Left-handers are fewer among older than younger subjects in every study of family handedness (see chapters 5 and 7). The Londoners attending a hospital dental clinic, mentioned above, declined from about 11% left-writers in young adults (15–24 years) to about 3% in older ones (55–64 years) (Fleminger, Dalton and Standage, 1977). Gilbert and Wysocki (1992) described data for over a million respondents in the USA, 10–86 years of age, to a questionnaire distributed with the *National Geographic* magazine. The questionnaire was about smell, but also included questions on handedness for writing and throwing. Left-hand preferences for both actions occurred in about 14% of males and 12% of females at younger ages, but about 6% for both sexes in the elderly. A questionnaire about hearing collected from a representative sample in the UK asked questions about age, handedness and twinning. Table 6.1 shows the findings for 33,401 UK adults in seven age groups from 18–30, to 81 years plus. The percentage of left-writers falls steadily from 11.2% in the youngest to 2.0% in the oldest group. The percentages differ for sex and for twinning, as mentioned in chapter 5. How are the changes with age to be explained?

Table 6.1 Percentage of left-handers as a function of age, sex and twinning: Davis and Annett, 1994

	Age group							
	18–30	*31–40*	*41–50*	*51–60*	*61–70*	*71–80*	*81+*	*Total*
N	8935	5530	4704	5788	4513	2966	905	33,401
Age (%)	11.2	9.0	7.7	5.5	3.7	2.6	2.0	7.2
Female sex (%)	9.9	8.0	6.7	5.2	3.5	1.9	1.6	6.3
Male sex (%)	12.5	10.0	8.8	5.8	3.9	3.7	3.3	8.3
Single birth (%)	11.0	8.9	7.5	5.4	3.6	2.2	1.9	7.1
Twin birth (%)	17.5	10.9	11.9	7.5	6.8	13.2	4.3	11.7

Several possible explanations must be considered. The first and least likely is that people learn to become right-handed as they get older. This would imply that young left-handers switch to right-hand use in later life. However the hand preferred for writing is usually fixed by the early school years and is very difficult to change thereafter. Hence it is not likely that hand preference changes in the course of an individual lifetime (except for traumatic influences like stroke). A second explanation is the secular trend considered above, that the expression of left preferences has increased during the 20th century because of increasing tolerance towards the use of the left-hand. The cultural change occurred around the time of WW2 because the idea that forced change of handedness might cause stuttering became widely disseminated in the 1930s. However, the difference in frequency between students and parents was clear in family data collected before 1940 and also after 1940. If cultural change were the only factor involved, it would have to be regarded as ongoing throughout the century. There are other factors that need to be considered in explaining the difference between genera- tions in family studies. One is under-reporting of left-handedness in parents by right-handed children, as will be considered in chapter 7. Another is the selection of students for higher education. Factors associated with the hypothesis of a balanced polymorphism with heterozygote advantage for the RS + gene (chapter 10) might imply that student samples include more left-handers than the general population (of whom parents would be more representative).

From certain points of view, handedness has been remarkably stable over time. Coren and Porac (1977) found handedness, as represented in works of art, stable over some 5000 years. Psychological studies over the past 100 years also do not show clear changes over time (Porac, Coren and Duncan, 1980). An early study reported a high incidence, leading Porac et al. to reject the hypothesis that changes with age are due to secular change with time. However, this study (Ramaley, 1913) classified 8.0% of parents and 15.7% of children left-handed, more than twice as many as Chamberlain (1928) and other contemporaries described above. The key point is that Ramaley did not explain his criteria of classification. Other studies from that time make it clear that left-handed writing was not expressed in more than about 3% of the population. The rejection of evidence for secular trend depended on taking Ramaley's data as if it depended on the writing hand when this could not be true.

The idea that higher rates of mortality in left-handers than right-handers might explain the smaller percentage of left-handers among parents than children was first suggested by Brackenridge (1981). She argued there could have been greater *perinatal* mortality of potential left-handers than right-handers in earlier times. The idea rested on the supposition that left-handers are more vulnerable at birth but that advances in obstetric care would have improved their prospects for survival. I do not know any follow-up work on this idea, nor how such a notion would be tested. The idea that left-handed adults are at risk of earlier mortality was suggested by Coren (Coren, 1992; Halpern and Coren, 1988, 1990). This idea generated considerable controversy, not to mention anxiety among left-handers.

The initial evidence for this hypothesis (Halpern and Coren, 1988) depended on data for baseball players whose handedness for play has been recorded over many years in encyclopaedia of the game, together with information on year of birth and death. The mean age at death was reported to be a few months younger for left-handed than right-handed players. Independent checks on the data did not support the finding (Fudin, Renninger, Lembessis et al., 1993; Hicks, Johnson, Cuevas et al., 1994; Wood, 1988). Data were then collected on the handedness and age of death of recently deceased persons in southern California, by sending a questionnaire to relatives (Coren and Halpern, 1991). The deceased was classified as left-handed if reported to have used that hand for writing, drawing or throwing. The mean age of death of right-handed persons was 75 years and of left-handed persons 66 years. The difference of 9 years was statistically significant. This result appeared to give strong support to the earlier mortality theory. However, the conclusion was wrong.

The fallacy rests on failure to take into account the distribution of handedness in the total population (Annett, 1993b; Salive, Guralnik and Glynn, 1993). Coren's argument that handedness had been stable throughout the 20th century depended on unspecified and variable criteria of handedness, as mentioned above, while he was now using a more strict criterion, that depended mainly on writing (how many relatives are aware of drawing and throwing?). Several sources agree that the proportion of left-handed writers in schools has grown from around 3% around the time of WW1 to around 10% today. What would be the effect of this gradual change in incidence on the distribution of handedness with age in the population?

Table 6.2 sets out the likely effects of this change in the form of a "thought experiment". The incidence of left writing is shown as increasing by 1% per decade, for nine decades from 2% in 1900 to 10% in 1980. Suppose there are 100 people from each decade still alive in 1990. How many will there be of each handedness? There will be 54 left-handers and 846 right-handers. The average age of the left- versus right-handers in 1990 can be found by counting the years of age of each group. The average age of the left-handers turns out to be about 38.9 years and of the right-handers about 50.7 years, a difference of 11.8 years.

Table 6.2 Illustration of the effect over time of relaxation of pressure against left-handed writing on the average age of right and left-handed writers in the current population: Annett, 1993b

Year of birth	N per 100 for writing hand		Age in 1990	Total years of age in 1990	
	Left	Right		Left-handers	Right-handers
1900	2	98	90	180	8820
1910	3	97	80	240	7760
1920	4	96	70	280	6720
1930	5	95	60	300	5700
1940	6	94	50	300	4700
1950	7	93	40	280	3720
1960	8	92	30	240	2760
1970	9	91	20	180	1820
1980	10	90	10	100	900
Total	54	846		2100	42,900
Mean age				38.9	50.7

Table 6.3 The average age and S.D. of left-handers and right-handers, twin and singleborn, as found in a population survey: Davis and Annett, 1994

	Left-handers		Right-handers	
	Singleton	Twin	Singleton	Twin
Mean years of age	38	42	47	46
S.D.	16	19	19	18
N	2366	109	30,841	841

The important point is that left-handers who are *alive* in the population are significantly younger than right-handers alive in the population. A sample of recently deceased persons from the population, divided into left-handers and right-handers would differ in the same way.

The thought experiment is borne out by findings for living left- and right-handers in the UK hearing survey (shown in Table 6.1). Table 6.3 gives the average ages of left- and right-handers. Among the singleborn, the mean age of left-handers was 38 years and of right-handers 47 years. This difference of nine years between *living* left- versus right-handers in the population matches that found by Coren for the *deceased*. Among twins, the left-handers averaged 4 years younger than right-handers. This is consistent with the hypothesis that the expression of left-hand preference has been stronger among twins throughout this period (see Table 6.1). Left-handers have a younger base-rate in the population. This difference needs to be taken into account in other studies of risks associated with handedness. For example, reports that breast cancer occurs at an earlier age in left-handed women (Kramer, Albrecht, Miller, 1985) and that left-handers have earlier menopause (Leidy, 1990) probably depend on the same difference in base-rates for age in the population. An analysis of cricketers for handedness and age of death (Aggleton, Kentridge and Neave, 1993) appeared to support Coren's findings for baseball players but was later acknowledged to depend on mistaken actuarial analysis (Aggleton, Bland, Kentridge et al., 1994).

THE EFFECTS OF SEX, TWINNING AND LOW BIRTH WEIGHT AS A FUNCTION OF MATURITY AT BIRTH

Table 6.1 showed that among the 33,401 persons of the UK hearing survey, left-handedness was more frequent in males than females by about 2% and in twins than the singleborn by about 4%. The genetic analyses of chapter 5 found that the RS model, as applied successfully to family data for the singleborn, could predict the twin distributions provided the extent of shift was smaller for twins than singletons. The observation that a similar reduction of shift is needed for DZ and MZ pairs led to the important general hypothesis that the expression of the RS + gene is a function of rate of growth in foetal life. This would imply that factors that reduce growth rate are likely to be associated with an increased proportion of left-handedness. Females tend to be more mature than males at birth and are more often right-handed for preference. It has been seen above that the left-hand is slower than the right-hand for both sexes at all ages, but that the left-hand of females is significantly slower than the left-hand of males.

Hand skill asymmetry for a square-marking test, conducted as part of the National Child Development Survey (NCDS) could be examined for the effects of sex and twin birth. Table 6.4 shows that the R–L differences were consistent with the hypotheses of stronger biases to dextrality in females and in the single-born. The largest difference was for singleton females (21.6) and the smallest for male twins (14.7) while twin females (18.9) and singleton males (18.4) were similar. The similarity of male singletons and female twins would not fit well with explanations of left-handedness as due to brain damage or other pathologies. They

Table 6.4 R–L asymmetry for square marking by sex and twinning: means and S.D. in NCDS UK survey: Annett, 1987a

	Singletons	Twins
Males		
N	6243	146
Mean	18.4	14.7
S.D.	20.7	21.9
Females		
N	5948	131
Mean	21.6	18.9
S.D.	20.5	19.4

are consistent with the idea that expression of the RS + gene is a function of relative maturity at birth, greater in females than males and the singleborn than twins.

Several studies of premature or low birthweight in infants have found a raised proportion of left-handers, not always statistically significant within studies, but with consistent trends between studies. O'Callaghan, Tudehope, Dugdale et al. (1987) described 39 children of extremely low birthweight (less than 1000g) assessed for handedness at four years of age; 54% were left-handed. This proportion is consistent with a simple chance distribution of handedness, as if the RS + gene had exerted no bias to dextrality in this group. Children over 1000g were about as biased to dextrality as normal samples. A later analysis for number of weeks' gestation found a linear trend for handedness: 53% left-handers for 26–27 weeks, 14% for 28–31 weeks and 8% for 32–43 weeks (O'Callaghan, Burn, Mohay et al., 1993). Ross, Lipper and Auld (1992) compared 88 premature with 80 matched full term children at 7–8 years of age. They found fewer consistent right-handers among the premature (69%) than full term (81%) children. These findings are consistent with the RS theory in two important respects. First, they support the assumption that was first suggested by the twin data, that the expression of the RS + gene is a function of foetal growth. Second, reduced expression of the RS gene implies a reversion to chance; the incidence of left-handedness is at most around 50%.

The learning disabled typically include a higher proportion of left- and mixed-handers than comparison groups and the difference has been attributed to early pathology, as mentioned in chapter 1. Pipe's (1987, 1990) reviews of this literature make several points relevant to the RS theory. First, a linear trend has been found in several studies such that the greater the handicap, the greater the percentage of left-handers, but never more than about 50% (consistent with random determination in the absence of RS). Second, the association of increased left-handedness with pathologies of development does not depend on specific damage to the left motor cortex; non-specific and bilateral brain damage may have the same effect, as expected if the cause is reduced expression of RS (see also Silva and Satz, 1979). Third, left-handers among the learning disabled have more left-handed relatives than right-handers (as do the non-disabled). As argued for twins above, it seems that the RS + gene is at work among the learning disabled, but that its expression is reduced in comparison with the non-disabled. This is to be expected if normal developmental progress is disturbed. In Figure 3.9 foetal development was likened to the fall of a ball through a pinball machine. A reduction of the typical bias to the right could occur in some cases because the rate of fall is slowed (in twins, or males compared to females) and in other cases because the pinball machine is jolted (in the learning disabled).

SUMMARY

This chapter asked fundamental questions about what aspects of handedness are stable and reliable versus unstable and subject to change. Scientific study must focus on the former and make proper allowance for the latter. Observations of hand preference and measures of peg moving time by each hand in several large samples of children and undergraduates, collected from the 1960s to the 1990s, allow examination of the effects of age, sex and time on the expression of handedness.

Peg moving time by the right and the left hands became faster with age as expected for a typical growth curve (a negative exponential). The fastest times were by young adults and there was a gradual slowing with increasing age in adulthood. Males and females were similar for the growth of right-hand time, but the mean left-hand times of females were slower than those of males at all ages. The difference between the hands, considered as a percentage of total time or R–L%, was constant with age, and larger in females (4.2%) than males (3.4%). These analyses lead to some important and unambiguous conclusions. First, R–L asymmetry is constant throughout the age range assessed here (3 years to 60 years). Second, R–L asymmetry for handedness is greater in females than males. Third, the stronger bias to dextrality in females than males is associated with relative weakness of the left-hand in females.

Hand preference for writing fluctuated between age groups due to accidents of sampling, but there was no evidence of increasing right-hand preference with age, as might be expected if people learned to become right-handed with age. Nor were there any consistent trends to decreasing right-handedness with age, as might be expected if there had been a continuing relaxation of pressure against the use of the left-hand over the latter half of the 20th century. There was an abrupt difference between Ps below and above 50 years of age. Only 2.9% of the 50+ group were left-handed writers. These Ps, mainly from the OU students assessed in 1974, would have been at school before WW2. The finding is consistent with other data from that time. The absence of gradual change with age among adults in these samples suggests a fairly abrupt change in attitudes to left-handedness around the time of WW2.

When left-handedness was defined in terms of faster peg moving time by the left-hand, there were 16.1% left-handers. The proportion in the 50+ age group was similar (12.9%). This suggests that the small proportion of left-writers in this group was not associated with greater dextrality for R–L% hand skill. It was more likely to be due to the effects of restrictions on the expression of left-hand preferences. In the sample as a whole, the contrast between 16.1% faster with the left-hand, and 10.8% left-writers, indicates that about one-third of people who are faster with the left-hand learn to write with the right-hand. This might be due to the effects of continuing subtle pressures toward right-handedness or to differences between the skills involved in peg moving and writing. The total proportion faster with the right-hand for peg moving (16.1%) matches the proportion of medieval skeletons from a Yorkshire graveyard with longer arm bones on the right than left, as described by Steele and Mays (1995).

The argument that left-handers are at risk of reduced longevity was found to be mistaken because it took reports of high incidence at face value, in spite of uncertain and variable criteria of assessment (especially in Ramaley, 1913), and then neglected the effects of secular trend on the stricter criterion of left-writing. The average age of left-handers who are *alive* in the population is younger than that of right-handers. Hence comparisons of the recently deceased for age are likely to find that left-handers are younger. A similar effect probably applies in other comparisons between handedness groups for age of onset of menopause, or breast cancer.

The greater bias to dextrality of females than males is unequivocal for peg moving asymmetry. This difference, together with the greater dextrality of the singleborn than twins, and well grown versus low birthweight neonates, suggests that the expression of the RS + gene is a function of relative maturity at birth. This would imply that expression depends on factors that influence brain growth *in utero*.

7 A single gene with variable expression for genotype, sex and twinning

The idea that the right shift of the handedness distribution depends on a single gene (RS +) whose main function is to induce the left cerebral hemisphere to serve speech was shown in chapter 5 to be consistent with findings for handedness in families. The genetic calculations did not distinguish the sex of parents or children, nor RS + − and RS + + genotypes for extent of shift, for reasons explained. However, certain findings in chapters 5 and 6 suggested that these distinctions should be made. The RS + gene is hypothesised to be dominant for cerebral asymmetry in the sense that one copy of the gene is sufficient to promote left CD in the course of normal growth. However, the gene could be additive in the sense that the mechanisms promoting cerebral asymmetry give greater displacement to the right for handedness, and perhaps larger asymmetries of cerebral anatomy, when there are two copies than only one. Further, there may be differences between the sexes and between twins and the singleborn in gene expression. That is, different levels of shift.

Figure 7.1 represents distributions of R–L hand skill for a gene that is fully additive (the RS + + mean twice that of RS + −) and is expressed more strongly in females than males by 20%. (The means of RS + − and RS + + genotypes are 1.0z and 2.0z respectively for males and 1.2z and 2.4z for females to the right of the mean for RS − −, 0.0z. Shifts for twins will be considered later in this chapter.) The relative sizes of the three distributions represent the genotype proportions, as deduced in chapter 5. The most frequent genotype is the heterozygote (RS + −, about 49.0% of the population) and both homozygotes are substantial (RS − − about 18.5% and RS + + genotype about 32.5%). These proportions suggest an advantage for the heterozygote and if this is true, the effect of two copies of the gene must be greater than one, on some aspect of gene expression. The question examined in this chapter is whether an additive model for handedness can explain family data as well as, or better than, the dominant model of chapter 5. Further, can it account for family handedness when the sex of parents and of children is taken into account? Can a revised model also account for handedness in twin pairs? These questions require close attention to quantitative data for several analyses. The model represented in Figure 7.1 will be shown to have strong predictive powers, here and in chapter 9. It offers the best estimates available of the parameters of the RS model.

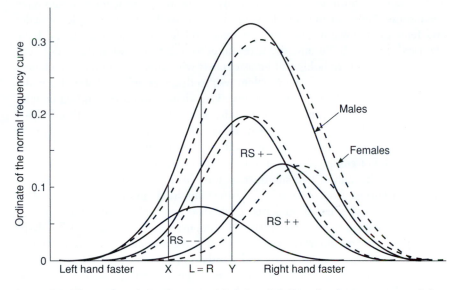

Figure 7.1 The predicted distributions of R–L hand skill in the three genotypes of the RS locus and in the total population for males and females: shifts are 0.0z, 1.0z, 2.0z for males and 0.0z, 1.2z and 2.4z for females for the RS – –, RS + –, and RS + + genotypes respectively.

An explanation is needed of how the parameters of Figure 7.1 were arrived at. The first point that must be emphasised is that the gene and genotype frequencies are exactly as derived in chapter 5, from the dysphasia analyses of chapter 4. This anchors the frequency of the RS – gene to the prevalence of right CD, as required for the argument that RS + is "for" left CD. The chief difference between the model as first envisaged in chapters 4 and 5 and the updated version in Figure 7.1 is that there are more precise estimates of shift, for RS + + and RS + – genotypes and for males and females. The estimate for the dominant model (1.97z) was based on percentages of left-handers in samples of patients with dysphasia following right versus left cerebral lesions. It was a rough and ready measure, but worked well enough to support the single gene hypothesis. The problem that needed solution was how more precise estimates of shift could be discovered. The derivation and tests of these values are the chief topic of this chapter.

Clues as to shift were sought in two sorts of empirical data, first distributions of R–L hand skill in large samples, and second thresholds for left-handedness in males and females drawn from the same sample. The shifts to be estimated involved two related questions. First, what are the means for people carrying one versus two copies of the gene? Second, how do these means differ between males and females? It was argued from chapter 2 that incidences of left-handedness vary between studies because investigators use different assessment criteria. Any particular incidence can be regarded as depending on a threshold (cut-off point) along the R–L continuum. But within any single study handedness should have been assessed using identical methods and criteria so that paired samples of males and females (fathers and mothers, or male and female offspring) should have identical thresholds. Because the sexes differ for gene expression (have different shifts), identical thresholds will be associated with slightly different incidences for males and females. So the problem was to discover values of shift for males and females that (1) agreed with observed incidences in corresponding samples of males and females from the same study, and (2) gave matching thresholds.

Annett and Kilshaw (1983) began the search for clues as to levels of shift by examining distributions of R–L hand skill for peg moving. The idea was to take large samples of empirical data and ask whether the R–L distribution was consistent with the sum of two sub-distributions (as represented in Figure 4.1) or three distributions (as in Figure 7.1). Using combined samples of schoolchildren and combined samples of students, each distinguished for sex, the question could be examined in four sets of data. A computer program predicted the shape of the total distribution as the sum of two or three normal curves, for particular values of proportions, mean shifts and standard deviations. (Certain constraints were adopted in fitting the model. The genotype proportions were fixed as explained above. The RS – – mean was always 0 by definition. Standard deviations were taken to be identical for the three genotypes. In tests of the dominant model, shifts were the same for RS + – and RS + +. For the additive model, they were twice as far to the right for RS + + than RS + –. Future work may show that these restrictions were too severe, but the very large number of possible analyses had to be limited.)

The hypothesis of a *single* normal curve could be rejected for both sexes, and also the theory that there are two distributions, one for right-handers and one for left-handers. Comparisons of the dominant and additive versions of the genetic model gave no grounds for preferring one more than the other, on the evidence of the peg moving distributions. With regard to the sex difference, females were more dextral than males in both the school and students samples. The means were similar in three of the four analyses, and roughly consistent with the shifts represented in Figure 7.1. But could precise shifts be discovered to give matching thresholds for paired samples of males and females as described above? A heuristic process of trial and error found the matching values required.

The first matches were found for three out of four sets of data of the Hawaii Family Study of Cognition (Ashton, 1982). The sample was large, personally interviewed, and not based on academics. Parents and children were asked:

1.   Which hand do you write with (right, left)?
2.   Which hand do you use most (right, left, use equally)?

This allowed tests of relative shift between the sexes for parents and for children at a stricter criterion (question 1) and also a more generous criterion (question 2). For three out of the four comparisons, males and females had virtually identical thresholds, when the values of shifts were as shown in Figure 7.1.

The comparison that did not match was for writing hand in parents where, unusually, mothers were slightly more often left-handed than fathers. Parents in this sample were drawn from several ethnic groups and among parents of Japanese origin only 1% wrote with the left-hand. Hence, it is not surprising if percentages for left-writing were unusual in these parents. The criterion "use most" classified 8.97% of fathers and 7.64% of mothers left-handed, consistent with thresholds at −0.52z and −0.53z for males and females respectively. Both criteria gave matching thresholds for children. Would these same values of shift give matching thresholds in other studies? The thresholds were found to match for parents in the McGee and Cozad (1980) sample, where incidences were 19.46% of fathers and 16.72% of mothers (thresholds at +0.09z for both). This was particularly encouraging because the classification here was for non-right-handedness and incidences were much higher (threshold well to the right) than for Ashton.

Table 7.1 lists values of thresholds from −1.0z to +1.0z and shows the percentages of left-handers expected for males, females and sexes together, for the shifts shown in Figure 7.1. (For sexes together the mean shifts are, RS + + 2.2z and RS + − 1.1z). Annett (1985a, Figure 16.3) plotted the thresholds for observed incidences for males and females in paired samples graphically in order to show

Table 7.1 Left-handers at thresholds along the R–L continuum for sexes separately and together: thresholds are measured from the mean of the RS − − distribution, RS is 1.0z, 2.0z for males, 1.2z, 2.4z for females and 1.1z, 2.2z for sexes combined, for the RS + − and RS + + genotypes respectively

Threshold (z)	Males	Females	Both sexes
−1.0	4.09	3.63	3.83
−0.9	4.87	4.29	4.55
−0.8	5.76	5.05	5.37
−0.7	6.77	5.91	6.30
−0.6	7.91	6.88	7.34
−0.5	9.18	7.95	8.50
−0.4	10.60	9.14	9.80
−0.3	12.16	10.45	11.23
−0.2	13.87	11.89	12.79
−0.1	15.74	13.46	14.50
0.0	17.76	15.15	16.35
0.1	19.94	16.98	18.34
0.2	22.26	18.94	20.47
0.3	24.73	21.03	22.74
0.4	27.34	23.24	25.15
0.5	30.08	25.58	27.68
0.6	32.93	28.03	30.32
0.7	35.89	30.59	33.08
0.8	38.94	33.24	35.93
0.9	42.05	35.99	38.86
1.0	45.22	38.80	41.85

Table 7.2 Observed incidences of left-handedness in paired samples of males and females, with corresponding thresholds and the difference between thresholds: (a) parents assessed by self-report, (b) parents assessed by indirect report, (c) children (mainly self-report)

	Males percent (threshold)	Females percent (threshold)	Difference between thresholds
(a) Parents assessed by self-report			
Annett (1978a)	4.52 (−0.94)	3.56 (−1.01)	+0.07
Ashton (1982)	5.26 (−0.85)	5.37 (−0.76)	−0.09
Annett (1985a)	9.03 (−0.51)	5.61 (−0.73)	+0.22
Ashton (1982)	8.97 (−0.52)	7.64 (−0.53)	+0.01
McGee and Cozad (1980)	19.46 (+0.09)	16.72 (+0.09)	0.0
Annett (1978a)	22.88 (+0.23)	24.52 (+0.45)	−0.22
Annett (1985a)	25.23 (+0.32)	26.17 (+0.52)	−0.20
Carter-Saltzman (1980)	34.15 (+0.64)	27.80 (+0.59)	+0.05
Mean diff.			−0.022 (S.E. 0.052)
(b) Parents assessed by indirect report			
Chamberlain (1928)	4.18 (−0.99)	2.94 (−1.12)	+0.13
Annett (1985a)	4.56 (−0.94)	2.95 (−1.12)	+0.18
Annett (1973a)	4.39 (−0.96)	3.71 (−0.99)	+0.03
Rife (1940)	5.38 (−0.84)	5.09 (−0.80)	−0.04
Annett (1979)	6.27 (−0.75)	6.27 (−0.66)	−0.09
Annett (1979)	9.53 (−0.47)	6.36 (−0.65)	+0.18
Spiegler and Yeni-Komshian (1983)	10.19 (−0.43)	8.20 (−0.48)	+0.05
Risch and Pringle (1985)	12.34 (−0.29)	7.29 (−0.56)	+0.27
Mean diff.			+0.0888* (S.E. 0.0432)
(c) Children (mainly self-report)			
Chamberlain (1928)	5.31 (−0.85)	3.77 (−0.98)	+0.13
Annett (1979)	8.45 (−0.56)	8.55 (−0.45)	−0.11
Annett (1985a)	9.20 (−0.50)	8.01 (−0.49)	−0.01
Rife (1940)	9.59 (−0.47)	7.59 (−0.53)	+0.06
Ashton (1982)	11.57 (−0.34)	9.93 (−0.34)	0.0
Annett (1973a)	11.30 (−0.35)	9.78 (−0.35)	0.0
Annett (1978a)	12.06 (−0.31)	14.67 (−0.03)	−0.28
Risch and Pringle (1985)	13.05 (−0.25)	11.86 (−0.20)	−0.05
Spiegler and Yeni-Komshian (1983)	15.20 (−0.13)	12.07 (−0.19)	+0.06
Ashton (1982)	16.65 (−0.05)	14.535 (−0.05)	0.0
Annett (1985a)	16.81 (−0.05)	8.72 (−0.43)	+0.38
Annett (1979)	19.56 (+0.08)	15.10 (0.0)	+0.08
McGee and Cozad (1980)	27.27 (+0.40)	21.44 (+0.32)	+0.08
Annett (1979)	33.06 (+0.60)	39.58 (+1.03)	−0.43
Annett (1985a)	39.50 (+0.82)	30.51 (+0.70)	+0.12
Annett (1978a)	39.53 (+0.82)	39.73 (+1.03)	−0.21
Mean diff.			−0.011 (S.E. 0.046)

Note
*p < 0.05.

the very high correlation between them (r = .973, S.E. 14). Here, the relevant data are presented in Table 7.2a–c in order to show that the matches between thresholds are excellent for samples where handedness was assessed by self report, but less good for indirect report data. For each paired sample of males and females the incidences are given with associated thresholds and the difference between the thresholds. For the self-report data in Table 7.2a and c the mean of the differences between the corresponding thresholds was close to 0. That is, they were well matched. For parents assessed by indirect report (Table 7.2b) the thresholds did not match. The mean threshold for mothers was significantly to the left of that for fathers. This suggests that left-handedness in mothers was under-estimated when assessment relied on the report of their children. However, the good matches for self-report data suggests that the estimated values of shift are likely to be reliable. The next question was whether these values would predict distributions of family handedness.

GENETIC PREDICTIONS DISTINGUISHING SEX OF PARENTS AND OFFSPRING

Annett (1985a, Table 16.7) examined the fit of the additive model just described to all the family data available that distinguished sex for parents and children. There were seven such studies with self-report of handedness in both generations, where fits could be examined for sons and for daughters. Predictions agreed well with observations for all of the 14 tests. There were seven studies with handedness assessed by indirect report for parents. These gave two poor fits for sons and six poor fits for daughters. The idea that poor fit might be due to inaccuracy of indirect report was tested by making small adjustments to parental incidences (Annett, 1985a, Table 16.10). Fits were improved but the procedure was *ad hoc* and therefore unsatisfactory. I returned to the question of poor fits for indirect report studies while drafting this book, and found a new approach to the problem (Annett, 1999c). However, with regard to the 1985a analyses, it is important to be clear that the RS additive genetic model, with shifts for each sex as shown in Figure 7.1 was successful in predicting all the available data for studies where handedness was assessed by self-report in both generations. (In the 1985a analyses for sexes separately, genetic predictions were made over all types of family in the total sample, not within family types as in chapter 5 and Appendix VIII. This was done with the intention of testing the idea that certain parental incidences were inaccurate, particularly for left-handed mothers. Using this method, small adjustments to parental incidences affected predictions for all family types. The 1999c changes were more specific and hypothesis driven, as explained below.)

For the new analyses all calculations were repeated, using the traditional method of testing predictions separately for each type of family (R × R, R × L, L × R and L × L, father × mothers). The steps of calculation were as outlined in chapter 5 (and shown as a worked example in Appendix VIII) except that the genotype distributions must distinguish between right and left-handed fathers and also right and left-handed mothers. Separate predictions must be made for R × L and L × R families. Similarly, predictions for offspring must match the genotype distribution of sons and daughters to the incidences observed. What are the expected genotype distributions for various incidences in each sex? Appendix III provides a look-up table for incidences from 1 to 40%, with geno-types of left-handers at each level of incidence for sexes together. Appendix IV gives the same information for sexes separately. (Right-handers are given in parentheses for sexes together, but can be obtained by subtraction from the genotype totals for sexes separately.) The numbers are expressed per 1000 to avoid decimals. For example, the "any use of the left-hand" criterion of Ashton (1982) found 8.97% (90 per 1000) left-handed fathers. Their genotypes are RS + + 2, RS + − 32 and RS − − 56. Right-handed fathers are RS + + 323, RS + − 458, RS − − 129. For mothers at this criterion there were 7.64% (76 per 1000) left-handers, made up of RS + + 1, RS + − 20, RS − − 55. Right-handed mothers are RS + + 324, RS + − 470, RS − − 130. To find the genotype distribu-tion of children of R × R parents the nine combinations of genotype pairs for right-handed parents must be calculated (+ + × + +, + + × + − . . . − − × − −, but treating the numbers as proportions of 1, as 0.323 × 0.324 etc.). Predictions were then worked out as proportions within each family type, as mentioned above.

Family predictions were tested for all available studies where sex was distin-guished in both generations. The findings are summarised in Table 7.3 and the numbers of sons and daughters in each family type are given in Appendix VII. The studies are grouped for self-report or indirect report of parental handed-ness, and both groups are examined at two levels of incidence. The results of chi-square tests of goodness of fit are given at several levels of analysis. Appendix VII shows the fits by sex and family type for each study separately. Table 7.3 summarises for sons and daughters within studies. It also gives the summed chi-squares over studies. Finally, the studies grouped together were combined to allow tests on substantial samples.

Consider first the tests of the model for samples with self-report in both generations (Table 7.3a). The studies were classified for two levels of parental handedness (below and above 10%). Except for one marginally poor fit (sons in Annett, 1985a, incidence below 10%) fits were good for every test. For these same sons classified for non-right-handedness (incidences above 10%) the fit was excellent. The sum chi-squares and the combined data for both sons and daughters all show excellent fits between the predictions of the RS additive genetic model and observed findings.

Turning now to the samples where assessment of parental handedness was indir-ect (Table 7.3b), parental incidences tended to be lower than for self-report studies so these samples were grouped as below and above 7% (for fathers). For five studies in the lower range, there were three poor fits for sons and also three poor fits for daughters. Individual studies with higher levels of parental incidence gave acceptable fits but with one outstanding exception, daughters for Spiegler and Yeni-Komshian (1983). However, the sum chi-square over

Table 7.3 Handedness in families distinguishing sex in both generations: summary of fits to the RS model (further details in Appendix VII) for (a) self-report in both generations and (b) parents by indirect report

Parental incidence	Incidences				Sons		Daughters	
	Father	Mother	Sons	Daughters	Chi-square	d.f.	Chi-square	d.f.
(a) Self-report in both generations								
(i) < 10%								
Annett (1978a)	4.52	3.56	12.06	14.67	0.655	2	2.370	2
Ashton (1982)	8.97	7.64	16.65	14.35	2.442	3	4.371	3
Annett (1985a)	9.03	5.61	16.81	8.72	6.082*	2	0.754	2
Sum chi-square					9.179	7	7.495	7
Combined data	8.42	6.45	15.53	13.47	0.9548	3	4.197	3
(ii) > 10%								
McGee and Cozad (1980)	19.64	16.72	27.27	21.44	2.684	3	0.278	3
Annett (1978a)	22.88	24.52	39.53	39.73	1.524	3	5.038	3
Annett (1985a)	25.23	26.17	39.50	30.51	2.206	3	2.012	3
Sum chi-square					6.414	9	7.328	9
Combined data	21.40	21.23	34.18	28.36	2.516	3	1.110	3
(b) Parents by indirect report								
(i) < 7%								
Chamberlain (1928)	4.18	2.94	5.31	3.77	7.115*	2	4.379	2
Annett (1985a)	4.56	2.95	9.20	8.01	0.036	2	12.636*	2
Annett (1973a)	4.39	3.71	11.30	9.78	7.362*	2	21.124*	2
Rife (1940)	5.38	5.09	9.59	7.59	1.651	2	11.698*	2
Annett (1979)	6.27	6.27	8.45	8.55	9.334*	2	5.306	2
Sum chi-square					25.498*	10	55.143*	10
Combined data	4.27	3.70	8.33	7.41	18.75*	3	43.00*	3
(ii) > 7%								
Annett (1979)	9.53	6.36	19.56	15.10	0.565	2	5.469	2
Spiegler & Yeni-Komshian (1983)	10.19	8.20	15.24	12.07	6.736	3	12.930*	3
Risch & Pringle (1985)	12.34	7.29	13.05	11.86	4.568	2	2.064	2
Sum chi-square					11.869	7	20.463*	7
Combined data	10.84	7.50	14.74	12.20	8.546*	3	15.93*	3

Note
*$p < 0.05$.

studies and the combined data gave poor fits for both sexes at both levels of parental incidence. Thus, the samples that relied on indirect report for parental handedness gave poor fits to the genetic predictions, in contrast to the good fits for the self-report studies. How did these poor fits arise?

It has been noticed for some years that the families of left-handed mothers tend to include a higher proportion of left-handed children than families of left-handed fathers (review by McGee and Cozad, 1980). One explanation might be that there are sex differences in the genetic expression of the relevant characteristics (as deduced for pyloric stenosis by Carter, 1961). A small Carter effect is expected for handedness, but not large enough to account for the present family data (see further below). The difference might, in principle, be due to a sex-linked gene (as hypothesised by McManus and Bryden, 1992). It could also be an artefact due to under-reporting of left-handedness in mothers.

Table 7.4 combines the indirect report studies at two levels of parental incidence (as in Table 7.3b) and gives details of the observed and expected proportions for sons and daughters in each of the four types of family. The four sum chi-squares (for each sex and each level) all show poor fits, but which family types are responsible? Looking first at sons when parental incidences were low, it is clear that almost all of the poor fit depended on the families of left-handed mothers (R × L). The proportion of left-handed sons observed in these families was much greater than the proportion predicted. For daughters in these families, there were even more left-handers than predicted. Predictions for the families of left-handed fathers (L × R) were good at this level.

Next consider the families where parental incidences were above 7%. The R × L families now gave excellent fits to predictions. The proportions of left-handed sons and also left-handed daughters agreed very well with those expected. The poor overall fits depended mainly on L × R families where left-handed fathers had *fewer* left-handed children than predicted (not *more* as for R × L families at the lower level of incidence). The contrast between family studies with lower and higher assessments of parental incidence leads to the important conclusion that there are no general rules that apply at both levels. The excess of left-handed children for left-handed mothers occurred only when parental incidences were low. Findings that reverse between R × L and L × R families at different levels of incidence, are unlikely to have a genetic explanation. Further, predictions at both levels were good for self-report studies. Hence, it is likely that the frequency of left-handedness has been under-estimated for mothers when parental incidences are low, and slightly over-estimated for fathers when parental incidences are high. How can this idea be tested?

Annett (1999c) performed what might be called a "thought experiment". All of the indirect report data (both groups in Table 7.4) were combined to give a grand total of 33,485 children. Children were counted as if there were only one per family. The number of children reporting a left-handed father was 2197 (6.56%) and a left-handed mother 1683 (5.03%). Table 7.5a gives the predicted and observed *numbers* of children. Fits were poor only in the families of

Table 7.4 Observed and predicted left-handedness in combined data: indirect report studies grouped for two levels of parental incidence

Father × Mother parental incidence	Sons					Daughters				
	N	Obs. prop.	Exp. prop.	Chi-square L (R)	d.f.	N	Obs. prop.	Exp. prop.	Chi-square L (R)	d.f.
(a) < 7% parental incidence										
R × R	11,837	0.076	0.079	1.159 (0.099)		8269	0.064	0.069	3.318 (0.247)	
R × L	416	0.209	0.139	14.264 (2.320)		343	0.242	0.131	32.114 (4.848)	
L × R	495	0.145	0.133	0.521 (0.080)		388	0.124	0.125	0.004 (0.001)	
L × L	29	0.276	0.231	0.238 (0.072)		18	0.389	0.232	1.895 (0.574)	
Total				18.75*	3				43.00*	3
(b) > 7%										
R × R	4708	0.136	0.133	0.534 (0.081)		4934	0.112	0.107	1.140 (0.137)	
R × L	378	0.230	0.220	0.185 (0.052)		403	0.211	0.192	0.779 (0.185)	
L × R	590	0.180	0.208	2.231 (0.610)		581	0.175	0.181	4.219 (0.931)	
L × L	56	0.196	0.334	3.172 (1.590)		40	0.100	0.315	5.852 (2.685)	
Total				8.546*	3				15.93*	3

Note
*p < 0.05.

Table 7.5 Combined indirect report samples showing the effect of transferring right-handed children from R × R to R × L

Father × Mother	Sons						Daughters					
	Total	Obs. right	Obs. left	Exp. left	Chi-square L (R)	d.f.	Total	Obs. right	Obs. left	Exp. left	Chi-square L (R)	d.f.
(a) Reported data: N = 33,485: N left-handed fathers = 2197 (6.56%); N left-handed mothers = 1683 (5.03%)												
R × R	16,545	15,006	1539	1579	1.039 (0.110)		13,203	12,119	1084	1125	1.476 (0.137)	
R × L	794	620	174	132	13.676 (2.716)		746	578	168	117	21.949 (4.094)	
L × R	1085	907	178	171	0.293 (0.055)		969	837	132	144	1.041 (0.182)	
L × L	85	66	19	23	0.580 (0.210)		58	47	11	16	1.368 (0.504)	
Total					18.68*	3					30.75*	3
(b) Transferring 200 right-handed sons and 200 right-handed daughters from R × R to R × L families. (Numbers changed from (a) in bold.) N = 33,485: N left-handed fathers = 2197 (6.56%); N left-handed mothers = 2083 (6.22%)												
R × R	**16,345**	**14,806**	1539	1548	0.051 (0.005)		**13,003**	**11,919**	1084	1097	0.153 (0.014)	
R × L	**994**	**820**	174	163	0.771 (0.151)		**946**	**778**	168	147	3.075 (0.565)	
L × R	1085	907	178	170	0.412 (0.076)		969	837	132	143	0.834 (0.144)	
L × L	85	66	19	22	0.507 (0.181)		58	47	11	15	1.269 (0.460)	
Total					2.155	3					6.514	3
Total both sexes											8.669	6

left-handed mothers. The number of left-handed children observed was much greater than predicted. But why was a low number predicted? This could be because the *predicted proportion* is wrong, of course, or it could be because the proportion is correct but the *total number* of children in R × L families is too low. Perhaps some children were not aware that their mother was left-handed. Who would be unaware of left-handedness in the mother? All the information we have on awareness of handedness (Kang and Harris, 1996; McGuire and McGuire, 1980) suggests that awareness is poor in right-handers but good in left-handers. This would imply that reports of the presence of left-handedness, in children and parents, are likely to be accurate, but that some right-handers are unaware that they have a left-handed parent. Table 7.5b shows the effect of taking 200 sons and 200 daughters from R × R families and re-assigning them to R × L families. The changes to numbers are shown in bold. No changes were made to numbers of left-handers within the body of the table, only to the numbers of right-handed children assigned to a left-handed mother. The re-assignment of right-handed children to R × L families raised the maternal incidence to 6.22%, just below the paternal incidence of 6.56%, approximately as expected for matching thresholds between the sexes in the parental genera-tion. By raising the total number of children in R × L families, the *proportions* of left-handers predicted now agreed with the numbers observed. The fits were improved not only for R × L families, but also for R × R families.

The transfer of more children would give even better fits. However, the "thought experiment" demonstrated that the transfer of 400 (1.2%) children would be sufficient to allow the RS additive model to predict the findings for indirect report samples, as well as it does for self-report samples. The sex-linked gene proposed by McManus and Bryden (1992) to modify the expression of right-handedness is less probable and also less effective in explaining the data than the present hypothesis of an artefact in samples assessed by indirect report. The argument is that maternal left-handedness has been under-reported by about 1%. In view of the good fits for all self-report data, and the small size of the adjustment for indirect report data, it seems safe to conclude that the additive model, as represented in Figure 7.1, can account for family distribu-tions, when sex is distinguished for parents and for children. With regard to the Carter effect, the RS theory expects there to be a higher proportion of left-handed children in the families of left-handed mothers than fathers, but by a very small amount (about 1.05:1, mothers:fathers). The numbers of left-handers observed in these families in the combined self-report samples were 276:264 (or 1.04:1) respectively.

ADDITIVE OR DOMINANT MODEL FOR HANDEDNESS?

The additive genetic model has been shown above to account very well for handedness in families, provided a small allowance was made for under-reporting of left-handed mothers when the assessment of parental handedness depended

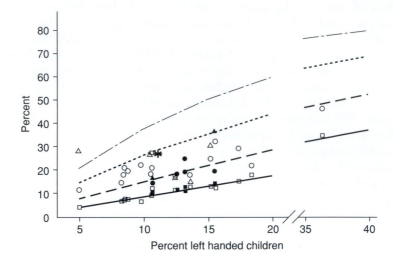

Figure 7.2 Predicted proportions of left-handed children in R × R (solid line),
R × L (bold dashed line) and L × L (dotted line) families for the additive
RS genetic model when parental incidence is 8.0%: predictions for the
dominant genetic model for L × L families are shown as a non-bold dashed
line; observed incidences are shown as squares, circles and triangles for
R × R, R × L and L × L families respectively; filled symbols indicate
self-report samples and open symbols indirect report; the bold star shows
the percentage of left-handed children in combined L × L families: studies
listed in Table 7.6.

on report by their children. But is the additive model more likely to be true
than the dominant model of chapter 5? Annett (1985a) found no empirical
grounds for preferring either version of the genetic model. In looking at this
question further, it was found that the predictions of the dominant and additive
versions of the model were similar for R × R and L × R (including R × L)
families but differed for L × L families. L × L families are infrequent in most
family data, so in order to compare the predictions of the two versions of the RS
model, it was necessary to combine data over studies and also over sex. (Shifts
were taken as the means for males and females, 2.2z, 1.2z, for RS + +, RS + −
genotypes respectively.)

Figure 7.2 represents the predicted proportions of left-handed children in the
three types of family when the parental incidence is 8% and filial incidence
ranges from 5 to 40%. The lower three lines give predictions for the additive
model, from the bottom up R × R, L × R and L × L respectively. The top line
gives the predictions of the dominant model for L × L families. The dominant
model gives a higher prediction than the additive model at all levels of incidence. (For other family types the difference between the two models is too small
to be represented.) Discrimination between the models depends, therefore, on
findings for L × L families, as said above.

Table 7.6 Children in L × L families when parental incidences range from 3.6 to 10.4%: studies are listed in order of filial incidence, as represented in Figure 7.2

	Filial incidence	Parent incidence	Children in L × L families	
			N total	N left
Chamberlain (1928)	4.8	3.6	25	7
Mascie-Taylor (cited McManus, 1985a)	8.3	9.3	4	1
Open University as filial generation	8.5	6.3	4	0
Lanchester parents as filial	8.6	3.7	2	1
Rife (1940)	8.8	5.2	11	6
Leiber and Axelrod (1981)	10.6	8.1	11	3
Ashton (1982) strict *	10.7	5.3	12	2
Chaurasia and Goswami (cited McManus, 1985a)	10.7	10.4	7	4
Annett (1973a)	10.7	4.1	5	1
Risch and Pringle (1985)	12.5	9.8	18	3
Lanchester self-report	12.6	7.5	5	1
Hull self-report	13.2	4.0	0	0
Carter-Saltzman (1980)	13.2	7.6	0	0
Spiegler and Yeni-Komishian (1983)	13.6	9.2	74	11
McManus (1985a)	15.2	10.0	23	7
Ashton (1982) generous	15.5	8.3	19	7
Ramaley (1913)	15.6	8.0	7	6
OU as parents	17.4	8.0	4	1
Coren and Porac (1980)	18.4	8.4	0	0
Open University as filial*	36.4	6.3	1	1
Sum excluding*			219	59
Percent				26.94%

Table 7.6 lists the data for L × L families in 20 studies, where parental incidences ranged from 3.6 to 10.4%. (They are not precisely 8%, the parental value for predictions in Figure 7.2, but they straddle this value and are close enough to give reasonably similar predictions.) Figure 7.2 plots the percentages of left-handed children for R × R and L × R families for the 20 studies, in order of incidence for children (left to right in the figure). Findings for L × L families were plotted by study only if the expected number of children in these families was at least three. The combined data gave 219 children with two left-handed parents, of whom 59 (26.9%) were left-handed. This proportion is shown as a bold star located at 11% on the x-axis (about the percentage of left-handed children over all the relevant samples). The observed percentage of left-handers in L × L families is almost exactly where predicted by the additive model. Inspection of the L × L percentages of individual studies (triangles in the figure) shows that except for Chamberlain (1928), none could be considered more

consistent with the dominant than the additive model. It may be noted that the proportions of left-handed children in L × L families reported by Rife (54%) and Ramaley (86%) are not represented here because the predicted Ns were less than three (as explained above). These studies were inconsistent with the combined data and depended on small numbers, but like Chamberlain, they were more in line with the dominant than additive version of the model. However, the combined findings for over 200 children were in full accord with the additive model.

Two samples were listed twice in Table 7.6, in order to show that fits were good at both strict and more generous criteria of sinistrality (but not counted twice in the data summary). These are the data for Ashton (1982) where the "left writing" criterion gave incidences of 10.7% and 5.3% for children and parents respectively, and the "use left" criterion 15.5% and 8.3% for children and parents respectively. These self-report data are shown in bold in Figure 7.2. Inspection shows that at the higher criterion, incidences were almost exactly as predicted for all types of family. At the lower criterion, fits were also good for R × R and L × R families. OU students were represented (and counted) at the strict criterion (8.5% for children and 6.3% for parents), but they were also represented (and not counted) at the non-right criterion for children (36.4% for children). The predictions for R × R and L × R families were acceptable at both levels. The parents of OU students could not be classified for the more generous criterion, but when parental handedness can be so classified, predictions must be examined for a higher level of parental incidence, as described in the next section.

THE ADDITIVE GENETIC MODEL APPLIED TO NON-RIGHT-HANDEDNESS AND TO EYE DOMINANCE

Reiss and Reiss (1997) reported a study of eye dominance in families. They suggested that the findings could not be explained by current genetic theories of handedness, including the RS theory, because there were more than 50% left eyed children in the families of L × L eyed parents. However, this was a misunderstanding because chance, for the RS theory, does not require a binary outcome like the toss of a coin, but rather a normal distribution of asymmetry. Predictions for incidence depend on thresholds, that may be below 50% for strict criteria and above 50% for generous ones.

I had not tried to predict eye preference in families because I had assumed that the parameters required would differ from those derived above for handedness. Many more people are left eyed than left-handed. The percentage of left eyedness is comparable to that of non-right-handedness, about 35%. Percentages of left and mixed eye dominance vary in an approximately linear fashion with subgroup hand preference (see Figure 8.1). This demonstrates that eye dominance is related to the underlying continuum of handedness asymmetry. However, I took the higher incidence of left eye preference over left-handedness

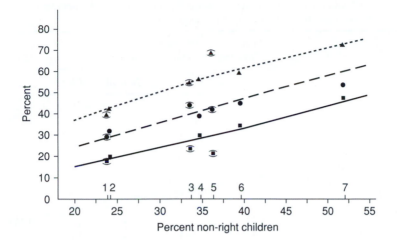

Figure 7.3 Predicted proportions of non-right-handedness and -eyedness (in parentheses) in families when the parental incidence is 25.0%: symbols as in Figure 7.2 and studies listed in Table 7.7.

to imply that the influence of the RS + gene on eye preference is weaker than its influence on handedness. But could a different level of shift give satisfactory predictions for eye dominance in families? This line of reasoning led me to approach the problem of predicting eye dominance in families by varying relative shifts, designed to "home in" on the optimal values. To my surprise, I found that the optimal values were the ones developed above for the additive model for handedness.

Figure 7.3 represents the predicted proportions of left-handers in R × R, L × R and L × L families for the additive model when the parental incidence is 25% and filial incidences range from 20 to 55%. Table 7.7 lists the filial and parental incidences for four studies of handedness and three studies of eyedness where parental incidences ranged from 18.2 to 33.7% (not exactly 25% but around this value). The table also gives the numbers of children in L × L (strictly non-right × non-right) families. In contrast to Table 7.6, the numbers of children in this family type were substantial for all studies. The combined data for the four studies of handedness included 219 children, 56.6% non-right-handers. For the three studies of eyedness there were 102 children in L × L families and 52.9% were non-right for eye preference. The chi-square values for fits of the model to findings in individual studies were acceptable in all cases, and very good for all but one. Findings for the three family types in the seven studies are represented in Figure 7.3. The proportions were as predicted in almost all cases. The fit was least good for the Reiss and Reiss data but still acceptable. Inspection of the fits for children in L × L families (triangles in Figure 7.3) confirms that for six out of the seven studies the findings were almost exactly as predicted by the additive genetic model.

Table 7.7 Children in L × L families classified for non-right-handedness and non-right-eyedness: studies represented in Figure 7.3

	Filial incidence	Parental incidence	Children in L × L families		Chi-square (d.f. 2)
			N total	N left	
Handedness					
McGee and Cozad (1980)	24.2	18.2	52	22	0.284
Lanchester self-report	34.8	25.7	52	29	0.975
Hull self-report	39.6	23.7	76	45	1.010
Carter-Saltzman (1980)	51.9	31.0	39	28	2.393
Sum			219	124	
Percent				56.6%	
Eyedness					
Brackenridge (1981)	23.9	23.9	43	17	0.358
Merrell (1957)	33.7	28.1	24	13	1.446
Reiss and Reiss (1997)	36.3	33.7	35	24	5.671
Sum			102	54	
Percent				52.9%	

These analyses were made with the aim of discriminating between the dominant and additive genetic models, as explained above. The findings for children in L × L families were examined for two levels of incidence in parents (8% and 25%, about as expected for left-writing and for non-right-handedness respectively) and at a wide range of incidences in children, from 5 to 52% (in Tables 7.6 and 7.7). The proportions of left- and non-right-handers were consistent with the additive model at both levels of parental incidence. Therefore, it appears safe to conclude that the RS + + genotype is shifted further to the right than the RS + − genotype, as represented in Figure 7.1.

The surprising discovery that the distribution of eye dominance in families was predictable by the additive genetic model suggested that the model might have wider applications to questions about laterality than I had anticipated. The idea opened up new possibilities for examining relationships between asymmetries, hand and eye, eye and foot, and others, as described in chapter 9.

HANDEDNESS IN TWIN PAIRS PREDICTED BY THE ADDITIVE MODEL

Handedness in twin pairs was shown in chapter 5 to be consistent with the dominant genetic model, provided the shift was reduced by about 50% from that of singletons. This reduction implied that the frequency of left-handedness is higher in twins than the singletons by a few percentage points. This prediction was strongly supported by the findings of a large UK survey (Davis and Annett, 1994). Table 6.1 showed that the incidence of left-handedness was higher in twins than singletons in all of seven age groups. For the additive genetic model, a reduction of shift by 33% was found sufficient to predict observed distributions for twin pairs. That is, when shifts for RS + + and RS + − genotypes are 2.0z and 1.0z for male and 2.4z and 1.2z for female singletons respectively, shifts are 1.33z and 0.67z for male and 1.6z and 0.8z for female twins respectively. Different shifts imply different incidences at thresholds along the laterality continuum. Appendix V provides a look-up table for incidences of left-handedness expected at thresholds between −1.0z and +1.0z, for female and male singletons and female and male twins. For example, at a threshold of −0.5z the expected incidences are about 8.0% for female singletons, 9.2% for male singletons, 11.0% for female twins and 12.9% for male twins. At +0.5z the expected incidences are 25.6% for female singletons, 30.1% for male singletons, 36.0% for female twins and 41.0% for male twins. These predictions will be testable when investigators select and assess twins and non-twins in the same way and classify both consistently for the same strict or generous criteria.

The fact that MZ twins often differ for handedness has seemed to many people sufficient reason to dismiss a genetic influence. As explained earlier, this is not true because the RS + gene is not "for" handedness but for cerebral dominance. The latter has a relatively constant effect on the handedness distribution. For this reason, the RS + gene is associated with little genetic variability. Most of the variability observed for handedness depends on random asymmetries of development that affect every individual independently, whatever the degree of genetic relatedness. Hence, twins may differ for handedness in the same way as pairs of siblings.

How does the RS additive model predict handedness in MZ twin pairs? First, we need to know the incidence of left-handedness in the sample, in order to discover the threshold and thus the proportion of each genotype called left-handed or right-handed. Appendix VI provides a look-up table for the expected genotype distribution of left-handed twins at incidences from 10 to 45%, expressed per 1000, for each sex separately and sexes combined. A random sample of 1000 of the general population (whether twin or singleton, male or female) is expected to consist of 325 RS + +, 490 RS + − and 185 RS − − genotypes (from the gene frequencies deduced in chapter 5). When 10% of twins are classified as left-handed, the 100 left-handers would include 6 RS + +, 44 RS + − and 50 RS − − genotypes respectively. Right-handers can be found by subtraction from the total. For male twins at this incidence there would be slightly fewer RS − − genotypes (47) and for female twins slightly more (53) (because thresholds differ between the sexes for the same incidence). A graphical plot of the data in Appendix VI would allow estimates of interpolated values.

The second step for predicting twin pairs is to discover how right- and left-handers assort within each genotype. An example of the calculations for MZ pairs is given in Table 7.8, for an incidence of 14%. The 140 left-handers (per 1000, sexes combined) include 10 RS + +, 65 RS + − and 65 RS − − genotypes. The genotypes of the 860 right-handers, by subtraction from the totals are 315 RS + +, 425 RS + − and 120 RS − −. The genotype distribution is set out at

Table 7.8 Handedness in MZ twin pairs when the incidence of left-handedness is 14%: genotype numbers and predictions of the RS additive model (Ns per 1000)

Genotype	Pop. total	Right-handers	Left-handers	Twin pair handedness		
				RR	RL	LL
				[Predicted]		
RS + +	325	315	10	305.3	19.4	0.31
RS + −	490	425	65	368.6	112.7	8.6
RS − −	185	120	65	77.8	84.3	22.8
Total	1000		140	751.7	216.4	31.7
				[Observed in 2627 pairs]		
				751.4	218.9	29.7

the left side of Table 7.8. The right side of the table gives the expected numbers of RR, RL and LL twin pairs for each genotype. A pair of MZ twins is identical for genotype, but within each genotype right- and left-handers combine at random. The probability of RR, RL and LL pairs, within genotypes, is given by the binomial theorem (as for two kinds of marble placed in a bag and pulled out in twos at random). For RS + + genotypes, the expected frequency of RR pairs is $(315 \times 315)/325 = 305.3$, RL pairs $2((315 \times 10)/325) = 19.4$, and LL pairs $(10 \times 10)/325 = 0.31$. The results of corresponding calculations for RS + − and RS − − genotypes are then combined. Summing over genotypes, the types of pairs expected per 1000 are RR 752, RL 216, and LL 32. In 12 studies combined, where the overall incidence of left-handedness was 13.9%, the observed pairs (per 1000) were RR 751, RL 219 and LL 30. The fit is excellent.

Table 7.9 lists the 12 studies and gives the chi-square tests of fit for each one individually, as well as for the studies grouped at three levels of incidence (9–12%, 13–15% and 16–24%) and also for the grand total. Calculations here are based on actual numbers, not per 1000 population. For the combined 2627 MZ pairs the fit was excellent (chi-square = 0.338, d.f. 2, n.s.). The fits were good for individual studies, and also for groups at the three levels of incidence. Table 7.10 lists 12 studies of DZ twins. The predictions for twin pairs are straightforward but take longer to calculate because genotypes may differ in DZ pairs and random combinations must be worked out for all possible combinations of genotype. Predictions per 1000 for DZ twins, for an incidence of left-handedness at 13.3%, the total for combined studies (Table 7.10), were RR 757, RL 220 and LL 23. The observed numbers (per 1000) were RR 755, RL 224 and LL 21. The test of fit, using actual numbers for 2394 DZ twins, found excellent agreement (chi-square = 0.696, d.f. 2, n.s.). Chi-square tests for individual studies, and for groups of studies at different levels of incidence, found that the fits were excellent for all but one analysis. For combined studies at the lowest level of incidence the fit was relatively poor (chi-square = 5.175, d.f. 2, p < 0.10 > 0.05). The mismatch between prediction and observation was almost entirely due to LL pairs, where 18 were predicted but only 10 were reported (in a total of 1097

Table 7.9 MZ twin pairs: distribution of handedness in pairs for studies grouped at three levels of incidence

	N pairs	Left (%)	RR	RL	LL	Chi-square (d.f. 2)
Wilson and Jones (1932)	70	10.7	56	13	1	0.165
Stocks (1933)	42	9.5	35	6	1	0.215
Neale (1988)	836	12.2	655	158	23	0.334
Rife (1950)	343	12.8	261	76	6	1.886
Total 9–12%	1291	12.2	1007	253	31	0.073
Zazzo (1960)	259	13.2	199	51	9	0.455
Loehlin and Nichols (1976)	514	14.1	380	123	11	3.011
NCDS: McManus (1985a)	43	15.1	32	9	2	0.210
Total 13–15%	816	13.9	611	183	22	0.820
Bouterwek (1938)	122	18.9	80	38	4	1.768
Thyss (1946)	103	18.4	72	24	7	1.049
Dechaume (1957)	33	24.2	19	12	2	0.396
Carter-Saltzman et al. (1976)	187	17.1	132	46	9	0.162
Springer and Searleman (1978)	75	16.7	53	19	3	0.026
Total 16–24%	520	18.2	356	139	25	0.052
Grand total (12 studies)	2627	13.9	1974	575	78	0.338

Table 7.10 DZ twin pairs: distribution of handedness in pairs for studies grouped at three levels of incidence

	N pairs	Left (%)	RR	RL	LL	Chi-quare (d.f. 2)
Wilson and Jones (1932)	123	11.4	97	24	2	0.011
Stocks (1933)	94	10.6	76	16	2	0.299
Zazzo (1960)	336	11.0	264	70	2	3.016
Rife (1950)	211	11.6	164	45	2	1.177
Loehlin and Nichols (1976)	333	11.1	261	70	2	3.074
Total 9–12%	1097	11.2	862	225	10	5.175
Neale (1988)	832	13.8	626	183	23	0.452
NCDS: McManus (1985a)	88	14.8	66	18	4	1.426
Total 13–15%	920	13.9	692	201	27	1.051
Bouterwek (1938)	35	17.1	23	12	0	2.074
Thyss (1946)	86	16.3	60	24	2	0.429
Dechaume (1957)	33	19.7	21	11	1	0.362
Carter-Saltzman et al. (1976)	176	19.3	115	54	7	0.260
Springer and Searleman (1978)	47	16.0	35	9	3	2.230
Total 16–24%	377	18.0	254	110	13	0.576
Grand total (12 studies)	2394	13.3	1808	536	50	0.696

pairs). At the same level of incidence of left-handedness for MZ pairs, 32 LL pairs were predicted and 30 observed (in a total of 1291 pairs). At the higher levels of incidence (13–15% and 16–24%) predictions for all types of pairs were excellent. The good fits in all but one set of grouped data suggest that investigators adopting strict criteria of left-handedness slightly under-estimated the number of LL pairs among DZ twins. (A study of Newman, Freeman and Holzinger, 1937 was excluded from these analyses because there was a large discrepancy between the incidence of left-handedness recorded for MZ twins, 19.0%, and DZ twins, 11.0%. This suggests that different criteria of left-handedness may have been used for the different types of twin. The other studies listed in Tables 7.9 and 7.10 did not differ by more than one level of classification between MZ and DZ pairs.)

Does the slightly greater genetic variability of DZ than MZ twins lead to a detectable difference in concordance for handedness? The RS model predicts more concordant LL pairs per 1000 in MZ twins (about 30 pairs) than DZ twins (about 20 pairs) when the sample incidence is about 14%. A difference of this order was observed in the combined samples, 78/2627 (3.0%) for MZ and 50/2394 (2.1%) for DZ pairs. Thus the difference observed is of the size expected by the RS model. The difference between the numbers of LL pairs in the MZ and DZ pairs in the combined data for twins (as summarised in Tables 7.9 and 7.10) was statistically significant (chi-square = 3.910, d.f. 1, p = < 0.05). Considered as an odds-ratio the proportion of MZ to DZ LL pairs was 1.43:1.

With regard to sex differences, few studies were large enough to distinguish pairs for both zygosity and sex but two large studies (Loehlin and Nichols, 1976; Neale, 1988) did make these distinctions. Because incidences of left-handedness were similar in these samples, 12.9% and 12.6% respectively, they were combined to give reasonable numbers for an examination of the sexes separately. Both studies recorded more left-handers in male than female twins; the combined incidences were 13.4% for males and 12.3% for females (consistent with a threshold between −0.4 and −0.5 in Appendix V). The numbers of pairs that could be examined for handedness were 501 MZ males, 849 MZ females, 325 DZ males and 550 DZ females. Predictions were based on the appropriate shifts for twins of each sex (above) and for the observed incidences in each group. All fits to the RS additive model were excellent (chi-squares 0.086-0.534).

Orlebeke, Knol, Koopmans et al. (1996) described a questionnaire study of handedness for twins in the families of parents of different handedness (the twin children not distinguished for zygosity). As far as I am aware, this is the only study that has looked at handedness in families for children who were of twin birth. The predictions of the RS model for left-handers in the sons and daughters of the four family types (R × R, R × L, L × R and L × L) are like those for singletons except for the reduced RS shifts of the children (because they were twins). Table 7.11 gives the predicted and observed numbers. For sons the fit was almost perfect (chi-square = 0.226, d.f. 3, n.s.). The fit for daughters was not quite so good but not significantly poor (total chi-square = 6.100, d.f. 3, n.s.). The model predicted 27 daughters in L × R families but only 17 were recorded.

Table 7.11 Handedness for twins in families: data of Orlebeke, Knol, Koopmans et al., 1996

Father × mother	Sons					Daughters				
	N total	N left obs.	N left exp.	Chi-square L (R)	d.f.	N total	N left obs.	N left exp.	Chi-square L (R)	d.f.
R × R	1018	144	143.4	0.002 (0.000)		1191	151	140.2	0.833 (0.111)	
R × L	110	24	22.7	0.078 (0.020)		120	23	22.2	0.030 (0.007)	
L × R	124	23	24.6	0.099 (0.024)		154	17	27.2	3.822 (0.820)	
L × L	14	4	3.9	0.001 (0.000)		20	4	5.4	0.349 (0.128)	
Total				0.226	3				6.100	3

All other predictions and observations were well matched. There are several ways in which this one mismatch might have occurred, but speculation on this point would take us beyond our present purpose. Orlebeke et al. stressed the role of the environment in producing the variability of handedness in twins. The RS model agrees. As said above, most of the variability for handedness is due to accidents of development that are independent for every individual, whether of multiple or single birth.

SUMMARY

Evidence that RS depends on a single gene (RS +) was found in chapter 5, when estimates of gene frequency were derived from the proportion of people with right hemisphere cerebral dominance (in chapter 4). The effectiveness of the gene in displacing a chance distribution for handedness in a dextral direction, the extent of shift, was estimated roughly in chapter 5. For reasons described in chapter 6, it was desirable to look for shifts appropriate for an additive version of the model (for handedness) with parameters that differed slightly with sex and twinning. This chapter described the search for these levels of shift through analyses of empirical data, and also tests of the values derived against data for handedness in families and in twins.

Measures of peg moving time in undergraduates and children, male and female, gave observed distributions of R–L asymmetry against which hypothetical distributions, with variable shifts for genotype and sex, could be tested. The results of these analyses gave clues to values of shift that were then examined for their ability to explain observed incidences of left-handedness in paired samples of males and females (such as fathers and mothers, or sons and daughters in a particular study). Assuming that the same criteria were used to assess handedness in both sexes in a single study, there should be identical thresholds for males and females. Incidences would differ, however, because of the stronger bias to dextrality of females than males. Could the values of shift deduced for the model predict observed differences for incidence in matched pairs of males and females? Good matches were found for several samples likely to be reliable because the data depended on self-report by parents and by children. The outcome of these tests of empirical data was that the shifts are likely to be as represented in Figure 7.1, the RS + + genotype shifted twice as far to the right as the RS + − genotype, and females shifted further to the right than males by 20%.

Could the model in Figure 7.1 predict handedness in families, when sex was distinguished in both generations? It had been shown earlier (Annett, 1985a) that the additive model predicted family data very well when assessment was by self-report. The findings for sons and for daughters in the four types of family (R × R, R × L, L × R and L × L) in seven studies gave 14 tests of family predictions and all gave good fits. This strong support for the model in self-report data was not found in studies where parental handedness was assessed by indirect report. Where did the problem arise? The hypothesis that the difficulty might be associated with under-reporting of left-handedness in mothers was supported by a comparison of thresholds of incidence in fathers and mothers; for indirect report but not self-report studies, the thresholds for mothers were further to the left than expected for those of fathers.

Genetic predictions were recalculated for the present analyses, using a more accurate computer program and including more data than available in 1985. Fits were excellent for self-report studies examined at several levels of analysis. They were often poor for indirect report studies. The latter were combined in two groups, for parental incidences below and above 7%, so as to have substantial data for tests of the model. At the lower parental incidences there were poor fits for the families of left-handed mothers, but not those of left-handed fathers. At the higher level, fits were excellent for left-handed mothers but tended to be poor for left-handed fathers. This very important observation showed that the problem of poor fit was not general, but varied with level of incidence in parents. The latter depend, in indirect report studies, on information supplied by their student children. A "thought experiment" was applied to the combined data for all indirect report studies. The idea was that the apparent excess of left-handed children born to left-handed mothers compared with left-handed fathers, arises not because there are in fact more left-handed children, but because there are too few right-handed children aware that they have a left-handed mother. Moving right-handed children from R × R to R × L families, sufficient to increase the *number* of children in these families to the level expected if the maternal incidence were higher by 1%, had the effect of making the *proportion of left-handed children* agree with that predicted. Hence, it seems likely that the poor fits of the RS model for some indirect report studies was due to under-estimation of maternal left-handedness.

Discrimination between the dominant version of the genetic model, as applied in chapter 5, and the additive model developed here, depends on predictions for children in L × L families. The dominant model expects a higher proportion of left-handers than the additive model in these families, while predictions for other family types are similar. Data were compiled from all available studies, and examined for two levels of parental incidence (8% in Figure 7.2 and 25% in Figure 7.3). The findings for combined data were in good accord with the additive model at both levels of analysis. At the lower level of parental incidence there were relatively few left-handers per study but 219 in the combined data for 20 studies. The percentage of left-handers (27%) was as predicted by the additive model. At the higher level of incidence, for non-right-handedness there were also 219 children in four studies, and the proportion non-right (57%) was again as predicted. These good fits suggest that the additive model is to be preferred. Surprisingly, it was found that eye dominance in families was also predicted by the additive model, with incidences and distributions similar to those for non-right-handedness.

The additive genetic model can account for handedness in twin pairs, if the extent of shift is reduced in twins compared with singletons by one-third (rather than the one-half of chapter 5). Look-up tables are provided in the Appendices to show the relative incidences expected for males and females, singleton and twin, at thresholds between −1z and +1z, and also to show the genotype distribution of twins, male, female and sexes together, at different levels of incidence. An example of the calculations for MZ twins is given to illustrate the method. The outcome is almost precisely as found in combined data for over 2000 twin pairs. The model is shown to predict DZ handedness equally well. Tests of the model for the sexes separately also show good fits. The family data reported by Orlebeke, Knol, Koopmans et al. (1996) agree well with predictions of the model except for a shortfall of left-handed daughters for left-handed fathers. Orlebeke and others have taken discordance for handedness in MZ twins to be contrary to genetic models of handedness but this is not so. The findings are just as predicted by the RS model because the major part of the variability is non-genetic. Random accidents of early growth occur in every individual independently, whether of single or multiple birth. The fact that there are more RR than LL twin pairs is due to the RS + gene but the assortment in pairs is largely binomial.

8   Other asymmetries of brain and behaviour

The asymmetries of chief interest for this book are handedness and cerebral speech laterality but there are many other asymmetries of human brain and behaviour. The theory developed in previous chapters suggests that there is no intrinsic relationship between hand preference and cerebral laterality for speech (CD). Both are influenced by a third variable, a gene that induces an asymmetry in favour of the left hemisphere during early growth. Left brain advantage leads to a typical pattern of hemisphere specialisation in the course of normal development and incidentally raises the probability of right-handedness. In the absence of the gene for left brain advantage, handedness and speech lateralise by chance. But what of all the other associated asymmetries? What is the pattern in the typical case, and in the absence of the typical pattern, do other lateralities assort together or do all lateralise by chance?

Laterality research has tended to explore two main questions. One asks what functions lateralise in which hemisphere in the typical case. This research tends to neglect individual differences and assume that findings will apply universally (except perhaps for pathological cases). The second research question acknowledges individual differences, but seeks evidence that atypical asymmetries reverse together. Many researchers have looked for asymmetries that might "index" CD. If an easily observable asymmetry were diagnostic of brain laterality, then cerebral dominance could be studied in "normal" samples. With regard to handedness, are there any asymmetries that reverse between right-handers and left-handers? From the viewpoint of the RS theory, both research strategies have limitations. The problem for the assumption of a universal pattern of CD is that it may not be present in almost one in five people. The second research strategy looks for reversed asymmetries that the RS theory does not expect to occur. The purpose of this chapter is to outline findings for asymmetries other than handedness and CD. Do any have strong associations with handedness or with CD, such that they could be regarded as "indexing" these variables? Or are relationships of the kind expected if asymmetries are *influenced by the RS + gene*, but otherwise mutually independent? The next chapter will test some of these associations quantitatively in the light of the RS theory.

EYE, FOOT AND OTHER OBSERVABLE ASYMMETRIES

Eye dominance was one of the first characteristics to be proposed as *the key* to handedness and other asymmetries (Harris, 1980a). Many other keys have been proposed also, including the side of hair parting, the manner of clasping the hands or folding the arms, and the direction of drawing circles. I have explored some of these asymmetries in laboratory classes with undergraduates, along with standard measures of eye and foot preference. This section describes findings for eye and foot, and briefly considers a miscellany of other observations.

With regard to eye preference, a simple test is to point a finger at a distant object and, holding the finger steady, close each eye in turn. It is apparent that only one eye was lined up with the object. Information from the other eye was suppressed, without any awareness of conflict. A commonly used criterion of eye dominance is sighting preference, the eye used to look through a telescope or through the sights of a gun. A possible objection to this criterion is that the hand holding the instrument might influence the eye used. The hole-in-card test avoids this bias by instructing participants to hold a piece of cardboard in both hands at arm length, and to sight a distant line, such as the edge of a window or door, through a small hole in the centre of the card. While maintaining fixation, the card is brought toward the face until it touches the nose. It is then evident which eye was doing the sighting. Alternatively, while P fixates through the hole, an examiner may cover each eye in turn with a small card and ask whether the line can still be seen. When several tests of eye preference are given, some individuals consistently use the right eye, some the left eye, and some show mixed preferences. The distribution of types of eye preference has not been studied as fully as types of hand preference. In my samples of students and personally tested families I found right-handers about 60% consistently right eyed, about 20% mixed eyed and 20% left eyed. Among left-handers there were about 55% consistently left eyed, 25% mixed eyed and 20% consistently right eyed. Overall, about one in three people have a preferred eye on the side opposite to the preferred hand. A study of French pre-school children found 40% left eyed (Dellatolas, Curt, Dargent-Paré et al., 1998).

Eye preference is independent of direct training for most people, and hence less influenced by social pressures than hand preference. So what causes eye preference? It seems intuitively reasonable to suppose that the dominant eye is the one with superior visual acuity, but this is not so, except when acuity differences are very great. Woo and Pearson (1927) described findings for visual acuity in over 6000 males, measured for acuity along with hand strength at the Health Exhibition of 1884. Acuity of the right and left eyes was about equal over the whole sample. The distribution of R–L acuity resembled that found for R–L strength, a normal curve. But whereas the curve for strength was displaced toward the right (like that for peg moving), the curve for acuity was not. It was centred at 0, with superior acuity in 23% for the right eye, 22% for the left eye and 55% equivalent. Thus, asymmetries of visual acuity were distributed without bias to either side, as if at random and not influenced by the RS + gene. Crovitz (1961) examined relative acuity and sighting dominance in the same subjects. He found that most people preferred the right eye for sighting, including some with better acuity in the left eye. When there were large differences in acuity favouring the left eye, the proportion of left eyed sighting increased, but the increase was smaller than for right eyed sighting in subjects with a large difference favouring the right eye. In other words, there was a bias to right eyed sighting across all levels of acuity difference.

Each eye has a different point of view, very different for objects close to the nose but more similar for distant objects. Both eyes send information to both sides of the brain. Everything to the right of the point an individual is looking at (the visual fixation point) falls into the right visual field (RVF) and information from the RVF of both eyes is sent to the left hemisphere. The visual field to the left of fixation (LVF) travels from both eyes to the right hemisphere. The anatomy provides for each hand to respond directly to events seen on its own side of the body, without the delay of transferring information to the other side of the brain. Since both eyes are connected with both hemispheres, there is no obvious *sensory* difference to explain why one eye should be preferred. However, the control of eye movements depends on several pairs of muscles whose actions must be co-ordinated. It is possible that sighting dominance depends on asymmetries of *motor* function (Money, 1972; Walls, 1951). The eye with the more efficient control system is likely to be preferred for decisions about what lies straight ahead. Thus eye preference might depend on relative motor skill, like hand preference.

Research on relationships between eye and hand preferences has sometimes found no association (Clark, 1957; Porac and Coren, 1976) but these negative results depended on samples with few left-handers. When large numbers of left-handers were available, eye preference was associated with hand preference, but with many exceptions, as mentioned above. Table 8.1 shows findings for sighting preference in a random sample of schoolchildren augmented by a complete sample of left-handers. The frequency of left eye preference rose from 36% in consistent right-handers to 68% in consistent left-handers. These data confirm that at least one-third of the population is discordant for laterality of hand and eye preference. When handedness is classified in the subgroup scheme devised in chapter 2, there is a roughly linear relationship between probability of left

Table 8.1 Eye and foot preferences in children classified for hand preference: based on Annett and Turner, 1974

Hand preference	N	Left eye for sighting (%)	Left foot for kicking (%)
Pure right	83	36.1	3.8
Mixed right	30	23.3	13.3
Mixed left	74	55.4	52.7
Pure left	37	67.6	83.8

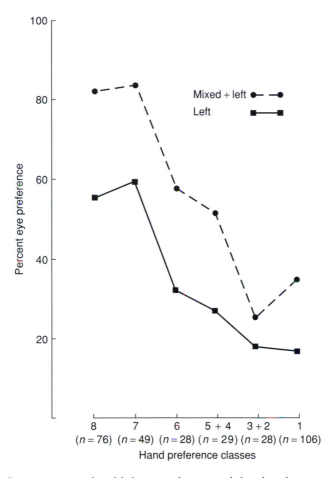

Figure 8.1 Percentage mixed and left eye preference with hand preference class in personally tested families.

eye dominance and level of subgroup handedness, as shown in Figure 8.1. Hand and eye preferences are clearly related, but in a continuous fashion, not a discrete one. More strong left-handers (classes 7 and 8) are left eyed than weak left-handers (class 6). The trend is clear also when eye preference is classified as left plus mixed preference. It should be recalled that eye preference in families was predictable, from the additive RS genetic model (see chapter 7). Relationships between hand and eye preference will be examined further in chapter 9.

Foot preferences were assessed in children, undergraduates, and personally visited families by asking which foot was used for kicking (as to score a goal in football), a suitable soft ball being provided when possible for demonstration. Findings for children are shown in Table 8.1. Only 4% of consistent right-handers

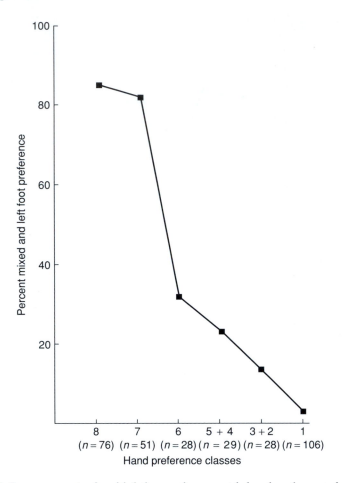

Figure 8.2 Percentage mixed and left foot preference with hand preference class in personally tested families.

but 84% of consistent left-handers were left footed. Data for OU students and for personally visited families confirmed that in right-handed writers some 90% were right footed and in left-handed writers about two-thirds were left footed. Figure 8.2 shows the distribution of non-right foot preference in personally visited families when individuals were classified for subgroup hand preference. There was an orderly relationship between levels of hand preference and frequency of left foot preference, consistent with the thesis that both preferences depend on a continuous distribution of relative asymmetry. As found for eye dominance, strong left-handers (classes 7 and 8) were more likely to be left footed than weak left-handers (class 6). However, the association between hand and foot is very much stronger than between hand and eye. It has been claimed that foot preference is more strongly associated with cerebral speech laterality than handedness (Elias and Bryden, 1998). The findings for people with left foot preference showed no bias to either side for ear advantage during dichotic listening (below). Foot preference cannot be regarded as an "index" of cerebral dominance on this evidence.

Chapman, Chapman and Allen (1987) gave psychology undergraduates several tasks requiring foot use (such as standing on one foot, kicking, writing one's name in a sand tray) and scored the responses to produce a "scale" of foot preference. This was examined against a similar scale for hand preference. About half of the students were consistently right-handed and right footed, but the remainder were distributed thinly over several levels of relative preference for both variables.

A miscellany of other asymmetries has been examined in different undergraduate practical classes. When clasping the hands there is a slight tendency for the left thumb to be placed on top, and similarly for the left arm when folding the arms. No relationship was found with hand preference. The hair at the crown of the head typically grows in a clockwise direction, and for most people the hair has a natural parting on the left side. However, anti-clockwise whorls and right-sided partings were not more frequent in left-handers, in my samples. Students were asked to write and to draw with both hands simultaneously on upright boards, angled away from the body midline to variable extents. Most (80%) produced better drawings with the preferred hand (whether right or left). Is the non-preferred hand likely to produce mirror writing in this simultaneous writing task? This was observed in 25% of right-handers and 34% of left-handers. The ability to write in mirror script deliberately (that is, script that would look normal if held up to a mirror) is a relatively rare skill that some people find they possess, usually to their surprise. Its cause and association with other asymmetries remains unknown, as far as I am aware. For comfort sucking in childhood, 32% of students reported that the right-hand was sucked and 16% the left-hand. Ear preference for listening to the telephone was investigated by asking students about the ear normally used when *not* writing messages at the same time. About 70% of both right-handers and left-handers reported holding the receiver in the preferred hand. This result was found in two of my samples. Porac and Coren (1981) found 59% of their questionnaire sample right-ear preferent for several listening tasks.

Among asymmetries not investigated in my practical classes are mouth asymmetries and fingerprints. Graves, Goodglass and Landis (1982) found the right side of the mouth more active than the left during spontaneous speech. With regard to fingerprints, both right- and left-handers tend to have certain patterns more often on the left than on the right palm, but this asymmetry was smaller in groups of left-handers than right-handers (Rife, 1955, 1978). Jantz, Fohl and Zahler (1979) counted the numbers of finger ridges on each side (radial and ulnar) of all 10 fingers in right and left-handed males and females. There were few statistically significant differences between groups, but there were consistent trends for right-handers to have higher and more variable ridge counts than left-handers in both sexes. As fingerprints develop at an early stage of foetal growth, these findings imply that handedness is influenced by prenatal factors (as argued for congenital determinants in chapter 3). Such influences could be genetic or environmental, but not learned or cultural.

PERCEPTUAL ASYMMETRIES OF HEARING, VISION AND TOUCH

Perceptual asymmetries are usually studied by presenting different information to the two sides of the body simultaneously so that there is competition for attention and/or perceptual processing. Reports of what the subject heard (in dichotic listening) or saw (in divided visual fields) or felt (in dichaptic manipulation) usually show a relative superiority of one side, and this is generally interpreted as a measure of hemisphere dominance for that type of perceptual processing. These types of experiment have generated huge numbers of studies of undergraduates, as well as clinic samples (reviews by Bryden, 1982; Hellige, 1993; Hugdahl, 1988; Springer and Deutsch, 1998).

Dichotic listening procedures were developed to study selective attention (Broadbent, 1956; Cherry, 1953). They were used by Kimura (1961) to investigate asymmetries of auditory perception in patients whose speech laterality had been assessed using the Wada method. A mean advantage for the right ear (REA) was found in normal participants and patients known to have left CD. In 12 patients with right CD, the trend was reversed, giving a mean advantage in favour of the left ear (LEA). REA for speech sounds is one of the most reliable findings in psychology, so consistent that dichotic listening has been used to investigate features of the speech system itself (Studdert-Kennedy and Shankweiler, 1970). However, the report of a reversal of directional asymmetry in patients with right hemisphere speech was taken to imply that dichotic listening might "index" CD, and thus throw light on cerebral asymmetry in normal samples. How far was this assumption justified?

The Wada test carries some risk, such that its use is restricted to certain preoperative investigations before brain surgery. Independent replications of Kimura's original experiment were few. Strauss, Gaddes and Wada (1987) found REA for dichotic listening in 74% of normal right-handers, 86% of patients known to have left CD, 71% of patients with bilateral speech and 50% in 10 patients with right CD. These findings suggest that atypical cerebral speech is not associated with a reversal of ear advantage, but rather with loss of the typical bias. The patients with right CD were at chance for ear asymmetry. The data of Strauss et al. were combined with findings from two other studies of dichotic listening for patients assessed for CD (Geffen and Caudrey, 1981; Zatorre, 1989) to give combined data for 187 patients as shown in Table 8.2. Speech laterality was left-sided in 66.8%, bilateral in 21.9%, and right-sided in 11.2% (Annett, 1991b). The last proportion is close to the estimates derived in chapter 4 for right CD in general population samples, but it should be noted that the patients studied for speech side and dichotic listening were likely to have sustained brain

Table 8.2 Summary of three studies of ear and speech side, N (%): based on Annett, 1991b

Ear advantage	Speech hemisphere			
	Left	*Bilateral*	*Right*	*Total*
Left	12	19	14	45 (24.1)
Right	113	22	7	142
Total	125 (66.8)	41 (21.9)	21 (11.2)	187

damage some years earlier. The point of interest for the present purpose is that the association between dichotic ear advantage and CD depended on 113 patients with both asymmetries in the typical direction, while all other combinations were consistent with chance distributions. Among patients with bilateral CD, the numbers with REA (22) and LEA (19) were similar. Among patients with LEA for dichotic listening, the frequencies of left CD (12) and right CD (14) were also similar. These findings do not suggest that LEA for dichotic listening is an "index" of atypical CD. They are consistent with random combination in the absence of typical biases to right ear and left hemisphere.

What has been found about auditory perception of nonverbal stimuli? A small bias to LEA was found for dichotic listening to non-speech material, sounds such as car engines starting up and tap water running (Knox and Kimura, 1970). There was also LEA for musical chords and phrases (Kimura, 1964). These findings agreed with previous studies of musical perception for patients with lateralised brain lesions (Milner, 1962). There were trends over groups, but never robust discriminations that might be diagnostic for individual cases.

When asymmetries of dichotic perception are examined in large samples of normal Ps, they are found to be continuously distributed (Shankweiler and Studdert-Kennedy, 1975). Distributions are normal, unimodal, with mean displaced to give REA in the majority. How do they differ between right- and left-handers? The distributions are alike, except that right-handers are more shifted to the right than left-handers, as can be seen in the data of Wexler and Halwes (1983), shown in Figure 8.3. Most reports do not give the continuous data, but classify for REA versus LEA. Lake and Bryden (1976) found that some 72% of right-handers had REA and 61% of left-handers similarly. These findings, typical of the field, can be summarised as showing that there is a statistically significant bias to REA for verbal material in groups of right-handers (but with many exceptions) and a smaller bias to REA, generally not statistically significant, in left-handers. The biases tend to reverse for certain types of nonverbal material.

Asymmetries of visual perception may be studied by presenting stimuli briefly to either side of a central fixation point, in order to contrast perception in the right versus left visual fields. As explained above the visual fields are the sides of

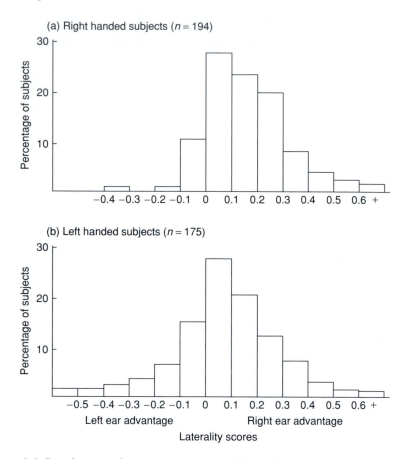

Figure 8.3 Distributions of asymmetry scores for dichotic listening in (a) right-handers and (b) left-handers: adapted from Wexler and Halwes, 1983.

space to either side of fixation. Early experiments using this technique found English words were read better to the right of fixation and Yiddish words to the left of fixation (Mishkin and Forgays, 1952). The effect seemed likely to be due to directional scan, associated with reading habits. Bryden (1964) suggested that a right visual field advantage (RVFA) for the perception of letters might be a function of left hemisphere CD, analogous to the REA of dichotic listening. Many subsequent studies have confirmed that RVFA is typically present for letters and words. Evidence for reversed asymmetries (LVFA) for nonverbal stimuli was found when Ps were asked to recall the location of dots in a spatial array (Kimura, 1973c). When these typical asymmetries are examined in relation to handedness and family handedness (left-handers with and without left-handed relatives), there is no consistent evidence for reversals of asymmetry (Annett, 1982).

As far as I am aware, there has been no direct test on patients with known speech laterality of the hypothesis that asymmetries of perception in the visual fields are directly related to CD. The role of overt scanning has been controlled by experimental procedures such as presenting stimuli very briefly and in vertical rather than horizontal arrays. However, these manipulations do not rule out a directional bias for scanning *internal* representations of stimuli, as argued by Efron (1990). Further, there is evidence for individual differences in such an internal scanning mechanism (Annett, 1983b; Annett and Annett, 1979).

Tests of tactile perception have found greater sensitivity on the left side in some studies (Ghent, 1961; Weinstein and Sersen, 1961) but not in others (Fennel, Satz and Wise, 1967). Witelson (1976) asked children to palpate two shapes simultaneously in each hand (dichaptically) and found left-hand superiority in boys, but no difference between the hands for girls. Harris (1980b) reviewed evidence for left-hand superiority in recognising Braille characters in normal subjects unfamiliar with these shapes. However, skilled readers of Braille tend to use the right-hand for reading, while the left-hand keeps track of lines. Asymmetries of perception probably differ between naïve and skilled performers in several fields, including music (Bever and Chiarello, 1974; Fabbro, Brusaferro and Bava, 1990) and Morse code (Papçun, Krashen, Terbeek et al., 1974). That is, skilled performance typically depends mainly on the left hemisphere.

In summary, findings for perceptual asymmetries in normal Ss may be interpreted as compatible with the hemisphere specialisations deduced from clinical studies. There are typical biases to more efficient processing of speech and linguistic symbols in the left than the right hemisphere, and the discrimination and location of nonverbal patterns in the right than the left hemisphere. Taken at face value as indicators of hemisphere specialisation (and putting aside the reasons for scepticism indicated above) have the perceptual studies added significantly to understanding of cerebral asymmetries? Have they thrown light on *individual differences* for asymmetries? The search for predictable reversals of asymmetry has been negative in all fields of enquiry. The implicit assumption that left-handers, or perhaps left-handers with left-handed relatives, "ought to have" asymmetries that are the opposite of those of right-handers has not been supported. Reports of reversed asymmetries in left-handers are few and all depended on small samples, where cases were too few for confidence in apparent reversals of trends. In left-handers, asymmetries are either absent or reduced versions of those seen in right-handers. These findings have been often attributed to "bilateral" CD in left-handers. They could equally depend on representation of speech in "either" hemisphere. The outcome of these attempts to "index" CD might appear at best as inconclusive, and at worst as failed. However, it is a failure only for those who regard CD and handedness as discrete variables, having distinct and opposite right and left-handed forms. When asymmetries are regarded as continuous variables, influenced by a directional bias (RS + gene) that may be present or absent, the outcome of the perceptual asymmetry research is neither failed nor inconclusive but just as expected.

ASYMMETRIES OF CEREBRAL FUNCTION

The fact that the symmetrical halves of the brain are each responsible for the functions of the contralateral side of the body (left hemisphere and right-hand, right hemisphere and left-hand) has been known for a very long time. The pattern is characteristic of vertebrates. However, even this universal feature of great antiquity appears to admit of exceptions. A Japanese patient was reported to have predominantly ipsilateral connections between brain and body (Hosokawa, Tsuji, Uozumi et al., 1996). Asymmetry between the human hemispheres for speech was recognised more than a century ago. For about one hundred years after Broca, research on cerebral function depended mainly on case studies in clinical neurology. With the advent of modern neuropsychology, and especially since the split-brain operations in California in the 1960s, the growth of research on hemisphere specialisation has been explosive. A full account of this work is beyond the scope of this book (see reviews in Kolb and Whishaw, 1996; Springer and Deutsch, 1998). The questions of interest here are, first, what are the main facts about specialisations in the typical case, and second, how do these specialisations vary in atypical cases. There is an important deeper question, whether it is possible to identify the "essence" of the difference in function between the hemispheres. This might give clues to the mechanism of action of the RS + gene.

What are the asymmetries of function expected in the majority of the population? Left-sided control of speech is associated with left lateralisation for many aspects of language function, including word knowledge (semantics), the ability to produce grammatical sentences (syntax), memory for stories, reading and writing. There is continuing debate about the extent of right hemisphere involvement in language. Patients who have lost speech due to lesions of the left hemisphere, or even removal of that side by hemispherectomy, may be able to sing familiar ditties and swear. Thus it is not the output of words, as such, that critically depends on the left hemisphere, but rather the output of words to express thoughts with meaning. The idea that the left side is responsible for propositional speech was suggested by John Hughlings Jackson, an English neurologist contemporary with Broca. Musical aspects of speech production (prosody) depend mainly on the right hemisphere.

Zaidel (1978) used a specially devised contact lens method to present stimuli to the LVF (and therefore right hemisphere) of split-brain patients, while they could move the eyes freely. When the left-hand was required to point to pictures to indicate the meanings of words it appeared that the right hemisphere could *understand* words, although it could not *say* them. Understanding varied between the levels expected for normal 8- to 16-year-olds in different patients. The left-hand could select a pattern from the Progressive Matrices test of nonverbal intelligence (Raven, 1958b) almost as well as the right-hand (and presumed left hemisphere). Zaidel also confirmed an important difference between the hemispheres, reported earlier by Levy, Trevarthen and Sperry (1972), that *only the left side is able to process speech sounds*.

It is important to recognise that, in spite of the popular characterisation of the left and right hemispheres as having "verbal" versus "nonverbal" or "visuospatial" functions, both sides of the brain are involved in the sensorimotor control of their respective sides of the body. The left side has a major role in some spatial tasks (Langdon and Warrington, 2000; Mehta, Newcombe and Damasio, 1987). The left hemisphere has a special role in purposeful, goal-directed movements. Disorders of voluntary movement, known as apraxias, affect many types of movement from simple repetitive tapping to complex sequences of action (reviews by De Renzi, 1989; McCarthy and Warrington, 1990). The ability to make a cup of coffee, to light a candle or a cigarette may be lost because the patient has some notion of the actions involved but makes mistakes like trying to strike the match on the candle. Experimental study of the ability to learn new action sequences found that patients with left brain lesions were especially poor, whether or not they also suffered from dysphasia (Kimura, 1977; Kolb and Milner, 1981). The control of complex goal-directed movements appears to depend on a network of frontal and parietal regions of the left hemisphere (Haaland, Harrington and Knight, 2000). For patients with atypical language dominance, the control of purposeful movements appears to be more associated with the speech side than with handedness (Meador, Loring, Lee et al., 1999).

Further evidence of the role of the left hemisphere in purposeful movements is found in the effects of brain lesions in people whose language is sign language for the deaf. Loss of the ability to communicate symbolically through sign (aphasia for the deaf-mute) was associated with left hemisphere lesions, but not comparable lesions of the right side (Poizner, Bellugi and Klima, 1989). Electrical stimulation of the exposed cortex of a deaf-signer found that errors of signing were associated with stimulation of Broca's area, and also the supramarginal gyrus (Corina, McBurney, Dodrill et al., 1999). Thus, it is clear that areas that in normal development are associated with spoken language, are also involved in sign language. These observations are consistent with the theory that speech is associated with other functions that may have had a role in primate nonverbal communication.

The idea that certain visual perceptual skills might depend on the right hemisphere was suggested by Hughlings Jackson. One of the main aims of modern neuropsychology was to investigate and substantiate this view. That the right hemisphere has particular expertise in aspects of visuospatial processing is now accepted (De Renzi, 1982; Milner and Taylor, 1972). A more detailed specification of the nature of this particular skill is not easy to give. Deficits identified include the detection of visual patterns and recognition of objects presented in ways that are partially obscured, by poor lighting, or unusual views (Warrington and Taylor, 1973). The right hemisphere appears to have special skills in visual recognition, especially for faces. It also has a role in drawing, assembling constructional puzzles, and negotiating complex routes through the environment. All of the above skills are characterised by a fairly high level of intellectual processing, in tasks where words are of little or no help. Lesions of the right parietal lobe may be associated with loss of awareness of the left side of space, such that patients neglect food on the left side of the plate, or draw clock faces with all the numbers on the right side. A type of apraxia mentioned in chapter 1, forgetting how to dress, is also associated with right-sided lesions. This is a skill learned so early, and normally practised at so automatic a level, that verbal instructions would be more likely to hinder than help the dressing process.

Given that several high level cognitive functions have a characteristic pattern of lateralisations in the typical brain, what can be said about atypical lateralisations? Among split-brain patients there were some marked individual differences (Gazzaniga, 1995). Most patients were fully dependent on the left hemisphere for speech, but a few developed an ability to control speech from the right side. The clinical literature has many examples of interesting cases with unusual combinations of lateral asymmetries (Alexander and Annett, 1996; Osmon, Panos, Kautz et al., 1998; Warrington, 2000). What does the RS theory predict about their combinations? My view is that it is better to make as few assumptions as possible until the evidence itself demands further complexity. For this reason I suggest that speech and other features of language, praxis and configurational abilities all lateralise at random when the typical pattern is absent, in that proportion of the population that is of RS − − genotype. This hypothesis will be testable when a large neurological service is prepared to keep systematic records for consecutive series of patients, examined in standard ways for the relevant abilities and lesion laterality. The evidence may take a few years to accumulate, but it is needed to test the theory of random functional asymmetry in atypical cases.

Are there any clues as to the "essence" of the difference between the hemispheres that might explain asymmetries of function? Left versus right hemisphere processing has been characterised by many dichotomies, such as analytic versus holistic, serial versus parallel, logical versus intuitive, that have passed into common folklore. These contrasts try to capture something fundamental about hemisphere differences. However, they are vague, speculative, and post hoc in the sense that they are descriptions of what might *follow from* the typical pattern of hemisphere specialisation. One important consequence of the typical pattern evident from study of split-brain patients (Gazzaniga, 1995) is that the left side constructs plausible stories about what both sides of the brain are doing (even when the right is operating independently of the left).

What can be said about differences that might *lead to* the typical pattern of asymmetry? There are two main candidates, one for motor output, and one for sensory input. The idea that speech laterality depends on an older system of communication through gesture has been mentioned above. Speech depends on complex gestures of the vocal organs and a facility for left-sided control of gesture might provide a critical impetus for left-sided speech lateralisation. The second candidate for a causal role in speech laterality is that the left hemisphere has a superior capacity to discriminate stimuli presented in very brief intervals of time (reviews by Nicholls, 1996; Tallal, Miller and Fitch, 1995). Evidence that the detection of rapid acoustic transitions depends on the left hemisphere has been found in normal volunteers studied by brain imaging (Belin, Zilbovicius, Crozier et al., 1998). Weaknesses in the processing of fast changing stimuli, both auditory and visual, would put the development of speech and reading at risk (Stein and McAnally, 1995).

ASYMMETRIES OF CEREBRAL ANATOMY

Broca and other pathologists looked for structural differences between the hemispheres but a review of the literature some 100 years later found that although many differences had been described, none seemed sufficient to explain the astonishing differences in function (Von Bonin, 1962). Hoadley and Pearson (1929) measured the internal lengths of the right and left halves of the skulls of 729 Egyptian males of the 26–30th dynasty, found by Sir Flinders Petrie. The differences between the sides were distributed continuously in an approximately normal distribution. The mean was displaced from the point of equality by about 0.58 standard deviations in favour of a longer right side. There was a negative skew. That is, although about 70% of the skulls were longer on the right, there were more skulls with a longer left side than expected for a truly normal distribution. They are as expected for a distribution that includes at least two subgroups, a larger one shifted and a smaller one not shifted away from a mean of 0, as deduced for R–L hand skill.

Two papers marked the start of the modern revival of interest in structural asymmetries of the brain (Geschwind and Levitsky, 1968; McRae, Branch and Milner, 1968). McRae et al. compared the lengths of the occipital horns of the lateral ventricles, as seen in air studies of 100 consecutive patients undergoing routine pre-operative assessments. The left horn was longer in 57, the right in 13, and 30 were judged equal. There were 13 left-handed and ambidextrous patients in this series, about equally divided between the groups, 5 left, 4 right and 4 equal, consistent with a random process.

Geschwind was interested in the planum temporale (PT) that lies on the upper surface of the temporal lobe, an area that is likely to be involved in language. PT is shown on a horizontal view of the brain in Figure 8.4. In 100 brains studied post mortem, PT was classified as larger on the left in 65, on the right in 11, and not clearly different in 24. Subsequent review of this same series of brains using more precise measurements found differences between the sides distributed as a continuous, unimodal, approximately normal curve. Classification for direction of asymmetry found 63 larger on the left, 21 on the right and 16 equal (Galaburda, Corsiglia, Rosen et al., 1987). Anatomical asymmetries occur in proportions reminiscent of the hand preference distribution of chapter 2, where about two-thirds were consistent right-handers and the remaining one-third divided between mixed- and left-handers (in various proportions varying with criteria of classification). Planum temporale asymmetries have been confirmed in several further studies of adult brains (reviews by Beaton, 1997; Zilles, Dabringhaus, Geyer et al., 1996). They have been found in the brains of

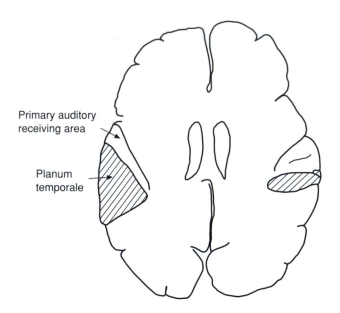

Primary auditory
receiving area

Planum
temporale

Figure 8.4 Asymmetry of the planum temporale shown on a horizontal section of the
brain at the level of the Sylvian fissure: based on Witelson, 1980.

neonates (Witelson and Pallie, 1973) and in foetal brains during the final quarter
of normal gestation (Chi, Dooling and Gilles, 1977; Wada, Clarke and Hamm,
1975). Loss or reductions of asymmetry have been associated with certain disorders, including dyslexia and schizophrenia.

Asymmetries of PT are associated with asymmetries of the lateral or Sylvian
fissure. This was noted by Cunningham (1902) to be longer on the left than on
the right in most brains. Rubens (1977) traced the line of the lateral fissure on
standard photographs of the hemispheres of preserved brains. The tracing for
the right side was then reversed and placed over the normal view of the left
side, as shown in Figure 8.5. It is evident that the lateral run of the fissure is
shorter on the right side, before it turns upward in what is called the posterior
ascending ramus. This turns upward earlier and ends at a higher level on the
right than the left side.

Witelson and Kigar (1992) made a post mortem study of Sylvian fissure morphology in patients who had agreed to donate their brains to research, and had
participated in psychological assessments some months before their deaths from
cancers not affecting the brain. There was considerable individual variability in
the length and shape of the fissures of both hemispheres. The most frequent
pattern was for the right fissure to turn upward more anteriorly than the left, as
in Figure 8.5. This was observed in 69% of 36 brains, the remaining 31% being
roughly symmetric. Handedness was classified as consistent right versus any
non-right preference (for the 12 actions of the AHPQ). Both handedness groups,
in both sexes, had longer horizontal segments on the left side, the typical pattern.

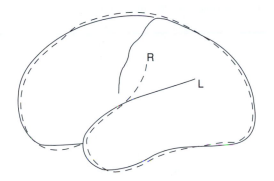

Figure 8.5 Asymmetry of the Sylvian or lateral fissure, illustrated on a composite tracing of hemisphere outlines, left (solid line) and right (dashed line): note the higher and shorter lateral fissure on the right: based on Rubens, 1977.

There was a curious finding for handedness, however, that consistently right-handed men had longer horizontal segments than non-right-handed men, and than females of both handedness groups. (The latter three groups were virtually identical when length was taken as proportion of overall brain size.) This finding is difficult to interpret. Witelson and Kigar suggested that it might be related to different patterns of specialisation for motor and perceptual functions between the sexes. An even more curious later finding (Witelson, Kigar and Harvey, 1999) was that in the brain of Albert Einstein the horizontal segment was absent in both hemispheres; the ascending branch of the Sylvian fissure was confluent with the postcentral sulcus. Consistently right-handed females and males did not differ for asymmetry of the horizontal segment, longer on the left in both sexes, in a study by Foundas, Falilhaber, Kulynych et al. (1999).

Sylvian fissure morphology is associated with an asymmetry of the angles formed by the posterior branches of the middle cerebral arteries as they loop over the fissure, wider on the right than the left in most people. The angle of arteries looping over the SF was wider on the right side in right-handed patients but not in left-handed patients (LeMay and Culebras, 1972). This finding was replicated in new data shown in Table 8.3. About two-thirds of right-handers showed the wider angle on the right, but the majority of left-handers were symmetric (Hochberg and LeMay, 1975). It was this asymmetry for the cerebral arteries that was studied by Ratcliff, Dila, Taylor et al. (1980), as described in chapter 4 (see Figure 4.2). For patients with left cerebral speech there was a normal distribution of asymmetry, displaced in the typical direction. For patients with right or bilateral speech there was also a normal distribution but with mean at 0, or no bias to either side. Handedness was also independent (55% right and 45% left) in atypical cases.

There are certain asymmetries of the skull that can be seen in Figure 8.4. The left side tends to be longer and wider in the occipital region, while the right side

Table 8.3 Sylvian point asymmetries in carotid arteriograms: based on Hochberg and LeMay, 1975

	N	R > L (%)	R = L (%)	R < L (%)
Right-handers	106	67	25	8
Left-handers	28	21	72	7

Table 8.4 Asymmetries of the skull: percentages of right-handers and of left-handers showing protrusions of the frontal and occipital bones on each side: based on LeMay, 1977

	Frontal			Occipital		
	R < L	R = L	R > L	R < L	R = L	R > L
Right-handers	14	20	66	77	11	12
Left-handers	36	27	37	36	29	35

is longer in the frontal region. The skull as a whole shows a torque (as if twisted slightly in an anti-clockwise direction). This asymmetry was noted by Clark (1934) but it was not easy to study *in vivo* until the advent of CAT scans. LeMay (1977) found occipital and frontal protrusions distributed as shown in Table 8.4. The typical pattern, protrusions of the right frontal and the left occiput, was present in about two-thirds of right-handers. Left-handers were about equally likely to have either asymmetry. About one-third of left-handers, and a substantial minority of right-handers, were symmetrical. These findings are generally described categorically (left or right larger). They are not discrete, however, but distributed continuously. The distribution for left-handers tends to be centred about 0, while that for right-handers is shifted toward a directional asymmetry. That is, the distributions are consistent with expectations for a population that includes two subgroups, one shifted and one not shifted to the right.

When PT asymmetries are studied *in vivo* by neuroimaging, right-handers tend to have larger PT on the left side, while non-right-handers have reduced asymmetries (Habib, Robichon, Levrier et al., 1995; Jäncke, Schlaug, Huang et al., 1994). Steinmetz, Volkman, Jäncke et al. (1991) found that PT asymmetry varied not only with personal handedness but also with the presence of left-handed relatives; it was largest in right-handers with no first degree left-handed relative and progressively reduced in those with left-handed relatives, left-handers without and then with such relatives. The last group included eight Ps, in whom PT was symmetrical about 0, as expected for a normal distribution without bias to either side (and absence of RS + on the RS theory). There were no statistically significant differences between groups but significant differences should not be expected because the four groups do not represent distinct "types".

For the RS theory, there are no types but chance distributions that are influenced to different extents by a single directional bias. The gradual but orderly trend was just as expected. The data of Habib et al. will be considered in chapter 9.

Are these anatomical asymmetries related to cerebral speech laterality, the assumption motivating their study? Tzourio, Nkanga-Ngila and Mazoyer (1998) examined PT and functional lateralisation, as measured by regional cerebral blood flow (rCBF), in nine right-handed and five left-handed male medical students, while they listened to stories. They found a positive correlation between the surface area of PT on the left side and an increase in rCBF in the left superior temporal gyrus, which they interpreted as a validation of Geschwind's hypothesis that PT asymmetry is associated with speech laterality. However, there was no correlation between PT asymmetry and functional asymmetry for handedness. The direction of PT asymmetry was typical (left side larger) for seven out of nine right-handers and for three out of five left-handers. Considered from the viewpoint of the four atypical cases, two were right- and two were left-handers. The numbers were small, but consistent with random asymmetry for hand preference in the absence of the RS + gene.

The only study of an anatomical asymmetry in a substantial sample of patients, classified for cerebral speech by Wada testing is that of Ratcliff, Dila, Taylor et al. (1980), as mentioned above. These and other findings reviewed here do not suggest that anatomical asymmetries "index" functional asymmetries in the sense that they are associated in the atypical direction. They are consistent with the idea that atypical asymmetries occur at random.

The search for R–L asymmetries in the anterior speech regions, Broca's area, has been less productive than for the posterior regions. Witelson and Kigar (1988) found no differences between the sides for measurements at the cortical surface, but sulci appear to be deeper on the left, suggesting a larger total area on the left than right sides (Falzi, Peronne and Vignolo, 1982). Two regions were distinguished within Broca's area by Brodmann, area 44 (pars opercularis or POP) and area 45 (pars triangularis or PTR). A detailed mapping of the cytoarchitecture of these regions in 10 brains, five males and five females post mortem, found considerable variability for volume and area (Amunts, Schleicher, Burgel et al., 1999). There was a significant bias to L > R for POP but not PTR in this small series.

Foundas, Eure, Luevano et al. (1998) measured the volumes of POP and PTR by functional magnetic resonance imaging in 16 right- and 16 left-handers. Their findings are shown in Table 8.5. There was a significant bias to L > R for PTR over all Ss. This was stronger in right-handers (only 1/16 with R > L) than left-handers (4/16 with R > L) but the directional trend was for the left side to be larger in both groups. For POP, there was no overall bias but an interaction between handedness and hemisphere. Inspection of Table 8.5 shows that 9/16 right-handers were L > R and 8/16 left-handers were R > L, while others were distributed in groups of equal and reverse asymmetry. This result gives the first indication of a possible reversal between right-handers and left-handers for a cortical asymmetry of the speech areas. Replication in a larger sample is needed

Table 8.5 Asymmetry of pars triangularis and pars opercularis of Broca's area: data of Foundas, Eure, Luevano et al., 1998

Group	Pars triangularis			Pars opercularis		
	L > R	L = R	R > L	L > R	L = R	R > L
Right-handers (n = 16)	11	4	1	9	4	3
Left-handers (n = 16)	9	3	4	3	5	8

before accepting this unique result. As a note of caution, it may be pointed out that the proportion of left-handers with atypical (R > L) bias remained 50%, consistent with a chance distribution.

There must be *some* features of cerebral anatomy that are closely associated with functional asymmetries for speech and for handedness. Searches for the cerebral substrate of hand preference in the motor cortex have found asymmetries in the depth of the central sulcus, where possibly relevant areas are larger on the left side than the right (White, Lucas, Richards et al., 1994; Yousry, Schmid, Alkadhi et al., 1997). How does this asymmetry differ between right- and left-handers? Foundas, Hong, Leonard et al. (1998) found a significant leftward asymmetry in right-handers, but no directional asymmetry in left-handers. That is, the results were consistent with those for most of the asymmetries reviewed above, a directional bias in right-handers but reversion to "default" randomness in left-handers. Amunts, Schlaug, Schleicher et al. (1996) compared 31 male right-handers and 14 male left-handers. They found the left central sulcus deeper than the right in right-handers. For left-handers the asymmetry was smaller, but reversed in direction. A subsequent study of 51 males and 52 females, classified for consistent right-, mixed- and consistent left-handedness, found the expected association between sulcal asymmetry and handedness in males, but not in females (Amunts, Jäncke, Mohlberg et al., 2000).

Several studies have compared the activity of the left and right motor cortex, as visualised by neuroimaging, while Ss made repeated movements with either hand. The interpretation of these findings is complicated by the fact that while each hemisphere is responsible for movements of the opposite (contralateral) side of the body, the left hemisphere (dominant in most people) tends to be activated during movements of the *same* (ipsilateral or left) side also. This is not surprising if the "dominant" side of the brain (left for most people) has overall control of the actions of both sides. This pattern of motor cortex activation during finger movements, visualised by MRI, was clear in right-handers, but weaker in left-handers (Kim, Ashe, Hendrich et al., 1993; Singh, Higano, Takahashi et al., 1998). During finger movements of the preferred versus non-preferred hands, right- and left-handers showed predominantly contralateral activation of the hemisphere opposite the preferred hand, but more bilateral activation for the non-preferred hand (Taniguchi, Yoshimine, Cheyne et al.,

1998). Dassonville, Zhu, Ugurbil et al. (1997) found that the ratio of contralateral activation to total activation (contralateral + ipsilateral) was highly correlated with degree of hand preference, as assessed by EHI (r = .694, p = 0.008). The direction of correlation suggested that the stronger the hand preference, the greater the relative contralateral control. A correlation between performance asymmetry on measures of hand skill, and the size of the hand area in the primary motor cortex (r = .76, p < 0.01) was found by Volkmann, Schnitzler, Witte et al. (1998), the greater the relative skill, the larger the area for the hand preferred. The last two studies analysed relationships between laterality variables as appropriate for continuous variables, not typological ones, consistent with the argument of the RS theory that handedness is a continuously distributed variable.

SUMMARY

Asymmetries of brain and behaviour have been reviewed in order to establish the patterns expected in the typical case and then consider what happens in atypical cases. Findings for eye and for foot preference were examined, together with several other observable asymmetries. Both eye and foot preferences are clearly related to hand preference, eye dominance relatively weakly and foot preference relatively strongly. These asymmetries are distributed continuously, but strong left-handers tend to have left eye and left foot preference, reversing the trends for right-handers. These relationships are analysed further in the next chapter.

Asymmetries of perception were reviewed with a view to noting the characteristic patterns in normals, and then asking whether the findings had made a contribution to the understanding of individual differences. The typical finding is a bias to one side in right-handers, that is reduced or absent in non-right-handers. There is no strong evidence for reversals of asymmetry, and all claims to the contrary depend on samples that are too small for confidence. No index of reversed cerebral asymmetry was revealed by these studies.

Functional specialisations of the cerebral hemispheres involve special dependence on the left hemisphere for speech and related language functions, and for the control of voluntary movements. The right hemisphere has special skills in cognitive processes that are independent of verbal control, and generally characterised as visuospatial. The left brain–verbal/right brain–nonverbal dichotomy of popular belief should not be exaggerated. The right hemisphere has considerable word knowledge and is involved in tonal qualities of speech production. The left hemisphere is responsible for coordinated movements in its own half space, as well as overall control of movements by both hands. Individual differences for functional cerebral asymmetries undoubtedly exist, but have not yet been systematically studied in a large neurological series.

Asymmetries of cerebral anatomy have generally been described as discrete variables although it is clear that the underlying distributions are continuous, unimodal and displaced along an underlying continuum in a characteristic direction. Distributions in left-handers resemble those of right-handers, but with reduced directional shift. The assumption that anatomical asymmetries are related to functional asymmetries has received remarkably little direct investigation. The only study of a substantial number of patients with known atypical speech laterality found them at chance for an anatomical asymmetry (Ratcliff, Dila, Taylor et al., 1980). This finding is consistent with predictions of the RS theory if anatomical asymmetries are influenced by the presence of the RS + gene, but independent of speech laterality in its absence. Relationships between handedness and planum temporale asymmetry are examined further in chapter 9.

9 Predicting associations between asymmetries

The previous chapter argued that several types of asymmetry, behavioural, perceptual and anatomical, are distributed in ways consistent with the RS analysis. But is it possible to be more precise, to predict associations between asymmetries? How are hand and eye preferences related, or asymmetries of handedness and cerebral anatomy? The aim of this chapter is to explain a recent discovery, that the joint distribution of certain asymmetries is predictable (Annett, 2000a). For some pairs of asymmetries the distributions are as expected for chance association, plus the influence of the right shift (RS +) gene on each variable independently. For other pairs the joint distributions are consistent with chance plus RS + gene, but with an additional association that I called a "pull to concordance".

The RS theory originated from the observation that some 25–30% of normal Ss are mixed-handers. They prefer to use different hands for the 12 actions of the AHPQ, different hands for actions such as writing and throwing, hammering and cutting with scissors and many more (see chapter 2). Peters (1990) suggested that inconsistent preferences for writing and throwing present a challenge to theories of handedness. A particular difficulty that concerned Peters was that the frequency of the pattern of preference for writing with the left-hand and throwing with the right-hand (LR) is higher than the frequency of the reverse pattern (RL). If atypical asymmetries depend on chance, should not these two patterns of preference be equally frequent? Eye dominance, writing and throwing were examined in a meta-analysis of some 12 studies by McManus, Porac, Bryden et al. (1999). A supposed "awkward" lack of symmetry about chance for writing and throwing was given considerable attention. Is lack of symmetry indeed awkward and was Peters' concern justified? A very large quantity of information is available on writing and throwing because over one million people responded to a questionnaire on smell distributed with the *National Geographic Magazine* that also asked about hand preference for these two actions (Gilbert and Wysocki, 1992). It will be shown below that there is no awkwardness for the RS theory, either in my own data, or in that of the *National Geographic* sample.

WRITING, THROWING AND EYE DOMINANCE IN FOUR OF MY SAMPLES COMBINED

Writing, throwing and eye dominance were assessed by the same methods in four of my samples that can be combined in order to have a substantial data base for examining relationships between the variables. The samples were as follows: 806 Open University (OU) students, aged 24–63 years (Annett, 1979); 426 10- to 11-year-old children in normal schools (Annett, Eglinton and Smythe, 1996); undergraduates, aged 17–53 years (80% 18–22 years), participating in psychology projects over several years at the University of Leicester (samples N = 317 and N = 299 in Annett, 1999b), a total N of 1849. Foot preferences were also observed in all but one of the last samples, giving a total N of 1532, as considered separately below. The numbers of males and females were approximately equal in the OU and school samples; among Leicester students there were about 3 females to 1 male. The sexes are not distinguished in the analyses below because preliminary work found only small and non-significant differences for the relevant variables.

Preferences were recorded for observed actions, either by students working together in practical classes, or by the author and trained assistants. The actions of interest here were to write the name, to throw a small ball into a paper-bin, to kick a small football, and to perform the hole in card test of eye dominance (Appendix I, assessment of eye preference d). "Either" (E) or uncertain preferences were checked by retesting, but if preferences remained undecided, E was recorded. Table 9.1A gives the joint data for writing and throwing, each recorded as R, E or L, for all 1849 participants. The sample can be regarded as representative of the children and students from whom it was drawn because none were omitted, unless there was a physical disability that might have affected performance. Consider first the E responses. Only two (0.1% or approximately 1 per 1000) participants showed that they could write with either hand. Eight-one (4.4%) threw the ball with either hand. What is to be done with these cases? Many investigators would omit them on the grounds they are ambiguous, as in some of the samples combined by McManus, Porac, Bryden et al. (1999). The RS theory demands that all are included because they are part of the normal distribution of asymmetry. In order to simplify analyses, E responses must be combined with responses for either R or L. The decision is arbitrary. Whichever is taken, the threshold will be matched to the observed incidence.

Table 9.1B shows the effect of combining E with R responses (R + E versus L) and converting all numbers to percentages. The percentage of L for writing was 8.4% and for throwing 7.7%. As a proportion of the total sample, left writers who throw right-handed (LR) were 2.3%; right-writers who throw left-handed (RL) were 1.6%. There were more of the former than the latter, as noted by Peters. Table 9.1C shows the effect of the alternative classification (R versus E + L) so that strictly speaking, L now means non-right-handed. There are now 8.5% non-right for writing and 12.1% non-right for throwing. Keeping the L versus R labels for simplicity, the joint frequencies of LR and RL are 1.8% and

Table 9.1 Write and throw: joint distribution of right, either and left responses in four combined samples

	Write			Total
	Right	*Either*	*Left*	
A. *Number*				
Throw				
Right	1592	0	34	1626
Either	70	2	9	81
Left	29	0	113	142
Total	1691	2	156	1849
B. *R + E v L (%)*	*R + E*		*L*	
Throw				
Right + Either	90.0		2.3	92.3
Left	1.6		6.1	7.7
Total	91.6		8.4	100
C. *R v E + L (%)*	*R*		*E + L*	
Throw				
Right	86.1		1.8	87.9
Either + Left	5.4		6.7	12.1
Total	91.5		8.5	100

5.4%. The direction of the awkward asymmetry was reversed. This will be considered further below. With regard to eye dominance, 5 (0.3%) were recorded as E and 33.3% as L. The following analyses are for the R + E versus L classification, but the alternative would give similar results. The peg moving test was given in all four samples and this performance asymmetry was recorded as right minus left percent (R–L% = (R – L)/(R + L) × 100).

Figure 9.1 shows the peg moving means of groups classified for writing, throwing and eye dominance. It gives the numbers of cases for each of the eight patterns (RRR, RRL, RLR etc., writing, throwing and eye dominance) and shows the group mean differences for hand skill (R–L%) with standard errors. All groups of right-writers were to the right (of 0 or no difference) and all left-writers to the left. Left-throwers were less biased to dextrality than right-throwers within each writing group. Within each writing and throwing group, those with left eye preference were less dextral than those with right eye preference. Analysis of variance for peg moving asymmetry, between groups classified for write (2) × throw (2) × eye (2), found effects for each variable. The effects were: writing (F = 169.702, d.f. 1:7, p < 0.001), throwing (F = 24.290, d.f. 1:7, p < 0.001) and eye preference (F = 3.810, d.f. 1:7, p = 0.051). This suggests that each of these asymmetries is related to peg moving, but each to some extent independently of the others.

The RRR group was the most frequent (62.7%) and also the most dextral for skill (R–L% = 4.65). The next most frequent group, RRL (27.3%), was a little less dextral for skill (R–L% = 4.36). The four groups discordant for writing and throwing were small in frequency, and standard errors were therefore relatively

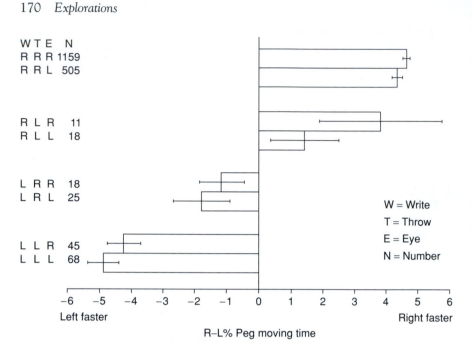

Figure 9.1 Groups classified for right and left preference for writing, throwing and eye dominance showing the frequency and peg moving asymmetry, means and standard errors.

large (but not significantly non-homogeneous). Three groups were close to symmetry for peg moving (RLL, LRR and LRL). The LLL were about as strongly biased to the left for skill (R–L% = −4.85) as the RRR were to the right. The important point about the data in Figure 9.1 is the linear trend of the R–L% means over the eight groups (weighted linear trend, F = 701.99, d.f. 1:7, p < 0.001). This orderly relationship between patterns of preference and R–L% skill suggests that the three variables have similar relationships with hand skill asymmetry, but not identical ones.

PREDICTING THE JOINT DISTRIBUTION OF TWO ASYMMETRIES

Quantitative predictions for pairs of asymmetries depend on mappings between incidences and thresholds for each variable. Any given incidence of left-handedness (or non-right-handedness) implies that a certain percentage of the population has been distinguished to the left of a cut-off point along the baseline of the asymmetry distribution. For any threshold, people to the left include genotypes in particular proportions and people to the right similarly. Look-up tables were provided to facilitate the mapping of incidences to genotype distributions for the genetic calculations (in chapter 7). For the present purpose, when sex is not distinguished, the table required is in Appendix III. The numbers are percentages multiplied by 10, to facilitate calculations by omitting decimals. The genotype frequencies per 1000 population are rounded to 185, 490 and 325 for RS − −, RS + − and RS + + respectively. Incidences at the left of the table are expressed as percentages (e.g. 5%) but at the right as proportions of 1000 (50) so the reader can check that the left-handers in the body of the table sum to this number. For each level of incidence, the numbers of people of each genotype called left or right-handed can be read off and intermediate values interpolated if required. (It should be noted that the genotype frequencies in Appendices III–VI relate incidences to population values. They cannot be applied to samples that were selected for handedness, unless the criteria of selection, such as left-writing or non-right preference, are associated with known incidences in the population from which the sample is drawn.)

The first step for predicting the joint distribution of two variables is to establish the genotype distribution for each one. Table 9.2 lists the numbers per genotype for 8.4% left-writers, 7.7% left-throwers and 33.3% left eye dominants. The 84 left writers include 1 RS + +, 26 RS + − and 57 RS − − genotypes. The 77 left-throwers are 1, 23 and 53 respectively, and similarly the 333 left eye dominant are 22, 170 and 141 respectively. Right-handers make up the genotype totals to 325, 490 and 185 respectively.

The second step is to calculate the chance combinations of right and left preferences for pairs of variables *within each genotype separately*. The RS theory suggests that asymmetry depends on chance plus the influence of the RS + gene.

Table 9.2 Paired associations of writing, throwing and eye dominance: predictions and tests of the RS model (Ns per 1000)

Genotype	Write (8.4%)		Throw (7.7%)		Eye (33.3%)	
	R	L	R	L	R	L
+ +	324	1	324	1	303	22
+ −	464	26	467	23	320	170
− −	128	57	132	53	44	141
		84		77		333

	Write × Eye		Throw × Eye		Write × Throw	
	Pred.	Obs.	Pred.	Obs.	Pred.	Obs.
RR	635	633	638	637	856	900
LR	32	34	29	30	67	23
RL	281	283	285	287	60	16
LL	52	50	48	46	17	61
Chi-square	0.222 d.f. 1, ns		0.133, d.f. 1, ns		117.36, d.f. 1, p < 0.001	

Table 9.3 Eye dominance with writing: example calculations for the joint distribution

	Write		Total
	R	L	

A. *Chance pairing of R and L for two variables, within each genotype separately*
i. RS + +

Eye	324	1	325
R	303 | 302	1	
L	22 | 22	0	

ii. RS + −

Eye	464	26	490
R	320 | 303	17	
L	170 | 161	9	

iii. RS − −

Eye	128	57	185
R	44 | 30	14	
L	141 | 98	43	

B. *Predicted pairings in total sample*

R	635	32	
L	281	52	333
		84	1000

C. *Observed pairings in total sample*

R	633	34	
L	283	50	333
		84	1000

Chi-square = 0.222, d.f. 1, ns

Within each genotype the latter is constant, so combinations depend on chance alone (as for MZ twin pairs, see Table 7.8). The calculations for predicting combinations of preferences for writing and eye dominance are given as a worked example in Table 9.3. The RS + + genotype includes 325 people of whom 324 are right and 1 left-handed for writing while 303 are right and 22 left eye dominant. Chance association would give 302 people RR for both variables ($324 \times 303/325 = 302$), 1 who is LR ($1 \times 303/325 = 1$), and similarly 22 RL, and 0 LL. The 490 people of RS + − genotype combine by chance to give 303, 17, 161 and 9 RR, LR, RL and LL pairs respectively. The 185 of RS − − genotype pair at random to give 30, 14, 98 and 43 respectively.

The third step is to sum the chance pairings for the three genotypes to find the predicted totals, 635, 32, 281 and 52. The observed values were 633, 34, 283 and 50 respectively. The fit was almost perfect; chi-square = 0.221, d.f. = 1, ns. (Where actual Ns exceed 1000, as here, the chi-square tests are based on the numbers predicted and found per 1000, for simplicity of exposition. Tests based on actual numbers must translate the predicted proportions into predicted numbers. For example, for write × eye, the predicted RR would be 1849 × 0.635 = 1174; 1170 were observed. A test of fit based on the actual numbers gives chi-square = 0.384, d.f. = 1, ns. When sample Ns are smaller than 1000 below, tests are for actual numbers.)

Predicted pairings for eye preference and throwing laterality were calculated as above. The predicted combinations (throw, eye) per 1000 were RR 638, LR 29, RL 285 and LL 48 and those observed were 637, 30, 287 and 46 respectively, as shown in Table 9.2. The match was again almost perfect (chi-square = 0.133, d.f. 1, ns). The third analysis in Table 9.2 for writing and throwing was very different. The predictions did not match observations (chi-square = 117.36. d.f. 1, p < 0.001). The discordant cases observed (LR 23 and RL 16) were fewer than predicted (67 and 60 respectively). Before examining this poor fit, we should note some good fits for handedness and two cerebral asymmetries.

HANDEDNESS AND CEREBRAL ANATOMY

The joint distributions of asymmetries of cerebral anatomy and handedness can be examined as above when samples are drawn at random with respect to these variables. I am aware of only one study that recruited normal volunteers irrespective of handedness, for a study of cerebral asymmetries by MRI scans (Habib, Robichon, Levrier et al., 1995). The important point for the present analysis is that the 40 participants were unselected for both of the variables of interest, handedness and cerebral anatomy. Handedness was classified by a laterality quotient, based on the French version of the EHI, using a criterion that identified 40% as non-right-handers. The planum temporale (PT) was larger on the left in 63% and equal or right larger in 37%, as found for the 100 brains studied post mortem by Galaburda, Corsiglia, Rosen et al. (1987). Habib et al. also measured the width of the parietal operculum (SR), from the end point of the Sylvian (lateral) fissure to that of Rolando (or central fissure). SR was larger on the left in 70%, and 30%, therefore, could be described as atypical. What are the expected combinations of these cerebral asymmetries, and each with handedness, if pairings depend on chance plus the influence of the RS + gene?

Table 9.4 summarises the relevant distributions for the three variables, taken from Figure 5 of Habib, Robichon, Levrier et al. (1995). When there are 40% non-right-handers, the 400 per 1000 include 33, 214 and 153 for the + +, + − and − − genotypes respectively (from Appendix III). For 37% (370) with atypical PT, there are 28, 194 and 148 respectively. Chance combinations of typical (T) and atypical (A) handedness and PT asymmetry within genotypes (calculated as in Table 9.3) give predictions for the total sample (hand, PT) as follows: TT 440, AT 190, TA 160 and AA 210. The predicted actual numbers are found by multiplying N (40) by the proportions per 1000 (e.g. 40 × 0.440 = 17.6).

Table 9.4 Handedness and asymmetries of cerebral anatomy for predicted and observed pairs: data of Habib, Robichon, Levrier et al., 1995

Genotype	Non-right-hand (40%)		Atypical PT (37%)		Atypical SR (30%)	
	R	L	T	A	T	A
+ +	292	33	297	28	308	17
+ −	276	214	296	194	341	149
− −	32	153	37	148	51	134
Total		400		370		300

	Hand × PT			PT × SR			Hand × SR		
	Pred.	Pre. N	Obs. N	Pred.	Pre. N	Obs. N	Pred.	Pre. N	Obs. N
TT	440	17.6	19	510	20.4	19	478	19.1	19
AT	190	7.6	6	140	5.6	6	222	8.9	9
TA	160	6.4	5	190	7.6	9	122	4.9	5
AA	210	8.4	10	160	6.4	6	178	7.1	7
Chi-square	1.059, d.f. 1, ns			0.408, d.f. 1, ns			0.007, d.f. 1, ns		

These were TT 17.6, AT 7.6, TA 6.4 and AA 8.4. The observed Ns were 19, 6, 5 and 10 respectively. The fit was good (chi-square = 1.059, d.f. 1, ns).

How do the two cerebral asymmetries PT (37%) and SR (30%) go together? Table 9.4 sets out the predictions 20.4, 5.6, 7.6 and 6.4 for TT, AT, TA and AA respectively. The observed Ns were 19, 6, 9 and 6 (chi-square = 0.408, d.f. 1, ns). Table 9.4 also shows the predictions for non-right-handedness with SR asymmetry as 19.1, 8.9, 4.9 and 7.1; the observed values were virtually identical (chi-square = 0.007, d.f. 1, ns). The pair-wise combinations of these three asymmetries were as expected if they combined at random, except for the common influence of the RS + gene.

WRITING AND THROWING IN MY SAMPLES AND IN THE *NATIONAL GEOGRAPHIC* DATA

For writing and throwing there were more concordant and fewer discordant pairings than expected, as said above. By how much did the observed and predicted values differ? Table 9.2 showed that for LR (writing, throwing), there were 67 predicted and 23 observed, a ratio of 67:23, or 2.9:1. For RL the ratio was 60:16, or 3.7:1. For LL, the ratio was 17:61, or 1:3.6. The difference between observed and predicted values for these three atypical asymmetries averaged 3.42:1. That is, the mismatch was by about one-third. This regularity suggests a possible rule. Could there be a "pull to concordance" such that one-third of LR

Table 9.5 Writing and throwing: the hypothesis of a one-third "pull to concordance" in MA and *National Geographic* samples (Ns per 1000)

	MA samples (Percent total)		National Geographic sample (Mean percent over sex and age)	
Left writing	8.4		8.5	
Left throwing	7.7		7.7	

Write × Throw

	MA samples		National Geographic samples	
	Pred.	Obs.	Pred.	Obs.
RR	856	900	856	896
LR	67	23	67	27
RL	60	16	60	19
LL	17	61	17	58

Predictions if 1/3 of LR and 1/3 of RL go to RR and similarly to LL

	RR	RL
RR = 856 + 22 + 20	= 898	898
LR = 67/3	= 22	22
RL = 60/3	= 20	20
LL = 17 + 22 + 20	= 59	59
Chi-square	0.917 d.f. 1, ns	1.221, d.f. 1, ns

pairs and one-third of RL pairs (as predicted by chance plus RS + gene) are drawn toward RR, one-third toward LL, and one-third remain discordant? The results of this adjustment are set out in Table 9.5. LR becomes 67/3 = 22; RL becomes 60/3 = 20; LL becomes 17 + 20 + 22 = 59 and RR becomes 856 + 20 + 22 = 898. The predicted and observed Ns now agree well (chi-square = 0.913, d.f. 1, ns). This manipulation was suggested by these particular data. Is there evidence for a pull to concordance by about one-third for writing and throwing in other data?

A questionnaire distributed with the *National Geographic Magazine* in September 1986 included questions on the hand used for writing and for throwing; the responses of more than a million respondents, age from 10 years to 86 years, were described by Gilbert and Wysocki (1992, hereafter GW). There are several ways in which findings from such a survey may not be representative of the general population but the intriguing findings in my samples described above led to the question whether they might be replicated in the GW data. GW listed the numbers of respondents showing the four patterns of preference (LL, LR, RL and RR, write, throw) for each sex and year group from 10 to 86 years (154 groups). My procedure was to derive the relevant percentages for each age and sex group separately and then average the percentages. (Because there were more females than males and because the Ns per group ranged from some 300 to 18,000, calculations based on the raw Ns would be unbalanced for both sex and age. The mean percentages over sex and age, however, are more representative overall.) These are listed in Table 9.5 along with the corresponding percentages for my samples. The first surprise about the GW data was that incidences for the total sample were virtually identical with those of my combined samples, as described above (8.437% MA versus 8.457% GW for writing and 7.680% MA versus 7.741% GW for throwing). Was the joint distribution of writing and throwing also similar? Table 9.5 gives the proportions, expressed per 1000, alongside those for my samples. Because incidences were the same in the two samples, the predicted joint distributions were the same, and also the predictions for the one-third rule. The GW findings fitted the predictions well (chi-square = 1.221, d.f. 1, ns.). This close similarity between two large samples gives confidence in both, and confidence in the "one-third" rule for both.

Does the RS model expect the proportions of LR and RL writers and throwers (or any other pair of discordant asymmetries) to be equal? No, because the relative proportions of LR and RL depend on the relative proportion of left-writers and of left-throwers in the sample. In the MA and GW data, there were more left-writers (8.4%) than left-throwers (7.7%). Since RR and LL are necessarily the same, there must be more LR than RL. It was shown in Table 9.1 that changing the classification of E responses from R to L in my samples changed the relative frequencies of left-writers and -throwers. For 8.5% and 12.1% *non-right-handed* writers and throwers, there were fewer LR (1.8%) than RL (5.4%). The direction of inequality was reversed.

The relative frequencies of writing and throwing differed with age in the GW data. For example, in 20- to 39-year-olds there were more left-writers (11.8%) than left-throwers (8.9%); in 60- to 79-year-olds, left-throwers (6.3%) exceeded left-writers (4.3%); in 57-year-olds the percentages of left-writers (8.0%) and left-throwers (7.95%) were equal. Table 9.6 sets out the percentages and predictions for the joint distributions, and then predictions adjusted by the "one-third" rule for the three age groups. Note first that the specific predictions and observations were very different between groups. However, in all three analyses the "one-third" rule predicted the proportions of both RR and LL. For the younger GW sample, there were more LR than RL predicted (31 and 21 respectively) but the observed inequality was even greater (41 and 11). The poor fit (chi-square = 7.999, d.f. 1, p < 0.005) was almost entirely due to the LR and RL groups. For the older GW sample, fewer LR than RL were predicted (12 and 18 respectively) and the observed inequality was again greater than predicted (10 and 30). The significant chi-square (p < 0.005) depended almost entirely on the RL group. For 57-year-olds, whose incidences for writing and throwing were the same, LR and RL should be equal. The prediction, after application of the "one-third" rule was 21 for both. This was found. The match to prediction was perfect for all four values. This excellent fit for the 57-year-olds was based on 14,776 questionnaires, not a trivial data base for this test of the model.

Table 9.6 Writing and throwing in three age groups of the *National Geographic* sample (Ns per 1000)

	20–39 years	60–79 years	57 years
Left-writers (%)	11.8	4.3	8.00
Left-throwers (%)	8.9	6.3	7.95

Write × Throw

	20–39 years		60–79 years		57 years	
	Pred.	Obs.	Pred.	Obs.	Pred.	Obs.
RR	819	870	902	927	857	899
LR	92	41	35	10	63	21
RL	63	11	55	30	63	21
LL	26	78	8	33	17	59

Predictions with 1/3 rule

	20–39 years		60–79 years		57 years	
	Pred.	Chi sq.	Pred.	Chi sq.	Pred.	Chi sq.
RR = 819 + 31 + 21	= 871	0.011	932	0.027	899	0
LR = 92/3	= 31	3.23	12	0.33	21	0
RL = 63/3	= 21	4.76	18	7.48	21	0
LL = 26 + 31 + 21	= 78	0.00	38	0.66	59	0
Chi-square	7.999, d.f. 1, p < 0.005		8.497, d.f. 1, p < 0.005		Perfect fit	

FOOT, EYE AND HAND PREFERENCES

Preference for kicking was recorded in the MA samples for N = 1532, as mentioned above. Preference for the left foot (when E was counted with R) was 11.03%. How does footedness associate with other preferences? Eye and foot preferences combined as expected by chance plus the RS + gene (calculated as in Table 9.3). The comparison of observed with predicted frequencies gave chi-square = 2.122, d.f. 1, ns. Thus eye dominance associated with foot preference in the same way that it did with writing and with throwing. No additional concordance was evident.

Preferences for kicking and writing hand were more strongly associated. The predicted combinations were RR (write, foot) 836, LR 54, RL 88 and LL 22, while the observed values were 858, 31, 59 and 52, respectively. There were more concordant and fewer discordant pairs than predicted as found above for writing and throwing. Some "pull to concordance" appeared to be operating, but not as strongly as the one-third rule for writing and throwing. The observed data were fitted well by the hypothesis that one-fifth of LR and one-fifth of RL pairs become RR and similarly LL, while the other three-fifths remain discordant (chi-square = 0.787, d.f. 1, ns). Because this adjustment was deduced from a single set of data, it was important to check its reliability. This was done by splitting the samples into two subgroups, the schoolchildren plus Leicester students (N = 726) versus the OU students (N = 806). The predictions for the "one-fifth" rule were examined for each subgroup separately. For the first group, the match between observations and predictions, adjusted by the "one-fifth" rule gave chi-square = 1.442, d.f. 1, ns, and for the second group, chi-square = 2.560. d.f. 1, ns (chi-squares based on actual Ns). Hence the "one-fifth" rule for writing and kicking can be taken to be reliable.

IMPLICATIONS FOR RELATIONSHIPS BETWEEN PAIRS OF ASYMMETRIES

This application of the RS theory to the problem of predicting the joint distribution of lateral asymmetries led to two important findings. First, for some pairs of asymmetries the association was predictable by the rules of chance, plus the influence of the RS + gene on each variable independently. Second, for other pairs of asymmetries the joint distribution was more concordant than expected by the above rules. The first group of associations included all variables paired with eye dominance and those between PT, SR and handedness. The second group included writing with throwing, and writing with foot preference.

Eye dominance was shown to be predictable in families (in chapter 7) and predictably associated with other asymmetries in this chapter. The success of these predictions implies that there are similar mappings between thresholds and genotypes for eye dominance and handedness, as said above. The incidence found here in the combined MA samples (33.3%) is almost identical to an estimate (33.2%) derived from a meta-analysis of some 43 samples (Bourassa, McManus and Bryden, 1996). This incidence implies a threshold about 0.7z to the right of the RS − − mean, in the region for non-right-handedness. However, eye dominance is not a simple binary (right or left) variable because, as mentioned above, some people have mixed eye preference, just as some are mixed-handers. Variability for eye preference has not been fully investigated. I would expect associations between hand and eye dominance to be predictable, whether strict criteria were adopted or generous ones, for either variable. In other words, they are likely to follow expectations for a threshold model of eye dominance, as they do for a threshold model of handedness.

The predictions for eye dominance with other asymmetries involved no extra pull-to-concordance, but simply chance plus the influence of the RS + gene on each variable separately. This implies that although different asymmetries have different thresholds of expression (different cut-offs on the underlying continuum) and although influenced by the RS + gene to a common extent (because the same genotype shifts apply to each one), chance affects each variable independently. That is, the effects of buffeting along the developmental path (see Figure 3.9) that influence eye preference are independent of those that influence writing, throwing and kicking. None of these variables can be interpreted as an *index* of the other. Their mutual association depends on the common influence of the RS + gene, and when the gene is absent there is no association.

Similarly, relationships between handedness and the anatomical asymmetries of PT and SR require no mutual association beyond the common influence of the RS + gene. This result is surprising in the light of the idea that these anatomical asymmetries might "index" CD. They are associated with CD in the sense that they are influenced by a gene that induces typical CD, but in the absence of that gene, there is no reason to suppose any instrinsic relation between these anatomical and the functional asymmetries. Atypical anatomy does not index a reversal of CD, nor atypical CD a reversal of anatomical bias. The findings are consistent with those of Ratcliff et al. (see Figure 4.2) for an anatomical asymmetry with patients with atypical CD. They imply lack of directional bias. Habib, Robichon, Levrier et al. (1995) noted that right-handedness was likely when both PT and SR were biased in the typical direction, but right- and non-right-handers were about equally likely for the several patterns of atypical asymmetry. Beaton's (1997) review of PT and other asymmetries found that although there were consistent trends for typical cases, atypical cases tended to assort by chance. If PT, SR and handedness are influenced by the RS + gene independently, none of these "index" one another. None is likely to be an index of CD.

Turning now to pairs of asymmetries with "extra" concordance (writing with throwing and with foot preference), it must be asked what kind of additional influence might be at work. The simplest possibility, in my view, is that the chance accidents of development that lateralise the skills involved in writing also influence the skills involved in throwing or kicking. That is, there are likely to be shared components in sensorimotor control systems. The relevant components lateralise by the rules above, but the shared components enhance concordance (both RR and LL) between pairs of asymmetries that would otherwise segregate independently. Note that in adjusting predicted frequencies to match observed frequencies above, the *proportions* moved from LR to RR and LL, and from RL to RR and LL were always kept constant (one-third for throwing and one-fifth for kicking). This was because the probability of shared components would depend on factors that are likely to be constant. Writing, throwing and kicking all depend on the motor cortex, but anatomically and functionally throwing is closer to writing than is kicking.

The "one-third" and "one-fifth" rules were checked by looking for replication. This was found for writing and kicking in two subgroups of the MA samples and for writing and throwing in several analyses of the GW data. The joint distribution over all of the GW groups matched the MA combined samples almost exactly, a surprising agreement in view of the different ways the two sets of data were collected. However, it may be noted that the MA combined samples included a wide age range, as did the GW sample. The "one-third" rule fitted the GW data well. For 57-year-olds, the year group with equal percentages for writing and throwing, the match between observed and predicted values, adjusted by the "one-third" rule, was perfect. For younger and older adults, application of the "one-third" rule gave good fits to RR and LL but the inequalities of LR and RL were even greater than predicted by the model and the "one-third" rule. The younger and older participants in the GW sample were likely to have experienced very different cultural pressures on the expression of left-handedness for writing. Further, GW commented that RL was twice as common among Asians than other groups. Pressures against left writing tend to be stronger in Asian than Western communities.

The "one-third" and "one-fifth" rules were found reliable for their respective pairs of asymmetries. These findings open up new questions for research. What other pairs of asymmetries are independent, apart from the common influence of the RS + gene? What pairs are more strongly associated and might be inferred, therefore, to share components? It was surprising to find that the anatomical asymmetries of PT and SR were associated with each other and with handedness in ways that suggest that all are influenced by the RS + gene but not otherwise associated. If the RS + gene is "for" left hemisphere specialisation, PT is not more closely linked with speech lateralisation than several other asymmetries, including handedness. None of these asymmetries is an index of the other. The findings are consistent with the conclusion that there is no direct association between PT and CD (see review of Beaton, 1997). The finding that 94% of 18 chimpanzee brains were larger on the left than right for PT (Gannon, Holloway, Broadfield et al., 1998) is a little easier to accept if PT is not directly related to cerebral speech in humans, but it remains puzzling why chimpanzees appear to be more asymmetrical than humans in this respect. When strong associations are claimed between laterality variables, as for handedness and POP (see Table 8.5), an important question is whether there is evidence of shared components, as inferred from the additional concordance of writing with throwing and writing with kicking above.

Do inequalities of LR and RL pose a problem for theories of handedness because they "ought to be" equal, or symmetrical about chance (McManus, Porac, Bryden et al., 1999; Peters, 1990)? How do these inequalities arise? The RS analysis suggests there is no mystery about the unequal prevalence of LR and RL. It follows directly from the relative frequencies of the two variables in the sample. Frequency depends on factors that influence the threshold of expression (culture, tests and criteria of classification, mentioned above). A simple re-assignment of E responses from R to L was sufficient to reverse a small excess of LR over RL to a large excess of RL over LR (see Table 9.1). In conclusion, inequalities between LR and RL are probably due to several different influences on the expression and assessment of hand preferences. For a threshold model of lateral asymmetry (as developed in chapters 2 and 3) these are practical matters of assessment. They are without serious theoretical significance. They present difficulties only to those who regard left- and right-handedness as discrete fixed types.

SUMMARY

This chapter has shown how to calculate the joint occurrence of pairs of asymmetries. The first requirement is estimates of incidence that are population representative. Incidences can then be mapped to thresholds along the R–L continuum and thence to genotype. Look-up tables in Appendices III and IV show this mapping for incidences from 1 to 40%. Predictions for the frequencies of combinations of variables in pairs (RR, RL etc.) depend on random combinations of preferences within each genotype. Summing over genotypes then gives the population frequency. For many pairs of variables, including eye dominance with all other variables considered (writing, throwing and footedness), and also the anatomical asymmetries of PT and SR with handedness, combinations were as expected if each variable is influenced by the RS + gene, but that otherwise lateralities associate at random. For some pairs of variables, writing and throwing, and writing and kicking, associations were more concordant than predicted by the simple rules of chance plus RS + gene. The extra association is likely to be due to shared components in the physical systems underlying the relevant actions. The estimated "pull to concordance" was stronger between writing and throwing than between writing and kicking, consistent with the idea that the former are closer functionally and anatomically than the latter.

Analyses for writing and throwing in my combined samples were checked against data for over a million respondents to a *National Geographic Magazine* questionnaire. There was a surprising similarity between the two sets of data. Incidences were almost identical, and consequently predictions were the same. The rule for one-third pull to concordance fitted both sets of data equally well. The relative frequencies of discordant pairs (LR versus RL) were shown in my samples to be sensitive to small changes in criteria of classification (E responses combined either with R or with L). The relative frequencies differed in the *National Geographic* data with age, because the relative frequencies of left writing and left throwing changed with age. For the age group where the incidences matched (about 8% for both variables in 57-year-olds), LR should equal RL. Identical proportions were found (2.1%) and both were exactly as expected by the "one-third" rule. Hence, the discordance of LR and RL in some samples presents no problem to the RS theory because it depends on specific influences on the expression and measurement of laterality in those samples. These concern practicalities of assessment, not fundamentals of theory.

To summarise, the analysis of the problem of variable incidences of handedness (chapter 2) led to the surprising discovery that the RS model can predict relationships between pairs of asymmetries quantitatively. The mapping between incidences, thresholds and genotypes depended on an analysis of atypical cerebral speech (chapter 4), the single gene theory of RS (chapter 5) and the further development of an additive model for handedness (in chapter 7). These linkages imply that the placement of the RS jigsaw puzzle pieces is firm and interlocked. But what does the new picture emerging from this pattern suggest? It leads on to new questions about the evolutionary mechanisms that might have produced these relationships. How did the system arise, and does it have implications for modern human learning and behaviour? The hypothesis of a balanced polymorphism for patterns of cerebral dominance is examined in the next five chapters.

Part IV

A genetic balanced polymorphism with heterozygote advantage

10 Why right shift and why genetic variability?

The advantages and disadvantages of the RS + gene

The research outlined so far began with the puzzle of relationships between handedness and cerebral speech laterality. Distributions of hand preference and hand skill led to the idea that the only thing that is special about human handedness, in comparison with other species, is that a universal chance distribution of asymmetry is displaced in humans in a dextral direction. This theory led to several useful and surprising discoveries. First, if the agent of displacement is a cerebral asymmetry that normally leads to left CD but is absent in some people, then relations between handedness and left versus right CD are predictable from the model. Second, if this agent is a single gene (RS +) with alternative alleles at the same locus (RS −) neutral for laterality, then findings for handedness in families are predictable. The model was strengthened by the fact that gene and genotype frequencies were deduced from the percentages of patients with typical versus atypical CD, not from the genetic data. The theory led to further productive findings, including differences in gene expression between the sexes and between twins and the singleborn, the predictability of eye dominance in families, and the predictability of right and left pairings between different asymmetries (as outlined in chapters 6–9). It cannot be doubted that the RS genetic model offers solutions to several problems. However, solutions to one set of problems often lead to the challenges of new problems. The gene and genotype frequencies deduced above pose a very profound puzzle. Why is the frequency of the RS + gene only 0.57, while 0.43 alleles remain neutral for laterality?

If the RS + gene were an unqualified "good" for humans, it should have spread throughout the population until everyone enjoyed its benefits. The fact that this has not happened suggests that there are costs for gene-carriers that have limited its spread. The most frequent genotype is the heterozygote (RS + −, 49%), about as high as possible (50%) for a single heterozygote at a single locus. Both homozygotes (RS − −, 19% and RS + +, 32%) are substantial. The genotype frequencies could be associated with a balanced polymorphism with heterozygote advantage (BP + HA). The classic example of a BP + HA is sickle cell anaemia, a condition found in regions where malaria is prevalent. A sickle-shaped deformation of blood cells carrying haemoglobin gives some protection from the parasites that carry malaria. Heterozygote carriers of the sickle gene have a reproductive advantage over homozygotes for the normal cell, but homozygotes for the sickle form are liable to be seriously anaemic. Sickle genes are lost from the population but the reproductive advantage for heterozygotes maintained the gene in populations exposed to malaria. A BP + HA for the RS + gene would imply a similar balance of advantages and disadvantages.

The idea of a genetic polymorphism associated with left-handedness is not new. Evidence that left-handers have been present as a small but stable minority since prehistoric times suggests there are advantages associated with sinistrality. The advantage could be with left-handers themselves, or it might be with some feature of the wider population that depends on the persistence of left-handers. The RS theory suggests that the relevant gene is for CD, not handedness. The three genotypes of the RS locus represent three patterns of hemisphere special-isation, a bias for left CD that is either absent (in RS − − genotypes), moderate (RS + − genotypes) or strong (RS + + genotypes). Until the relevant genes are identified, their influence on reproductive success cannot be investigated directly. However, a BP + HA for CD is likely to be expressed through indi-vidual differences for psychological variables, speech, motor skills, cognitive and social behaviours. Maynard-Smith and Szathmáry (1995, p. 252) made the key point when they wrote, "One should . . . ponder the biological significance of the phrase 'chatting up'." In a similar vein, I have used the term "sweet talk". Differences in reproductive success in humans must depend at least in part on psychological qualities associated with a smooth tongue. A medieval knight was judged by his skills in verse as well as jousting. Human evolutionary success has depended on a combination of verbal skills and practical skills for tool making and tool using. Could the need to balance these two aspects of human ability explain the genetic variability at the RS locus?

A search for evidence relevant to a BP + HA for the RS + gene has been the main focus of my research for over 20 years. The diversity of human skills and the improbability that any one individual could be good at everything makes it reasonable to suggest that different genotypes, for different patterns of CD, are associated with various strengths and weaknesses that complement and bal-ance one another in the population as a whole. It is important to avoid certain prejudices that usually surface in discussions about genes and behaviour. The genotypes under consideration here are likely to be present in every family and every social group. They could not stratify in society. A glance at the principles of genetic assortment confirms that the optimal combination of RS + and RS − alleles would depend on inter-mating of all three genotypes. The most successful matings for producing heterozygote children would be between the two homozygotes (RS − − × RS + + parents) because *all of the children* would be heterozygote. By contrast, the mating of two heterozygotes (RS + − × RS + − parents) would produce children with genotypes in the classic proportions de-duced by Mendel for heterozygote crosses (RS − − 25%, RS + − 50%, RS + + 25%). Half of these children would *not* carry the most advantageous genotype.

People take up different roles within families and groups, depending on their particular interests and expertise. Fortey (1997/1998, pp. 3–4) described the roles that emerge in a group of scientists sharing the hardships of a field expedition, leader, practical man, chef, joker and so on. Similar roles are likely to emerge in any relatively stable group. They certainly did in the extended family of my childhood. It is the different talents which people bring to the group that are advantageous to all. If a BP + HA for the RS + gene has a social message, it would be that we should not tamper with nature's balance but rather respect the different sorts of talents that humans bring to the common endeavour. But before indulging in such speculations, we must find evidence for the hypothesised BP + HA. The hypothesis requires an impartial examination of many kinds of evidence. It represents a new approach to the psychology of individual differences. Much of this new field needed exploring from scratch. I do not claim to have all the answers or to be correct in all surmises (Annett, 1993c). However, the BP + HA hypothesis offers solutions to several puzzles about laterality and abilities, as outlined in this and following chapters.

What are the main questions? The two fundamental questions are first, what is the evolutionary *advantage* of the RS + gene and second, what is its *disadvantage*? From the beginning (Annett, 1972) it was obvious that a factor that induced RS for handedness was likely to be a factor for left hemisphere speech. If some people lacked the factor, they might be at risk for speech and language development. Such people would also be less strongly biased to right-handedness, like the "motor-intergrades" described by Orton (1937) among people with developmental problems of speech and reading. The RS approach seemed likely to throw light on long-standing controversies about handedness and dyslexia and indeed it does (see chapter 13). But what could be the *disadvantage* associated with the RS + gene? The idea of costs for human CD was unprecedented. Annett (1978b, p. 18) surmised there could be, "an over-commitment of cognitive capacities to language skills at the expense of those other skills on which human evolution depended, the manufacture and use of tools. The heterozygote and neutral homozygote (RS – – genotype) probably have advantages in skilled performance (as in famous left-handers such as Michaelangelo, Leonardo Da Vinci, Charlie Chaplin and Jimmy Connors) which far outweigh the advantages of ready speech in the dominant homozygote." The rest of this chapter examines evidence for the overall thesis that the advantage of the RS + gene is for speech, and its disadvantage is for performance skills, especially those depending on the right hemisphere.

THE ADVANTAGE OF RS + FOR SPEECH LEARNING

Popular culture now takes for granted that there are complementary roles for the left and right cerebral hemispheres, the left "verbal" and the right "nonverbal" and the contrast between the hemispheres has been attributed to many dualities such as analytic versus holistic, rational versus emotional, as considered in chapter 8. These are at best rough simplifications of the roles of the cerebral hemispheres in the "typical" brain. The question of interest here is how and why people *differ* for patterns of CD. Why are some people atypical for cerebral specialisation and does it matter? We need to discover the essence of the advantage conferred by left hemisphere specialisation. There is a potential minefield of issues here about the "why", the "how" and the "what for" of cerebral asymmetry. The argument that CD is primarily an aid to speech acquisition depends on three main sources of evidence, first research on children with hemiplegic cerebral palsy, second on certain findings for split-brain patients, and third findings from direct stimulation mapping of the cerebral cortex.

Children who suffer early damage to one side of the brain learn to talk, whether the left or right hemisphere is affected, although adults suffering strokes may show only limited recovery from a left hemisphere lesion. But do children with early unilateral brain lesions learn to speak with equal speed and efficiency when lesions are left-sided or right-sided (giving right or left hemiplegias respectively)? I spent some years personally examining all children diagnosed as hemiplegic at four paediatric centres in Yorkshire, UK (Annett, 1973b). I expected that careful testing of a population sample would reveal differences in verbal and nonverbal intelligence, reading and spatial perception. Levels of physical impairment of the hands were assessed by a peg moving task (see Figure 3.1) that was specifically designed for this research. Performance times were compared with norms established in schoolchildren. The peg moving task revealed that 39% of the children diagnosed as hemiplegic were in fact disabled in both hands. When equated for disability, there were no differences for intelligence between right and left-sided cases.

Table 10.1 shows the children classified for impairment of the better hand in three groups, none, mild-to-moderate and severe. When the better hand was

Table 10.1 Verbal IQ and verbal minus performance IQ in children with right and left hemiplegias, classified for three grades of peg moving by the better hand

Better hand	Hemiplegia	N	Affected hand (Z score) Mean (S.D.)	Better hand (standardised score) Mean (S.D.)	Verbal WISC IQ Mean (S.D.)	Verbal minus performance IQ Mean (S.D.)
Normal						
Within 2 S.D.s	Right	36	26.0	96.4	88.1	−2.6
of normal mean			(27.2)	(12.9)	(17.7)	(12.5)
	Left	29	26.7	91.0	88.0	−2.8
			(28.7)	(13.2)	(16.3)	(10.9)
Slightly impaired						
Between 2.0	Right	16	51.2	45.9	70.9	7.6
and 6.7 S.D.s			(37.5)	(20.8)	(19.5)	(16.4)
below the	Left	12	46.5	49.7	74.1	7.3
normal mean			(34.5)	(16.4)	(14.0)	(13.4)
Severely impaired						
More than 6.7	Right	7	73.1	< 1	49.7	1.7
S.D.s below the			(37.6)		(9.2)	(7.8)
normal mean	Left	6	76.9	< 1	57.5	5.8
			(36.2)		(9.9)	(8.3)

normal (suggesting that the brain damage was indeed restricted to one side) the mean verbal IQ of 36 children with left-sided lesions was 88.1; for 29 children with right-sided lesions it was 88.0. The groups were virtually identical for performance scale IQ also. This remarkable similarity was not anticipated but rather contrary to my expectations. Children with mild-to-moderate impairment of the better hand had lower IQs, bordering on mental handicap. This fall was particularly large for performance scale IQ, suggesting that nonverbal skills might be especially sensitive to bilateral lesions. The children with severe impairment of the better hand were likely to be seriously learning disabled.

Other comparisons of children with right and left hemiplegias have also found no significant differences for intelligence (Cruikshank and Raus, 1955; Hammil and Irwin, 1966; Perlstein and Hood, 1957; Reed and Reitan, 1969). In spite of the traditional view that the left hemisphere is "dominant" or "leading" and the right hemisphere "non-dominant" or "subordinate", no differences have been detected in their capacities to support intelligence, as measured by psychological tests. The evidence suggests that the hemispheres have equivalent capacities for language and intelligence.

There was only one statistically significant difference between left and right-sided cases, a history of speech problems. Children with right hemiplegias (left brain damage) were delayed in learning to talk or experienced problems of articulation significantly more often than children with left hemiplegias. Among children with normal better hand speed, 39% of left lesion and 7% of right lesion cases had a history of speech problems. These findings suggested that although the two half-brains are equally capable of serving verbal intelligence, the left has some special role in facilitating *speech learning*. Most of the speech difficulties had cleared at the time of testing, suggesting that the left hemisphere advantage affected early stages of speech acquisition but was not persistent. Other studies of speech disorders in childhood hemiplegia found similar differences between left and right-sided cases. Dennis and Whitaker (1977) reviewed nine studies in the 19th century and five in the 20th century. There were small but statistically significant increases in the frequency of speech disorders in children with lesions of the left in comparison with the right hemisphere. Thus, the left hemisphere appears to have an advantage over the right in readiness to serve speech.

The contrary view, that the hemispheres are fully equipotential at birth (Lenneberg, 1967) dominated the literature for many years. This view relied heavily on a survey of brain-damaged children seen at the National Hospital for Nervous Diseases, London, some treated by removal of the affected hemisphere, hemispherectomy. A review of hospital case records found no evidence of differences for speech between right and left-sided cases (Basser, 1962). This was a series of severely handicapped children, not likely to be representative of the majority of children with early unilateral lesions. Hécaen (1983) re-appraised his cases of aphasia in childhood and concluded that the hypothesis of equipotentiality was mistaken. Rasmussen and Milner (1977) described the laterality of cerebral speech, as assessed by the Wada technique, in patients who

Table 10.2 Cerebral speech laterality in 134 cases with definite evidence of early left hemisphere lesion: based on Rasmussen and Milner, 1977

Handedness	No. cases	Speech representation (%)		
		Left	Bilateral	Right
Right	42	81	7	12
Left or mixed	92	28	19	53

had suffered cerebral lesions of early origin, probably before the age of 2 years, as shown in Table 10.2. If the hemispheres were fully equipotential, it might be expected that all cases of early left-sided lesion would depend on the right hemisphere for speech. The table shows higher incidences of bilateral and right-sided speech, in comparison with cases without early lesion (see Table 1.2) but the majority of right-handers, and even some left-handers, continued to depend on the left side for speech, despite the early left-sided lesion. The left hemisphere does not easily give up its role in speech. Lenneberg's inference that the hemispheres are equipotential is probably correct for *language*, but it is incorrect for *speech*.

Studies of split-brain patients have explored many differences between the hemispheres. The critical difference for the present argument was revealed by experiments that presented two different objects to the two hemispheres simultaneously, by constructing chimeras made up of the left and right halves of different stimuli. Patients were unaware of the join because the midline coincided with the fixation point that had to be viewed during the brief presentation. After each presentation, the patient was asked to point to the object that had been seen among a set of pictures of the whole objects (Levy, Trevarthen and Sperry, 1972). A clear advantage for the stimuli presented to the left hemisphere (in the RVF) appeared when the task was to choose the picture (toes, pie or key) whose name *rhymed* with the picture seen as a chimera (rose, eye or bee). For most patients, only the left hemisphere could match pictures by the sound of their names. These findings pinpoint a critical difference between the hemispheres, that only the left could generate an internal representation of the sound of the word.

The third reason for believing that CD is for speech control, rather than language in general, depends on findings for electrical stimulation of the exposed cortex, prior to elective surgery. When surgical removal of part of the cerebral cortex is planned for the treatment of epilepsy, it is necessary for the surgeon to explore the brain surface with a gently stimulating electrode, to map the specific locations of cortical functions in that patient. This is done under local anaesthetic so that the patient can report sensations associated with the stimulation. Cortical stimulation does not lead to speech, in the sense of meaningful words, but stimulation over a wide area may stop the patient's ongoing speech. Some studies required patients to perform a standard series of tasks that had been practised before the operation (Ojemann, 1983a, 1983b; Ojemann and

Mateer, 1979). The tasks included naming objects represented by slide projector, reading an incomplete sentence and supplying an appropriate ending, and then recalling the object previously named. Slides were also shown of mouth movements, such as protrusion of the tongue or pursing the lips, which were to be imitated either alone or in sequences. An audio-tape presented elements of speech sounds (phonemes such as /p/, /b/, /d/) for identification. The electrical stimulation was applied at several stages of testing, and the person scoring the patient's response was unaware of the time or location of stimulation.

One of the striking findings of electrical mapping was the variability between people in the locations of these various functions, within the broad area associated with language. A second striking finding was the discreteness of localisation. Very small shifts in the placing of the electrode might lead to abrupt changes in the function affected. Ojemann described the findings for a 30-year-old woman whose first language was English, but second language Greek. Stimulation at some sites disturbed her ability to name objects in English but not in Greek while stimulation at other sites affected her ability to name objects in Greek, but not in English. Stimulation in part of Broca's area inhibited all types of speech output and also the imitation of mouth movements. Some sites were associated with reading and others with memory.

In contrast to the many sites with discrete localisations there were some sites that were critical for *two* functions, identification of phonemes and mimicry of sequences of mouth movements. The finding that the recognition of speech sounds depends on *the same cortical units* as are required for imitation of mouth movements suggests that the recognition of speech sounds is intimately linked with our ability to make the vocal gestures that are required to produce them. The idea that speech perception depends on motor processes associated with speech production was proposed some years ago (Liberman, Cooper, Shankweiler et al., 1967) and updated by Liberman and Mattingley (1985). The theory is controversial and the processes involved unclear (Doupe and Kuhl, 1999; Mateer, 1983). However, the finding that phoneme identification and the imitation of mouth movements often depend on the same cortical sites is consistent with the idea that speech is associated, in most people, with an intimate link between input and output mechanisms. The link depends on lateralisation to one side, typically the left. Stimulation mapping of the right hemisphere found discrete localisations for certain nonverbal functions (Fried, Mateer, Ojemann et al., 1982). The perception and recognition of lines, faces, and emotional expressions were affected by stimulation in areas corresponding to those that on the left side were associated with speech and language.

Distinctions between speech, language and cerebral dominance were outlined in chapter 1. Speech and language are human universals, because everyone with normal developmental exposure to speech learns to understand and, given a functioning vocal tract, to speak their native language. Speech is also unique among primates and several attempts to teach chimpanzees to talk have failed. There has been greater success in teaching higher apes to use sign languages (Fouts and Mills, 1997). The ability to develop language is probably an inherent property of a large primate brain. Cerebral dominance, in the sense of the typical pattern of hemisphere specialisation, is not essential for speech or language, because a substantial minority of people do not have it. Left CD is not a human universal, but subject to individual differences. It has been inferred above that left CD aids speech learning, but it is an aid that many people must do without. The logical implication is that there are likely to be individual differences in the rate and efficiency of speech learning. With regard to the hypothesised RS + gene, there are two basic questions. First, how does its presence help, and help to such an extent that it evolved as a new genetic change, unique to humans among primates (recall that other mammals and primates have no RS for handedness). Second, what are the risks for speech acquisition in its absence?

Why should an aid to speech acquisition be useful? Speech depends on some very complex gestures by the vocal tract (tongue, lips, vocal cords and pharynx). When we hear and understand what someone says, we decode a sequence of phonemes. However, research on the spectrum of sounds produced during speech shows that phonemes are produced in ways that are very variable. The same phoneme may be produced in quite different ways, to fit in with the phonemes that precede and follow it (A.M. Liberman, 1989). When a linguist looks at a visible recording of the sound spectrum of a particular spoken phrase, it is very difficult to "read" because of the lack of consistency of the output. Further, the quality of speech sound varies with the size of the vocal tract, the shape of the palate and nasal cavities and the control of breath; all of these differ with body size, age and sex. Males and females, children and adults differ in acoustic features of the sounds produced. In spite of all this variability, infants learn in their first year to distinguish most of the phonemes of their native language and by 1 year of age they have lost the ability to produce phonemes that are not used in their native tongue. The acquisition of speech sounds is a beautiful example of the interaction of a genetically programmed developmental sequence that relies on the experience of the individual child in the family for its realisation. How has "nature" accomplished such a wonderful development as human speech?

One part of the move from higher ape to human primate involved the remodelling of the human vocal tract. The changes include the descent of the larynx and enhanced mobility of the tongue and the lips. The dangers associated with these modifications are serious, as witnessed by the first lesson in first aid, to turn unconscious people on their side. It may be inferred that there was strong evolutionary pressure toward the acquisition of speech. My argument for the RS + gene is that it promotes cerebral lateralisation for speech because it is a useful aid to speech learning but it has not become fixed (universal) because it carries dangers even greater than the remodelled vocal tract. How does lateralisation of cerebral functions aid speech learning? The brain of a newborn is analogous, in some respects, to that of a split-brain adult because the cerebral commissures are largely unmyelinated (Yakovlev and Lecours, ...). Transfer of information from one side to the other would be slow and unreliable. Just how speech learning proceeds is not known, but it is likely that a single focus would expedite the process. There would be a smaller network ...

program for a half brain than for a whole brain. In discovering how the mouth must be shaped to produce the fine differences between /b/ and /p/, or between /l/ and /r/, it would be advantageous to have a close link between the somatosensory feedback from the mouth and the auditory feedback from the ear. Brain imaging by positron emission tomography (PET) revealed that anterior speech areas (Broca) and posterior speech areas (Wernicke) were both involved in *listening* to words, as well as when repeating them (Price, Wise, Warburton et al., 1996).

I have suggested earlier (Annett, 1985a, chapter 21) that if the mouth were being controlled from one side and the sound analysed on the other, this intimate link would be absent. Babies vary in their practice of speech sounds through babbling, and my personal observations suggest that this might vary with handedness but this is a research question I have not been able to pursue. Lateralisation of speech processes to one side would be likely to facilitate this conjunction of motor and perceptual processes. A more direct feedback for vocalisation might make babbling more enjoyable for the infant and so promote speech sound learning. Evidence from hemiplegic children, dichotic listening, and split-brain patients suggests that there is something special about the left hemisphere of most people, that makes it more fitted than the right to serve speech. There are parallels here between the acquisition of speech in humans and song learning in certain species of birds (review by Doupe and Kuhl, 1999). Some songbirds learn to recognise and produce particular streams of sound that match the songs produced by their parents, sometimes with particular dialects characteristic of the neighbourhood. The output is lateralised in birds, with elements of song depending more on the left side than the right side of the syrinx, the vocal organ (Nottebohm, 1970, 1977). Lateralisation to one side of the brain for the control of vocal output in species as widely separated as the songbirds and humans supports the thesis that lateralisation facilitates such control.

But if nearly one in five people are not gene-carriers then what is expected for speech and language development in the absence of left lateralisation? The first important point to recall is that in RS − − genotypes asymmetries are expected to occur by chance. Some chance combinations of asymmetries would provide adequate bases for speech learning. Brain imaging studies found a surprisingly high proportion of normal subjects had bilateral speech activations (Frackowiak, 1997, p. 293). Risks would arise only in some cases. There is abundant evidence for individual differences in the speed and efficiency of speech learning in childhood and speech use in adulthood.

There is a small but long established sex difference in favour of girls for first words and early stages of learning to talk. Some children may have problems with articulation or the smooth production of speech, as in stuttering. Speech defects, as well as reading problems are very much more frequent in boys than girls. Aside from the controversies about developmental problems (to be considered in chapter 13) there is considerable variability in the use of speech by normal adults. It is as obvious as it is generally unremarkable that adults vary greatly in their ability to articulate their ideas, to tell stories or to persuade people by argument. Consider how many people could be politicians, or give live commentaries by radio? Skills with words appear to be independent of intelligence and other cognitive abilities. The Greek orator and philosopher Demosthenes was said to have overcome a tendency to stutter. Moses was an exception that proves the rule, a leader who needed a spokesperson to put his ideas across to the people. Differences in the efficiency of spoken output may be related to differences in ability to represent words mentally. Inner speech took on a new importance with the invention of writing, as will be discussed in relation to problems of phonological processing in dyslexics (chapter 13). The argument here is that left hemisphere CD evolved as an aid to speech acquisition in childhood and that it may continue to have consequences for verbal expression in telling a good story, in leading a social group, as well as in "chatting up" and "sweet talk". However, in an important sense, left-sided CD is relatively trivial because it is not essential for speech.

The nature of the mechanism that promotes the control of speech by the left hemisphere is unknown. A relatively small developmental "nudge" that gives an advantage to one side could be sufficient to promote a developmental cascade of events toward typical lateralisations. One influential theory is that the left hemisphere's role in speech rests on some fundamental difference in the perception of sounds at the two ears. Comparisons of the perception of synthetic speech sounds when distinctive features were manipulated experimentally suggest that the typical advantage for the right ear (REA) depends on the detection of very fine differences in the timing of sounds (Allard and Scott, 1975; Bryden, 1982; Lackner and Teuber, 1973; Schouten, 1980; Tallal, Miller and Fitch, 1995). For example, the difference between /ga/ and /ka/ depends on a very small difference in the timing of voice onset. Subjects may show LEA for the pitch of dichotically presented musical sounds, and also for vowel-like sounds but switch to REA when fine time discriminations are required. It is possible that speech is special (among other sounds) only in its temporal complexity. However, whatever the initial cause, the result of the mechanism has to be such as to give an advantage to the left side for language learning, even in the deaf-mute who hears no speech and communicates by sign language (Poizner, Bellugi and Klima, 1989). It is clear that sign language learning is lateralised to the left side, like spoken language. It also needs to embrace the possibility that the human speech system is founded on an earlier primate system for communication that depended on the interpretation of manual and facial gestures (Rizzolatti and Arbib, 1998) as mentioned in chapter 1. The argument that hemisphere specialisation evolved as an aid to speech learning, does not beg questions about the origins of the mechanisms "nature" adapted for this purpose, nor questions about their possible implications for other cerebral functions. Crow asked "Is schizophrenia the price that *Homo sapiens* pays for language?" in the title of his (1997b) paper. The present argument implies that this should be amended to "Is schizophrenia the price that *Homo sapiens* pays for ready speech?" These issues will be reconsidered in the light of later evidence as to the role of the RS + gene in mental illness in chapter 14. First, we must consider the nature of the possible *disadvantage* associated with cerebral specialisation.

DISADVANTAGES OF THE RS + GENE FOR LEFT-HAND AND RIGHT HEMISPHERE

The first surmise as to the dangers of the RS + gene (Annett, 1978b) was that it led to an over-commitment to verbal skills at the expense of nonverbal skills, as said above. A programme of research was begun, looking for evidence of relative deficits associated with strong right-handedness, as defined by peg moving asymmetry. A review of findings in my samples was initiated with the assist-ance of Diana Kilshaw, herself a left-hander. Diana noticed that left-handers tended to have faster peg moving times than right-handers, when examined for the actual performance of each hand (Kilshaw and Annett, 1983). The samples available at that time fell into two groups, called the "combined main samples" (teenage children and undergraduates) and the "birthday samples" (other school-children, mostly in the primary stage, selected for testing by date of birth).

Figure 10.1a shows the times taken by the preferred and non-preferred hands in the combined main samples and Figure 10.1b gives the same information for the birthday samples. The samples are classified for hand preference in three groups, consistent right-handers, right-mixed handers and left-handers (based on the writing hand or the drawing hand for Figure 10.1a and b respectively). Longer times imply poorer performance, higher on the graphs. The most striking feature was the slowness of the non-preferred hand of consistent right-handers. In all four sets of data (two sexes in two samples) there was a linear relationship between bias to right-hand preference and slowness of the non-preferred hand. Female consistent right-handers had especially slow left hands. The findings for the non-preferred hand in both sexes and in both sets of samples suggested that consistent right-handedness is associated with slowness of the non-preferred (left) hand, rather than speed of the right-hand. These observations suggested that the notion of *advantage* for the right-hand and left hemisphere should be reconsidered. Perhaps RS is induced not by some factor that boosts the left hemisphere but rather by some factor that *handicaps the right hemisphere*. This interpretation of the evidence for hand skill gave a completely new perspective on cerebral lateralisation. Perhaps language is lateralised to the left side by some factor that slows down or otherwise impedes the growth of the right hemisphere. These observations gave the first clue why the RS + gene might be disadvantage-ous. Its spread in the population may have been limited and its expression reduced in males compared with females, because its action is to *impair* the function of the right hemisphere.

The findings above, for left-hand weakness in consistent right-handers needed checking in a new sample. A representative sample of schoolchildren, aged 5–11 years, was tested for hand preference and hand skill, as well as for other abilities that will be described in later chapters (Annett and Manning, 1989).

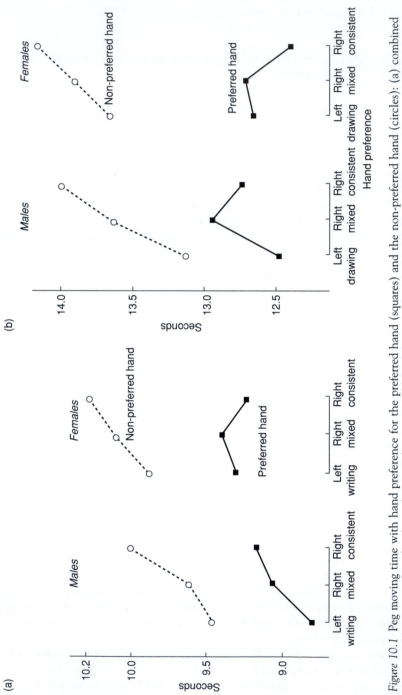

Figure 10.1 Peg moving time with hand preference for the preferred hand (squares) and the non-preferred hand (circles): (a) combined main samples of undergraduates and teenagers, (b) birthdays samples of schoolchildren: Kilshaw and Annett, 1983.

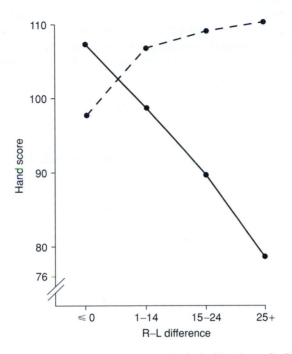

Figure 10.2 Left-hand (solid line) and right-hand (dashed line) standardised scores for peg moving time in children classified for L–R difference (in $^1/10s$).

Because actual peg moving times differ over this age range (see Figure 6.1), times were converted to standardised scores for age. Because we wanted to know how the left and right hands differed for actual skill, a common standard was needed for both hands. That is, a comparison of the skill of the right and left hands required scores to be standardised using the same set of norms for both hands. The norms used could have been for the left or the right, the choice was arbitrary, but we used those for the right-hand. The whole sample of children was classified for R–L difference into four groups, representing about 20, 30, 30 and 20 per cent of the sample. The groups can be described (1–4 from left to right) as having absent, mild, moderate and strong bias to dextrality, respectively. Figure 10.2 shows the mean standardised scores in the four groups, with higher scores (faster times) at the top of the graph (good and poor reversed from the previous graph). Inspection shows that right-hand scores rose from group 1 to group 2, but there was relatively little further change between groups 2–4. Left-hand scores fell strongly and linearly over all groups, from left to right. These findings support those above for samples classified for hand preference (both parts of Figure 10.1). They confirm that strong right-handedness is associated with weak left-hand skill.

This result has now been repeated many times in further samples of teenagers and students whose actual hand speeds change little with age, making score transformations unnecessary (Annett, 1991a, 1992c). These replications should put to rest suspicions that the findings of Annett and Manning were a product of the method of deriving the standardised scores (Bishop, 1990b). The findings have also been repeated in several independent studies, all otherwise critical of the RS approach (Leask and Crow, 1997; McManus, Shergill and Bryden, 1993; Palmer and Corballis, 1996; Resch, Haffner, Parzer et al., 1997). The pattern of findings was also found in tests of hand skill other than peg moving, including square marking, dotting, line drawing and hole punching. The pattern of hand skill in relation to the R–L difference is consistent with the theory that asymmetry arises by chance but that a bias in favour of the right-hand in the majority is a function of left-hand weakness rather than right-hand strength.

The findings for asymmetry of the hands bear a strong resemblance to findings for PT asymmetry, as described by Galaburda, Corsiglia, Rosen et al. (1987). Annett (1992b) summarised this parallel, as shown in Table 10.3. The table lists correlations between the coefficient of PT asymmetry derived by Galaburda and various measures of PT size. The corresponding correlations between L–R

Table 10.3 Correlations between left/right asymmetry and actual size for the planum temporale (data of Galaburda, Corsiglia, Rosen et al., 1987) and for hand skill (data of Annett, 1992d)

	Asymmetry	PT R–L/0.5(R + L)		Peg moving L–R time
A	*Total for R + L*			
	(i) All cases	0.369**		0.191**
		(100)		(454)
	(ii) Typical cases	0.550**		0.295**
		(63)		(353)
	(iii) Atypical cases	−0.325		−0.211*
		(21)		(91)
B	*Each side, all cases*			
	(i) Left PT	−0.509**	R hand	−0.394**
		(100)		(454)
	(ii) Right PT	0.861**	L hand	0.633**
		(100)		(454)
C	*Each side, typical cases*			
	(i) Left PT	0.069	R hand	−0.132*
		(63)		(353)
	(ii) Right PT	0.873**	L hand	0.601**
		(63)		(353)
D	*Each side, atypical cases*			
	(i) Left PT	−0.793**	R hand	−0.507**
		(21)		(91)
	(ii) Right PT	0.323	L hand	0.157
		(21)		(91)

Notes
*$p < 0.05$; **$p < 0.01$.
(N) in parentheses.

time for peg moving and actual times for the right and left hands are listed alongside. The clearest contrast between the sides, but parallel for the two measures, is given in section C. For PT there was no correlation between left PT size and asymmetry, but a strong correlation (r = .873) between right PT size and asymmetry. For hand skill there was a small negative correlation between the right-hand and L–R difference (−.132) but a large positive correlation for the left-hand (.601). Similar patterns of correlation were found for 12 further analyses using five different tests of hand skill in several samples (Annett, 1992d).

These observations consistently suggest that there is greater variability of the right hemisphere and the left-hand, than of left hemisphere and right-hand. Symmetrical brains tended to have large PT on both sides, and people relatively symmetrical for hand skill were reasonably fast with both hands (see Figure 10.2). How are these observations to be interpreted? If symmetry is the default condition, then brain and hand appear to be well endowed on both sides (for size and speed). Asymmetry appears to be associated with some loss of size (for right hemisphere PT) and loss of speed (for the left-hand). The results are consistent with the idea that the typical bias to left CD depends on some mechanism that handicaps the right hemisphere. The potential importance of these observations can hardly be over-stated. They suggest a fundamental reason why the spread of RS + gene has been limited in the population, and perhaps especially limited for expression in males, in spite of its potential benefits for speech. The danger of the RS + gene might be a serious cost to the functions of the right hemisphere, and perhaps to brain power or intelligence as a whole.

Leask and Crow (1997) challenged the idea that there is a specific weakness of the left-hand in strong right-handers by showing that strong left-handers were poor with their non-preferred right hands, in a square marking test of hand skill, given to 11-year-olds in the NCDS survey. A similar observation was made for left-handers by Tan (1990). Annett (1992b) showed that when left-handers were classified for asymmetry on the same criteria as right-handers but with reversed sign, extreme left-handers were as poor with their right-hand as extreme right-handers with the left. Thus strong right-handers cannot be said to have specific weakness for hand skill that does not occur in left-handers. The primary cause of asymmetry, for the RS theory, is chance. Strong left- and strong right-handers are expected under opposite tails of a normal distribution of asymmetry. However, the RS of the distribution implies that for any level of asymmetry (distance from R = L) there will be *more cases to the right than to the left*. Whatever mechanism the RS + gene uses to displace the R–L distribution to the right does not alter the shape of the chance distribution itself. Extreme asymmetries can occur in both directions. RS induces a relative right hemisphere deficit in more people than occurs by chance for relative left hemisphere deficit. The RS + gene might induce the displacement of the chance distribution to the right either through some new agent of right hemisphere weakness or by merely increasing the natural probability of right hemisphere weakness. The distinction now sounds like hair-splitting, but it may be important when the gene and its effects are clearer. However, the practical conclusion is that strong asymmetry

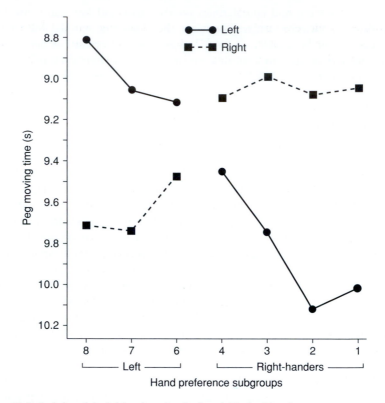

Figure 10.3 Left-hand (solid line) and right-hand (dashed line) peg moving times in hand preference subgroups: new combined samples (age 11 years or older).

in the typical direction is associated with a small PT in the right hemisphere and a weak left-hand. The mirror pattern in left-handers may occur, but much less frequently. The parallels between PT and handedness asymmetry described by Annett (1992b) were made long before the discoveries as to how asymmetries for PT and handedness combine (Annett, 2000a) as described in chapter 9. The more recent work suggests that the directional biases of both PT asymmetry and handedness are a function of the presence or absence of the RS + gene, but that they are otherwise independent.

Figure 10.3 expands on the earlier analyses by showing peg moving time in the hand preference subgroups defined in chapter 2 (instead of the three preference groups of Figures 10.1). Actual times for each hand are given for all available data for participants at least 11 years of age. No score transformations were needed here because times change little over this age range (see Figure 6.1). Figure 10.3 shows that the preferred hand was faster than the non-preferred hand in both left- and right-handers as expected. The means were very similar for the preferred hand over all groups, but consistent left-handers (class 8) were fastest. Post hoc t-tests found class 8 faster than groups 1, 2, 4 and 6 for the preferred hand. For the non-preferred hand, the most striking feature was the slowness of the left-hand of classes 1 and 2. These two groups differed from all others by post hoc comparisons. It was shown above that consistent right-handers were slow with the left-hand. The present analysis shows this is true also of class 2 right-handers (left-hand preferences for broom, spade or needle only). Class 2 is of particular interest in the analysis of spatial ability (chapter 12). The seven hand preference groups (originally eight) were distinguished because they differed for relative R–L hand time. This analysis shows that the R–L differences between groups depend mainly on the variability of the left-hand. Class 2 resembles class 1 for left-hand speed. It is closer to consistent right-handers other than mixed-handers.

The argument that poor mean hand speeds are due to accidental pathologies in extreme cases is quite unsustainable. At the right extreme, there were some 1700 Ss in classes 1 and 2 (69% of the total sample). The standard errors of the times in Figure 10.3 are too small to be represented clearly in the graph and they were not larger in the extreme groups than the centre. At the left extreme, the performance of consistent left-handers is not likely to be due to pathology because this group was fastest overall. The thesis of Kilshaw and Annett (1983) that left-handers are faster than right-handers overall can be examined by summing the times for both hands to give total hand time. Total hand time found left-handers faster than right-handers in these new combined data. Inspection of Figure 10.3 shows that the difference depends on the poor left-hand times of subgroups 1 and 2.

SUMMARY

The first main point of this chapter is that the genetic model suggests there might be a balanced polymorphism with heterozygote advantage for the RS locus. This is because the frequency of the single allele (RS +), that was deduced from neurological evidence for dysphasia and applied successfully to the problem of the distribution of handedness in families, implies that the heterozygote (RS + – genotype) is more prevalent than the dominant homozygote (RS + + genotype). This suggests that whatever the mechanism by which RS + is expressed, one dose is more advantageous than two doses.

The second main point concerns the advantage conferred by the RS + gene. It is argued that the functional outcome of the expression of RS + is an advantage to the left cerebral hemisphere for the control of speech. Several sources of evidence were reviewed which point to the conclusion that the specific superiority of the left hemisphere relates to the perception and production of speech sounds. With speech depending on the left side, other language functions are likely to lateralise to the left side also, but the primary asymmetry is likely to be for speech.

The third main point concerns the disadvantage associated with the gene. Why did it not spread throughout the population, to give everyone the advantages of left lateralised speech? The surprising outcome of research on the actual skill of each hand in relation to the difference between the hands was that the bias to the right-hand is a function of left-hand weakness, not right-hand skill. The pattern of asymmetry for hand skill was shown to resemble that for asymmetry of the planum temporale (PT). Typical asymmetry, left side larger than right, is associated with a reduction of PT on the right, not enlargement on the left. The advantage for the left hemisphere depends on a disadvantage of the right hemisphere. This suggests that the price of left hemisphere specialisation for speech is some cost to right hemisphere function, at least in the speech areas.

These two elements, advantage for speech but cost for the right hemisphere, imply that the patterns of cerebral dominance associated with the three genotypes of the RS locus could give rise to some interesting combinations of strength and weakness for different abilities, speech and language based versus non-speech based abilities. The next few chapters review evidence for relationships between handedness and abilities.

11 Heterozygote advantage

The hypothesis that there is a genetic balanced polymorphism with heterozygote advantage (BP + HA) for the RS locus cannot be examined directly because the relevant alleles are unknown. What can be asked at present is whether there are associations between laterality and ability that are consistent with a BP + HA. There is a large literature on laterality and abilities, but there are few undisputed findings. Previous research has looked for statistically significant differences between left- versus right-handers, treating handedness as a type variable. The RS model and BP + HA hypothesis expect relationships to be more subtle because handedness is not a type, and the relevant genotypes are not "for" handedness but "for" different patterns of cerebral specialisation. The RS − −, RS + − and RS + + genotypes imply that a bias to left CD is absent, moderate and strong respectively. Because of the substantial overlap between genotypes (see Figure 7.1) contrasts for handedness are expected to be small. However, the model makes predictions about the different types of ability that might be at risk versus advantage in the two homozygotes. The overall advantage for heterozygotes might depend, therefore, on minimising both types of risk and achieving overall balance for cognitive and other abilities. The present chapter looks for evidence of heterozygote advantage, but it is useful to begin with a summary of the assumptions involved in the BP + HA hypothesis, so that the strategies for research described in this and the next two chapters can be seen as a whole.

Figure 11.1 outlines four levels of analysis required for the RS theory, genetic, cerebral, cognitive and behavioural. At the genetic level, the three genotypes follow from the idea that there is a single gene (RS +) that may be present or absent. The genotype frequencies follow from the deductions for percentage of patients with atypical CD, 9.27%, doubled to give the RS − − genotype proportion in the population, 0.1854, as argued in chapters 4–5. At the cerebral level, the hypothesis of left hemisphere advantage for gene carriers follows from the assumption that the gene is something that promotes left CD. The hypothesis of right hemisphere disadvantage follows from the evidence that the biases to right hand skill and to larger left PT depend on weaknesses of relevant regions of the right hemisphere. Notice that the general principle of a balance of costs and benefits is inherent in the assumption that RS − − genotypes lack left hemisphere advantage but also lack right hemisphere disadvantage, whereas RS + + genotypes

Level of analysis

Genetic

genotype proportions	RS − − 0.1854	RS + − 0.4904	RS + + 0.3242

Cerebral

left hemisphere advantage	absent	moderate	strong
right hemisphere disadvantage	absent	moderate	strong

Cognitive

risks to phonology	present	absent	absent
risks to visuospatial	absent	moderate	strong

Behaviour

RS for R–L skill	absent	moderate	strong

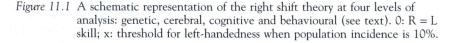

	0 x	0 x	0 x

Percent left-writers	34	8	1

Figure 11.1 A schematic representation of the right shift theory at four levels of analysis: genetic, cerebral, cognitive and behavioural (see text). 0: R = L skill; x: threshold for left-handedness when population incidence is 10%.

have strong advantages for the left hemisphere but risk strong disadvantages for the right hemisphere. How do these costs and benefits translate into abilities and disabilities at the cognitive level? These are the questions that need investigation psychologically. The main contrasts suggested here are for risks to speech based processes versus visuospatial abilities. The idea that speech and speech related functions are at risk in RS − − genotypes follows directly from the hypothesis that the RS + gene evolved to aid the acquisition of speech (but not verbal intelligence, for reasons explained in chapter 10). The nature of the cognitive risk associated with the RS + gene is more problematic. Analyses of actual hand skill showed that strong right-handers have weak left-hand skills. Perhaps RS + + genotypes are unlikely to excel in sports and other performances that require skilled control of both sides of the body. If right hemisphere deficits are involved, in areas corresponding to those involved in speech on the left side, it is reasonable to look for visuospatial problems. However, the deficits associated with the RS + gene may be more general than implied by the term "visuospatial". If there is a loss of neurons, or neuronal connectivity, there may be a general loss of intellectual power. There is no clear way to distinguish these possibilities at present. Hence visuospatial in Figure 11.1 should be seen as a provisional label for what could turn out to be more complex and varied risks associated with the RS + gene.

Predictions for handedness depend on the behavioural level of analysis. The overlapping distributions of the three genotypes were shown in Figure 7.1, but here the predictions are illustrated for each genotype independently. All have normal (chance) distributions of R–L hand skill, along the continuous baseline. The differences for hand preference depend on their relative shifts. The mean is at 0 (by definition) for RS – –, 1 standard deviation (z) to the right of 0 for RS + –, and $2z$ for RS + + (shifts expected for males, see chapter 7). Actual levels of hand preference in the three genotypes depend on the sample threshold, and this varies, as discussed earlier, with methods of assessment and criteria adopted by investigators. When the criterion distinguishes about 10% of the population, then the threshold (x) is about $0.5z$ to the left of 0. This implies that the proportions of left-handers in the three genotypes are about 34% for RS – –, 8% for RS + –, and 0–1% for RS + + , as shown. Considered in terms of the total population, 34% of RS – – implies about 6 left-handers, 8% of RS + – implies 3–4 and 1% of RS + + implies 0–1, giving 10 left-handers overall. For other incidences the numbers would differ, as shown in Appendices III and IV. For example, 30 per 100 non-right-handers would include 13, 15 and 2 RS – –, RS + –, and RS + + genotypes respectively.

In the light of this model, how might it be possible to test for relationships between laterality and ability? The prediction would be relatively straightforward for a group with a specific difficulty in phonological processing if it can be assumed for the sake of the present argument that there are no other major causes of poor phonology. Such a group would include about one in three left-handers. Similarly, a group with a specific deficit in visuospatial processing and no problem of phonology would rarely include a left-hander. But what is expected of heterozygotes? The analysis suggests that about 8% of them would be left-handed writers when the population incidence is 10%. With regard to R–L hand skill, the heterozygote mean is $1.0z$ (for males) when the population mean (all genotypes combined is $1.2z$). Hence a group of heterozygotes would not differ significantly for incidence of left-hand preference or for mean R–L hand skill from a random sample of the population. The predictions have to do with the spread of relative hand skill, fewer strong left-handers and fewer strong right-handers are expected in heterozygotes than in the general population. Evidence must be sought in studies of hand skill, looking for evidence that intellectual advantage, as shown by superior educational progress is more often found toward the centre of the laterality distribution than to either the left or the right sides.

The analyses below all depend on data that was collected for other purposes and examined later for its bearing on the question of heterozygote advantage.

The analyses fall into two main groups. First, samples that had been tested for peg moving asymmetry could be classified for R–L hand skill, and the resulting groups compared for ability. Second, some samples could be classified for what will be termed "educational advantage" and compared for hand preference. Both sets of analyses point to the conclusion that there are advantages for those with moderate rather than strong bias to dextrality.

CLASSIFYING FOR LATERALITY AND COMPARING FOR ABILITY

Vocabulary in representative school samples

The BP + HA hypothesis followed from the single gene hypothesis (Annett, 1978b). The Peabody Picture Vocabulary Test (PPVT; Dunn, 1959) had been given to schoolchildren in Hull some ten years earlier (Annett, 1970b). The test asks the child to point to one of four pictures to indicate the meaning of a word spoken by the examiner. The test was also given to another sample of children in schools in a village close to Hull (Annett and Turner, 1974). The children in these two samples were combined and classified for peg moving asymmetry ($^1/_{10}$s in 1s intervals) as shown in Figure 11.2a. The leftmost group was biased to the left-hand for skill (< 0) and the three other groups can be described as

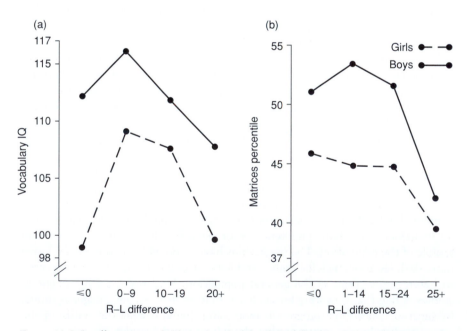

Figure 11.2 Intelligence in children classified for R–L difference for peg moving: (a) Peabody Picture Vocabulary Test (PPVT), (b) Raven's Coloured Progressive Matrices: Annett, 1995a.

having mild, moderate and strong biases to dextrality. Vocabulary IQ was distributed in the shape of an inverted U, higher toward the centre and lower to either side. This was true for both sexes. The quadratic trend was highly significant statistically for sexes combined and for females considered alone (Annett and Kilshaw, 1984). The trend for males was partly U-shaped but also partly linear, declining toward the right. These findings for old data, reanalysed in the light of a new hypothesis, was one of the "happy surprises" afforded by the RS theory. Data for both sexes were consistent with the hypothesis of heterozygote advantage, disadvantages associated with strong bias to dextrality, compared with relative advantages in the centre. The findings were retrospective. Could they be replicated in a new sample using a different test of ability?

Raven's Matrices in primary schoolchildren

A new sample of children, 5–11 years of age, was given Raven's Coloured Matrices test (Raven, 1963). The children were drawn from six primary schools in different areas of a midland town, Rugby, far from the port of Hull. They were described in the last chapter for standardised peg moving scores (see Figure 10.2). As for PPVT, the Matrices test asks the child to point to one of alternative choices. We also observed hand preference for several actions and tested for word reading, as described in chapter 13. In addition to our own tests, we asked head teachers if scores for recent tests of educational attainment given in school might be made available to us. Scores for English, maths and other Richmond Tests of educational skills (Hieronymous, Lindquist and France, 1991) were supplied for 9- to 11-year-olds in several schools. The first report of the Matrices test in this sample (Annett and Manning, 1989) required correction (Annett, 1993d) after an error was found in the template that had been used for marking. The corrected findings are shown in Figure 11.2b. The pattern for males resembled that for PPVT, the highest mean was for mild dextrals (group 2) and there was a linear trend from left to right. For females, scores were fairly flat over groups 1–3, but lower for group 4. The contrast between groups 2 and 4, for sexes combined, was statistically significant. This supported the hypothesis that children with mild bias to dextrality have some advantage over children with strong bias to dextrality.

A surprising feature of the findings for the Matrices test, as well as for PPVT, was the overall superiority of males over females, although it is generally expected that the sexes would be about equivalent at the primary stage, or girls slightly ahead because of their earlier maturity. Differences, if present, would be expected to favour girls for verbal ability. It was of some interest, therefore, to compare the sexes and handedness groups for English and for maths scores. Figures 11.3a and b show that girls tended to perform better than boys for both of these school based tests, but not significantly. There was a striking decline of ability from left to right across the R–L hand skill continuum for both English and maths. In this sample, there was clear support for the idea that strong dextrality, as represented by the most dextral 20% of the sample, was associated with poorer performance on all measures, Matrices, English and maths.

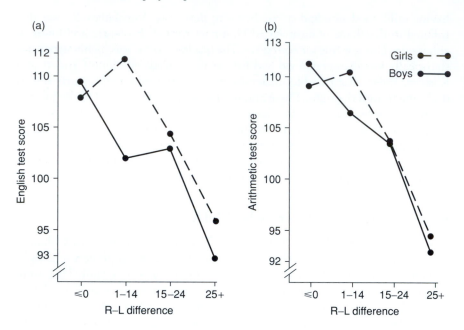

Figure 11.3 Educational attainment in children classified for R–L difference for peg moving: (a) English, (b) arithmetic: Annett, 1995a.

Scores on 11 Richmond tests, administered by teachers, were available for just over 100 children. We divided the children into two groups, below and above the mean for R–L hand asymmetry (that is, to the left and to the right of the R–L distributions above) and compared the groups for test scores. The mean scores for all of the 11 tests were in favour of the less dextral group, and in 6 out of 11 cases, the difference was significant statistically. These findings support the thesis that stronger bias to dextrality is associated with poorer educational performance. Evidence for weakness at the left side of the distribution was not clear for these measures, although it was found for reading in this sample (described in chapter 13).

Selection for grammar school

A sample of pupils attending secondary schools in Rugby was recruited shortly after the primary school sample above. The purpose was to examine relations between spatial ability and laterality (as described in chapter 12). The majority of education authorities in the UK gave up selection for secondary education in the 1960s–1970s but Rugby retained grammar school selection, based on tests and educational reports at 12 years. In order to have a representative sample for my study of spatial ability in 14- to 15-year-olds, tests were given to a whole age cohort in two large coeducational high schools and two small grammar schools, one for each sex. The children observed one another for hand preference and timed each other for peg moving, under supervision by the author, research assistant and teacher. Complete handedness data was obtained for 507 children, 157 attending grammar and 350 attending unselected high schools. After completing the analyses for spatial ability (Annett, 1992c) it occurred to me that the BP + HA hypothesis would predict the grammar school pupils, who had made exceptional educational progress at age 12 years, to be distributed differently for R–L hand skill from the unselected children. They should be more frequent in the centre than at either side (Annett, 1993a).

This hypothesis was tested by computing the difference between the hands as a percentage of total time (R–L%). The total sample was classified as evenly as possible (Ns = 126, 127, 127 and 127) to give 25% in each of four groups, ordered for hand skill asymmetry. The prediction was that the grammar school children would be over-represented in the central groups and the unselected children under-represented. Figure 11.4 shows that the predicted pattern was found. The comparison between selected and unselected children was statistically

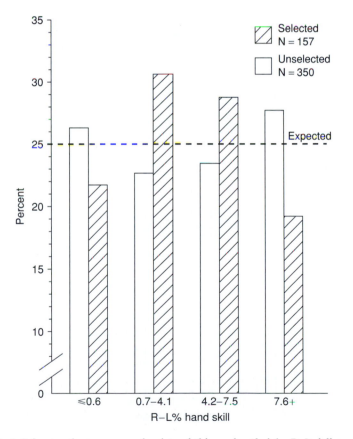

Figure 11.4 Selection for grammar school in children classified for R–L difference for peg moving.

significant (chi-square = 8.095, d.f. 3, p = 0.044). Note that the highest proportion of grammar school pupils occurred in group 2, mild dextrals, just to the left
of the mean for R–L% skill (as for the highest abilities in Figures 11.2 and
11.3). The pattern was present for both sexes.

   The selection tests for grammar schools were taken when the children were
12 years old, some 2 years before my tests. Two years later, at 16 years, these
same children took national examinations for scholastic achievement (General
Certificate of Secondary Education, GCSE). Does relative success at GCSE
differ with asymmetry for hand skill? The grammar school children must be
omitted here because they had been taught separately. The 350 children in
unselected schools were divided into two groups, 57% who obtained at least one
pass at grade C in GCSE, versus the 43% who did not reach this level. A 25%
division for R–L% hand skill was made as before and the proportions of successful and unsuccessful children compared, as shown in Figure 11.5. This shows

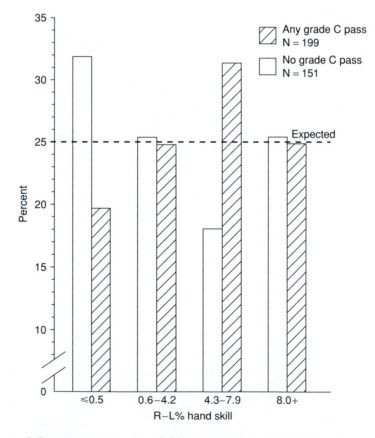

Figure 11.5 Examination success in children classified for R–L difference for
      peg moving.

that examination success was not independent of laterality. There were more successful pupils in the centre, in group 3, than at the left extreme, group 1. Again the pattern was present in both sexes.

Sixty-three children obtained eight or more GCSEs at grade C or D, about the level required for progress to further and higher education. In comparison with the 287 children not meeting this level, the successful children were significantly more frequent in the centre of the distribution than extremes (p = 0.038). Annett (1993a) described these data from further points of view, examining and rejecting possible objections. In particular, it should be noted that these findings can not be attributed to "pathology", because the relevant contrasts depended on very large numbers of children in each group. When the analyses were repeated, omitting children with slow peg moving times, significant contrasts remained. The role of pathology will be considered in chapter 16.

A factor for ability in undergraduates

The studies of teenagers above show that the more successful, those selected for grammar schools at 12 years, or more successful in national examinations at 16 years, were not distributed at random for R–L hand skill, but were more often at the centre of the distribution. Could this be true among university students, already selected for higher education? The analyses described next, previously unpublished, were suggested by students working with me on final year projects. For several years it was among my duties at the University of Leicester to guide groups of final year students in the design, running and analysis of short research projects. The brief was to train the students in research methods by using them as quasi research assistants, before they ran their own individual research projects. For some years, I used this opportunity to investigate questions about handedness and abilities, with particular attention to the role of phonological processing in reading (Annett, 1999b and chapter 13).

The final year students tested groups of first year student volunteers, under close supervision by myself and research assistants. The projects were given titles that were neutral for handedness and reading (e.g. "Sound and Sight") so that the volunteer sample should not be biased in these respects. Some tests were constant over several years and others changed, but they typically included a test of spatial ability, standard assessments of hand preference and peg moving, and various measures of lexical processing. The final year students, having collaborated in collecting, scoring and entering the results in a common data base, were invited to individually select aspects of the data they found interesting for their personal write-up. Two students independently asked if they could examine the findings as measures of general ability or intelligence. I suggested that the test results available for five tests given to 295 participants over three project years be entered into a factor analysis (SPSS principal components analysis). The first unrotated factor was taken as a measure of overall ability, analogous to Spearman's "g".

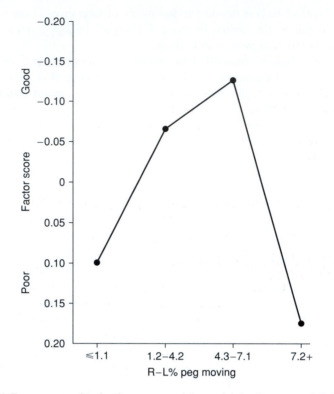

Figure 11.6 Factor scores for the first unrotated factor (g) for five tests of ability in undergraduates classified for R–L difference for peg moving.

Figure 11.6 shows the findings for Ps classified in four groups for peg moving asymmetry (20/30/30/20 percent groups for R–L%, Ns 60, 88, 86 and 61 respectively). The factor scores are based on errors so negative scores imply above average performance. The distribution is an inverted U, with better performance in the two central groups than at either extreme. The weighted quadratic trend reached the conventional level of significance (p = 0.05). What did this first factor measure? Three of the five tests involved word knowledge (spelling, phonology and word discrimination for homophonic words). All of these three had similar high loading on the first factor (0.73–0.77). The loading for the nonverbal test was 0.35 and for the fifth test of phoneme discrimination nil (0.06). Therefore, the first factor was measuring mainly lexical abilities. The several lexical processing tests were planned to tap different types of word skill, phonological versus non-phonological, that were expected to differ for associations with laterality. Contrasting deficits between the tests at the left and right of the R–L distribution will be revealed in chapter 13. The present analysis for their combined scores is complementary to the analyses for different specific deficits because it shows that students who performed well on *all of these tests of different types of word skill* were in the centre of the distribution. This is consistent with the thesis that they were free from the different risks associated with both extremes. In terms of R–L% skill, they were where heterozygotes are expected, in the centre of laterality continuum.

The reliability of the findings was checked by analysing the sums of the relevant test scores. The standardised (z) scores of the four tests that loaded on the first factor were summed and compared between the four R–L% groups. The summed scores were clearly quadratic over the laterality distribution (p = 0.032). The finding supports the thesis that good all-round ability is more likely at the centre than at the extremes of the laterality distribution, even among undergraduates.

EDUCATIONAL ADVANTAGE AND HANDEDNESS

The BP + HA hypothesis, together with the findings above, suggests that heterozygotes are more likely to be selected for higher education than homozygotes and have better all-round abilities at university. The evidence depended on classifications for hand skill asymmetry and comparison of the resulting groups for ability. Might it be possible to test the evidence in the reverse direction? That is, could one start with groups distinguished for educational advantage and test for differences in handedness? In principle it should be straightforward. Select people of comparable age and sex at random from the non-student population and give them exactly the same handedness assessment as a random sample of students. In practice, it is virtually impossible to find a cohort of non-students because after the school years there is no single organisation that is representative of the general population (except perhaps for males in countries where conscription for the services is required). It will not do to send out questionnaires and rely on the information from returns because non-returns are probably not independent of the questions. My own efforts to get funding for general population studies were not supported, so the present analyses rely on incidental evidence from other studies.

The samples I have assessed for handedness over many years were designed to be as representative as possible of the populations from which they were drawn, school or university. There was one non-academic sample of adults, service recruits who completed the AHPQ along with other tests in classes run by a colleague. The data were collected immediately on completion. The recruits were compared with students at the University of Hull and found slightly but significantly more dextral than undergraduates, 71% versus 66% consistently right-handed (Annett, 1970a).

Three levels of education were sampled, primary, secondary and higher, during two main periods, 1966–1976 and 1986–1993. For each period of time, and at each educational level, a broad distinction can be made between two streams, one more advantaged than the other. Figure 11.7 shows the percentages of left-handed writers and also the percentage of non-right-handers for combined samples including over 3000 Ss. The samples are distinguished for educational

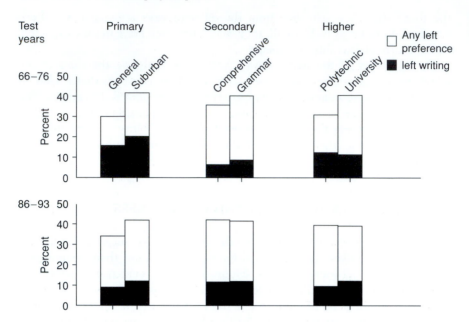

Figure 11.7 Handedness by educational advantage at primary, secondary and higher
levels of education for two periods of time, 1966–1976 and 1986–1993.

advantage, at three levels of education and for two periods of time. The original
purpose of this analysis was to investigate whether the frequency of left-hand
preferences has changed with time, between the earlier and later periods of my
research. Secular change between the first and second halves of the 20th century has certainly occurred (see chapter 6) and it was of interest to discover if
this change was continuing. Possible secular change was suggested by Bishop
(1990b) as a reason to question the validity of using children seen around 1970
as controls for dyslexics seen around 1980 (Annett and Kilshaw, 1984). There
was no change with time in my samples, but the distinction for time allows
us to examine certain consistencies between the two periods for educational
advantage.

The criteria of educational advantage must be explained. At the higher level
the distinction refers to what might be called a fast track entry to academic
study versus a slower track. The fast track groups were students attending established redbrick universities (Hull in the earlier period and Leicester in the later
period), most having entered directly from school at about 18 years of age. The
slow track entry, labelled "polytechnic" for simplicity, includes students taking
less conventional routes to higher education, through Coventry Polytechnic
(now Coventry University) or the Open University (OU, established in the
1960s for study via distance learning). All of the latter and many of the former
were "mature" students. At the secondary level the distinction is between comprehensive or general high schools and grammar schools. At the primary level,

the distinction is between the majority of city or town schools and those I have labelled suburban. The suburban schools were of the kind that academic parents would wish their own children to attend. They were in leafy suburbs, or dormitory villages where professional and middle-class families often chose to live, schools that had a good track record for getting children well placed at the next stage of their education. Thus, at the primary level, the classification that I have called "educational advantage" depends on the location of the family home. Why did I see a need to make such a distinction?

The primary schools were visited in different time periods and in different locations. The studies around 1970 were in Hull (an east coast port and its dormitory village suburb). I noticed at the time that the proportion of left and mixed handed children was remarkably high for schools in the suburb. Not much can be made of a single observation of this sort, because "significant" results can occur by chance. It was my policy to look for replication before taking such observations seriously. The replication was apparent when I visited schools in Rugby and its dormitory suburb some 20 years later. In Hull, there were 30.2% non-right-handers among 225 children in the general schools but 41.5% among 135 children in the suburban schools (chi-square = 4.737, d.f. 1, p = 0.029). In Rugby, there were 30.1% non-right-handers among 272 children in general schools and 42% among 81 children in the suburban schools (chi-square = 3.958, d.f. 1, p = 0.047). These differences are clear in Figure 11.7.

At the secondary and higher levels of education there tended to be more non-right-handers in the more advantaged groups in the 1966–1976 period. This was not so evident for non-right-handers at these levels in the 1986–1993 period. However, there were trends toward more left-writers in the advantaged groups at this time.

Figure 11.8 summarises the findings over all levels of education, for the sexes separately. The distinction for sex gives another check on the reliability of the trends. Figure 11.8 shows the percentage of left-writers, right mixed-handers and pure right-handers in the advantaged versus general groups. For both sexes it is clear that the more advantaged groups included fewer consistent right-handers and more of both types of non-right-hander. For sexes together (N = 3101) the contrast over the three types of handedness was very significant statistically (chi-square 12.664, d.f. 2, p = 0.0018). For males alone the contrast was strong (p = 0.005). For females the contrast was present but less strong (p = 0.078). However, the trends were consistent between the sexes. Females were slightly more biased to dextrality than males at both levels of educational advantage, as expected. The differences were small, but consistent for both variables, sex and educational advantage. There were fewer consistent right-handers, and more left-writers and non-right-handers among the educationally advantaged groups. The pattern of results is consistent with the hypothesis that there is a factor that displaces the human handedness distribution toward dextrality, but that this factor is not so prevalent (or not expressed as strongly) among those who make faster educational progress. The findings are consistent with the hypothesis of a BP + HA for the RS locus.

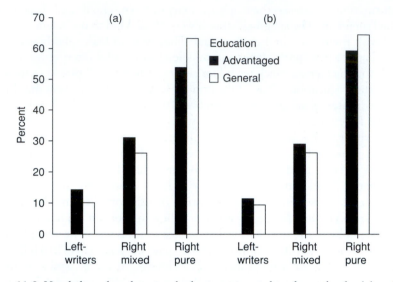

Figure 11.8 Handedness by educational advantage in combined samples for (a) males and (b) females.

SUMMARY

The search for evidence of heterozygote advantage depended on comparisons between groups classified for R–L hand skill among children and undergraduates. All the present analyses were retrospective because they depended on reanalyses of data collected for other purposes. Children classified for peg moving asymmetry were shown to differ for intelligence, measured by vocabulary test, and by matrices test, in two different representative samples. Educational progress in the real world, as shown by school assessments, selection for grammar school at 12 years, and by examination success at 16 years, differed across the R–L continuum, as expected if those in the centre, more likely to be heterozygotes (RS + − genotypes) were more successful. A similar pattern was shown among first year university students, tested on a variety of tests of word knowledge.

Comparisons of samples for relative educational advantage, at three levels of education, and in two periods of time, found that the more advantaged group was less likely to be biased to strong dextrality. The trends were present in both sexes, along with the expected stronger shift to dextrality in females than males.

12 What are the disadvantages of right shift?

Spatial and mathematical reasoning, art, music, surgery and sport

The balanced polymorphism hypothesis for the RS locus implies that RS − − and RS + + genotypes differ for risks of particular strengths and weaknesses. The predictions summarised in Figure 11.1 suggested that RS + + genotypes have strong left hemisphere advantages, but also strong risks of right hemisphere disadvantages. This chapter seeks to clarify what the latter might be. The main research strategy is to ask whether certain positive skills are associated with a high frequency of left-handedness. These may be clues to advantages for RS − − genotypes relative to risks for RS + + genotypes. The converse question, what are the risks for RS − − compared with advantages for RS + + will be asked in the next chapter.

The possibility of *deficits* associated with the agent of human cerebral dominance was a surprising idea, without precedent in the scientific literature. There are informal beliefs, however, about skills likely to be associated with a raised incidence of left-handers, including architecture, art, mathematics, music, surgery and sport. Annett (1978b) surmised that the risks versus benefits of the RS + gene might depend on a broad distinction between "doing" versus "talking". Ready speech may be promoted by the RS + gene, but human evolutionary success depended on practical skills, such as making tools, shelter and clothes, travelling through hostile environments, and physical prowess in combat. When the crunch comes, getting things done is more critical to survival than talking about them. Perhaps there is a trade-off between the "doer" and the "talker" that is pivotal for the balance associated with the RS locus. Can we find evidence to support folk wisdom that left-handedness is more frequent among groups with certain special talents in performance? What sort of incidences would the RS theory predict?

Previous research on handedness and abilities has looked for evidence of superior skills in left-handers compared with right-handers. The RS approach differs in two main ways, first because the relevant variable is not handedness but rather pattern of cerebral dominance, and second because it does not predict positive advantages for atypical cases but rather *disadvantages for typical cases*. The relevant contrast might be between RS − − genotypes and gene carriers (RS + − and RS + + genotypes). Or it might be between those with absent or mild doses (RS − − and RS + − genotypes) versus those with strong doses (RS + +

genotypes). These alternatives cannot be distinguished at present, pending the discovery of reliable gene markers. However, certain predictions can be made about the relative prevalence of left- and non-right-handers in the relevant groups.

Consider first the predictions for poor performance in RS + + genotypes. This genotype spans most of the R–L continuum (see Figure 7.1) and may include an occasional left-hander, but for the present purpose can be taken to consist of right-handed writers. The prediction is that RS + + genotypes are reduced or absent from groups with certain performance skills that do not depend on words. If outstanding performers include RS + – and RS – – genotypes only, what would be the handedness distribution? For example, if RS + + genotypes are absent from tennis players at tournament level, then this genotype (32% of the population) must be taken out of calculations as to frequency. When 8% (8/100) of the general population use a racquet in the left-hand, then the frequency of left-handed players among tennis professionals should be 8/(100 − 32) = 8/68 = 11.8%. Or if the base rate in the population is 10%, the prediction would be 10/68 = 15%. Figure 12.1 shows the distribution expected for samples drawn at random from the population for RS + – and RS – – genotypes but with RS + + missing. For the *same thresholds* (X, Y) that cut off about 9% and 30% in general samples of males (see Figure 7.1) the proportions for Figure 12.1 would be 13.3% and 41%, respectively. For females the proportions would be slightly smaller, about 8% left-writers and 26% non-right-handers in the general population but

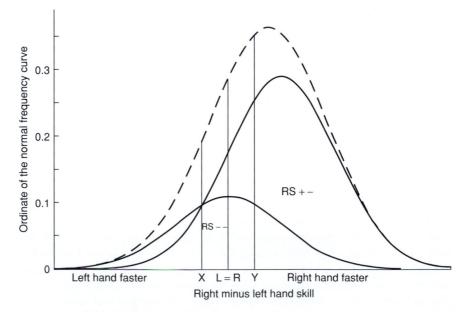

Figure 12.1 The distribution of R–L hand skill in samples where the RS + + genotype is missing, as hypothesised for certain talented groups (see text).

12% and 36% respectively for skilled groups (if RS + − and RS + + are shifted further to the right by 0.2z and 0.4z, respectively, see chapter 7). Differences of this order of magnitude are not likely to be statistically significant unless samples are very large. However, as will be shown below, these are the levels of incidence observed in many special groups that have been suggested to have a raised frequency of left-handedness.

If proportions rise above these levels, then it must be considered whether the RS + gene is disadvantageous even in single dose and whether RS − − genotypes have the greatest advantage. Findings for some outstanding sports-people are consistent with this possibility, as reviewed below. The overlap of genotypes (in Figure 7.1) implies that left-handers include gene-carriers, while non-gene-carriers are more often right than left-handed (as discussed in chapter 4). The overlap suggests there might be differences *within* left-handers and *within* right-handers, associated with the presence versus absence of the RS + gene.

SPATIAL ABILITY

The term "visuospatial" in Figure 11.1 gave a useful starting point for exploring the possible disadvantages associated with the RS + gene but it should not be taken as more than an initial surmise. The present section has two main themes that are apparently contradictory. First, we should not expect to find simple relationships between handedness and spatial abilities. Second, I have found evidence that performance on certain visuospatial tests is inversely related to the probable presence of the RS + gene. The important point is that the issues are not simple, and should not be expected to be simple at this stage of knowledge.

There are many reasons why differences for handedness and hemispheres should not be expected on tests of spatial ability. First, spatial abilities involve many practical skills that are intrinsic to the survival of all animals that travel in the real environment. The evolutionary foundations of these abilities must have a history of enormous length compared with the tiny period of the evolution of human speech. The effects of the hypothesised RS + gene in lateralising speech and associated functions to the left hemisphere must overlay ancient dual brain systems for spatial awareness. Second, investigations of right hemisphere functions have not pinpointed any single skill that is specific to the right side, comparable with the loss of speech with left-sided lesions. Thus the relevant skills cannot be easily identified and measured. As outlined in previous sections, classical neurology found few disorders associated with right-sided brain lesions. One of the most striking disorders, neglect of the left side of personal space, involves profound deficits of spatial awareness, but ones that are not easily understood or translatable into tests for normal subjects. Experiments on split-brain patients led Sperry (1974) to conclude that the right hemisphere was involved in "nonverbal ideation", but the task of specifying precisely what this means has proved difficult (Gazzaniga, 1995). Neuropsychologists have found subtle perceptual deficits associated with right-sided lesions, as in the ability to identify objects visually and tactually from degraded information (McCarthy and Warrington, 1990). However, there is no certain method for testing these functions in the general population.

A third reason for caution is that the psychological description of spatial ability is itself controversial. When large numbers of abilities are tested in samples of normal participants and the scores are subjected to factor analysis, two groups of tests are distinguished, some that are language based and others that are not directly language based. The latter are variously described as requiring nonverbal, spatial, mechanical, perceptual, visuospatial or performance abilities. The interpretation of factor analyses is highly controversial (see Mackintosh, 1998 for review). There may well be several types of spatial ability. The main type to emerge in factor analysis is usually labelled "spatial visualisation", exemplified by tasks like mental paper folding, where the outcome of various manipulations must be envisaged. Other types of nonverbal ability are more directly perceptual, requiring the perception of hidden figures, or objects seen from unusual viewpoints. A particularly challenging task is mental rotation, distinguishing rotated figures from their mirror images. How these various classroom and laboratory tasks relate to ability to finding one's way in the real environment (spatial orientation) is unknown. Several test batteries, including the Verbal and Performance Scales of the various Wechsler intelligence tests were designed to tap the broad division between two types of ability, verbal and nonverbal, but it should not be assumed that the so-called "performance" scales are equivalent to "spatial" ability.

A fourth reason for caution is that costs to the right hemisphere could show themselves, either as a handicap to specific right hemisphere functions, or as a deficit of general intelligence, as mentioned above. A BP + HA could balance the benefits of ready speech with deficits to nonverbal ability, or alternatively, loss of overall brain power. Two sets of evidence suggest to me that spatial ability itself may depend on total brain power, rather than the right hemisphere alone. First, a massive study of cognitive abilities in 997 families in Hawaii, including parents and children (14 years plus) from three ethnic groups, found very similar factor profiles in the largest groups (Caucasians and Japanese) including a spatial visualisation factor in both. Girls were poorer on this factor than their brothers, but better than their mothers; they were about the same as their fathers (Wilson, De Fries, McClearn et al., 1975). Thus spatial ability varied not only with sex but also with age, consistent with the idea that it depends on some overall level of cerebral efficiency. My second reason for suggesting that spatial ability depends on overall brain power depends on the hemiplegic children that I personally examined for intelligence and for peg moving hand skill (see Table 10.1). When the better hand was in the normal range, IQs were virtually identical on both verbal and performance scales, and also virtually identical whether the good hand was the right or the left. When the better hand fell below the normal range and both hemispheres were likely to be affected, both types of intelligence declined, but performance more strongly than verbal IQ, whichever hemisphere was affected. This suggested that nonverbal abilities might be especially sensitive

to overall loss of intelligence. This reinforces the argument that simplistic assumptions about types of ability and brain laterality should be treated with caution.

My fifth reason for caution about associations between spatial ability and
handedness depended on my own negative findings. I looked for relationships
between handedness and different types of ability, starting in the early 1960s,
many years before formulating the RS theory. My hunch at that time was that
mixed-handers might have advantages over consistent-handers, because I thought
they might have more variable cerebral organisation to match their more variable
handedness (the heterozygote variability hypothesis of Annett, 1964). Some
300 first year students at the University of Aberdeen were given a vocabulary
test (Mill Hill scale; Raven, 1958a) and a spatial test (the Shapes test, Morrisby,
1955), along with an eight-item handedness questionnaire as part of a laboratory class exercise. Students in other years (N = 411) had taken routine tests of
cognitive abilities and also completed a handedness questionnaire. Findings
for several tests were compared between consistent versus mixed-handers, left-
versus right-writers, and right- versus non-right-handers. There was a significant
male superiority on the spatial test, but nothing else, and certainly no effects for
handedness. I was also able to examine the scores of some 400 recruits to the
armed forces on several tests of ability, including verbal and nonverbal reasoning, along with handedness questionnaire data. I could find no relationship
between handedness and ability. These negative findings were not published,
because the train of ideas that led me to look at the data was highly speculative
and because there was no general interest in laterality and ability at that time.
The findings for students, together with further studies of schoolchildren (Annett,
1970b; Annett and Turner, 1974) that also found no substantial differences,
suggested that normal left-, mixed- and right-handers are essentially equal for
intellectual abilities. The Hawaii cognitive study found no significant difference
between 246 left-handers and 3005 right-handers for any of four cognitive factors
(Kocel, 1977). Thus I was convinced, and remain convinced, that there are no
grounds for believing that left- and right-handers differ for cognitive abilities.
This does not mean that spatial and other abilities are uninfluenced by the RS
locus, but it does mean that left- versus right-handedness is a very poor indicator
of the relevant variables.

Levy (1969) reported Wechsler test findings for 15 right-handed and 10 left-
handed graduate science students who were similar for Verbal Scale IQs (138
and 142 respectively) but differed for Performance Scale IQ (130 and 117
respectively). She suggested that left-handers have poorer spatial abilities than
right-handers. In the light of my own extensive negative findings in very large
samples, as outlined above, I expected this report to be quickly discounted.
There were failures to replicate in large samples (Gibson, 1973; Roberts, 1974)
but the idea of visuospatial deficit in left-handers became current in the literature. From my experience as a clinical psychologist working in Oxford I knew
that undergraduates tend to have a pattern of scores like Levy's left-handers, as
was confirmed in Gibson's data for both handedness groups. What was odd
about Levy's data was the high performance IQs of the 15 right-handers. They

were a small and unusual sample, graduate students at a prestigious institution and without independent replication, their high scores should be treated as due to sampling variation. My hunch is that further questions about hand preference would have found many of this talented group non-right-handed.

A substantial literature on spatial ability and laterality followed Levy's report, with mostly weak or negative findings. Reviews concluded that relationships are far from clear, possibly because they are moderated by other variables, including sex, intellectual level, familial sinistrality and strength of handedness (Lewis and Harris, 1990; O'Boyle and Benbow, 1990). I would add that most of the experiments depended on university students, not expected by the BP + HA hypothesis to be representative of the general population for spatial or other abilities. The effect of educational level was examined but the pattern of findings was not easily interpretable (Harshman, Hampson and Berenbaum, 1983). Given all of these theoretical cautions and negative findings, why should spatial ability be considered a risk factor for the RS + gene? I now have to describe some findings for spatial ability in children and undergraduates, distinguished for subgroup handedness.

In order to study spatial ability in a representative sample of the population it is necessary to seek a general school sample. The children must be old enough to attempt appropriate tasks, but young enough to obtain a complete cohort, before school leaving age and also before the pressures of final year examinations precluded time for testing. Annett (1992c) studied a cohort of 14- to 15-year-olds in four secondary schools, two large high schools for both sexes and two small selected (grammar) schools, one for each sex. The spatial test required mental paper folding, expected to tap spatial visualisation. Hand preferences were observed and peg moving was measured as in previous samples. Spatial ability did not vary with left- or right-handedness or with sex, although there was the usual trend to male superiority. Thus far, the findings agreed with my earlier negative findings for handedness.

The surprise was that spatial ability differed *between the hand preference subgroups* identified in chapter 2. The pattern can be described roughly as a "W" with a peak in the centre. The findings are shown in Figure 12.2 for the sexes separately, because the similarity of the findings for males and females was the first reason to take them seriously. The means are joined together in the W because of the argument that handedness is a continuous variable, from consistent left (eight) to consistent right (one). Recall that classes 1–4 are right-handers and 6–8 left-handers (and class 5 was revised into classes 3 and 4). Considering each set of subgroups in turn, it can be seen that the highest means for spatial ability were for *the more sinistral groups for both types of handedness*. The highest scoring left-handers were class 8 in both sexes and also class 7 for males. The highest scoring right-handers were class 4 in both sexes and also class 3 for males. Class 6 left-handers and class 2 right-handers were poor in both sexes. Could this unexpected W pattern be found elsewhere?

The Rey-Osterreith (Rey) figure is a complex geometrical design known to be difficult for patients with right brain lesions. It had been copied by first year

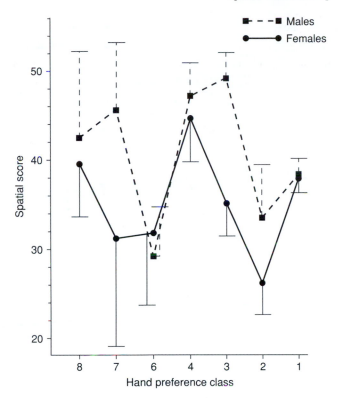

Figure 12.2 Spatial ability by subgroup handedness in teenagers, male and female: mean and standard error bars.

psychology students as part of experiments at the University of Leicester. After some 40 minutes of other tests, the students were asked to redraw the figure from memory and without prior warning. Data were available for 96 male and 332 female students. The copy scores did not differ, indicating the subgroups were equivalent for the initial drawing. The recall scores differed between subgroups, as shown in Figure 12.3. For females there was again a rough W pattern, class 4 right-handers out-performing the rest. For males there was a gradual fall from left to right, with consistent left-handers (eight) superior. Among right-handed males, the mean was highest for class 4, as for females. The reversal between classes 1 and 2, observed for teenagers in Figure 12.2, was present for males but not females. Thus, many features of the W pattern in the school sample were repeated in the university sample.

The subgroup analysis suggested that spatial ability declines from left to right across levels of preference in left-handers and in right-handers. The laterality groups were originally discriminated because they differed for R–L hand skill. One of the curious features of that analysis (chapter 2) was that class 2 right-handers were actually more dextral that consistent right-handers. (It may be recalled

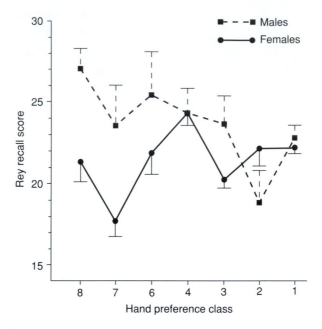

Figure 12.3 Spatial ability by subgroup handedness in undergraduates, male and female: mean and standard error bars.

that class 2 included the mixed-handers remaining after other mixed-handers with smaller R–L differences for peg moving had been removed.) The poorer spatial ability of class 2 here might agree with their greater dextrality, if spatial ability declines from left to right across the laterality spectrum. Figure 12.4 plots mean spatial test scores, standardised for sex and sample against observed R–L% peg moving asymmetry. Among right-handers, 16 groups comprising four classes in two sexes and two samples, class 2 tended to be at the extreme right for R–L% hand skill as well as poorest for spatial test performance. Class 4, by contrast, tended to be least dextral and superior for spatial ability. There was a significant linear trend over handedness subgroups (r(16) = –.67, p = 0.005). The more biased to dextrality, the poorer the mean spatial ability.

Among the 12 groups of left-handers there was no overall trend. Although class 8 tended to be superior and class 6 inferior for spatial ability there were exceptions. The lack of trend was due partly to the fact that the left-handed children were more strongly sinistral than left-handed undergraduates for R–L% asymmetry. Associations between R–L% and spatial test scores in left-handers were examined for each sample separately. The correlation for schoolchildren was r(52) = –.282, p = 0.043, and for students, r(57) = –.274, p = 0.065. The trend was clear and consistent in both, the stronger the bias to dextrality the poorer spatial ability, even among left-handers.

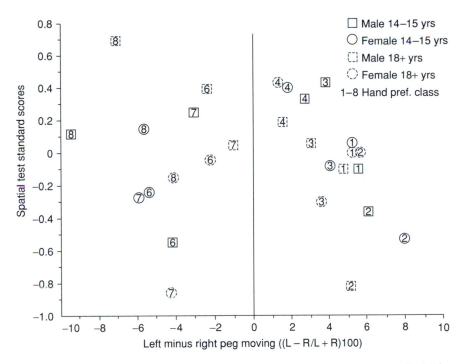

Figure 12.4 Spatial test standardised scores by L–R difference for peg moving (R–L%) in teenagers and undergraduates classified for subgroup hand preference.

These findings were the first to suggest that there could be a decline of ability from left to right, not over the whole laterality spectrum but within each handedness group separately. How is this to be interpreted? Looking at the three overlapping genotype distributions and the threshold for left-handedness at X (about 10% of the population, see Figure 7.1) it can be seen that left-writers include RS + – as well as RS – – genotypes. The former would tend to be to the right of the latter for hand skill asymmetry, more likely to be class 6 than class 7 or 8 left-handers. To the right of X are the 90% of the population that are right-handers. Some 12 of these 90 would be RS – – genotypes. These would tend to be to the left of other right-handers for hand skill, more likely to be class 4 or 3 than 1 or 2. Thus, the findings suggest that the tendency for spatial ability to decline from left to right within both handedness groups might depend on the superior performance of RS – – genotypes in comparison with RS + –. That is, presence of the RS + gene, even in single dose, could be associated with less than optimal spatial ability. How could these ideas be tested further?

If the hand preference subgroups differ for spatial ability because they differ for genotypes, as hypothesised above, they should also differ for number of left-handed relatives. It was this line of reasoning that prompted a reanalysis of family handedness data collected several years earlier, where respondents could be classified for subgroup handedness and where the handedness of relatives had

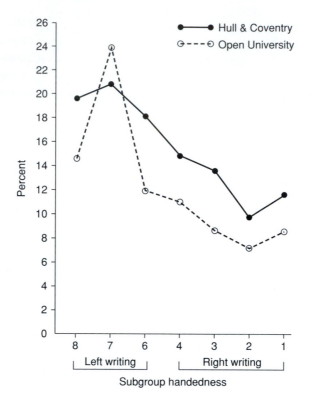

Figure 12.5 Percentage left-handed relatives by subgroup handedness in two samples: Annett, 1994.

been reported (Annett, 1994). The percentages of non-right-handed relatives for Ss classified for hand preference subgroup is shown in Figure 12.5. There were linear falls from left to right for both samples. Class 7 (left writers with weak right tendencies) had most left-handed relatives in both samples. Among right-handers, the highest percentage was for class 4. In both samples there was a dip for class 2, as found for spatial ability. In comparison with the W pattern for spatial ability, what was missing in the data for relatives was the contrast between class 6 left-handers and class 4 right-handers. There was a problem of method here because many of the participants in these samples had grown up at a time when there were strong pressures against the use of the left-hand for writing. If there was any report of early pressure to use the right-hand, I took the view that participants should be classified as if they were left-handed writers. This was a conservative decision that put several class 4 right-handers into groups 6–8. If these had been counted as class 4, the approximation to the spatial ability "W" may have been closer. Hence the hypothesised contrast between classes 4 and 6 could not be clearly resolved by these data. It remains to be investigated further. Aside from the relative positions of classes 6 and 4, the distribution of left-handed relatives shares important features of the findings for spatial ability, namely a linear trend from left to right, with a peak for class 7 and trough for class 2.

I have had no further opportunity to check the above findings by replication in a comparable sample. Similar findings have been evident, however, in later samples of left-handers. A sample of 9- to 10-year-old children (Annett, Eglinton and Smythe, 1996; see chapter 13) was asked to draw four nonsense shapes from memory, and to perform a hole punching test of hand skill (Annett, 1992d). Both of these were short tests given in class. There were 45 children left-handed for hole-punching (all subsequently found left-handed for writing) for whom the correlation between the spatial test score and R–L% was negative (r(45) = −.343, p = −0.021), as above. In a sample of female students, there was a negative correlation in left-handers between scores for drawing the same four shapes and R–L% peg moving (r(22) = −.466, p = 0.029). In another sample of female students given a different test of spatial ability (drawing a house plan), the correlation was again negative but smaller (r(38) = −.216, p = 0.193). The weight of evidence over these several samples supports the inference that spatial ability declines within left-handers, as the bias to dextrality increases. Replication within right-handers depends mainly on the superiority of class 4 and the inferiority of class 2 right-handers. This pattern has not been clearly replicated in the above samples. Independent tests of spatial ability in the light of the RS theory will be considered in chapter 15.

MATHEMATICS

An association between left-handedness and mathematical ability was a possibility that interested me several years before the advent of the RS theory and BP + HA hypothesis. In my questionnaire studies of university and school samples, maths students often included more left-handers than non-maths students but the differences in frequency were generally small. Having thought of the BP + HA hypothesis, mathematical ability seemed a strong candidate for RS + disadvantage. Annett and Kilshaw (1982) investigated this idea with further questionnaire studies of students and through personal assessments of teachers of mathematics and maths related subjects.

Questionnaire responses that depend on voluntary returns may inflate proportions of left-handers, but in general surveys any such bias should be common to both maths and non-maths students. For males there were significantly more left-writers among maths students (21%) than non-maths (11%) and significantly more non-right-handers (44% versus 24% respectively). For females the contrasts were smaller but the percentages (11% left-writers for maths versus 8% for non-maths students) consistent with the hypothesis of absent RS + + genotype as explained above.

Teachers of mathematics and related sciences in several universities and polytechnics were asked to take part in a personal interview. Hand use was observed for the 12 actions of the AHPQ and peg moving was measured for both hands. Ninety-seven males and twenty-seven females were recruited, including five teachers of advanced (A-level) maths in schools. Control academics, 50 male and 20 female, were from non-maths departments. Mean asymmetry for peg moving was smaller for mathematicians than controls of both sexes, the difference significant statistically for males. The maths teachers were subdivided for sex and speciality in 10 groups. Mean peg moving times were smaller in nine out of ten comparisons with controls. Male pure mathematicians included 18% left-writers and 48.5% were non-right-handers. The distribution of L–R peg moving times for all male maths teachers was tested for compatibility with the two genotype model in Figure 12.1 and the fit was good.

Benbow (1986) distributed EHI handedness questionnaires to young people who scored at extremely high levels for maths and for verbal abilities on the US scholastic achievement tests (SATs). Among 145 males precocious in maths there were 13.8% left-handers (defined as LQ < 0) and 5.9% in 17 females. Among those precocious in verbal tasks there were 23.5% left-handers in 51 males and 12.3% in 57 females. Thus, high scorers on the verbal tests as well as the number tests tended to included more left-handers than controls (about 10%), but the differences were not significant statistically in these small samples. Benbow made another comparison for percentage of *strong right-handers*. There were only 23% strong dextrals in the 305 extremely precocious students compared with 42% in controls. This supports the present thesis that the relevant difference is not an excess of left-handers in talented groups but rather a shortfall of strong right-handers.

Temple (1990) distributed the EHI to staff in several departments at the University of Oxford, in order to contrast those with mathematical orientations versus verbal ones (law and modern languages). The proportions with LQ < 0 were virtually identical at about 12% in both groups of respondents. These observations, like those of Benbow above, suggest that the proportion of left-handers is raised in many talented groups, whether the talents are specifically for maths or non-maths skills. The differences in frequency were not large, but consistent with the theory of a reduction in the proportion of strong right-handers.

In the Annett and Manning (1990b) sample maths test scores were supplied by teachers. The findings for groups classified for R–L hand skill were shown in Figure 11.3b. There was a strong linear decline from left to right in both sexes. The total group in this analysis (N = 149) included 8% left-writers. Among those superior at maths (one standard deviation above the mean or 116+, N = 39) there were 13% left-writers. The difference is about as predicted if RS + + genotypes were missing from the latter.

ART AND MUSIC

The handedness of 103 art students in Boston, Massachusetts, was compared with that of 101 students attending a liberal arts college (Mebert and Michel,

1980). The arts students included 30% left-handers and the controls 10%, a highly significant difference. The contrast was of similar order for all the 12 actions of the AHPQ. This very marked difference between groups was surprising. If replicated, it would suggest that art students are predominantly of RS − − genotype.

Are musicians more likely to be left-handed? Byrne (1974) found a raised incidence of mixed-handedness in instrumentalists. Aggleton, Kentridge and Good (1994) distributed the EHI to musicians in 17 orchestras, 10 leading choirs and 2 associations of composers. The return rates were 51% for orchestral players, 61% for choristers and 92% for the small sample of composers, clearly not complete samples. The incidences of left-handedness (by LQ < 0) were 12.2% for males and 11.8% for females among musicians. In comparison with controls, taken from a survey of people registered with a large general medical practice (Ellis, Ellis and Marshall, 1988), the strongest effects were for degree of handedness. That is, musicians were less often strongly right-handed than controls. The findings are consistent with the general thesis, that talent is associated with reduced RS.

There are a number of suggestions that higher musical ability is associated with reduced bias to dextrality. Deutsch (1978, 1980) found that mixed-handers (mildly rather than strongly left-handed as assessed by questionnaire) made fewer errors than strongly right or left-handed subjects on a test of pitch identification. Craig (1980) found left-handers superior to right-handers for identifying rhythms when beats were presented to both ears simultaneously. Laguitton, Demany, Semal et al. (1998) found differences between right- and left-handers in the perception of complex tones, which they interpreted as suggesting that left-handers are more analytic than right-handers in tone perception.

Measurement of the presumed hand region of the motor cortex by magnetic resonance imaging in professional keyboard players found larger motor strips on both sides, especially the right, than for controls (Amunts, Schlaug, Jäncke et al., 1997). Whereas there was a pronounced asymmetry in favour of left side larger in controls, the musicians were more symmetrical. Amunts et al. attribute the findings to the effects of years of practice on the relevant areas, but it is possible that relative symmetry was also a pre-requisite of talent. It should be noted, however, that in musicians with perfect pitch, there was a strong asymmetry of the planum temporale in the typical direction (L > R) (Steinmetz, 1996).

SURGERY

Personal observations and informal reports suggest that surgeons include a high proportion of non-right-handers. I looked for evidence in a sample of veterinary surgeons. The AHPQ was distributed to members of an association for small-animal veterinarians, with an additional question, whether or not surgery was a main interest. Twenty-three vets said that surgery was not a main interest, and of these 8.7% were left-handed writers and 26.1% showed some sinistral preference. Among 87 vets for whom surgery was a main interest, 13.8% were left-handed writers, and 41.4% reported some left-handed preference. The differences were not statistically different in this small sample, but the size and direction of difference were as expected. The percentages of left and mixed hand preference found among non-surgeons agreed with expectations for the general population, while those for surgeons were consistent with absence of RS + + genotypes.

SPORT

The physical prowess required for success in sport can be assumed to have advantages for reproductive and hence evolutionary success. Many folk tales tell how the favours of the princess were won by the champion at arms. Some modern sporting heroes have confessed to astonishing numbers of sexual partners. If certain sports are associated with a higher frequency of left-handedness, then the skills involved are likely to be relevant to the BP + HA of the RS + gene. It should be recalled that the left-handed slingers in the army of the Children of Benjamin were highly skilled, they "could sling stones at an hair-breadth and not miss". The sports particularly associated with raised incidences of left-handedness are ones that take the form of personal duels, as in tennis, boxing and especially fencing. About a third of top class fencers with foils and sword play with the left-hand (Azemar, 1993; Azemar, Ripoll, Simonet et al., 1983). However, good footballers kick with either foot and good boxers lead with either hand. Porac and Coren (1981) distributed questionnaires to athletes in a variety of sports in order to investigate whether the more proficient, at higher levels of achievement, differed for handedness from those at lower levels. The only notable difference was for more left-handers among top level boxers. Looking at consistent versus inconsistent preferences, greater ability in the majority of sports was associated with a higher frequency of inconsistent or mixed hand preferences. This agrees with the present argument that there should be fewer strong right-handers, rather than a positive excess of left-handers.

The most frequently offered explanation of the excess of left-handers in sport is a strategic one, that left-handers have an advantage over right-handers because the latter are less practised in playing against left- than right-handers. The alternative hypothesis is that left-handers have a constitutional advantage, perhaps for reaction time or balance that gives an edge in competitive sports. A variant of this hypothesis is that the left-hand is preferred in certain sports, even by people otherwise right-handed, because the left-hand and right hemisphere respond faster than the right-hand and left hemisphere (Carson, Chua, Elliott et al., 1990). If this were true of the "typical" brain, and were indeed the reason why one-third of fencers use the left-hand, the question arises why two-thirds continue to use the right-hand. Analyses of hand skill in chapter 10 suggested that the RS + gene shifts a chance distribution toward dextrality by weakening the left-hand (see Figure 10.4). This implies that RS + gene-carriers may be disadvantaged in tasks requiring skilled performance on the left side of the body. There might be a lack of speed or a lack of balance that precludes exceptional performance. In contrast to other constitutional theories that look for positive advantages in left-handers, and then have the problem that most good sports-people are right-handed, the RS version of the constitutional explanation looks rather for disadvantage in some right-handers. Mild and moderate right-handers are expected to be free of these weaknesses, and to share the same relative advantages as left-handers.

The late Mr. C.M. Jones took a particular interest in the handedness of tennis players. He indicated for me, on the 1978 Wimbledon programme, the hand used by singles players that season. There were 15.6% male and 9.4% female left-handers. The proportion was higher than in my student samples (8.1%; Annett, 1970a) but not by a large margin. 1 looked for evidence that the percentage was greater in players of higher than lower rank (Annett, 1985a) but my analysis of the rankings was flawed, as pointed out to me by Charles Wood. Wood and Aggleton (1989) examined the handedness of the top rank 100 players for several years and found left-handers in the ranges 13.0–16.5% for men and 11.1–11.2% for women. In comparison with control data (8.9% for male and 8.1% for female students) the incidences in tennis professionals were judged not to differ significantly. However, the trend to higher incidence was present in every comparison. I have checked the playing hand of the top ranked 100 men and also women players for November 1999 (ATP and WTA guides). There were 15 men and 11 women left-handed players. These findings agree with those of Wood and Aggleton and give confidence in their reliability. They are as expected for absence of the RS + + genotype, as outlined above.

The handedness of baseball and cricket players has received particular attention as part of the controversy about life expectancy and handedness (chapter 6). Encyclopaedia record statistics for players, including handedness for play and years of birth and death. Among 4219 baseball players there were 18.1% left-handed throwers and only one who threw with either hand (Wood, 1988). An analysis for bowling side in English cricketers found 18.4% left-handers among 3599 deceased and 18.2% among 2574 living players (Aggleton, Bland, Kentridge et al., 1994). Incidences for players recorded over five seasons between 1937 and 1985 ranged from 15.3 to 26.1% for bowlers and from 18.7 to 19.6% for batsmen (Wood and Aggleton, 1989). By contrast, schoolboy cricketers included 10.6% left-handed bowlers and 9.8% left-handed batsmen. There is little room for doubt that left-handed play is more frequent in talented cricketers and baseball players than expected in the general population. How is side of play related to preferences for writing and other actions?

In the mid 1980s, left-handed English cricketers were sent a version of my handedness questionnaire (AHPQ) by Norman Harris, cricket correspondent of the *Sunday Times* newspaper. The sample was not intended to be representative of all cricketers, but to investigate certain ideas of Mr. Harris about left-handed players. Some right-handed players were included for comparative purposes. Table 12.1 classifies the respondents for side of play (batting, bowling, N) RR 26, LR 27, RL 24, LL 11 and for subgroup handedness. Several findings are of

Table 12.1 Hand preference subgroup with batting and bowling side in first class cricketers: N (percent)

Batting	Bowling	Left cons.	Left weak R	Left strong R	Right strong L	Right mod. L	Right weak L	Right cons.	N
Right	Right	1	—	3	2	5	1	14 (54)	26
Left	Right	—	—	—	6	3	2	16 (59)	27
Right	Left	14 (58)	6	3	1	—	—	—	24
Left	Left	4 (36)	2	1	3	1	—	—	11

interest. First, there was a strong association between the bowling side and writing hand. There were 35 left-sided bowlers, of whom 30 (85.7%) were left-handed writers. The remaining five had strong to moderate left-handed tendencies. None were class 1 or 2 right-handers. Among the 53 right-handed bowlers, 49 (92.5%) wrote with the right-hand and 3 of the 4 left-writers had strong right tendencies (class 6). Discordance for bowling and writing was not due to forced changes of handedness because the questionnaire specifically asked for information on this point. The RR player classified as a consistent left-hander (class 8) reported that he originally bowled with the left-hand and subsequently switched to the right. As he was left-handed for all other actions of the questionnaire and clearly ambidextrous for bowling he fulfilled the criteria for class 8.

In contrast to the strong association between bowling and writing, there was no direct association between the batting side and writing. Among 38 left-sided batsmen, there were only 7 (18.4%) left-writers. When the bowling and batting hands differed, writing hand agreed with the bowling hand in all except one instance, and the exception was a class 4 right-hander with strong sinistral tendencies. It should be recalled that these proportions are not representative of the population because the questionnaire was addressed mainly to left-sided players. However, the writing hand was not known in advance.

The RR players are particularly interesting for the BP + HA hypothesis. The 26 RR cricketers included 4 (15.4%) left-handed for writing and 12 (46.1%) with some sinistral preference. These left-sided preferences for the actions of the AHPQ are consistent with predictions for a sample drawn from the population that includes RS − − and RS + − genotypes, but not RS + + genotypes (see Figure 12.1 and text). The critical point here is that these left-handed preferences for questionnaire items have nothing to do with strategic advantages for play, because all of these players were right-handed for both bowling and batting. They are consistent with the idea that skilled sports-people are less strongly biased to the right-hand than the general population. My conclusions are that tendencies to non-right-handedness are high in all cricketers, even those who play right-handed.

MORE ABOUT CRICKET: A COHORT OF TEST PLAYERS

The questionnaire sample above was not representative of all cricketers, but selected for left-sided players, as mentioned. In order to estimate frequencies for side of play and also to assess the relative success of left- versus right-handers, information is needed for a complete set of players. A list of all cricketers who played for England in test matches between 1877 and 1996 was compiled by Woolgar (1997), together with statistics of performance. The players represent the best in over a century of test cricket because they were invited to play for the national team. The sample is large, complete and selected only for cricket skills (not handedness). Selectors of test teams must look for various talents, batting, bowling, fielding and wicket keeping. The rules require every player to bat and the batting hand was noted in every case. Not every player must bowl and a bowling hand was not always recorded. In the sample as a whole (N = 582) there were 84 (14.4%) left-handed batsmen and 87 (14.9%) recorded as left-handed bowlers (unknown bowlers counted as right for this purpose). One player bowled with either hand, just as there was one switch pitcher in the baseball data. Thus, the base rates for left-sided batting and bowling were similar, and about the frequency expected if these exceptional sportsmen included R − − and RS + − genotypes but not RS + + genotypes (as explained at the start of this chapter).

The rates for the total cohort represent a minimum, because the players were selected for different skills. Were the proportions higher among more successful players? Among batsmen, 304 players had a batting average at the median or above (17+ runs) and these included 15.5% left-handers. For the top 30% of players (25+ runs) there were 36/189 (19.0%) left-handers. Among bowlers, the base rate for left and ambidextrous bowlers when non-bowlers were excluded was 88/504 (17.5%). Among those who took at least two test wickets (the median and above) there were 55/294 (18.7%) left-handers and among those taking at least ten wickets (the top 30% of bowlers) there were 41/189 (21.7%) left-handers. Overall, the proportion of left-handers rose from a base rate of about 14% to about 20% with increasing skill, for both batsmen and bowlers. Among all-rounders (above the median for batting and bowling) the percentage of left-handers did not rise further.

Edwards and Beaton (1996) distinguished bowlers whose effectiveness depends on speed of delivery (fast bowlers or "seamers") and those who induce the ball to bounce in directions that are difficult for the batsman to counter (slow and "spin" bowlers). They found the latter more often left-handed than the former among English cricketers playing in four seasons between 1981 and 1991. Woolgar classified the test cricketers for bowling action in eight categories for speed and types of spin. There were marked differences in proportions of left-handers between the groups. Reducing the groups to two, one for speed of delivery ("fast", "fast medium" and "medium" bowlers) versus all the rest (slow bowlers and those with various types of spin), found 12.3% left-bowlers in the former and 26.6% in the latter, consistent with the findings of Edwards and Beaton. For bowlers taking 10+ wickets, there was little change for seamers (14.5% left-bowlers) but a marked increase for spinners (35.4%). The latter proportion is about the level predicted for left-handed writers in RS − − genotypes (see Figure 11.1).

The argument that the raised proportion of left-handed players is due to their strategic advantages in playing against right-handed opponents, needs to be addressed by posing the question of success the other way around. Were left-handers indeed more successful than right-handers in over a century of test matches? Did left-handers outperform right-handers for either batting averages or bowling averages? Batting averages were compared between right- and left-sided bats for all players, and also for players with good levels of performance (to exclude players selected for other talents such as wicket-keepers). No significant differences were found. For all right-handers (498), the mean batting average was 19.9, S.D. 13.7, and for all left-handers (84) the mean was 21.4, S.D. 14.2. Thus, there was no reason to believe that batting side was associated with a strategic advantage.

For bowlers, the question whether left-handers were more successful than right-handers must be asked for seamers versus spinners separately. It should be noted first that there were seven star bowlers, defined as taking over 200 wickets. None of these were spinners and only one was left-handed (14.3%). After excluded these seven, because their extreme scores would distort the general pattern, bowling averages were virtually identical between the seamers and spinners. Left and right-handed seamers were virtually identical for wickets taken. Among spinners and slow bowlers, however, there was a significant difference in favour of left-handers. (The 135 right-handers took an average of 14.9, S.D. 31.9 wickets and the 49 left-handers took 29.5, S.D. 44.4: t = 2.462, d.f. 182, p = 0.015.) Thus for most comparisons, right versus left-handed batsmen or bowlers did not differ for successful play. The only category in which left-handers were more successful than right-handers was that of slow and spin bowlers. It appears that greater success depends not on being a slow bowler, or on being a left-handed bowler, but on the combination "left-handed slow bowler". The effectiveness of this combination might well depend on its rarity. Its relative frequency in the test series might also depend on the interest of test selectors in this valuable type of player. However, if and when it is possible to identify the RS + gene, it would be interesting to see if the gene is particularly infrequent in this group.

In summary, this unique set of test cricketers included a relatively high base rate of left-handed batsmen and bowlers, at about the level expected by the BP + HA hypothesis if RS + + genotypes are absent from this group. Among the most successful batsmen and bowlers percentages of left-handed players rose to about 20%. But left-handers were not more successful in runs scored or wickets taken than their right-handed counterparts. There was only one group of left-handers who enjoyed exceptional success, left-handed slow and spin bowlers. Among the most successful slow and spin bowlers there were about one in three left-handers, a proportion consistent with expectations for the RS − − genotype.

SUMMARY

This chapter investigated possible deficits associated with the RS + gene by looking for groups with higher frequencies of left-handedness than the general population. It has been shown previously (in chapter 10) that strong right-handers (subgroups 1 and 2) have weaker non-preferred hands than mild and moderate right-handers. Does the weakness of the left-hand imply weakness of the right hemisphere, or loss of physical and mental power for spatial and mathematical reasoning, performance in the arts, music and sport?

There are several theoretical reasons not to expect simple relationships between handedness and abilities. Notwithstanding certain beliefs in the literature that left-handers have poorer spatial abilities than right-handers, the quantity of substantial negative evidence leads to the conclusion that there are no differences that can be attributed to handedness as such. The RS theory suggests that there might be differences associated with absence of the RS + gene, or with its presence in double dose. If RS + + genotypes are not present in certain talented groups, whether top level tennis players or academic mathematicians, the proportion of left-handers should be raised by about 50%, compared with the general population (e.g. from 10% to 15%). If the RS + gene is disadvantageous even in single dose, then about 30% of talented groups might be left-handed (as found in some data for art students, top fencers with foils, and the best slow bowlers in cricket).

Spatial ability in a cohort of teenagers, and in a large sample of undergraduates, was examined for hand preference subgroups. The pattern of ability, roughly W-shaped, suggested that spatial ability declines from left to right across the laterality spectrum, in left-handed writers and in right-handed writers. Negative correlations between ability and bias to dextrality were found in further samples of left-handers. These findings are consistent with the idea that spatial ability is advantaged in people of RS − − genotype, and declines with increasing doses of RS +.

For most of the abilities considered, the question of relative disadvantage for the RS + gene could be approached only through a comparison for incidences of left-handedness or non-right-handedness. Differences were of the order expected for absence of RS + + genotypes for several groups, including veterinary surgeons, professional musicians, academically precocious young people, and talented players of tennis, cricket and baseball. By conventional criteria of statistical significance, most of these results were non-significant. However, they were consistent with predictions of the RS model.

Handedness in cricketers was examined in two ways. First, all prominent left-handed players, together with some right-handed players, were invited to complete a version of the AHPQ. This revealed a strong association between the side for bowling and for writing, but not between side for batting and writing. Among players who were right-sided for batting and bowling, the proportions of left-handed writers and non-right-handers were consistent with expectations for absence of RS + + genotypes, as argued for other sports-people above. That is, the raised proportions of left preferences for actions of the AHPQ had nothing to do with strategic advantages for play, because play was right-sided. It was consistent with the argument for disadvantages for RS + + genotypes in skilled sports performance.

Second, in a cohort of cricketers selected to play in test matches spanning some 120 years, the base rates for left-handed batsmen and left-handed bowlers were about 14%. When analyses were restricted to players with good performance records, incidences rose to around 20%. The argument that left-handers have strategic advantages could not be sustained in these data, because the batting averages and the bowling averages of left- versus right-handers did not differ. There was one group, however, where the proportion of left-handers rose to over 30%, the most successful slow or spin bowlers. A similar percentage has been reported for the most successful fencers with foils and sword. Incidences of this order suggest that any dose of the RS + gene could be a handicap for these very special talents. The argument whether the advantage is strategic or genetic will not be settled until the presence of the RS + gene can be detected.

13 Speech, phonology and varieties of dyslexia

The costs and benefits of the RS + gene

The idea that problems of speech and literacy might be due to atypical cerebral dominance was suggested soon after it was known that speech and language depend in most people on the left hemisphere (Ireland, 1881, cited in Harris, 1980a). A report that stuttering was more common in "dextro-sinistrals" than other children (Ballard, 1911–12, in Harris, 1980a) led to the idea that stuttering might be caused by forcing a naturally left-handed child to write with the right-hand. The popularisation of this theory during the 1920s and 1930s was probably the most important single cause of the relaxation of pressures against the use of the left-hand in the United States of America and the United Kingdom (Travis, 1959). These pressures were still severe in the 1920s, according to bitter accounts in letters written to me in the 1960s, in response to my appeals in the media for left-handed parents. However, one mother told me she was *forced to use her left-hand*, in the 1930s, because her teachers noticed she had some tendencies to left handedness and they were anxious she should not stutter. She continued to use the left for writing, but believed she should have used the right. For peg moving she was equally fast with both hands. Some teachers continue to "encourage" children to use the right-hand today. The supposed link between forced change of writing hand and stuttering is unproven, but in my view "nature" knows best and children should be allowed to follow their inclination for hand use.

Non-right or inconsistent preferences for hand, eye and foot were found to be more frequent in stutterers than controls (Morley, 1957) and in children with specific developmental disorders of speech, "specific" meaning unassociated with other problems (Ingram, 1959a, 1959b). Differences were small, however, and of questionable statistical significance (Bishop, 1990a). An unpublished study I made of children attending for speech therapy in Sheffield, in the early 1960s, found that 53 stutterers included 13.2% left-handers, compared with 5.7% among the other 228 children in the sample. The difference was in the predicted direction but not significant statistically.

The neurologist Samuel T. Orton (1925, 1937) noted that many of the children referred to him for developmental language problems were what he termed "motor-intergrades", not clearly right or left-sided. Two major studies, in Sweden (Hallgren, 1950) and London (Naidoo, 1972), found 18% of poor readers and spellers left-handed in comparison with 9% of controls left-handed.

There is a deep puzzle here, because if atypical handedness is an important factor in developmental language problems, why are most children with such problems right-handed, and why are most left- and mixed-handers in the general population not affected? Surveys of large school populations typically find no association between laterality and literacy (Clark, 1970; Rutter, Tizard and Whitmore, 1970). A review of the early literature concluded that relationships were "extremely obscure" (Vernon, 1957, p. 107). A recent review, taking a critical look at carefully selected studies, concluded that it is doubtful that reliable relationships exist, and suggested that if they do, effects are so small as to be negligible (Bishop, 1990a). The RS theory expects effects to be small but meta-analysis shows that effects for handedness are reliable (Eglinton and Annett, 1994).

The concept of "dyslexia" as a type of reading disorder is controversial. For most of the 20th century, teachers and educational psychologists argued that dyslexia is a myth created by neurologists. The term "congenital word blindness" (Hinshelwood, 1917) referred to a specific deficit of the "visual memory centre" for words, that was unexpected in the light of other abilities and educational opportunities. Should we call poor readers dyslexic only if they are of high intelligence? But how high should this be and on what tests? Are all children who fail to learn to read, given normal opportunities, dyslexic? Neither educational practice nor psychological research has revealed a distinct group among poor readers in class (Stanovich, 1994). Another possible source of confusion is that the term "dyslexic" is applied to poor spellers as well as poor readers. Poor readers are usually also poor spellers, but many poor spellers are not poor readers. I shall use the terms "poor reader" and "dyslexic" interchangeably, but use "poor speller" for those who are poor at spelling alone.

What are the causes of poor reading and spelling? Literacy normally implies that the language we speak can be understood when represented by written symbols. Writing systems may take many different forms, but the basic requirement is that spoken words are represented visually. Learning to read might be impeded if there were problems with either or both of the representation of speech sounds or visual word forms. That is, problems could arise in either or both the auditory and visual domains. Difficulties might be due to relatively superficial weaknesses of perception, as in discriminating rapidly changing stimuli, but they might depend on deeper processes through which speech and writing are represented and associated.

Theories of dyslexia are many and have changed with time and fashion. Early theories looked for visual difficulties, possibly arising from confusions between shapes and their mirror images. Letters such as "b and d, p and q", and words such as "was" and "saw", might be confused because of conflicting representations in both hemispheres when cerebral dominance is weak (Orton, 1937; see review in Corballis, 1983). A widely accepted current view is that the roots of dyslexia lie in the analysis and processing of speech sounds, phonology (I.Y. Liberman, 1989; Snowling, 1981; Wagner and Torgersen, 1987). Both visual and speech based processing continue to be investigated as causes of dyslexia (Stein and Walsh, 1997; Willows, Kruk and Corcos, 1993). Reading is one of the main research fields of modern cognitive psychology. It is of interest from the viewpoints of neuropsychology and genetics as well as education and remedial teaching. The main purpose of the present account is to outline my research, as prompted by the RS theory. Wider implications will then be considered briefly.

From the start, the RS theory was expected to have implications for theories of speech and reading disorders. The 1972 analysis distinguished two main factors, a chance distribution of handedness asymmetry that humans share with other species, and an agent specific to humans that shifts the distribution to the right. The obvious place to look for an agent of right shift was left hemisphere lateralisation for speech. If some people lack left hemisphere specialisation, they might be disadvantaged for speech learning, and for other skills that depend on the efficiency of speech, including phonological processing. Handedness in people lacking the RS "factor" would be unshifted to the right. Many would have mixed-hand preferences; they would be motor-intergrades in Orton's terminology. Poor language learning and inconsistent lateral preferences would go together because they both stem from the same cause, absence of the RS factor. As Brain (1945) put it, there would be lack of hemisphere dominance on either side. This hypothesis resolves the puzzle as to why the frequency of mixed-handers is raised among dyslexics although mixed-handers in the general population are not dyslexic. Inspection of Figure 7.1 shows that the genotype at risk (RS − −) overlaps extensively with the genotypes of gene-carriers. The majority of RS − − are expected to be mixed-handers, but the majority of mixed-handers should enjoy the benefits of the RS + gene. Could I find evidence to support the RS interpretation? Investigations from the early 1970s to the present have strengthened but also qualified the initial hypothesis. There is abundant evidence to support the theory that people with poor phonology tend to be toward the left of the laterality spectrum but there is also evidence, not anticipated, for risks to reading toward the right of the spectrum also. This implies at least two types of dyslexia, one associated with atypical cerebral dominance and one that might be called "over-typical" cerebral dominance. However, before this became clear, the RS theory made another contribution to the debate about laterality and dyslexia, by distinguishing the logic of arguing from disorder to handedness from the logic of arguing from handedness to disorder.

CLINIC VERSUS SCHOOL: THE LOGIC OF DISORDER TO HANDEDNESS VERSUS HANDEDNESS TO DISORDER

A contrast between the strategies underlying research in clinic versus school was noted by Annett and Turner (1974). They investigated laterality and ability in a school sample that was representative (selected by date of birth), but with the addition for certain analyses of all remaining left-handed writers (the complete cohort of left-handers). Reading attainment scores were supplied by teachers for older children. There were no differences between right-handers and left-handers for reading ability. The story was different, however, when children were selected for poor reading relative to vocabulary intelligence. Reading quotients were available for 66 right-handers and 79 left-handers. Quotients more than 30 points below vocabulary IQ were found in 6.1% of the right-handers but in 15.2% of left-handers. This difference was not quite statistically significant. The interesting point, however, was that the difference appeared only when children were selected for disability, as they would be in a clinic sample. The negative findings for reading and laterality in the literature, as here, were for children classified for handedness and then compared for ability. The positive trend was for groups classified for disability and then compared for handedness. In the clinic children are selected, of course, for disability.

Reports of atypical laterality in cases of speech and reading disorder, as outlined above, originated from the medical profession. The key point is that children were referred because they had a problem. Among those so selected, clinicians noted a high proportion not consistently right-sided. If certain developmental language disorders are more likely to occur in RS − − genotypes, then children referred for such problems are likely to include a high proportion of this genotype. Inspection of Figure 7.1 suggests that up to about 75% of RS − − genotypes might be non-right-handed.

By contrast, investigations designed to test the clinical reports typically used the "survey" approach in school. The argument was along these lines, "If there is an association between developmental language disorder and atypical laterality, then we will make a stringent examination of normal school samples to discover whether *left-handers* are more likely to have problems." The results of such enquiries were negative because groups of left- and mixed-handers in normal schools do not have particular problems with language. This is because the majority of left- and mixed-handers are of RS + − and RS + + genotypes. Further, many RS − − genotypes are not affected because absence of the RS + gene is a risk factor, not a determinant. When cerebral asymmetries lateralise at random, only some patterns are likely to be unfortunate.

Another version of the selection fallacy is to take a sample of clinic children, already known to have developmental language problems or other learning disabilities, classify them for laterality within the sample and look for differences in ability (Capobianco, 1966). No differences are expected by the RS theory because *handedness is not a cause*, but only a weak associate of the causal factors. Increased non-right-handedness is a result of the increased randomness of cerebral organisation. The conclusion that handedness is irrelevant to learning difficulty is correct. However, the laterality of cerebral speech is likely to be of the greatest importance for the efficiency of speech, or why would the RS + gene have evolved? Misunderstandings have arisen because handedness was taken to be an "index" of cerebral dominance, whereas these two variables are only weakly and incidentally related.

An example of the contrast between findings for the school versus clinic approach can be found in Clark's (1970) survey of 7-year-olds in a school district in Scotland. When the very large sample was classified for hand, eye and foot preferences, the various groups achieved virtually identical reading scores. Laterality did not predict differences for reading. However, follow-up at age 9 years revealed 19 severely retarded readers of normal intelligence. These included 15.8% left-handers, compared to 8.8% for the total sample. Similarly, Rutter, Tizard and Whitmore (1970) surveyed a school population in the Isle of Wight and found 9.3% left-handers among children with specific reading retardation (identified by regression of reading scores on intelligence) compared with 4.8% in controls. The overall rates of left handedness differ but the outcome is the same, about twice as many left-handers among children with reading problems as controls, as for Hallgren (1950) and Naidoo (1972) above.

A DYSLEXIA CLINIC SAMPLE: STRONG DEXTRALS AMONG POOR READERS

An opportunity to study diagnosed "dyslexics" (who may have been poor readers or poor spellers) arose when Mrs. Beve Hornsby invited me to study young people attending her remedial clinic in London. Annett and Kilshaw (1984) asked people waiting for treatment sessions to perform the peg moving test of hand skill, and to demonstrate their hand use for the 12 items of the AHPQ, as well as eye and foot preference. We assessed 109 males and 20 females and compared them with combined data from my previous samples of children and students, 1480 controls. There were highly significant differences for left-handed writing (18.6% versus 8.2%, dyslexics and controls respectively), consistent right-handedness (48.8% versus 62.8%), consistent left-handedness (7.0% versus 3.2%) and also left or either foot preference (26.4% versus 16.7%). Further, all of these differences between the groups were about as expected if a normal curve that is shifted to the right for the general population were pulled back toward the left by about 0.35z. That is, the various pairs of percentages look very different, but they are mutually consistent for areas under two normal distributions, offset by about one-third of a standard deviation.

If the findings for preference above depended simply on the difference between two normal distributions, dyslexics should have a smaller difference between the hands for R–L peg moving than controls. To our great surprise, this was not found. A careful analysis of peg moving times found that some of the dyslexics were very strongly right-handed for skill. The distribution overall was consistent with the idea that the dyslexic sample included an excess of RS − − genotypes (as predicted) but also an excess of RS + + genotypes (not predicted). The BP + HA hypothesis suggested that RS + + genotypes are at risk for certain skills, unknown, but to be researched (as in chapter 12). Could the RS + + genotype be at risk for learning to read? This surprising idea was interesting because it might throw light on controversies about handedness and dyslexia. The presence of strong dextrals would mask the excess of non-right-handers in group comparisons. Further, if both RS − − genotypes and RS + + genotypes were at risk, in comparison with the advantaged RS + − genotype, they should have different types of dyslexia.

Absence of a gene for speech learning must have different consequences from a double dose of that same gene. These ideas demanded new investigations.

POOR READING AT BOTH SIDES OF THE LATERALITY SPECTRUM IN NORMAL SAMPLES

The surprising presence of strong right-handers in a dyslexia clinic needed to be checked out in a new school sample. The RS theory is about distributions in the population. If RS + + genotypes are at risk for reading, then strong right-handers in normal schools should tend to include poor readers. Of course, about two-thirds of the general population are consistently right-handed so that measures of preference alone would not be sensitive to the distinctions required. Measures of hand skill, however, should discriminate strong right-handers. Primary school children were classified for R–L peg moving asymmetry in four groups as equally as possible (quartiles). Figure 13.1a shows that reading quotients were distributed like an inverted U. Children with mild and moderate bias to dextrality tended to be better readers than those at both the left and right ends of the distribution (Annett and Manning 1990a, corrigendum, 1994). The analysis was repeated for reading quotients regressed on Matrices test scores. The standardised residuals (stresids) are shown in Figure 13.1b. The U-shape relationship with laterality was still present. The findings for this general school sample supported those of the clinic sample, because there were risks to reading at both ends of the laterality spectrum. This was consistent with the hypothesis that both RS – – genotypes and RS + + genotypes make slower progress in learning to read than RS + – genotypes.

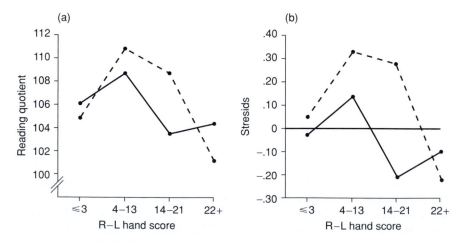

Figure 13.1 Reading in primary schoolchildren, males (solid line) and females (dashed line), classified for R–L hand peg moving: (a) reading quotient, (b) standardised residuals (stresids): Annett and Manning, 1990a.

Undergraduates were also investigated for reading skills across the hand skill distribution by asking them to read text, under time pressure, when it was presented in the normal orientation, or upside down, or in mirror reversal (Annett, 1991a). The experiment was run as a practical class exercise for second year students, so that a whole year cohort was involved. There was an inverted U-shaped trend over laterality groups for upside down reading, the strong right-handers being especially poor. No differences were found for normal reading or for mirror reading, probably because they were too easy and too hard respectively in this experiment. The findings for upside down reading in undergraduates agreed with those for children, that reading is at risk at both sides of the laterality spectrum. What could these risks be?

PHONOLOGY VERSUS HOMOPHONE DISCRIMINATION ALONG THE LATERALITY SPECTRUM

If literacy is at risk in both RS − − and RS + + genotypes, then different types of risk are likely to be involved, because the first lacks typical cerebral dominance while the second has "over-dominance". RS − − genotypes are expected to be at risk for speech based tasks, including phonological processing. A double dose of this same gene in RS + + genotypes might entail over-commitment to speech at the expense of other non-speech functions. What might be the risks of the RS + + genotype? Evidence that the RS + gene weakens left-hand and right hemisphere function and the overall arguments of the BP + HA hypothesis (see Figure 11.1) suggest the RS + + genotype might be at risk for poor visual memory for words.

The question whether there are subtypes of developmental dyslexia is controversial. Several classifications have been suggested (Seymour, 1986) but a similar contrast runs through many of them, "auditory" versus "visual" (Johnson and Myklebust, 1967), "dysphonetic" versus "dyseidetic" (Boder, 1973) and "phonological" versus "surface" (Castles and Coltheart, 1993). These distinctions have a common theme, a contrast between two types of problem. The dyslexics with auditory, dysphonetic or phonological problems are poor at relating speech sounds, phonemes relevant to word meaning, to the letters and groups of letters, graphemes, that represent them in writing. The hallmark of this type of problem is weakness in attempting to read new words or nonsense words (e.g. "fape", "slint"). This is believed to indicate poor grasp of the speech sounds involved and weak strategies for building words from elementary sound–letter relationships. By contrast, visual, dyseidetic or surface dyslexics are reasonably competent in grapheme–phoneme conversion and can therefore attempt to build new words, but they have difficulty in reading irregular words that do not follow typical sound–grapheme rules. Many English words have irregular pronunciations, such as "have" in comparison with "gave", "save", "slave", and "pint" in comparison with "mint", "lint", "stint". Surface dyslexics are likely to regularise the pronunciation of irregular words, as if they are over-reliant on letter–sound relationships. These two contrasting types of difficulty have been found not only in children, but also in undergraduates with continuing weaknesses in reading and spelling (Hanley and Gard, 1995). The question for the RS theory is whether these contrasts for types of difficulty map onto the contrasts expected between the two homozygote genotypes for handedness.

At this stage in the development of the RS theory it was important: (a) not to beg too many questions about the nature of the underlying problems, but (b) to discover whether two varieties of difficulty could be distinguished, one associated with poor phonology and one not so associated. The question is whether the two types of problem dissociate for handedness, the first less biased and the second more biased to dextrality than controls. Those with weak phonology will be referred to as "phonols". Those without weak phonology will be referred to as "visuals", on the hypothesis that their problem is to do with visual memory for words, or more neutrally as "non-phonols". The first task was to show that people with the two types of problem could be distinguished (phonological and non-phonological) and that they differed for laterality, the first less biased and the second more biased to the right than controls.

Controversies about types of dyslexia are part of a wider issue, the distribution of the relative skills in the general population. "Cases" with recognised problems may be like the visible part of icebergs, resting on much larger masses of relative strengths and weaknesses for cognitive processing. Although it has been argued above that the "survey" research strategy (that classifies for handedness and looks for differences in ability) is likely to be negative when it relies on assessments of hand preference, measures of hand skill might be sensitive enough to detect trends across the population. Analyses for reading and intelligence described earlier depended on this approach. However, effects are likely to be stronger for the "case" or clinic approach. The strategy was to collect samples large enough to be examined in both ways. First, classify all subjects for laterality and compare for the efficiency of different types of lexical processing (to address the population question) and second, compare selected "cases" with specific difficulties of each type (to address the clinic question).

In order to investigate differences in the relative strength and weakness of cognitive processes in large samples, it was necessary to develop group tests that could be given to classes of children and undergraduates. The relevant differences were likely to be small and their detection would require large representative samples that could only be assembled by group testing. What tests to use? Group tests of hand skill must depend on paper and pen or pencil. This has the obvious disadvantage that subjects are already well practised in the use of writing implements in the preferred hand. Several paper and pencil tests were piloted on undergraduates and schoolchildren (Annett, 1992d). Whereas the peg moving task gives a unimodal distribution of R–L differences with considerable overlap between left and right-handed writers, all of the paper and pencil tasks gave bimodal distributions. However, all were moderately sensitive to degrees of R–L asymmetry because the hand preference subgroups that were defined so as to be ordered for peg moving asymmetry (see chapter 2) were ordered similarly for the paper and pencil tests (Annett, 1992d). A line drawing test (Lines) was given to the first school sample, to be described next. A hole punching task (Holes) was used for a second school sample described in the following section. The Lines test asked the child to "join up" a series of target circles between a row at the bottom of the page and another row at the top, making zigzag lines across the page, and hitting as many targets as possible in the short time allowed. The difference between the hands in skill was calculated as a proportion of total time for both hands, R–L%.

What group tests could distinguish between phonological and non-phonological difficulties in word processing? Two new tests were devised, for Word Order (WO) memory and for word discrimination (WD). The WO test was intended to tap phonological abilities. Subjects were given a sheet with a list of 18 sets of four words, such as "SUN GUN FUN NUN" and "CAP LOT DEN TUN". In alternate sets the four words shared one or two phonemes, and were likely to be phonologically "confusable"; the other sets were "non-confusable" in this sense. Subjects listened to the words spoken from a tape recorder, while holding a pencil in the air with elbow on the desk. The words were spoken in a different order from that printed (e.g. "gun, nun, fun, sun"). The task was to write the numbers 1–4 above the printed words, to show the order they were heard, immediately at the end of each set. The test required the sounds of spoken words to be retained long enough for the sequence to be mapped onto the printed words on the page.

The word discrimination (WD) test used real word homophones. Homophonic words like "root" and "route", or "saw" and "sore" sound the same but they are spelled differently. The phonology is constant but the meanings and spellings vary. This test does not make demands on the "inner ear" but rather on the "inner eye". Dyslexics of the "surface" type find homophonic words particularly difficult. The hunch was that poor word discrimination might depend on visual memory problems and associate with strong dextrality.

The Lines, WO and WD tests were given to classes of 9- to 11-year-olds (Annett, 1992a). The findings for the WO test in the whole sample, when classified in quartiles for R–L% Lines, are shown in Figure 13.2. The most sinistral group was significantly poorer than the other three groups that did not differ between themselves. All groups found the confusable items more difficult, but there was no interaction between confusability and laterality. The most sinistral group was not only poorer overall, but had a significantly larger standard deviation. Increased variability was expected because not all RS – – genotypes have problems, only those with unfortunate chance lateralisations of the relevant functions.

For the WD test, the means over the laterality quartiles were virtually identical. There was no evidence that homophonic word discrimination was specifically poor at either end of the laterality spectrum. However, for relative performance on the two tests (WO minus WD) there was a linear trend (p = 0.084) such that children at the left were relatively poorer for phonology than word discrimination, while children at the right tended to the reverse.

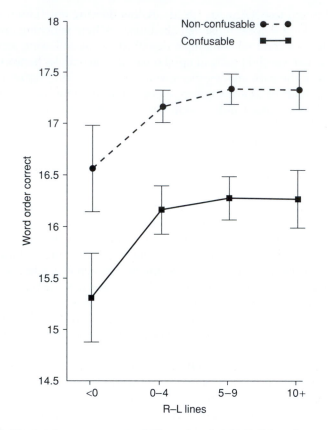

Figure 13.2 Word order test scores in children classified for R–L line drawing skill: confusable sets (solid line) and non-confusable (dashed line): Annett, 1992a.

What happens if we look for cases of children with specific difficulties on one test versus the other test? Do the cases differ for laterality? How can extreme cases be identified in sufficient numbers for the statistical significance necessary for psychological attention? How is the selection to be made objectively and consistently between different samples? Of several methods tried over some years, the one that met most of the above requirements was to take the difference between standardised scores on the two tests, and then select a fixed percentage of cases at each extreme. (Standard scores ensure that both tests have the same mean (0) and the same standard deviation (1). A difference of 2.0z, for example, could be obtained by a participant with an average score on test A and a very poor score on test B. Another participant might have an exceptionally good score on test A and an average score on test B, or vice versa for −2.0z.)

In the total sample of 160 children, the Lines test found 19.4% left-handed (L–R > 0, for targets hit). Four children were poorer on the phonology test than homophone test by 2.0z and *all* happened to be left-handed. At the other side of the distribution there were also four children with a difference greater than 2.0z in favour of good phonology but poor homophone discrimination and none of these was left-handed. Selecting the 5% extremes, there were eight children with poor phonology who included five (62.5%) left-handers while eight children at the extreme for good phonology included none (0%). Comparison between these groups and controls (18.1%) gave chi-square = 11.607, d.f. 2, p = 0.003. Selecting the extremes at 10%, the contrast was between 31.3% left-handers among phonols versus 12.5% among non-phonols. These analyses for selected "cases" were important, but were they convincing for this relatively small sample? The findings were described in conference talks but not published. Two new series of investigations were initiated in order to test the reliability of the findings. One was of undergraduates who were taking part in student projects as described next. The second was a large representative school sample, described in the following section.

The WO and WD tests were revised for undergraduates. The WO test was made more difficult by adding sets up to seven words in length. The new WD test presented 60 pairs of real word homophones, along with a definition of one of the words and an instruction to circle the word that agreed with the definition (e.g. "There, Their—a place", "Fowl, Foul—loathsome"). This revised WD test was used for all undergraduate samples below. The WO test was used for two cohorts of students, but alternative tests of phonology were given in subsequent years. Combined over several cohorts, there were 265 students who took the WO test, 285 who were asked to judge whether nonsense words sounded like real words (e.g. "caik", "burb") and 297 who were asked whether nonsense words rhymed (e.g. "swoin"—"toyne", "quoz"—"fint") (materials from Besner, Davies and Daniels, 1981). The experiments were run along with others available to students taking first year courses in psychology, open to departments across the university. Participation was encouraged, but not mandatory. The experiments were run with the assistance of year 3 students, for whom the projects were supervised research experience. Posters advertising the experiment said nothing about handedness or reading, because volunteers must be unselected in these respects.

As explained above, associations between ability and laterality may be examined using a survey approach or a case approach. For the general survey, the whole sample was classified in R–L% quartiles for peg moving and the quartiles compared for standardised scores on the two tests. Standardised scores were derived by regressing the error scores for each test on age and saving the standardised residuals (zresids). (Standardisation for age was required because mature students tended to be better at homophone discrimination than students straight from school.) Differences between zresids for WO–WD (zdiffs) indicated whether relative performance on the two types of word knowledge differed over the laterality spectrum. Figure 13.3 shows the zresids and zdiffs over the four groups. For the WO test, the two groups with lesser bias to dextrality (absent and mild) were below the mean and the two groups with greater bias (moderate and strong) were above the mean. The differences were in the predicted direction

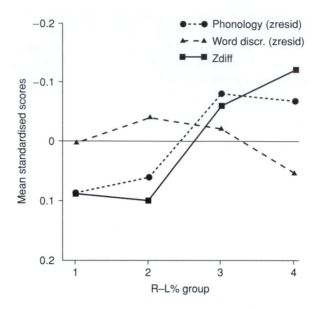

Figure 13.3 Phonology versus word discrimination in undergraduates: standardised scores (zresids) and the difference between standardised scores for the two tests (zdiff): Annett, 1999b.

but the trend was small (p = 0.101). For WD there was no clear trend but the most dextral group was poorest. Differences between the tests (zdiffs), showed a strong linear trend (p = 0.005). As expected, people toward the left of the laterality spectrum tended to be poorer for phonology than homophone discrimination and people at the right tended to be better at phonology than homophones.

Turning now to the case approach, how could students with *specific difficulty* for either type of word processing be distinguished? The procedure was as described above for the school sample, selecting fixed percentages from the two extremes of the zdiff distribution. The 10% extremes for each of the three groups of samples were combined in order to have the substantial groups needed to detect laterality effects (85 phonols, 85 visuals and 677 controls). Table 13.1 shows the findings for several measures of hand preference and hand skill. All were consistent with the prediction that phonols have reduced bias to dextrality while visuals are more strongly biased to dextrality. The differences were significant statistically for consistent right-hand preference (46%, 60% and 69% for phonols, controls and visuals respectively) and also for subgroup hand preferences (hand preference classes 1–7 treated as a parametric variable). The trends were *almost* statistically significant for left writing (13%, 9% and 5% respectively) and for faster peg moving with the left-hand (21%, 15% and 11%). Particularly important for a genetic model, there were significant differences for left-handedness in siblings (20%, 13% and 8% respectively).

Table 13.1 Handedness in groups of undergraduates classified for relative weakness of phonology versus discrimination between real word homophones

	Phonols	Controls	Visuals	p	Linear trend
Participants (N)	85	677	85		
Hand pref. subgroup mean (S.D.)	2.48 (0.92)	2.08 (0.70)	1.73 (0.55)	0.009*	0.002*
Consistent right (%)	45.9	59.8	69.4	0.007	0.002
Left-writers (%)	12.9	9.2	4.7	0.173	0.062
L–R < 0% (peg moving time)	21.2	15.4	10.6	0.159	0.056
Parents (N)	163	1318	168		
Left or mixed (%)	14.1	11.7	10.7	ns	0.341
Siblings (N)	135	1022	123		
Left or mixed (%)	20.0	13.0	8.1	0.017	0.005

* F ratio, others Chi-square

These several samples of children and students were collected over a period of some 10 years (along with the school study to be described next). Each sample considered alone gave trends that would not convince a sceptic that there was "anything of significance". However, taken together, they were consistently in the direction predicted. People with poor phonology were further to the left of the laterality spectrum than people with adequate phonology. Can we say that homophone discrimination takes the reverse pattern, better at the left than the right? Both the school and university samples suggest rather that weaknesses of word knowledge may occur anywhere across the spectrum of laterality. At the left such weaknesses are associated with poor phonology and at the right with good phonology. However, it should be noted that the analyses above concerned the relative strengths and weaknesses of different types of lexical processing in normal samples. Can the approach be adapted for schoolchildren, so as to identify some with problems severe enough to be classifiable as "dyslexia"?

PHONOLOGY, READING, SPELLING AND LATERALITY IN SCHOOL

A new study was undertaken of a large, representative sample of children aged 9–10 years, followed for 3 years. The question was whether certain cognitive abilities relevant to literacy could be mapped in a population sample, and then related to poor reading and spelling. The prediction was that different types of cognitive weakness would be associated with different types of dyslexia, and that the contrasting types would differ for handedness, as expected by the BP + HA hypothesis. The research plan was to screen a large and complete cohort of children for hand skill and for various measures of word knowledge using group tests given in class. A second series of tests was given in individual examinations the following year, including all children with poor scores on any of the first year tests (one standard deviation below the mean) and controls from the same class. The results of the second series of tests were then used to identify children with severe problems of reading and spelling. These were seen for a third time to check the "diagnosis" and to give further cognitive tests, again with control children from the same classes and also younger children of comparable reading age to the dyslexics. We consulted teachers about children with physical or learning disabilities, and we checked with educational psychologists about children with special needs (statement) or otherwise known to have learning difficulties. In the third year of testing we also distributed handedness questionnaires to the families of the whole of the original cohort, with requests for completion by both parents and siblings.

The first year group tests included all 9- to 10-year-olds in nine schools (N = 479) located in rural, suburban and inner city areas of the same local authority, schools selected by the Senior Educational Psychologist as representative of the region. Tests were for handedness (Holes test), phonology (WO), word discrimination (WD), spelling, nonword spelling and a drawing test of memory for shapes. The spelling test was intended to be moderately difficult for this age group (year 10 spelling test; Schonell and Schonell, 1952) in order to elicit errors. We wanted to know if the errors would be what Boder (1973) called "good phonetic equivalents" (GFEs). GFEs indicate that the child has a reasonable grasp of letter–sound relationships, counter-indicating poor phonology. In the Holes test of hand skill a ballpoint pen is used to punch holes through small circles on stiff paper, clipped to a board with holes beneath the circles. The punches were to zigzag between rows, analogous to the peg moving task. The Holes test gave a bimodal division between left-handers and right-handers. Although we could not make direct observations of handedness in the first round of tests, children punching more Holes with the left-hand were confirmed later to be left-handed writers. Twenty children were excluded because they did not have English as a first language or because physical or mental disabilities made testing unreliable, leaving 459 children for analysis. The first question we asked was whether children identified by teachers as having serious literacy problems would be atypical for handedness compared with those without problems. There were 15.5% left-handed writers among the former and 9.2% in the latter. Like many comparisons in the literature, the difference was in the predicted direction but not statistically significant. However, for hand skill (R–L% for Holes) the poor literacy group was significantly less dextral (p = .035).

Our test findings, obtained over three years, permitted several alternative classifications of dyslexia. The regression of reading test scores on matrices (IQ) scores was used to distinguish specific reading retardates (in the manner of Rutter and Yule, 1975). When these were classified for good versus poor phonology on the WO test, there were highly significant differences for laterality in the direction expected. The specific cases excluded a small number of poor readers who were borderline on the regression criterion, but otherwise resembled them. The published account (Annett, Eglinton and Smythe, 1996, hereafter AES) took a wider view and included all poor readers *and* also those poor relative to intelligence. Figure 13.4 shows the classification adopted by AES, 40 poor readers, 57 poor spellers (at least nine out of ten spelling errors but not poor readers) and 362 controls (not poor readers or spellers by these criteria). Possible concerns about pathological handedness were countered by excluding children with slow peg moving times from all analyses. Similarly, concerns about intelligence were countered by excluding *all* children with Matrices at or below the fifth percentile. Nine children were excluded on this criterion but it is worth noting that they included only two poor readers and one poor speller. The fact that six out of nine children with very low Matrices scores were not poor readers or spellers shows that intelligence as measured by this test is not a sufficient cause of poor literacy. After exclusions, there were 35 poor readers and 53 poor spellers.

Phonology was assessed by three main tests during the successive phases of testing (tests for word order, phoneme segmentation and nonword reading). Poor scores on at least two of these tests were taken as the criterion of poor phonology. There were 17 poor readers with phonological problems, of whom 5 (29.4%) were left-handed writers. There were 18 poor readers without significant phonological problems, and none were left-handed (0%). Among the 53 poor spellers left-handers were 13.6% and in controls 9.7%. The differences over the four groups, and between phonological and non-phonological dyslexics separately, were statistically significant. There were further significant differences for hand skill asymmetry and also for presence of left-handed relatives, consistent with the theory that those with poor phonology lack a genetic bias to dextrality.

The contrast for handedness between those with good versus poor phonology was examined independently in poor spellers (excluding those who were also poor readers). Spelling errors in year I were classified by Elizabeth Eglinton, blind to information on laterality and other test findings. Errors were classified as GFEs if the intended word was intelligible from the child's attempt. The reliability of the classification was checked with the help of independent judges. For the present purpose, the poor spellers with 50% or fewer GFEs were classified as having poor phonology (poor phonol poor spellers, PPPS) and if greater than 50% as good phonol poor spellers (GPPS). There were 30 PPPS, of whom 7 (23.3%) were left-handed, while the 27 GPPS included no left-handers (0%). The contrast for phonology in poor spellers replicates that for poor readers. Figure 13.5 represents the bias to dextrality for R–L% Holes, distinguishing the two types of poor reader, two types of poor speller and controls. There were no exclusions here for hand speeds or intelligence. (AES showed that effects were significant *with* exclusions. It is shown here that effects are significant *without* exclusions.) Overall F ratios between groups were significant for R–L% Holes (p = 0.027), R–L% Pegs (p = 0.032) and also for subgroup handedness (p = 0.037). AES showed that poor readers with and without poor phonology straddled controls (and poor spellers). Figure 13.5 shows that poor spellers with and without poor phonology straddle controls also. The GPPS were the most dextral group on all three measures of asymmetry.

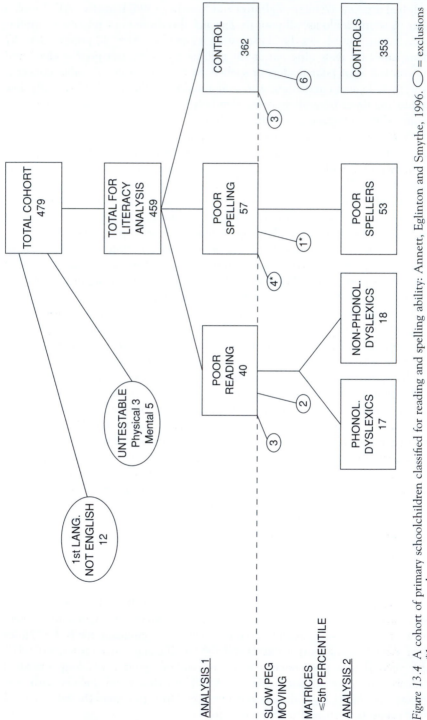

Figure 13.4 A cohort of primary schoolchildren classified for reading and spelling ability: Annett, Eglinton and Smythe, 1996. ◯ = exclusions *1 case repeated.

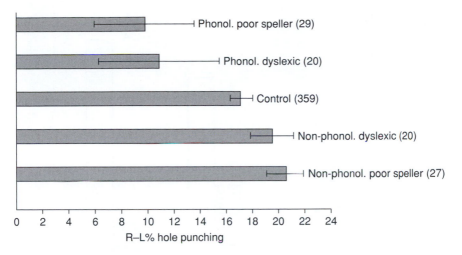

Figure 13.5 Types of dyslexia with R–L hand difference for hole punching: bias to dextrality differs between those with and without poor phonology in both poor readers and poor spellers.

These analyses strongly support the overall thesis, that two types of threat to literacy can be distinguished, one with poor phonology and one without poor phonology. The types differ for handedness, consistent with the theory that they are associated with RS − − genotypes and RS + + genotypes respectively. This contrast was evident in poor readers and also in poor spellers who were adequate readers. Further, as shown in the last section, the contrast for handedness between those with and without poor phonology was present among undergraduates who were adequate readers and spellers. This suggests that relative strength and weakness of phonological processing is associated with the RS + + and RS − − genotypes, through all levels of ability and achievement.

FURTHER EXPERIMENTS ON PHONOLOGY: OUTPUT PHONOLOGY IN UNDERGRADUATES AND RHYME AWARENESS IN EARLY SCHOOL YEARS

A Reverend Spooner of the University of Oxford had an unfortunate tendency to exchange the initial sounds of words. People vary in their ability to produce "Spoonerisms" deliberately. A test was devised by Perin (1983) for teenagers, using the names of popular entertainers, such as David Bowie (required response, Bavid Dowie) or Chuck Berry (Buck Cherry). This test was given to undergraduates, who were also tested for dichotic listening ear asymmetry (Annett, 1991b). The latter involved listening to pairs of digits played one to each ear simultaneously, and pressing a response button when a "one" or a "nine" was

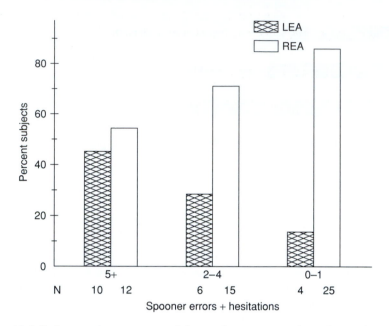

Figure 13.6 Right ear advantage versus left ear advantage in undergraduates classified for errors on a Spooner task: Annett, 1991b.

heard. Most people tend to hear digits at the right ear more accurately than at the left, such that group data typically shows a right ear advantage or REA (see chapter 8). The experiment was run at two different institutions (Coventry Polytechnic and Leicester University) with similar findings at both. The combined sample gave 72 Ps classifiable for errors on the dichotic test, 52 with REA and 20 with LEA (including equal errors in 4 cases).

The association between ear advantage and Spooner task performance is shown in Figure 13.6. Participants who could do the Spooner task easily (not more than one error or significant hesitation) included few with LEA. Those who were not quite so good included more with LEA. Ps who were rather poor at the task (five or more errors or hesitations) were about equally divided for REA and LEA. The last finding is consistent with the theory that people who have weak phonology due to absence of a gene "for" speech laterality have random biases to either side. There were no significant differences for handedness, but trends were in the expected direction. The Spooner task has been used again at Leicester, along with other tests of phonological processing and with careful screening for hearing difficulties, with similar results (Smythe, 2001).

The Bradley (1984) test of rhyme awareness asks young children to listen to sets of four words (e.g. "hat, mat, fan, cat" or "mop, hop tap, lop") and say which word differs from the rest. Annett (1992a) showed that 5- to 8-year-olds who were poor on this task were less biased to dextrality for peg moving asymmetry than those not so poor. The findings again are consistent with the theory that poor phonology is associated with reduced bias to dextrality.

IMPLICATIONS FOR THEORIES OF DYSLEXIA

These experiments, together with others described above, support the basic hypothesis that phonological abilities vary among normal children and under-graduates, as well as among those with poor reading and spelling. In all of these groups, weak phonology is associated with reduced bias to right-handedness. It is not being said that people with weak phonology are *left-handed*. They are as expected for a normal distribution of asymmetry, but a distribution not dis-placed as far to the right as for those with good phonology. This distinction is important for understanding the supposed failure of the literature to support Orton's finding for motor-intergrades. Tests of Orton's observations were usually designed to examine a stronger and less likely hypothesis, that dyslexics are left-handed. That is not what Orton observed, and it is not what the RS theory pre-dicts. It is what most sceptics have looked for. Relationships between dyslexia and handedness were indeed obscure (Bishop, 1990a; Vernon, 1957) but they are consistent with predictions of the RS theory.

The wider implications of these findings for theories of dyslexia are greater than can be fully reviewed here. My aim is to indicate issues that need further consideration. An over-arching concern has been the relationship of poor reading to low intelligence, such that it is common practice to require children classified as dyslexic to be near average for scores on nonverbal tests. However, it has been shown here that in the general school population, a low score for Raven's Matrices was not sufficient to cause poor reading. Most of the children with Matrices scores below the 5th percentile in the AES sample were *not* poor readers. Neither is brain damage a sufficient cause because children with hemiplegias of early onset may be good readers (Annett, 1970c). At the upper end of the intellectual spectrum, undergraduates may have persisting weaknesses in lexical processing, although the strength of other abilities allowed entry to higher education. My conclusion is that the skills involved in literacy vary throughout the population, in ways that defy simple classification as dyslexic/not dyslexic and also simple explanations in terms of IQ or brain damage.

The subtype question, whether there are different types of threat to literacy must be answered in the affirmative. There are at least two main types, one associated with poor phonology and one not so associated. There may well be other types also (see Seymour, 1986). The critical point for the RS theory is that the phonological and surface types of poor literacy differ for handedness as expected if the first is associated with the RS − − genotype and the second with the RS + + genotype. Compared with the general population, the former has a smaller shift to dextrality, as expected for absence of an RS factor that induces modal cerebral dominance. The latter has a stronger bias to dextrality, as expected if there is over-commitment to left hemisphere dominance. Comparison of dysphonetic and dyseidetic dyslexics by EEG (electroencephalography) suggested that the latter appear to over use linguistic strategies, consistent with the present thesis (Flynn and Boder, 1991; Flynn and Deering, 1989).

As to genetic foundations, the RS theory makes no specific claims beyond the assertion that a single genetic locus is sufficient to account for individual differences for human lateral asymmetries. This locus is also likely to be involved in individual differences for the efficiency of speech learning, and related speech based processes. Several studies of the genetics of dyslexia have identified two main regions of interest, one on chromosome 6 (Cardon, Smith, Fulker et al., 1994; Fisher, Marlow, Lamb et al., 1999; Gayan, Smith, Cherny et al., 1999) and one on chromosome 15 (Nopola-Hemmi, Taipale, Haltia et al., 2000; Schult-Körne, Grimm, Nothen et al., 1998). Grigorenko, Wood, Meyer et al. (1997) found linkage on both chromosomes 6 and 15. The latter study suggested that a gene on chromosome 6 might be associated with poor phonology, while that on chromosome 15 might be associated with poor word recognition. Is either locus likely to be relevant to the RS + gene? The one associated with poor phonology would be the more probable, of course. The presence of a second genetic locus, independent of phonological processing, but associated with poor word recognition, might be interpreted as consistent with the contrast between findings for phonology versus word discrimination above. Poor word recognition (as shown by poor homophone discrimination) did not vary with laterality in my school or university samples. Perhaps weaknesses of written word recognition can occur anywhere along the laterality continuum. The differences between phonol and non-phonol (or visual) cases might depend on the relative use of phonology in coping with poor word recognition skills. At the left there might be weak phonology, but attempts to use compensating strengths in visual representations (Campbell and Butterworth, 1985; Goulandris and Snowling, 1991). At the right of the spectrum, poor word recognition in the presence of strong phonology might lead to over-reliance on sublexical analysis. A genetic influence on literacy was found to be stronger for spelling than for reading (Stevenson, Graham, Fredman et al., 1987). Reading requires words to be recognised, but spelling requires them to be recalled accurately from a lexical store; the latter would make greater demands on the accuracy of the reconstruction of stored visual representations. The genetic evidence is consistent with the overall thesis that there may be at least two types of difficulty, one involving some visual type of memory for word structure, and the other a phonological analysis of the sounds representing these structures.

Future progress in understanding how genes influence learning and behaviour will depend on careful analyses of that behaviour. What are the difficulties in learning to read and spell that must be explained? Theories of dyslexia have developed through many stages, from early notions about confusions between mirror images in the two cerebral hemispheres, through information theory to artificial neural networks (further below). A fundamental and persisting issue is how far brain functions can be analysed into different components and in what sense the brain works as a whole. For most of the 20th century attempts to distinguish centres for different kinds of brain activity and map the links between them were scorned as "diagram making". The foundation of modern neuropsychology depended on a renewal of attempts to discover the "wiring diagram" of the brain. For example, neurologists have known for some time that reading and writing centres are distinct because patients with brain lesions may lose one without the other; some patients can read but not write, while others can write but not then read what they have written (Geschwind, 1965).

Modern neuropsychological studies of reading disorders were inspired by analyses of the types of error made by cases of dyslexia acquired as the result of head injuries sustained many years earlier in WW2 (Marshall and Newcombe, 1973). The use and misuse of phonology was pivotal in the distinctions made between deep dyslexics (with impaired use of letter–sound relations) and surface dyslexics (over-use of letter–sound relations). For deep dyslexics, the mismatch between the word they see and the word they say can be so great as to give semantic errors such reading "chair" for "table", or "moon" for "sun". The words produced were related in meaning (semantics) but not in sound (phonology). It is as though the phonological system was by-passed completely and the response depended on some route through the store of word meanings (semantic lexicon). Errors of this type have been found recently in a young person whose left hemisphere was removed surgically, such that language and reading had to depend on the right hemisphere (Patterson, Varga-Khadem and Polkey, 1989). Coltheart (1980, 1983, 2000) had surmised that semantic errors might be mediated by the right hemisphere. The importance of these findings for our purpose is that they suggest that the right hemisphere might be involved in certain aspects of lexical processing, but aspects that are independent of phonology in most people.

Analysis of the errors of adults with dyslexias acquired through brain injury was aided by an information theory approach to cognitive functions. That is, key processes likely to be involved in the task were represented as boxes, with arrows indicating probable connections between them. The contrast between patients whose reading errors involved too little or too much reliance on phonology, as described above, required two pathways through the information system, a "dual-route" model of reading. One was a lexical route that gives direct access to known words, as represented in an orthographic lexicon (a kind of direct "look-up" word store). The other route was used to build words from sublexical elements, letters and groups of letters. The sublexical route would be involved in reading new words and nonsense words. For the skilled reader, both routes were expected to be available, but the errors of acquired dyslexics suggested that the two routes may operate independently.

Is the dual-route model, developed from studies of acquired dyslexias in brain damaged adults, relevant to reading in children? Teachers distinguished two methods of teaching children to read, long before their interest to neuropsychology, the "look and say" method, and the "phonic analysis" method. The terms imply a contrast between a direct link between seeing a word and its pronunciation, versus a breakdown of the word into letter–sound units and their assembly into the spoken word. A distinction was also made for normal readers between those using a "Chinese" (relying on the visual appearance of words) versus a "Phoenician" (relying on letter–sound relationships) approach to reading (Baron and Strawson, 1976). Controversies about the relevance of these distinctions depend on problems inherent in any typology, the danger of exaggerating the differences when the majority of cases may show mixed features. That is, although mental processes may be conceptualised as "boxes", dyslexics with associated problems are not necessarily classifiable into discrete boxes or types (Wilding, 1989). In the same way that biologists classify living things into species, but find there may be no absolute distinctions between them, so psychologists must accept that differences between people for cognitive processing may vary along continuous dimensions. This was evident for the analysis of phonological versus surface subtypes among dyslexic boys studied by Castles and Coltheart (1993). It was recognised in their title as "Varieties of Developmental Dyslexia" (not "Types of . . ."). The important point for the RS theory is that differences between groups of interest should be recognised as depending on *distributions* of relative strengths and weakness. It has been shown above that the different types of cognitive weakness relevant to poor reading can be found in both schools and universities, so they are not limited to dyslexics, nor to a particular level of intelligence. Further, they occur in some people who are poor readers and poor spellers, and in others who are poor spellers but not poor readers. Hence the distinction between poor phonology versus not poor phonology has wider relevance than dyslexia itself.

The box and arrow diagrams of information theory are useful tools in the analysis of complex behaviours, but is the modern "diagram-making" going too far? A challenge to the information theory approach is offered by demonstrations that some apparently complex learning processes can be simulated in relatively simple but artificial computer generated networks. One of the attractive features of such networks is that banks of units that have little intrinsic structure can be "trained" to reproduce stimuli by simple exposure over several trials. They show how a very simply programmed self-organising system can learn to produce outputs analogous to words, and in the course of this learning reproduce some of the features observed in real learners, such as the faster learning of more frequent and more regular words (Seidenburg and McClelland, 1989). The relevance of such modelling to developmental dyslexia depends on whether networks can be trained to produce words, as a child would learn to say and then to read them. Can such a network be disturbed so as to produce errors like those of reading disabled children? A test for such a model would depend on two sets of data, first for the types and frequencies of errors produced by real children, and second, for the resemblance of the errors produced by the model to those of the child sample. That is, can a connectionist network reproduce the different types of error associated with developmental "phonological" versus "surface" dyslexia?

Patterns of error found in dyslexic boys versus control boys by Castles and Coltheart (1993) were checked and replicated by Manis, Seidenberg, Doi et al. (1996). An attempt was then made to model the development of speech and reading skills in an artificial network in such a way as to discover how the patterns of error might have arisen (Harm and Seidenberg, 1999). It was clear that phonological and surface type errors could be simulated by the model.

From the viewpoint of the RS theory, it is not important to discover exactly how types of dyslexia are simulated by connectionist models, nor to map the simulation to actual cerebral systems. It should be acknowledged, however, that at least two types of threat to literacy may occur. One depends on the efficiency of a speech-based system that governs phonological processing. The second depends on the efficiency of the internal representations of words in a visual lexical semantic store. The former is likely to be enhanced by the presence of the RS + gene and at risk in its absence. Might there be an association between risks to the visual memory store and the RS + + genotype? If the RS + gene lateralises speech and language to the left cerebral hemisphere by handicapping relevant areas of the right hemisphere, and if the lexical-semantic store depends at least in part on the right hemisphere, then over-commitment to the left side might put the latter at risk. Neuroimaging studies suggest that language and reading depend on widely distributed functions in both hemispheres (Frackowiak, 1994; Paulesu, Frith, Snowling et al., 1996; Posner and Raichle, 1994; Price, 1997; Shaywitz, Shaywitz, Pugh et al., 1998). Perhaps the role of the right hemisphere in the neural network is restricted by over expression of the RS + gene in some cases. Mild impairments of a visual word store might allow recognition but not recall of complex word forms. Such people would be able to read but not spell difficult words. In others, more severe impairments could affect both reading and spelling. The greater demands of recall than recognition would explain why there are many more poor spellers than poor readers.

Both neuroimaging and connectionist models suggest that literacy involves widely distributed units that are mutually connected through complex circuits. Malfunctions of the system could be due to weak links between the units as much as loss or malfunction of the units themselves. Paulesu, Frith, Snowling et al. (1996) interpreted their findings for dyslexics by PET scanning as showing weak connectivity between anterior and posterior language areas. Poor connectivity in some dyslexics is consistent with the overall thesis that they lack an advantage that is normally conferred by the typical pattern of left hemisphere lateralisation.

SUMMARY

This chapter has reviewed research investigating dyslexia in the light of the RS theory. The RS analysis offers several suggestions for clarifying confusions and controversies in this field. If it is accepted that RS − − genotypes are at risk for speech learning, and for the representation of speech-based material in phonological processing, then problems of dyslexia can be considered in the light of the RS model of patterns of cerebral dominance. Relationships between handedness and cerebral dominance are such that there is great overlap between genotypes and classifications of left-, mixed- and right-handedness. Inspection of representations of these relationships (as in Figure 7.1) shows why classifying Ss for handedness and looking for differences in ability is likely to be unfruitful (as in most school-based or survey type research). However, children with certain developmental language problems are likely to include an excess of RS − − genotypes. A group of such children attending for clinical investigation would be likely to include an excess of left- and mixed-handers. Hence, it is important to distinguish the research logic of the educational survey from that of the selected clinic sample. Many controversies in the literature arise from a failure to make this distinction.

The second main contribution of the RS theory was to discover that dyslexics may include some of RS + + genotype, as well as the expected excess of RS − − genotypes. The presence of some strong right-handers in dyslexia samples would obscure the effects associated with reduced dextrality in RS − − genotypes. Dyslexics differing for patterns of cerebral dominance (associated with the different genotypes) should also differ for type of reading problem. Could the long-standing distinctions between approaches to reading known as "phonics" versus "look-and-say", or distinctions between "phonological" and "dyseidectic" problems relate to a underlying distinction between speech based and visually based processing? The RS theory suggested that people with problems of the former should be less shifted, and the latter more shifted to dextrality than controls.

The predicted differences for handedness between groups with and without poor phonology was investigated in several samples of children and undergraduates. Evidence for an association between relative skill in phonology and relative bias to dextrality was found in several analyses. The effects were present in normal samples as well as in groups of poor readers and poor spellers. It was shown that poor readers with and without poor phonology, and also poor spellers with and without poor phonology straddled controls for R–L hand skill, as predicted.

The two main routes to reading proposed by the dual-route model are consistent with the idea that reading may be impaired in two main ways, and that these ways dissociate for relative bias to dextrality. Connectionist models of reading also need to allow at least two main types of threat to literacy. These findings have important implications, for ideas about relationships between reading difficulties and intelligence, genetics, and remediation. The RS theory's contribution to these debates is to assert that at least two types of difficulty are involved and that these are associated with different patterns of cerebral specialisation.

14 Schizophrenia and autism

The theory of an agnosic
RS + gene

Schizophrenia is a disorder at the heart of concepts of "madness" but one that is difficult to define precisely because it is variable in expression and severity. Until recently it was classified as a functional disorder, meaning that no organic basis was known. It was distinguished from the other main group of functional psychoses, the affective or emotional disorders, over a century ago. Schizophrenics may be emotionally disturbed, but the primary problem is one of thought rather than emotion. There is often a curious divorce between emotion and thought with inappropriate laughing, crying or flat unconcern. Running through the various manifestations of schizophrenia are certain core features that involve disorders of speech, thought, belief and social awareness (Frith, 1992). Speech may follow a bizarre train of ideas. Voices may be heard that tell the patient what to do or that talk critically about what the patient is doing. Schizophrenia is a disorder that devastates the individual sufferer, imposes great strain on the family, and is costly to society. It has been attributed to many causes, styles of parenting, society, diet, unknown viruses and genes, but no theory is universally accepted. Evidence from family and adoption studies indicates a genetic influence.

With the advent of computerised axial-tomography (CAT-scans) in the 1970s and later techniques of brain imaging, groups of schizophrenics were found to have subtle differences in cerebral anatomy. The ventricles (fluid filled spaces in the brain) tend to be larger, indicating smaller volumes of neurons and other brain tissue (Johnstone, Crow, Frith et al., 1976). The changes are most frequent in the left temporal lobe, in areas believed critical for language functions. These physical changes imply that schizophrenia is not a purely functional disorder. The changes were associated with loss or reduction of typical brain asymmetries, especially in temporal regions but also in frontal regions where the right side normally tends to be larger than the left (Luchins, Weinberger and Wyatt, 1979). Loss of asymmetry in schizophrenics was confirmed by post mortem study (Brown, Colter, Corsellis et al., 1986). These observations led to a new theory of the causes of schizophrenia, that it is a disorder of the mechanisms responsible for the development of lateral asymmetries (Crow, 1984). Developing this idea over several years Crow (1997a, 1997b) asked "Is schizophrenia the price that *Homo sapiens* pays for language?"

If schizophrenia is a disorder of the mechanisms that induce normal cerebral dominance (CD) and if the RS theory is correct that the only specific influence on human CD is a single gene, then schizophrenia may be among the costs of the RS + gene. My research on a possible BP + HA for the RS locus, reviewed in chapters 10–13, sought evidence that there are costs associated with the RS + gene by looking for weaknesses in strong right-handers in comparison with relative benefits for left- and mixed-handers. However, if it is true that the RS + gene is associated with risks for serious mental illness, these risks alone might be sufficient to check the spread of the gene in the population and ensure the persistence of left-handedness. I was sceptical of Crow's theory, at first, because many non-genetic factors could disturb the development of cerebral asymmetries (as in shaking the pinball machine of Figure 3.9b). However, on hearing evidence that relatives, who were not themselves schizophrenic but likely to be gene-carriers, have reduced cerebral asymmetries (Murray, 1996), it was necessary to think again. How might schizophrenia be caused by a disorder of the RS + gene? To my great surprise, I soon thought of a mechanism for Crow's theory that also accounted for the risk of schizophrenia for relatives of schizophrenics. Further, and even more surprising, this development of the RS theory appeared to demand extension to the problem of childhood autism.

Crow's argument depended on the inter-relationships of many findings. First, surveys of schizophrenia in different countries show that it is a disorder that occurs with similar features in all human groups and with consistent life-time risk at about 1% (Jablensky, Sartorius, Ernberg et al., 1992). It is unlikely, therefore, to be the product of particular types of rearing, nutrition, climate or social environment. Second, the main cause is probably genetic because risks are higher for relatives than the general population and the risks rise in proportion to genetic proximity, from about 2% for first cousins, through 5% for grandchildren and 15% for children to about 50% for monozygotic (MZ) twins (Gottesman, 1991). A third important part of Crow's argument is that schizophrenia is associated with a reduction of fecundity. The overall risk of schizophrenia is the same for both sexes but males tend to have earlier onsets than females and many male patients have no children. Reduced fertility implies that relevant genes are lost from the gene pool. The fact that the incidence remains stable between cultures and over time implies that the genes are replaced. This suggests that they are associated with some selective advantage, as would be the case if they were genes "for" language. Fourth, the differences of cerebral anatomy mentioned above particularly affect the language areas of the left temporal lobe, while the right temporal lobe shows variable differences from controls (Falkai, Bogerts, Schneider et al., 1995; Suddath, Christison, Torrey et al., 1990). Other cerebral asymmetries present in most brains tend to be absent in the brains of schizophrenics (Bullmore, Brammer, Harvey et al., 1995; Crow, Ball, Bloom et al., 1989). A sixth important point is that these differences in anatomy are not due to active disease, but appear to originate from factors influencing development in foetal life (Murray, 1994; Weinberger, 1995). Children who were assessed routinely in national surveys and later became schizophrenic tended to have been below average in intellectual, physical and social functions (Crow & Done, 1995; Jones, Rodgers, Murray et al., 1994). The illness is typically manifest in early adulthood, when the highest levels of language, thought, and social interaction normally mature.

Other possibly relevant findings include anomalies in the hippocampus, particularly on the left side (Fukuzako, Kodama, Fukuzako et al., 1995; Maier, Ron, Barker et al., 1995) and reduction in area of the corpus callosum, the neural bridge between the hemispheres through which the two sides communicate (Woodruff, McManus and David, 1995). The severity of hallucinations and delusions is strongly correlated with diminished cortical volume in the left temporal lobe and reduced thickness of the corpus callosum (Wright, McGuire, Poline et al., 1995). Brain imaging studies of schizophrenics while they were experiencing auditory hallucinations found activity in areas normally associated with speech production (McGuire, Syed and Murray, 1993) and also in subcortical, limbic and orbito-frontal cortex (Silbersweig, Stern, Frith et al., 1995). Theories of auditory hallucinations suggest that the patient might hear inner speech as if it were coming from outside or alternatively, that mechanisms of speech perception distort the interpretation of neutral sound (Hoffman, 2001). Schizophrenia involves malfunction in a network of recently evolved brain areas called heteromodal cortex (including prefrontal cortex, anterior cingulate gyrus, superior temporal and inferior parietal cortex and limbic system) that are likely to serve high level functions, language and decision making.

These findings support Crow's thesis that schizophrenia is a disorder of humanity and one that cannot be attributed to variable external factors. There are no clear parallels in other species. Rats, for example, can be made to behave in strange ways if they are fed an excess of amphetamines, or other substances whose effects in humans sometimes mimic schizophrenic symptoms. Nonhuman primates may have hemisphere asymmetries like those found in humans, but it is uncertain that there are species biases to one side rather than the random biases expected by the RS theory. Humans share some 98–99% of genes with chimpanzees but any genes that are involved in human biases to the right-hand, left hemisphere and schizophrenia are likely to be among those we *do not share* with chimpanzees. Crow (1999, 2000) suggested that the relevant genes are associated with changes to the structure of the Y chromosome in humans, compared with higher apes. These speculations about the location of the genes "for" schizophrenia and/or cerebral dominance go beyond what is required by the RS theory. The theory remains neutral as to location of the genes involved.

Autism was first described by Kanner (1943) and independently by Asperger (1944). The disorders described by these two child psychiatrists are now recognised as essentially the same (Frith, 1991) but cases with relatively good language are often referred to as "Asperger's syndrome". Kanner's young patients, by contrast, tended to have little useful speech. Autism is a child psychosis of early onset, around the age of 2 years, characterised by profound impairments of communication, social interaction and imaginative play (Frith, 1989). The child's behaviour is dominated by idiosyncratic routines of repetitive action. There are secondary features that are more variable between cases. There may be a continuum along which cases differ for severity and for number of autistic features (Wing, 1981, 1991). Intellectual level ranges between profound mental handicap to normal for nonverbal abilities. There may be striking talents for specific skills such as drawing, music or calculation.

The population rate for autism, when strictly defined for the full Kanner syndrome, was estimated at 2–4 per 10,000 (Rutter, 1991). For weaker criteria the rate is a little higher. Twin studies suggest that autism is a strongly genetic disorder. Eccentric behaviour was noted in some parents of autistics by both Asperger and Kanner and these impressions were confirmed in recent studies (Gillberg, 1991; Gillberg, Gillberg and Steffenburg, 1992; Piven, Wzorek, Landa et al., 1994). However, some cases of autism may be non-genetic and arise from infections and other trauma of early childhood.

Autism was initially confused with childhood schizophrenia, but it was understood later to be a quite different condition. It differs from childhood schizophrenia for major symptoms and for age of onset (Kolvin, 1971). Autism is typically evident from late infancy when the usual growth of speech and pretend play do not occur. Childhood schizophrenia is rare and occurs, at the earliest, not before 7–8 years of age. However, it has been argued that a single fundamental disability could be common to both disorders while the different symptoms could be due to the different ages of onset and hence different developmental paths (Frith and Frith, 1991). A problem for this hypothesis is the observation that schizophrenia and autism do not go together in families more often than expected for base rates in the population (Rutter, 1991). The conditions are not absolutely distinct because some autistic children have developed schizophrenia (Petty, Ornitz, Michelman et al., 1984). The boundaries between "schizoid" and "schizotypal" personalities and Asperger's syndrome are unclear (Wolff and McGuire, 1995). There may also be overlap with other serious developmental disorders of early childhood (Howlin, Mawhood and Rutter, 2000; Mawhood, Howlin and Rutter, 2000; Szatmari, MacLean, Jones et al., 2000). Brain imaging is not easily done in autistic children because it requires a willing and compliant subject. Reduced cortical volume has been found, particularly of the left temporal lobe as described above for schizophrenics (Chiron, Leboyer, Leon et al., 1995; Zilbovicius, Boddaert, Belin et al., 2000).

THE THEORY OF AN AGNOSIC RIGHT SHIFT GENE IN SCHIZOPHRENIA AND AUTISM

If schizophrenia is a disorder of the mechanisms of cerebral dominance (CD), as argued by Crow, and if CD depends on the RS + gene, how might the gene become disordered? It has been argued in chapter 10 that the RS + gene evolved to assist the acquisition of speech by inducing left hemisphere CD, but at the expense of areas relevant to speech and to hand skill in the right hemisphere. The RS + gene is likely to be a specifically human modification of the genetic blueprint that emerged along with the development of speech. Speech probably evolved in several stages, perhaps beginning with our earliest hominid ancestors, but even if the process began some 3–5 million years ago, it would still be "new" in the evolutionary time-scale. Such a gene might be unstable. Moreover it has a difficult job to do, to specify a left–right asymmetry. Morgan (1977) argued that genes could not specify left or right, that they must be *left–right agnosic*. ("Agnosia" means a lack of recognition, an inability to tell left from right. It is often confused with, or "corrected" by spell-checkers to, "agnostic" meaning lack of belief, something quite different.) Genes governing left–right asymmetry were unknown at the time Morgan was writing but some have since been discovered that influence asymmetries of the heart and other viscera (Beddington, 1996; Yost, 1998). The RS theory postulates the existence of a gene for cerebral asymmetry, but the precise mechanism remains unknown. Its recency in the evolutionary time-scale makes it reasonable to suggest that it might be liable to mutation, a mutation that loses some of the distinctive characteristics of its hard-won human species form. The normal instruction carried by the RS + gene says, in effect, "Impair speech related cortex of one cerebral hemisphere, the right." Suppose the directional part of this instruction were lost, the gene would say, "Impair speech related cortex of one cerebral hemisphere, side unspecified." Because chance is the default for all asymmetries on the RS theory, an agnosic RS + gene would impair either hemisphere at random (Annett, 1996b, 1997a, 1999d).

The key postulates relevant to the present argument are summarised in Figure 14.1. These ideas have been introduced in previous chapters, but it is useful to

Environment	• main cause of lateral asymmetries, universal in primates including humans • asymmetries arise from random accidents of embryological growth • these lead to a Gaussian distribution of R–L differences
Genes at RS locus **RS –** **(RS minus)**	• ancestral primate allele(s), neutral for laterality
RS + **(RS plus)**	• a human species allele • it carries an instruction to "impair the growth of the *right* hemisphere" • left-hand weakness shifts the R–L distribution toward dextrality
RS +*a* **(RS agnosic)**	• a mutation of RS + • it gives an instruction to "impair the growth of *one* hemisphere" • the left *or* the right hemisphere is impaired at random

Figure 14.1 The theory of an agnosic RS + gene.

review them here with reference to the extension to schizophrenia. The main causes of asymmetries of hand and brain are *environmental*. They are accidental differences between the two sides of the body due to random differences in the translation of a common genetic blueprint during foetal development and perhaps early postnatal life. It is not necessary to look for specific environmental causes for individual differences in asymmetry, they are intrinsic to this model of human development. Random asymmetries account for the 50/50 distribution of right/left-hand preferences and the *absence of genetic influences* in other species (Collins, 1969; Peterson, 1934). They occur in the growth of every individual human, including every individual twin, MZ and DZ. They give a normal distribution of R–L differences in the population. The weighting toward dextrality introduced by the RS + allele is *added to* the asymmetry that arises by chance. There is chance for all bilaterally symmetrical species, human and nonhuman, *and* additionally, right shift for most humans. (Contrasts between the RS theory and other theories of directional *or* random asymmetry are considered in chapter 16.) The randomness of cerebral asymmetries is important for applications of the RS theory to psychosis because chance asymmetries could be an essential environmental ingredient in the causal recipe. It allows for a high degree of variability in the pattern and severity of symptoms.

The allele(s) called RS – are expected to be neutral for laterality. They probably represent the ancestral primate forms of the gene before an allele was modified to become RS +. The argument that the gene induces *right hemisphere disadvantage* rather than left hemisphere advantage is crucial to the new proposal for schizophrenia. The typical pattern of asymmetry was found to be associated with a planum temporale that was smaller on the right side, and with relatively weak left-hand skill. Symmetry, by contrast, was associated with large PT and good hand skill on both sides (see chapter 10). Thus, it was inferred that the normal shift to the right for handedness could be due to a slight weakening of the right hemisphere and the left-hand.

The RS +*a* allele is a mutant RS + that has lost the directional part of the code. The normal RS + allele impairs the *right* hemisphere but the agnosic mutant (RS +*a*) impairs *one* hemisphere, left or right at random. The RS mutant does not cause schizophrenia directly, but only when it is paired with a normal RS + allele, and then only in 50% of cases. *Schizophrenia is hypothesised to occur when the speech mechanisms are impaired on both sides of the brain.* This would occur in RS + *a* + genotypes for the 50% of cases in whom by chance both hemispheres are impaired. When paired with an RS – allele (RS +*a* – genotype) one hemisphere remains intact, so permitting normal development.

Table 14.1 lists the hypothesised gene and genotype frequencies as deduced for the RS genetic model, but with the addition of an agnosic mutant. The hypothesis of bilateral impairment by chance, implies that about 1% of the population would develop schizophrenia if the frequency of the agnosic gene were 0.02. The intact RS + proportion would be reduced from 0.57 to 0.55. Apart from this single modification, the genotype frequencies are identical to those deduced above (chapter 5).

Table 14.1 Gene and genotype frequencies

Gene frequencies	Proportion	Genotype frequencies	Percent
RS −	0.43 deduced as $\sqrt{(2 \times \text{prop. right hemisphere speakers})}$	RS − RS −	18.5
		RS + RS −	47.3
RS +	0.55	RS + RS +	30.3
RS +*a*	0.02		
		RS +*a* RS −	1.7
		RS +*a* RS +	2.2
		RS +*a* RS +*a*	0.04

The patterns of cerebral deficit associated with the several genotypes are represented in Figure 14.2. The top row shows the three normal genotypes not carrying the agnosic gene. Predictions for these genotypes were reviewed in chapters 10–13. Briefly, the R − − genotype (nearly one in five of the population) carries no instruction for cerebral impairment. It probably has the highest potential for motor skill and for intellectual growth but it is at risk for speech delay and poor phonological processing. The RS + − genotype (nearly one in two) enjoys the benefit of left hemisphere speech laterality with minimal cost to right hemisphere function. This genotype is expected to have an overall heterozygote advantage. The RS + + genotype (about one in three) carries a double dose of right hemisphere deficit. This is associated with significant weakening of the left-hand and certain right hemisphere skills, whose precise nature remains to be determined.

The second and third rows of Figure 14.2 represent carriers of the agnosic mutant. The genotypes of the second row carry only one copy of the mutant gene (heterozygotes for RS +*a*). When the agnosic gene is paired with an RS − allele (RS +*a* − genotype, in 1.7% of the population) there is impairment to either hemisphere at random. Only one hemisphere is compromised and speech learning should proceed normally on the unaffected side. (Right hemisphere CD in this genotype, 0.85%, will require a small adjustment to calculations of RS − gene frequency as described above, but this can be ignored for the present purpose.) Heterozygote carriers of the RS − allele may enjoy advantages similar to those of the RS + − genotype.

When the agnosic gene is paired with a normal RS + gene (RS +*a* + genotype, in 2.2% of the population) the normal gene induces right hemisphere deficit in all (100%). The agnosic gene affects the left or the right hemisphere with 50% probability. If it impairs the right hemisphere, the outcome resembles the normal RS + + genotype. One hemisphere is unimpaired and the individual is non-psychotic. If the agnosic gene affects the left side *both* hemispheres will be impaired. This would occur, on the gene frequencies suggested here, to

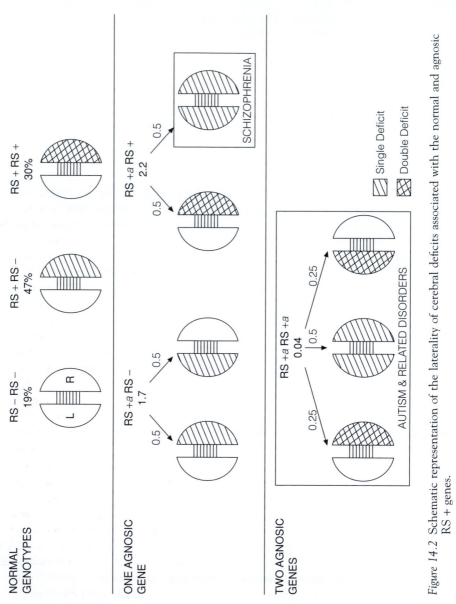

Figure 14.2 Schematic representation of the laterality of cerebral deficits associated with the normal and agnosic RS + genes.

give schizophrenia in 1.1% of the population. Individuals of RS +*a* + genotype have 50% probability of developing schizophrenia, but all have the same probability of affected relatives. Schizophrenics are shown in Figure 14.2 as having bilateral deficit, a single dose of cerebral impairment to both hemispheres. This implies that typical patterns of brain asymmetry would be absent in individuals with bilateral impairment (and liability to schizophrenia). Stronger than average asymmetries should occur in people of the same genotype but a double dose of right-sided impairment, and therefore no schizophrenia (see Figure 14.2).

Homozygotes for the agnosic gene are represented in the bottom row of Figure 14.2. The RS +*a* +*a* genotype (0.04% or 4 per 10,000) suffers a double dose of random cerebral impairment. By chance there may be a single deficit to both sides (50% of cases) or a double deficit to the left hemisphere (25%) or to the right hemisphere (25%). What patterns of impairment are expected for these cerebral deficits? Those with bilateral deficits might resemble schizophrenics, and those with a double deficit to one side but one intact hemisphere might resemble the normal RS + RS + genotype. However, the striking coincidence of the estimates for the frequency of this genotype with estimates for the prevalence of autism suggests that a double dose of the agnosic gene might disrupt early brain growth severely enough to cause major developmental anomalies. The different patterns of random cerebral deficit represented in Figure 14.2 would allow for the observed variability of cognitive function in autistics who show a bewildering variety of disorders and talents. One relatively "normal" hemisphere might serve a special talent, although there was a double dose of impairment to other systems. It is interesting to note that the talents most often observed in autistics, for music, drawing and calculation, are among those considered advantaged by the absence of the normal RS + gene (see chapter 12). Their disabilities for speech and language are also associated with the absence of the normal RS + gene (see chapter 13). Thus the disabilities and the talents of autistics are consistent with absence of the normal bias to left CD and right handedness. But clearly, their disabilities are of a different order of magnitude from normal R − − genotypes. Whereas the normal R − − is hypothesised to carry no copy of the RS + gene, the autistic is hypothesised to possess two disordered copies of the RS + gene. Both lack the typical bias to asymmetry, but for very different reasons.

The genotype frequencies and the random pattern of double cerebral impairments represented in Figure 14.2 are logical consequences of the RS genetic model as already developed to account for handedness and cerebral dominance. They *follow from* the idea that a mutant of the RS + gene may be agnosic for left or right asymmetry. The existence of the agnosic gene, its role in producing schizophrenia in heterozygotes for the agnosic and normal versions of RS +, and its role in producing autism in homozygotes for the agnosic gene are conjectures. They are conjectures that must be tested quantitatively. The hypothesis that homozygotes for the agnosic gene develop autistic spectrum disorders is the working assumption in the following calculations.

Table 14.2 Predicted and observed concordance for schizophrenia in relatives

	Predicted %	Observed %*
MZ twins	50	48
Offspring of dual matings	38–50	46
DZ twins	16–20	17
Siblings	16–20	9
Children	14–15	13
Grandchildren	4–8	5
Nephews/nieces	5–6	4
General population	1	1

Note
* Gottesman (1991).

PREDICTIONS FOR SCHIZOPHRENIA

Table 14.2 lists the predictions of the above model for schizophrenia in the relatives of index cases. The "observed" risks are those estimated by Gottesman (1991) from a review of European studies. True risks of schizophrenia in relatives are difficult to ascertain because of problems such as ambiguities of diagnosis, changes in clinical manifestations with time and place, and variable age of onset. Gottesman made adjustments for age because some relatives who were normal at the time of study would be expected to develop schizophrenia subsequently. Hence, the best available "observed" values are themselves approximate. The predicted values depend on straightforward Mendelian principles of segregation in families, when the genotypes at risk for schizophrenia and autism are as shown in Figure 14.2. The calculations were made twice, for maximum and minimum values. The maximum values are those expected if all genotypes contribute to the gene pool in proportion to their frequency (ignoring the low reproductive rate of schizophrenics and virtual absence of children of autistics). The minimum values are those expected if *no* schizophrenics or autistics reproduce (that is, 50% of RS +a RS + genotypes and all of RS +a RS +a genotypes are excluded from the parent generation). The true value lies somewhere in between.

For MZ twins the prediction is straightforward, that half of the co-twins with identical genotype should be normal and half schizophrenic. The offspring of two schizophrenic parents (both RS +a + heterozygotes) should show the classic distribution described by Mendel for heterozygote crosses. One-quarter would be of RS + + genotype and fully normal. Half would be RS +a + genotype and 50% of these would be schizophrenic and the others normal. Thus, at least 50% of the children of two schizophrenic parents should *not* have schizophrenia. One-quarter of the children of two schizophrenic parents would be RS +a +a homozygotes and at risk of autism. If all developed autistic spectrum disorders, then as many as 50% of all children of two schizophrenic parents would be abnormal. If fewer than half were disordered, the affected proportion would be smaller (see estimates for MZ co-twins of autistics below). Gottesman (1991, p. 101) reported that one-third of the children of two schizophrenic parents were affected while 46% was the estimate for lifetime risk. He found it "amazing" that as many as one-quarter of the children of two schizophrenic parents were fully normal. This is just as expected for a classic Mendelian heterozygote cross.

For DZ co-twins of schizophrenics, the weighted average risk of 17% is well within the predicted range of 16–20%. Predictions are the same for siblings but the observed value (9%) is smaller. The shortfall is not likely to be statistically significant. For other relatives, the predicted and observed risks are in good agreement.

Gottesman and Bertelsen (1989) described children born to MZ and DZ twins who had been previously studied for schizophrenia. The percentages of schizophrenic children were about the same (16–17%) for both the affected and unaffected MZ twins and for the affected DZ twins, while the rate for the children of unaffected DZ twins was about 2%. This is predicted by the model because both members of the MZ pairs and the affected DZ twin should be of identical genotype (RS +a +), while the children of unaffected DZ twins would have the same risk as nephews and nieces. Kringlen and Cramer (1989) found a similar percentage of schizophrenics (17.9%) among the children of affected MZ twins, but fewer than expected (4.4%) in the offspring of unaffected co-twins.

PREDICTIONS FOR AUTISM

Some autism may not be genetic, as mentioned above. Putting aside this complication for the present, what are the implications of the theory that autism depends on homozygosity for the agnosic gene? Autistics become parents so rarely that there is only one study of their children, to my knowledge. Ritvo, Ritvo, Freeman et al. (1994) traced 14 parents of autistic children whom they described as "mild autistics" themselves. They represented less than 0.5% of several thousand parents of autistics surveyed. Among these rare families, there tended to be multiple affected children, as would be expected if these parents were recessive homozygotes mated with a carrier of the agnosic gene.

Most cases of genetic autism are likely to occur in the families of parents who are both heterozygote for the agnosic gene (RS +a – or RS +a + genotypes). If parental genotypes were proportionate to the frequencies in the middle row of Figure 14.2, some 28% of the parents of autistics should be schizophrenic. However, the reduced fertility of schizophrenics implies that the actual proportion would be smaller. At least half of the parents of autistics are likely to be RS +a – heterozygotes, who do not carry the normal RS + allele. In these families there would be *no schizophrenic parents or children* (as brothers or sisters of the autistics) because the model suggests that schizophrenia occurs only when the agnosic gene is paired with a normal RS +. One-quarter of the children would be at risk for autism, however. Parents with RS +a – genotypes could enjoy the intellectual advantages expected for heterozygotes. It is a matter of some controversy whether the high proportion of professional and skilled parents noted in early studies is a reliable associate of autism, or whether it is a product of selective factors influencing referral for treatment (Frith, 1991). However, the RS model offers an explanation for a high proportion of talented parents.

Evidence that autism is inherited depends primarily on the rare cases of autistics who are also twins. Higher concordance was found for MZ than DZ pairs (Bailey, Le Couteur, Gottesman et al., 1995; Ritvo, Freeman, Mason-Brothers et al., 1985; Steffenburg, Gillberg, Hellgren et al., 1989). Ritvo, Spence, Freeman et al. (1985) inferred that there is autosomal recessive inheritance. This would apply to the present model if autistics must be homozygote for the agnosic gene (as in Figure 14.2). But what proportion of recessive homozygotes are likely to show autistic symptoms? Are these expected in the 50% with impairment of both hemispheres (by analogy with schizophrenics) or are 100% likely to show some autistic symptoms, even if not the full syndrome? Evidence from MZ twins offers clues as to the frequency of expression. Full expression would imply that 100% of MZ co-twins and 25% on average of DZ co-twins and siblings should be at risk, because they share the same genotype. Ritvo, Freeman, Mason-Brothers et al. (1985) found 96% of MZ pairs and 24% of DZ pairs concordant for autism, as expected for full expression in the RS +a RS +a genotype. Steffenburg, Gillberg, Hellgren et al. (1989) also found a high degree of concordance in MZ pairs (91% in 11 pairs) but no concordance in DZ pairs (0 in 10 pairs). The combined data for two national surveys in the UK (Bailey et al., 1995) found that 60% of MZ co-twins were concordant but 0% of DZ twins, when strict criteria were applied in the diagnosis of autism. Taking the weaker criterion of any symptoms of social or cognitive impairment, 92% of MZ co-twins and 10% of DZ co-twins were concordant. These findings suggest that at least half of RS +a RS +a genotypes are strongly affected, while almost 100% are affected to some degree.

If this is true, then 12.5% of DZ co-twins and full siblings should develop autism and 25% should show some autistic features. In the Steffenburg et al. series of 10 pairs of DZ twins, one fully autistic co-twin would have been expected and two with at least some autistic symptoms. Similarly in the UK series of 20 DZ pairs, the predictions would be two and four respectively. A concordant DZ twin pair was discovered later in the UK (Rutter, 1996). In view of the small numbers available, the evidence as to DZ concordance must be regarded as inconclusive.

Among the siblings of autistics in a UK national case control study (Bolton, MacDonald, Pickles et al., 1994) at least one of the three cardinal symptoms of autism (defects of cognition, sociability, or presence of stereotyped behaviour) was present in 20.4%, close to the 25% expected. Severe disorder was present in 5.8% of siblings for the UK series, and 4.5% in a US series (Jorde, Hasstedt, Ritvo et al., 1991).

COMMENTS, CRITICISMS AND COUNTER-ARGUMENTS

The idea of an agnosic RS + gene first occurred to me in May 1996 and it was described at a conference a few months later (Annett, 1996b). It was published

(Annett, 1997a) along with five critical commentaries (Corballis, 1997b; Elvevåg and Weinberger, 1997; Green, 1997; McManus, 1997; Sham, 1997) and an author's rejoinder (Annett, 1997b). It would not be appropriate to review the commentaries in detail here, but I will consider some important questions that were raised, often by several contributors.

First, is the whole edifice a "House of Cards", an image used by Corballis. There is no doubt that there is a great deal of speculation and circumstantial evidence in the theory of schizophrenia proposed by Crow, and also in the theory of CD proposed by Annett. Either or both theories could be wrong but both were tightly argued. The RS theory was assembled from several clearly interlocking pieces. The surprise about the agnosic gene theory was that the two theories, of Crow and of Annett, could be brought together directly. Three commentators described the theory as "ingenious", which the *Concise Oxford Dictionary* defines as "cleverly contrived". Now the most surprising thing to my mind was that the theory was not contrived but rather "hit me between the eyes". Within a couple of hours of considering the idea that the gene might lose its directional sense, rough calculations showed that the RS model as already developed (chapters 5 and 7 above) could account for the frequency of schizophrenia in the relatives of schizophrenics (in Table 14.2). This is the key problem for any genetic theory of schizophrenia. The idea of an agnosic gene offered an immediate solution. What makes the arguments above worth consideration is the remarkable fit of predictions of the model to the estimated risks of schizophrenia for relatives. It worked quantitatively, given the RS theory as already developed to account for the many phenomena considered in previous chapters.

The realisation that the theory might embrace autism came later, as the implications of the calculations for schizophrenia became clearer. There were three features of the model that seemed particularly striking as applied to autism. First, my estimate of the frequency of agnosic gene, as required to predict the incidence of schizophrenia, implied that homozygotes would be 4 in 10,000, matching estimates for the prevalence of autism. Second, it was clear that many autistic children would have parents who were heterozygote carriers of the agnosic gene, paired with the RS − gene. They could be expected to enjoy the heterozygote advantages inferred for normal RS + − genotypes (chapter 11). The high proportion of professional parents has been a particularly puzzling feature of autism. Third, the patterns of random cerebral impairment that are intrinsic to the model might explain the strange variability of talents seen in autistic children, along with the core deficits. Criticisms of the model need to be considered in two stages. The application to schizophrenia should be considered first because this could stand alone, independently of any extension to autism. The application to autism is a second issue. This might be invalid, without causing the whole edifice to collapse as in a house of cards.

There is a feature of Crow's theory that should be kept distinct from the present argument, speculations about the location of the relevant gene(s) on the sex chromosomes. Crow (1999, 2000) argued that cerebral dominance genes are located on regions of the sex chromosomes that are homologous for X and Y but not exchanged between the sexes in the production of gametes. This is an interesting speculation but one that is independent of the argument of the RS theory above. It is clear that the RS + gene is unlikely to be transmitted as a typical sex-linked gene because this would give very substantial sex differences for handedness and CD, that are not present. However, expression of the gene is almost certainly sex-modified. Sex-modification is implied by the stronger expression of the normal RS + gene in females than males, and the associated relative advantages for females in speech and language related skills and relative disadvantages of females compared to males in maths and spatial abilities. The relevance of these sex differences to arguments about schizophrenia is unclear. There is no difference between the sexes in liability to schizophrenia, except for the earlier age of onset in males. For autism there are major differences between the sexes because boys are very much more likely to be diagnosed autistic than girls. The origin of this sex difference is unknown. It could not be accommodated in the predictions of Figure 14.2, unless it is supposed that female homozygotes for the agnosic gene are either lost (perhaps through foetal mortality because of the stronger expression of the agnosic gene in females) or manifest other forms of developmental disorder.

Several commentators raised questions about handedness in schizophrenics and autistics, and considered whether they were compatible with the model. Although the RS model arose from analyses of handedness, I said nothing about handedness in the application to schizophrenia. The literature on the handedness of schizophrenics is controversial and confusing, but so are most treatments of handedness. As argued in previous chapters of this book, variable assessments of handedness are likely to be due to variable methods and criteria. However, it should be acknowledged that the predominant finding in the literature is that schizophrenics are less clearly lateralised than controls for handedness (Cannon, Byrne, Cassidy et al., 1995; Gur, 1977; Taylor and Amir, 1995) and also for dichotic listening asymmetry (Loberg, Hugdahl and Green, 1999; Wexler, Giller and Southwick, 1991). Two studies should have particular mention because they followed certain leads suggested by my approach to handedness, as expounded above. Orr, Cannon, Gilvarry et al. (1999) restricted their definition of mixed-handedness to my classes 5 and 6 (from the subgroup analyses of chapter 2). That is, mixed-handers in their scheme were ones who were inconsistent in their preferences for the primary actions (writing, throwing, racket, match, hammer, toothbrush), while the other six actions were ignored for this purpose. Schizophrenics were very much more likely to be inconsistent for primary actions than controls, and there was also a strong trend for the relatives of schizophrenics to be inconsistent in this way also. Inspection of Figure 14.2 suggests that schizophrenics should be without strong bias to either side. Hence, increased mixed-handedness is consistent with the present theory. A study of peg moving in autistic children found them without significant bias to either side, consistent with randomness as represented in the bottom row of Figure 14.2 (McManus, Murray, Doyle et al., 1992). Dichotic listening asymmetry in autistic children was also consistent with random bias (5 REA, 7 LEA and 7 with no difference between sides; Prior and Bradshaw, 1979).

McManus (1997) referred to analyses by Boklage (1977) of the handedness of twins, discordant for schizophrenia. If unaffected co-twins in MZ pairs (with RS +*a* + genotypes) resemble normal RS + + genotypes, they should be shifted more strongly to dextrality than the general population. McManus (1997) pointed out that the frequency of left-handedness should be about 1%, as indeed was shown for this genotype in Figure 11.1. However, Boklage (1977) reported that 5/12 (42%) of such co-twins were left-handed, in the Maudsley twin series of Gottesman and Shields (1972). The numbers of cases were small but the mismatch between prediction and observation looks serious at first sight. However, both Boklage and McManus neglected the critical question of the *criterion* of left-handedness. Boklage talked about left foot preference and ambidexterity as well as left-handedness and then claimed that (p. 24), "a single important departure from full right-side motor preference may place an adult in a minority of 8–10%". This is nonsense, of course, because the 8–10% incidence depends on the criterion of left writing, while *any* left preference may include 40–50% of the population. Boklage is actually referring to "mixed-handers", generously defined. RS + +*a* genotypes include many mixed-handers, especially among twins because of the reduced RS of twins compared with the singleborn. Thus, the Boklage analysis is not inconsistent with the model.

The most critical question for the agnosic gene theory, raised by several commentators, is whether the genetic predictions fit the evidence. Sham pointed out that quantitative fits to incidences of schizophrenia in relatives could be found for any model with a "suitable environmental (or random) component and an appropriate degree of gene–gene interaction" and indeed McManus proposed to devise one in his commentary. Of course such a model could be *invented* but the RS theory's combination of randomness and genetic influence was deduced many years earlier to solve independent problems. It was the fact that the puzzle pieces fell into place immediately, once the idea of an agnosic gene occurred, that was to me the most compelling feature. Sham, and also Elvevåg and Weinberger, suggested that previous studies of the genetics of schizophrenia rule out the presence of a major gene. However, the agnosic gene theory makes some very specific predictions that would not have been tested in earlier data analyses. The agnosic gene is expected to present in some 4% of the population, to lead to schizophrenia only in 50% of people in whom this gene is paired with a normal RS + gene, but not when paired with an RS – allele, nor when paired with another agnosic gene. What a strange recipe! In view of the specific predictions of the RS hypothesis, and the absence of an accepted alternative, it is surely worth another look at the evidence.

Elvevåg and Weinberger doubted the theory on several of the grounds considered above, but questioned particularly the implications for cerebral asymmetry. Is there likely to be a gene for right hemisphere disadvantage when several cerebral asymmetries favour the right side? The hypothesis of right brain impairment followed from empirical observations of the weakness of the left-hand and the smallness of right PT, reviewed in chapter 10. The physical basis of the impairment of right language cortex might be subtle, affecting perhaps only one critical aspect of speech function. The timing of this impairment is unknown, but the RS theory agrees that it is likely to be in foetal life. The fact that reversals of asymmetry are associated with other conditions such as dyslexia and other disorders of speech and literacy is not a reason to doubt the theory. On the contrary, these reductions were predicted by the theory, long before the application to schizophrenia was envisaged.

The inconsistency of findings between studies of cerebral asymmetry in schizophrenia presents problems for the evaluation of evidence. However, these inconsistencies do not throw doubt on the agnosic gene theory but are rather predicted by the RS model because all effects have to be detected against a background of random asymmetry. Inspection of Figure 14.2 will remind the reader that normal people may have any of three different patterns of cerebral dominance. Thus normal controls will differ, by chance in these respects. Contrasts between the *left* hemispheres of schizophrenic and controls should be fairly clear because no normal group has the hypothesised left-sided impairment associated with the agnosic gene (except for 50% of the RS +a – genotype in about 0.9% of the population). Contrasts for the *right* hemisphere may differ considerably between groups of controls, depending on the genotypes sampled. In some samples (Crow, Ball, Bloom et al., 1989; Johnstone, Owens, Crow et al., 1989) the right hemisphere was apparently more "impaired" in controls than in schizophrenics. This would be expected if controls happened to include a high proportion of RS + + genotypes. Among MZ twins discordant for schizophrenia, the unaffected twin should have a double dose of right-sided impairment, compared with a single dose for the schizophrenic twin. Hence, the affected twin should have reduced asymmetry while the unaffected twin should have exaggerated asymmetry, compared with controls. Bartley, Jones, Torrey et al. (1993) examined the length of the Sylvian fissure in ten MZ twins discordant for schizophrenia. The proportion larger on the left side (the typical pattern) was 50% for schizophrenic twins (chance, as predicted in Figure 14.2), 65% in normals (comparable with Geschwind and Levitsky's, 1968, findings for PT), and 80% in the unaffected discordant twins (more strongly asymmetrical, as expected for the individual of RS +a + genotype who does not become schizophenic). The numbers were too small for statistical significance but the trend, not noted by Bartley et al., was consistent with the RS thesis.

McManus and Sham were particularly concerned that the evidence for co-occurrence of autism and schizophrenia in families is weak. If both conditions depend on the presence of an agnosic (RS +a) gene, these conditions should have some association in families. The association is difficult to predict because of uncertainty as to the reproductive rate of schizophrenics. If there were no limitations on the fertility of schizophenics, then about 28% of the parents and about 13% of the siblings of autistics should be schizophrenic, as explained above. However, if the fertility of schizophrenics is reduced, the proportions would be correspondingly smaller. If the majority of parents of autistics were of

RS +*a* – genotype, there would be *no* schizophrenic parents or siblings (because no normal RS + gene, as said above). Actual levels of association are difficult to assess because the disabled children of disabled parents are likely to be placed in care. Even if these children enter research series, their parents are likely to be untraceable or uncooperative. Studies of the families of autistics always lose some cases through non-compliance and institutionalisation. Thus it is possible that the true proportion of schizophrenic relatives of autistics has been under-estimated. It is premature to dismiss the theory on these grounds.

Elvevåg and Weinberger asked why abnormalities of the language cortex might lead to psychosis at maturity, rather than to developmental language disorder. That is indeed an interesting question and the answer depends on the mechanism of gene action. There is a related question, why the effects of a single dose of the agnosic gene should lead to schizophrenia, while a double dose of the same gene should lead to a profound developmental disorder from infancy. The operational mechanisms of the RS + gene are expected to be effective during foetal growth. We know that children destined to develop schizophrenia were relatively impaired throughout childhood, so there can be no doubt as to the early influence of the gene, even if psychosis is not manifest until adulthood. If homozygotes for the agnosic gene are liable to autism, as suggested, then it must be inferred that a double dose of the disruption to foetal development has serious effects, that lead to a profound disorder of development, perhaps through a cascade of influences on subsequent growth. It should also be noted that the schizophrenic, on this theory, has one copy of the normal RS + gene, while the autistic has none.

FURTHER POSSIBLE IMPLICATIONS

The theory of an agnosic RS gene offers a mechanism for Crow's hypothesis that schizophrenia is a disorder of cerebral dominance for language. It suggests that schizophrenia is due to a gene that arose in the course of human evolution, a gene associated with language, vulnerable to mutation, and associated with damage to the language cortex of the left hemisphere. The agnosic gene does not cause schizophrenia directly because there must be the joint presence of the normal RS + gene, and only 50% of agnosic gene carriers are then affected. The pattern of risk for relatives, fitted by no previous genetic model, follows the pattern of inheritance expected for a classic co-dominant gene when all other features of the model are as deduced for the RS theory from data independent of schizophrenia.

When considering the variety of subtypes of schizophrenia, it is important to recall that according to the RS theory all genetic effects are expressed against a background of accidental developmental asymmetries, in addition to the genetic randomness introduced by the agnosic right shift mutation. Random cerebral asymmetries may exacerbate or ameliorate the difficulties associated with the genotypes discussed above. When combined with other variability for intelligence,

personality and life experience, it is not surprising that the schizophrenic phenotype shows diverse modes of expression, while sharing certain core features.

The relevance of the model to other psychiatric disorders will need consideration. The puzzles of relationships between schizotypy, related personality
disorders, and schizophrenia might be clarified if the presence of the agnosic
gene, paired with an RS – gene, sometimes produces oddities of thought and
behaviour but without psychosis (see Figure 14.2). The observation of manic-
depressive psychoses in the relatives of schizophrenics, including identical
twins and triplets (Torrey, Bowler, Taylor et al., 1994), suggests that the RS +a
RS + genotype might be at risk for affective disorder, perhaps among those with
a *double dose of right hemisphere impairment* (in contrast to schizophrenics who
suffer a single impairment to each hemisphere). The observation of affective
disorders in the parents of autistics (Bailey, Phillips and Rutter, 1996) would
accord with this possibility. Crow (1995a) has suggested that the psychoses are
diverse expressions of a single underlying entity. Perhaps the agnosic gene (RS +a)
is that entity.

The RS theory was prompted by studies of handedness, but the theory itself
implies that little can be deduced from handedness alone (Annett, 1985a, 1995a).
Differences for handedness are *weak effects but not causes* of the variables of
interest. Absence of cerebral asymmetries in normal RS – – genotypes occurs
because *neither* hemisphere is impaired. For this reason, non-gene-carriers are
expected to have high potential for the development of physical and intellectual
skills. The absence or reduction of cerebral asymmetries in schizophrenics, by
contrast, are hypothesised to occur because *both* hemispheres are impaired. In
comparison with controls, only the left hemisphere differs, because deficits of
the right hemisphere occur in controls also. Close attention to the actual sizes
of the relevant brain areas, instead of the usual derived "index" measures of
lateral asymmetry, is needed to test this aspect of the theory. Cutting (1994) has
argued that schizophrenics suffer cognitive and other dysfunction associated
with right hemisphere impairment. The present theory suggests that *both* hemispheres of schizophrenics resemble the typical right hemisphere. There are sex
differences in all of the phenomena under discussion, but the mechanisms remain
to be worked out.

What is the nature of the deficit that has such disastrous consequences when
applied at random to either or both hemispheres? A gene for left hemisphere
CD could produce its effects in many different ways. Is it possible to identify a
handicap that might lead to all of the relevant deficits, for speech, learning and
schizophrenia? Schizophrenia and autism are associated with rafts of problems,
and there are many theories as to the nature of the core deficits (reviews in
David and Cutting, 1994). Frith (1992) has argued that the critical problem for
schizophrenics might lie in the processes by which we generate intentions to
act, and monitor the effect of those intentions. In learning to talk infants must
attend to the sounds made by carers. When trying to reproduce these sound
they must monitor the feedback in a self-generated, self-correcting learning
process, whose basis is not yet clear (Doupe and Kuhl, 1999). Perhaps "nature"

impairs the ability of the right hemisphere to generate and monitor this learning process, forcing the infant to use the left hemisphere when learning to make speech sounds. A break in the feedback circuits through which we internally monitor our own behaviour might be a key component process that is compromised in schizophrenia. This might affect mechanisms of attention, will, self-initiated and latent learning (Gray, Feldon, Rawlins et al., 1991), as well as the acquisition of speech and language.

An analogy used over 100 years ago by Fechner, was that the two brains in one skull are like two horses in the shafts of a cart (cited by Beaton, 1979). Both must proceed at the same pace, but it is usual for one horse to take the lead and the other to follow, for the smooth progression of both. A more modern analogy might be that the human brain operates like a twin-engine vehicle, each engine with its own steering system. Both systems are involved in low level and relatively automatic activities like walking and some types of conditioned learning, but learning to talk with two hemispheres (simultaneously or alternately) would be difficult, because of time constraints on the mechanisms of speech production and perception. It could be to the advantage of the system as a whole if the steering system on one side were slightly disabled. A single, dominant system would give a unified central executive for initiating actions and monitoring their outcomes in both hemispheres. There is abundant evidence that the left hemisphere (dominant in most people) exerts some ipsilateral control over the left-hand as well as typical contralateral control of the right-hand while the right hemisphere's role is restricted to the opposite, left side. However, the advantages of unified control, produced by slightly disabling one side, would be bought at grave costs if the gene responsible became right–left agnosic. Schizophrenics, according to the present model, do not have a reliable steering system on either side. There would be a frightening experience of loss of control. Damping down the system, as in the chronic poverty syndrome or through drugs, might give relief but not cure.

This model suggests that autistics begin life with steering systems that are so severely disabled that they barely learn to drive, nor understand what it means for others to drive. If their intentions to act meet with little reliable success, it is not surprising that they become fixed in repetitive behaviours and insist on sameness. Without reliable mechanisms for producing and monitoring their own intentional behaviour, they would fail to understand that of others. It would not be possible to communicate intentions. This could contribute to their difficulties in interpreting the beliefs and mental states of others and their continuing weaknesses of social relationships throughout life (Frith, 1989, 1991).

Tests of the theory will require brain imagers and others to grasp the nettle of individual differences in order to study the range of variation of human cerebral functional specialisation. In searching for the gene(s) involved, three sources of asymmetry must be considered. First, there is non-genetic random asymmetry that is universal. Second there is genetic directional asymmetry present in some 80% of humans that is associated with left hemisphere specialisation for speech. Third, there is a mutant variant of the latter causing cerebral deficits at random.

The genetic locus is expected to carry some alleles shared with other primates, at least one common allele specific to humans, and a mutant variant of the latter, with a frequency of about 2%.

SUMMARY

This chapter reviewed the theory proposed by Crow that schizophrenia is caused by a disorder of the mechanisms of cerebral dominance. If this is correct, and the RS theory is correct, then schizophrenia could be caused by a disorder of the RS + gene. It is shown how a mutant form of this gene, that is agnosic for (unable to distinguish) the left versus right hemispheres, could be the mechanism required for Crow's theory. This hypothesis required no changes to the RS theory, other than the idea of an agnosic mutant with an allelic frequency of about 2%. All other features of the genetic model were as already deduced from evidence for dysphasia and handedness in families. The reason the model should be considered seriously is that risks for schizophrenia in the relatives of schizophrenics, as estimated by Gottesman (1991), were immediately predictable.

The application to schizophrenia rests on the idea that the RS + gene acts to lateralise speech in the left cerebral hemisphere by handicapping some feature of the speech relevant cortex on the right hemisphere. The agnosic mutant has lost its directional coding, so by chance, may impair the left hemisphere instead of the right. This does not matter, provided there is one intact hemisphere. However, if the agnosic mutant is paired with a normal RS + gene, that always impairs the right side, then in 50% of cases, both hemispheres will be impaired. Hence, the suggestion is that schizophrenia is likely to develop when the speech relevant cortex is damaged on both sides of the brain.

The model as developed above, together with the estimated frequency of the agnosic gene, implied that homozygotes for the agnosic mutant would occur in about 4 in 10,000 persons. This happens to be about the rate observed for childhood autism. There are several features of the model that could be useful in explaining otherwise puzzling features of autism. These include the probable heterozygote advantage of many parents of autistics, the variety of manifestations due to chance patterns of cerebral dominance, and the evidence that the transmission of autism in families is as expected for a recessive homozygote. These ideas are new, and were challenged by a number of commentators. Most of the objections, however, depended on misunderstanding of the RS theory.

These possible extensions of the RS model into puzzles of psychosis offer exciting new opportunities for research. The jigsaw puzzle of handedness and cerebral dominance has grown considerably, in the light of the RS theory, but it is far from complete.

Part V

Independent replications, challenges and theories

15 Independent tests and challenges

This chapter reviews independent tests and challenges to the RS theory. Studies that have sought to replicate my findings have reported positive and negative results. Claims to "fail" the RS theory are examined.

HAND PREFERENCE AND HAND SKILL IN GUATEMALA

The first major replication of my research was done for a doctoral thesis (Demarest, 1982), testing children in Guatemala for lateral preferences and for hand skills. The question whether findings for handedness in English children would be replicated in Guatemala was examined for children of two racial groups, Ladinos and Maya. Most Guatemalans are Ladinos, of mixed Spanish and Indian ancestry, who speak Spanish. The native Indians are Maya who speak some 20 Mayan languages but must learn Spanish if they are to be educated in school. Demarest set out in 1976 to check my findings for English school children (Annett, 1970b; Annett and Turner, 1974). The data were also examined retrospectively for findings of Kilshaw and Annett (1983), that left-handers tend to be faster for actual hand speeds than right-handers. An account of Demarest's findings was given in Annett (1985a, chapter 20). The present account is based on the same material from Guatemala, but the comparisons with my samples are updated to include the larger groups described earlier in this book (especially in chapter 6).

The findings that Demarest set out to test were as follows, (1) distributions of hand preference and relative hand skill remain constant with age during the school years, (2) females are more biased to right-handedness than males, (3) right-, mixed-, and left-handers (defined as consistent right or left, versus inconsistent-handers) are in binomial proportions, (4) degrees of hand preference and degrees of L–R skill are systematically related, and (5) children with relatively poor language skills include more non-right-handers than children with good language skills. A sixth test was added later to check the observation that left-handers are faster than right-handers for actual hand speed for both the preferred and non-preferred hands.

Four samples of children were tested in different parts of Guatemala. The first sample (Ladinos I, N = 146) was of pre-school children tested in their homes in

North Guatemala City. The second sample (Ladinos II, N = 485) was of pupils attending an elementary school in South Guatemala City. The third sample (Ladinos III, N = 172) was of schoolchildren in San Pedro Soloma, a township in the mountains north of Guatemala City. The Mayan sample (Maya, N = 280, but 233 of known age) was of children attending schools in and around Soloma. A peg moving test was given to all children, the apparatus and method based on the description of Annett (1970b). Demarest devised another test of hand skill using beans, a material very familiar to children in Guatemala, to check the generality and consistency of findings for the peg task. The bean moving test required children to pick up seven dried beans and place them in a narrow-necked aspirin bottle. Five trials were given for each hand, timed by stopwatch. All except the first Guatemalan sample were tested for bean moving.

Observations of lateral preferences were introduced for the second sample and continued for other samples. The actions were to wave goodbye, throw a ball, kick a soccer ball, insert beans in a bottle, screw on the lid of a jar, sight through a tube, eat with a spoon, and use a pencil. As the findings for hand preference were not described separately from those for foot and eye preference, and as the hand tests included a gesture (waving) that requires no skill, the findings for preference cannot be compared directly with my samples. The findings of particular interest here are those for hand skill. The first group of questions concerns age, sex, and racial group. The second group of questions concerns the balanced polymorphism hypothesis. Among Mayan children slow to learn Spanish, was L–R skill smaller than in those who learned Spanish easily, as expected if the latter but not the former enjoyed the benefits of the RS + gene? Third, among children left-handed for preference, were absolute hand speeds faster than among right-handed children? This surprising finding for my samples was discovered long after the data were gathered. Would Demarest also find an absolute hand speed advantage for left-handers, also several years after making the measurements?

Sex, age and racial group

The question whether there are *sex* differences in extent of right shift can be answered as unequivocally for the Guatemalan samples as for my English ones. In all four samples girls had larger L–R differences than boys for the peg moving task. On the bean test, girls showed larger differences than males in the two Ladino samples tested, but the Maya did not differ for sex on this test. Demarest checked that the sex difference for relative skill was not due to different numbers of left-handers. When left-handers were excluded and L–R differences were examined for right-handers only, the relatively greater bias of females to the right was still evident. On the RS theory, of course, the sex difference is due to stronger expression of the RS + gene in females, so that sex differences are expected among right-handers but not among left-handers.

Asymmetry for peg moving and bean moving (where available) is summarised by sample and age in Table 15.1, together with data for six age groups in my

Table 15.1 R–L% for peg moving and bean moving in Guatemala and UK

Sample	Grade	Age (yr.mth)	N	R–L% pegs	R–L% beans
Ladinos I		3.9–5.5	44	5.64	—
		5.6–6.8	51	5.78	—
		6.9–9.7	51	5.12	—
Ladinos II	K		35	5.83	6.67
	1		86	5.62	6.57
	2		72	4.76	6.19
	3		85	5.00	7.55
	4		85	4.55	6.93
	5		68	4.80	6.25
	6		54	4.00	5.38
Ladinos III	K–1		59	4.55	5.26
	2–3		57	4.23	4.59
	4–6		56	6.72	4.95
Maya		5.0–8.1	76	3.10	3.40
		8.5–10.10	78	2.84	3.03
		10.11–16.7	79	2.49	3.51
English		3.9–4.8	35	4.45	—
		5.9–7.5	265	3.83	—
		8.6–9.5	165	4.49	—
		9.6–11.5	201	3.64	—
		11.6–13.5	221	3.88	—
		13.6–14.5	486	3.70	—

Note
K   kindergarten.

samples, corresponding to those tested in Guatemala. The analysis is based on Demarest's Tables 10–13, as was that by Annett (1985a, Table 20.1), except that the measure of asymmetry used here is R–L% and the English samples included more children. (Sex is not distinguished in Table 15.1 because the difference was relatively constant over samples.) An analysis of variance of the means was run for the Guatemalan samples alone and then with the English samples, in order to explore possible differences between racial groups. For the four Guatemalan samples there was a significant difference between groups (F = 8.552, d.f. 3:15, p = 0.003). Post hoc comparisons with Bonferroni corrections found the Maya less biased to dextrality than all three samples of Ladinos. The Ladinos did not differ from each other. When English children were included in the analysis they were intermediate between the Ladinos and Maya. The English children differed significantly from the Ladinos I sample only (the most dextral). Analysis of variance for the bean test, available for two samples of Ladinos and the Maya, found a highly significant difference between groups. All three groups differed. The Ladinos II were exceptionally right shifted on this test (R–L% = 6.5) while Ladinos III were similar for bean asymmetry (R–L% = 4.9) and peg asymmetry (R–L% = 5.2). The Maya were less asymmetrical than both of the Ladino samples for beans (R–L% = 3.3), as they were for pegs (R–L% = 2.8).

There can be little doubt that the Maya are less right shifted than the Ladinos, because this was found for two different measures.

Analyses for changes with age were based on the Ladinos alone because the Maya differed significantly and because, of course, the English samples have been described already (chapter 6). The interesting question was whether R–L% varied with age over the three Ladino samples, considered together. Analysis of variance (weighted for number within the various age groups of Ladinos) found no differences between groups and no overall trend. The mean difference between the hands over all Ladino groups was 5.1% (while for English ones, in Figure 6.2 it was just under 4%). The Guatemalan and English data agree that asymmetry is constant with age.

Differences between racial groups could occur either because there are differences in the frequency of the RS + gene or because there are differences in the expressivity of the gene. Differences in expression have been postulated between the sexes and between twins and the singleborn, and these have been attributed to differences in relative growth and/or maturity at birth. Cross-cultural studies of neonatal maturity and development in infancy have reported several differences between racial groups, but the evidence is insufficient to reach any firm conclusions about the relative rates of maturation of Ladino and Mayan children (Super, 1981). Assuming that lesser RS is associated with lesser maturity at birth (as postulated for males and twins), Mayan babies would be expected to be slightly less mature than Ladino babies. Studies of Maya Indians in Mexico (Brazelton, Robey, and Collier, 1969) and of Hopi Indians in the United States (Dennis, 1940) both concluded that development in infancy paralleled that of Caucasian children but was delayed approximately 1 month. This delay was found in the latter sample for infants who had been tied to a cradle-board and also for those for whom this traditional practice had been abandoned. The newborns observed by Brazelton et al. were very small, about 5lbs, though not premature. On tests of development, items concerning quality of vocalisation could not be scored because of the *paucity of social babbling*. The main aim of the mothers seemed to be to keep the infants quiet, but it seems remarkable that the voice play that is so evident in Caucasian children in the second half of the first year should be so reduced. It would be consistent with reduced expression of the RS + gene.

Other studies of native Americans have reported reduced or absent REA for dichotic listening (Scott, Hynd, Hunt et al., 1979; Volate, 1984) but this was not confirmed by McKeever and Hunt (1984). The Kwakiutl were reported to include a high proportion of non-right-handers (Marrion, 1986). By contrast, natives of the Amazon rain forest were described as having low incidences of left-handedness (Ardila, Ardila, Bryden et al., 1989).

Peg moving asymmetry was assessed for young people in Papua New Guinea (PNG) and compared with that of English schoolchildren with findings that were strikingly similar to those just described above for the Maya (Connolly and Bishop, 1992). The difference between the hands was about half as large as for English children, a difference that was highly significant statistically. My calculations of the difference between the hands as a proportion of total time

(R–L%) in the data of Connolly and Bishop found 4.8% for English children and 2.1% and 2.5% for two groups in PNG. It is important to note that the total time taken by both hands was almost identical between groups so that the difference in asymmetry was not an artefact of differences for actual time on the task.

The tests of lateral preference used by Demarest included measures of foot and eye preference, as well as the unskilled action of waving goodbye, as mentioned above. The findings for 179 children in the Ladinos II sample were in general accord with those of English school children (Annett, 1970b) but detailed comparisons are not appropriate in view of the different criteria.

Language learning and levels of hand skill: Aspects of the BP + HA hypothesis

Demarest was guided by the analysis of Annett and Turner (1974) when examining relationships between laterality and language skills. Annett and Turner distinguished two different approaches to research on handedness and abilities, as discussed in chapter 13. One type of analysis, the school-based survey, classifies for handedness and compares for ability. Typically, no differences are found. The second type of analysis, the clinical comparison, starts with a group of children known to have a problem (reading, spelling, speech disorder, etc.) and compares them with controls for handedness. The clinic sample is typically less shifted to dextrality.

Education in Guatemala depends on learning Spanish, as mentioned above. A vocabulary test was given to 123 Indian children in their first year in school. Children were asked whether members of their families knew Spanish, and there were no differences in handedness between children with and without Spanish-speaking relatives. They were asked to name 48 familiar items in their native language, Kanjobal, and for all items correctly named they were asked to give the name in Spanish. Hand preference groups did not differ for number of errors, the finding expected for the survey approach. The critical test for the RS theory depended on the difference between 99 children who did well on the Spanish vocabulary test and 24 who did not (the clinic comparison). The prediction that the latter would show a lesser right shift was confirmed. The L–R means of high scorers (9.5) and low scorers (3.8) differed significantly in the predicted direction ($t = 1.69$, d.f. $= 121$, $p = 0.047$, one-tailed test).

Demarest looked at the actual times taken by the preferred and non-preferred hands of left- and right-handers, for the pegboard and bean tests after receiving a pre-publication copy of (Kilshaw and Annett, 1983). For the Guatemalan samples, as for the English ones, the analyses were made long after the original data were collected. Even if it might be argued that the differences found for English samples depended on some improbable conjunction of accidents, the chances that such accidents would be repeated in an independent test of children from two other cultures is so unlikely as to merit no serious consideration. Demarest compared left- and right-handers on the pegboard task in four samples and on the bean test in three samples, giving seven comparisons for the preferred hand and seven for the non-preferred hand. In 13 out of 14 comparisons absolute mean times favoured left-handers, and in the 14th case there was no difference. As for English samples, differences tended to be clearer for the non-preferred hand than for the preferred hand. (The difference in favour of left-handers was statistically significant for three out of seven comparisons for the non-preferred hand and only one out of seven for the preferred hand.) The advantage to left-handers was as clear in the Maya as in the Ladinos. Thus, faster hand speed in left- than right-handers, evident for both hands but more marked for the non-preferred hand, has been found in three racial groups.

THE POSTULATE OF VARIABLE EXPRESSION OF THE RS + GENE

The idea that the RS theory was seriously weakened by the need for an "extra" postulate for twins, reduced expression of the RS + gene compared with singletons, was suggested by McManus (1980a). The criticism was reiterated (McManus, 1985a) and extended to embrace the hypothesis of stronger expression in females than males (McManus and Bryden, 1992). In this last paper it was implied that the hypothesis of variable shifts with sex and twinning, and between dominant and additive versions of the model, represented several different and mutually inconsistent versions of the RS theory. However, variable shifts do not represent different theories but hypotheses about a single gene whose effect in shifting the handedness distribution was unknown but needed to be estimated from different sets of data. Differences in expressivity for the same gene in different environments, and in different genotypes, are well known phenomena (Weaver and Hedrick, 1992). McManus and Bryden misunderstood the RS theory in this respect.

With regard to twinning, the supposed weakness of the RS theory turned out to be a strength because it led to a clear prediction, that left-handedness should be more frequent in twins than singletons by some 4–5%. This was subsequently upheld in a very large representative sample (Davis and Annett, 1994). The hypothesis of variable expression between the sexes was supported by the discovery of levels of shift that gave matching thresholds for paired samples of males and females, as explained in chapter 7. These led, in turn, to the ability to predict distributions of handedness in families when the sex of parents and of children was distinguished, in all samples where assessment was by self-report. The hypothesis that variable expression of the RS + gene is associated with relative maturity at birth gives a simple and consistent explanation for differences for handedness associated with sex, twinning, low birth weight and possibly differences between racial groups.

QUESTIONS ABOUT HAND SKILL

The first specific claim to "fail the right shift model" was by McManus (1985b; rejoinder Annett, 1985b, and reply McManus, 1985c). The claim depended on analyses of empirical data for R–L peg moving skill, for 617 males and 863 females, published as an appendix to Annett and Kilshaw (1983). McManus sought to show that these distributions were likely to consist of mixtures of two distributions, with means to the left and right of R = L, as might be expected for left-handers versus right-handers. This contrasted with the RS theory of a mixture of two or three distributions, as represented in Figures 4.1 or 7.1 respectively. Because McManus followed the common-sense view that there are two discrete types of handedness, right versus left, his theory requires the former outcome. For the square marking test given to the NCDS sample, where response depends on making small marks on paper, observed distributions are clearly bimodal. This bimodality is evident in all tests that use pens and pencils, or other familiar tools where one hand has enjoyed special practice. The bimodality is evident without need for statistical analysis. For the peg moving task there is a unimodal distribution (see Figure 3.5). Annett and Kilshaw sought to discover whether the RS model of two or three subdistributions was consistent with empirical data.

McManus used a maximum likelihood method of model fitting and reported better support for his own model (symmetrically bimodal about 0) than for either of the RS models. Annett (1985b) examined the peg moving data against the various models derived by McManus and compared them with the heuristic solutions derived by Annett and Kilshaw. The Kolmogorov test showed that most of the former gave poorer fits than the latter. In fact, neither model could be clearly rejected on this evidence. Some years earlier I had sought advice on the feasibility of using R–L data of this kind for testing hypotheses about the mixture of distributions likely to be present. The advice was that very much larger samples would be required to make satisfactory tests and that my data was far from sufficient for this purpose. The evidence as to the mixture distributions for R–L peg moving remains unclear because the samples examined in 1985 were not large enough for firm conclusions to be drawn. However, the success of the predictions for sex differences, matching thresholds, and handedness in families as described in chapter 7, strongly supports the RS hypothesis as represented in Figure 7.1.

Several authors checked the pattern of relative hand skill shown in Figure 10.2, namely that the right-hand changes relatively little with increasing bias to dextrality while the left-hand falls strongly and linearly. This pattern was confirmed in every sample in which it was looked for (Leask and Crow, 1997; McManus, Shergill and Bryden, 1993; Palmer and Corballis, 1996; Resch, Haffner, Parzer et al., 1997). There can be little doubt, therefore, of the reliability of these empirical observations. The challenge from Leask and Crow concerned its interpretation. They showed that strong left-handers for square marking in the NCDS sample were as poor with the right-hand, as strong right-handers were with the left-hand. The theoretical importance of the issues depends on the cause of the poor left-hand performance of most right-handers. The RS theory supposed that the cause depends on the mechanisms of the RS + gene, but the nature of these mechanisms is unknown.

QUESTIONS OF ABILITY AND THE BALANCED
POLYMORPHISM HYPOTHESIS

A review of my findings for the hypothesis of a balanced polymorphism with heterozygote advantage (Annett, 1995a) was published with some 20 commentaries and author's reply (Annett, 1995b). It should be noted that the hypothesis was prompted by inspection of the genotype frequencies. The latter were deduced from evidence described in chapters 4 and 5. The hypothesis was proposed (Annett, 1978b) before any relevant data were examined. The hypothesis was supported by an analysis of retrospective data (Annett and Kilshaw, 1984) and also by new prospective data reviewed in chapters 10–13. The question for independent replication was whether the findings for abilities and educational attainments in representative samples of English schoolchildren would be matched in new samples.

With regard to abilities, McManus, Shergill and Bryden (1993, rejoinder Annett, 1993c) proposed to test the BP + HA hypothesis by giving advanced intelligence tests to 45 right-handed medical students classified as weak, moderate and strong right-handers on a pencil dotting test. No differences were found. McManus et al. argued that it was implausible that differences between groups would be detected, unless differences for intelligence between genotypes were implausibly large, or group sizes were enormous. It must be agreed that my observed differences were surprising, but it is not surprising that they were not replicated in a small sample of right-handed medical students.

Casey (1995) described two samples of children drawn from the school population of Boston, USA, 464 15-year-olds, and 218 9-year-olds, tested for intellectual ability. The samples were classified for handedness in three groups: non-right-handers, moderate and strong right-handers on the basis of the laterality index of the EHI. There were similar quadratic trends with almost identical mean IQs for the three handedness groups in the two samples. The moderate right-handers outperformed those to the left and to the right. Although effect sizes were modest, the moderate right-handers were superior to the other two groups combined. The findings were consistent with the hypothesis of heterozygote advantage.

Three studies sought a quadratic trend for reading or spelling over hand skill groups. The first sampled 11- to 13-year-olds in three schools in Auckland, New Zealand (Palmer and Corballis, 1996). The schools were drawn from different suburbs but all were described as "middle class". Among 345 children targeted, only 207 returned parental consent forms, 125 girls and 78 boys. More than half of the boys and over a quarter of the girls selected themselves out of the study. The participants were given the Burt reading test, on which most were near ceiling. These various constraints were likely to seriously limit the range of ability sampled. Further, schools in leafy suburbs may differ for laterality from those of general city schools (see Figure 11.7). A full range of social strata is needed to detect the curvilinear relationship between laterality and reading.

The second study sampled 16- to 30-year-olds in Heidelberg, Germany, in various types of high school and in one university class for students of pedagogy (Resch, Haffner, Parzer et al., 1997). They were tested for spelling in German. The total sample was large (N = 545) and drawn from 39 whole classes, so there should have been no volunteer bias within classes. The sample was said (p. 624) to cover "a representative sample of different professional groups and educational levels", but (p. 633) was "not representative in any strict interpretation of the phrase". German law requires attendance at school or other vocational institution by all young people up to the age of 18 years. A sample of 16- to 18-year-olds, drawn from representative types of school, might have been population representative. The addition of 84 university students of pedagogy introduced a substantial group of almost certainly superior spelling ability compared with the rest. There were strong sex differences within the sample for R–L skill, the female mean twice as large as the male mean, and also very marked sex differences for spelling, females greatly superior to males. When the sample was divided into quartiles for R–L skill, the most sinistral group was about two-thirds male, and the most dextral group two-thirds female. Not surprisingly, the strong trend in the data was for increasing spelling ability, and educational level from left to right over the sample. For a test of nonverbal intelligence there was a significant quadratic trend, but strong dextrals were not significantly poorer than other groups (as they were in the samples described by Annett and Manning). I should like to see these data described for sexes separately in 16- to 18-year-olds only. A further point about this study is that it concerned spelling in German by young adults, whereas the Annett and Manning literacy study was about reading in English by 6- to 11-year-olds. Poor reading and spelling do not always go together.

The third study looked at literacy in a large sample of children being studied longitudinally in Vienna (Klicpera and Gasteiger-Klicpera, 1994). Strong right-handers, as assessed for manual skill, were not poorer for reading or spelling. There were trends, however, for reading and spelling to be poorer toward the left than the right over the laterality continuum. It was concluded that the RS theory was not supported, but it was also suggested that left-handed children have a greater chance of being referred for remediation for dyslexia than right-handed children. This poses an interesting question as to the direction of cause and effect. The failure of Natsopoulos, Kiosseoglou, Xeromeritou et al. (1998) to find poor literacy in extreme right-handers was answered by Annett (1998c), who pointed out that their most dextral group was drawn from 40% of the population at the right of the laterality continuum (not 20–25% as in my studies).

Whittington and Richards (1991) tested the hypothesis that mathematical ability is likely to be poor in strong right-handers. They selected groups of strongly dextral versus strongly sinistral children from the NCDS sample, omitting all cases with low scores for either abilities or hand skills that might be associated with pathology. The groups did not differ for mean mathematics scores. Maths scores and reading comprehension scores were then regressed on scores for a test of general ability. The trends were weak, but in the direction predicted if strong right-handers had relative advantage for reading compared with maths, and strong left-handers relative weakness for reading compared with maths. Whittington and Richards concluded that the findings failed to demonstrate significant deficit for maths in putative RS + + genotypes, but there were contrasting trends for different types of ability between handedness groups consistent with the BP + HA hypothesis.

Cerone and McKeever (1999) reported failure to support the BP + HA hypothesis in a study of verbal and spatial abilities in 259 university students, said to have a broad range of ability. The sample was restricted to right-handers who were classified for hand preference in the four subgroups of Annett (1970a, classes 1–4 as revised in Table 2.5 above). Hand preferences were assessed by questionnaire (not observation) and hand skill was tested for one trial per hand of the Purdue peg board (not three–five trials for the Annett peg moving test). My interpretation of the findings was more positive than that of Cerone and McKeever. The findings of Annett (1992c) for spatial ability in right-handers can be represented as taking the shape of a left-handed "tick" (the right half of a roughly W shape, see Figure 12.2). A full tick would find the highest scores in class 4 (the most sinistral right-handers for R–L skill) and the lowest for class 2. Cerone and McKeever used two tests of spatial ability (Stafford Identical Blocks and Vandenberg Mental Rotation) and two tests of verbal abilities (Shipley Hartford Vocabulary and Word Fluency). For all four tests, the mean was lowest for class 2, followed by class 1 and then class 3. This gave most of the expected "tick" (but a right-handed tick as plotted by Cerone and McKeever's Figures 1–4). The complete "tick" depended on the superiority of class 4. This was present for the Stafford Identical Blocks and for Shipley Hartford Vocabulary, thus giving the full pattern for two of the four tests. Class 4 was relatively poor for word fluency, but this was not a test of spatial ability. Poor performance is consistent with the hypothesis of weak phonology for the RS − − genotype (if class 4 includes many R − − right-handers). The only feature inconsistent with the Annett (1992c) data was relatively poor performance by Class 4 on the Vandenberg Rotation test. My conclusion on seeing a pre-publication version of this paper (giving fuller information and for sexes separately) was that the findings replicated my spatial test findings better than my own more recent data. Why the write-up was negative for the RS theory is a mystery.

SUMMARY

An independent replication of the birthday sample studies (Annett, 1970a; Annett and Turner 1974) was made on Guatemalan children, Ladinos and Maya, by William Demarest (1982). Females were more strongly biased to the right-hand than males on *two* tests of L–R skill, the peg moving task and a bean moving task. No systematic changes were found for L–R skill with age. There was evidence of racial differences in L–R skill because the means of Mayan children were significantly smaller than those of Ladino children for both peg moving and bean moving. My English samples were intermediate for peg moving. If confirmed, the differences imply differences between races, either in the frequency of the RS + gene or in its expression. The evidence that Mayan children are slightly less mature than others as infants would be consistent with the thesis that differences in relative maturity underlie differences for handedness between the sexes, twins, and low birthweight infants.

It was especially interesting that two important findings in English children for relationships between laterality and ability were replicated in Guatemalan children. First, the report of Annett and Turner that there is no difference for language ability between right and left-handed children in general samples but a reduced right shift for children identified as having special language difficulties, was supported in a study of Mayan children's progress in learning Spanish. Second, when the actual hand speeds of right and left-handed children were compared for peg moving and for bean placing, the left-handers tended to be faster than right-handers in 13 out of 14 comparisons. Faster times for left-handers were found in Mayan and in Ladino children, as in English children. Thus the assumptions basic to the balanced polymorphism hypothesis, that the bias to the right-hand gives advantages to language learning but at costs to actual hand speed, were supported by this independent cross-cultural study.

Several challenges to the RS theory were reviewed. None were substantial but, of course, readers cannot expect me to be impartial in this respect. The negative reports were not surprising because the BP + HA hypothesis is about relatively weak trends over the population, that need to be tested in large and representative samples. Samples should be representative of the general population, as in schools that serve whole communities. If samples are drawn from a university population, then a wide range of abilities within that population is needed, as in some large first year courses in psychology. Tests must be of appropriate levels of difficulty. There are many ways in which studies may not meet these requirements.

16 Alternative theories or variations on a theme?

The recipe for a cake requires several ingredients to be combined in a particular order and cooked for a specified time and temperature. The RS theory suggests that the recipe for human handedness also requires ingredients to be combined in sequence and developed through certain environmental and cultural influences. The chief ingredients are represented in Figure 16.1, from the top down, as follows: (1) accidental buffeting during early growth, (2) a single gene that gives directional bias but may be absent, or present in single or double dose, (3) genetic expressivity, or extent of shift, that varies with factors influencing rate of growth including sex and twinning, and (4) sociocultural influences on the use of the left-hand that affect thresholds for the expression of sinistral tendencies. No other theory has proposed exactly the same ingredients and developmental processes as the RS theory. Some theories, however, share certain features. This chapter reviews other theories with the aim of acknowledging similarities but also pinpointing critical differences.

There are two fundamental distinctions that must be borne in mind throughout this discussion. The first is whether the proposals concern handedness or cerebral dominance. Most theories do not make this distinction, assuming that rules for one apply also to the other. The RS theory does make this distinction because the RS + gene is for left CD, not for right-handedness. The presence of the RS + gene merely weights the probabilities toward right-hand preference (like a bias on a coin that causes it to fall to one side more often than 50% but not 100%). The second important distinction is between theories that treat left-handedness as a natural variant and those that regard it as "abnormal" or "pathological". There are many speculations about the causes of right-handedness that offer no specific explanation of left-handedness. Left-handedness is treated as an aberration, a pathological failure to establish right-handedness. The pathology assumption is implicit in most of the literature. By contrast, theories that recognise left-handedness and other atypical asymmetries as natural (normal) phenomena often invoke a genetic explanation. It is these theories that are likely to be confused with the RS theory. This chapter begins by reviewing theories of right-handedness and pathology. It then considers genetic theories, distinguishing those proposed before the RS theory from those that followed. Before the RS theory none included a systematically applied "chance" postulate,

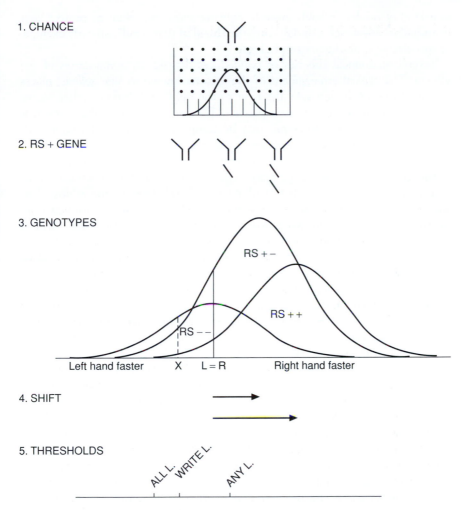

1. CHANCE

2. RS + GENE

3. GENOTYPES

RS + −

RS + +

RS − −

Left hand faster   X   L = R   Right hand faster

4. SHIFT

5. THRESHOLDS

ALL L. WRITE L. ANY L.

Figure 16.1 A schematic representation of the right shift theory.

although there may have been uncertainties of expression such as imperfect penetrance. After the RS theory, all theories have invoked a chance postulate.

THEORIES OF RIGHT-HANDEDNESS AND PATHOLOGY

Speculations about right-hand preference have a long history. Early theories ranged from the anatomical, through the developmental to the cultural, like their modern counterparts (see Harris, 1980a for review). An often quoted musing by Thomas Carlyle in 1871 (cited in Harris, 1980a, p. 40) asked, "Why that particular hand was chosen is a question not to be settled, not worth asking except as a kind of riddle; probably arose in fighting; most important to protect your heart and its adjacencies, and to carry the shield in that hand", an early example of speculative evolutionary psychology.

Several anatomical theories of handedness depend on asymmetries of the viscera. The typical arrangement of the viscera, known as *situs sollitus*, places the heart toward the left side, the liver to the right, and disposes other organs and intestines in a characteristic pattern. The mirror image of this pattern is known as *situs inversus*. Reversals may be complete or partial. The typical arrangement has certain consequences for the relative weight of the two sides of the body, the directness of the blood supply to the left and right arms, and also to the left and right sides of the brain. These asymmetries have been associated with a variety of proposals that attribute right-handedness to the relative balance or efficiency of the two sides of the body. None of the theories gave an explanation of non-right-handedness, because none showed that atypical handedness is associated with atypical situs.

The fallacy of supposing that the position of the heart and liver could be a cause of handedness was pointed out, in the 17th century, by Sir Thomas Browne, a Norfolk country physician. He noted that left-handedness is fairly common but, "the seate of the liver on the left side is monstrous and rare to be met with in the observations of physitians" (Browne, 1646/1981, p. 305). A survey of *situs inversus* in Norway, as revealed by routine X-rays, estimated the prevalence at about 1 in 10,000 (Torgersen, 1950). Among 160 individuals with complete *inversus*, 6.9% were left-handed, about the same level as the rest of the population. The idea that *situs inversus* is due to mirror imaging in twins was contradicted by the observation that the proportion of twins with anomalies of *situs* was comparable with that of the general population. A study of dichotic listening asymmetries in nine people with *situs inversus* showed that they were as likely to have REA as controls (Tanaka, Kanzaki, Yoshibayashi et al., 1999). Thus atypical arrangements of the viscera are independent of twinning, handedness and dichotic listening asymmetry.

Genes involved in the development of visceral asymmetries, the *iv* gene (Layton, 1976) and a gene called "lefty" (Meno, Saijoh, Fujii et al., 1996) are under investigation and there are some interesting parallels with the probable genetic mechanisms of handedness, as will be considered further below. However, the mechanisms cannot be *the same* for hand, brain and gut, for the reasons given by Sir Thomas Browne. Sir Thomas believed that hand preference was more likely to depend on the brain than the viscera.

Among developmental theories, it was suggested early in the 19th century that bodily asymmetries might depend on the position of the yolk sac in the egg (Von Baer, 1826, cited Harris, 1980a). Embryological growth is guided by chemical gradients (see Wolpert, 1991 for review). Morgan (1977) proposed that asymmetries, including human right-handedness and left CD depend on a left–right maturational gradient that is common to the vertebrate kingdom, a gradient that determines asymmetries from the earliest growth of the fertilised egg. On this theory human right-handedness is caused by the earlier and better development of the left hemisphere of the brain (which controls the right hand). Further expositions of the theory (Corballis and Morgan, 1978; Morgan and Corballis, 1978) were published with commentaries that drew attention to some of the difficulties. The main problem from the present viewpoint is that a mechanism universal among vertebrates is proposed to govern asymmetries in humans for viscera, brain and hands. The independence of the three levels of asymmetry has been argued above. If handedness was due to a vertebrate maturational gradient why has a bias to right paw preference not been found in any other vertebrate? Why do humans show individual differences for asymmetries of hand and brain? Corballis and Morgan suggested that disturbance of the mechanisms giving typical biases might be associated with a reversion to chance asymmetries, of the type proposed by the RS theory. There would be a "left shift" from the expected right-handedness. Thus chance was used as a default explanation for atypical cases, but the theory was otherwise non-specific. No attempt was made, to my knowledge, to develop predictions for atypical cases, nor for left-handedness in families.

Is handedness a by-product of asymmetries of the senses? One influential view was that eye dominance is the cause of handedness (Parsons, 1924). Woo and Pearson (1927) described findings for nearly 7000 men tested for visual acuity and for hand strength as measured by pressing a dynamometer. No correlation was found between asymmetries for these two variables. Later work showed that visual acuity and ocular dominance are not strongly related, nor are ocular dominance and handedness (see chapter 8). The analyses of chapter 9 found that eye dominance and handedness are related as expected if both are influenced by the RS + gene, but otherwise independent. A recent variant on the theme that handedness is a by-product of sensory asymmetries concerns the ear and its inner labyrinth (Previc, 1991). Right ear preference and left hemisphere dominance were argued to depend on positional asymmetries in foetal life due to the posture of an upright-walking mother. No systematic theory of exceptions was offered.

The idea that training is the cause of hand preferences, either unwitting or deliberate by nurses, parents, teachers, has a history said to start with Plato. John Watson, the father of behaviourism, asserted that there are no fixed preferences until, "Society . . . steps in and says, 'Thou shalt use thy right-hand.' . . . We force it to eat with the right-hand. This is a potent enough conditioning factor to account for handedness" (Watson, in Harris, 1980a). A recent exponent of the training view argues that the chief evolutionary advantage of humans in comparison with other species is a capacity for learning (Provins, 1997). Provins interpreted Collins' (1975) findings for mice as showing that paw preferences are learned. If learning is sufficient for mice, why suppose that more is required for humans? The RS argument also depends on the findings of Collins but interprets them differently. Collins did not show that paw preferences were learned, but rather that a disposition to prefer one paw was present before exposure to the learning situation. The disposition was acquired in the course of congenital growth. It was of environmental rather than genetic origin, but predated learning experience in the laboratory. The effect of congenital environmental experience is represented for the RS theory by accidental buffeting in the fall through the pinball machine (see Figure 16.1).

If preferences are learned, why is the right-hand preferred in every known society? Provins suggested that the bias to dextrality has been culturally determined throughout human history by religious symbolism for everything sacred (right) versus profane (left). The idea supposes extraordinary stability for this aspect of human culture from remote antiquity. Cerebral lateralisation cannot be a product of society, of course. The learning hypothesis must suppose that human left CD is a by-product of right-handedness. "The cerebral lateralisation of speech may be expected to be related to whatever manual habits are being acquired at that particular stage of development" (Provins, 1997, p. 563). If this were true, there would be no puzzle about the relationship between lateralities of hand and brain but perfect concordance. The puzzle at the heart of the research described in this book would not exist. But it does exist. Of course humans learn their motor skills, and develop hand preferences through experience, practice and habit. Of course cultural pressures incline those indifferent to the use of either hand to the right side. But why do some humans use the right-hand and right brain, and some the left-hand and left brain, in consistent proportions through many samples? Where are quantitative analyses of atypical cases for either the dysphasia literature or the family handedness literature?

Pathology theories of handedness fall into two main groups, broadly social deviance or brain damage. If the typical bias to the right-hand is due to learning, then exceptions must be due to failures of learning. Social deviance explanations were prevalent in the first half of the 20th century. Burt (1937), whose long chapter on left-handedness was extremely influential in educational psychology, reported that his case summaries of left-handed children often included descriptions such as stubborn, wilful, contra-suggestible or "just cussed". "Even left-handed girls . . . often possess a strong, self-willed and almost masculine disposition" (Burt, 1937, p. 317). Burt acknowledged, however, that these character traits could be the result of having to put up with constant corrections of hand use, rather than being the cause of left-handedness. An extreme form of the social deviance view was taken by the American psychiatrist Abram Blau (1946, p. 115) who argued that, "Sinistrality is . . . nothing more than an expression of infantile negativism and falls into the same category . . . as contrariety in feeding and elimination."

The brain damage theory of left-handedness follows from the assumption that right-handedness and left CD are human species characteristics. If this is true, then left-handedness must be an abnormality due to cerebral impairment. In special schools for the mentally handicapped in London, 18.2% of children threw a blackboard duster with the left-hand, in comparison with 7.3% in normal schools (Gordon, 1921). The learning disability and the shift of hand preference to the left were interpreted as due to damage to the left hemisphere, an idea that was widely accepted (Brain, 1945). However, there are several reasons for not taking these implications at face value. The findings for learning disabled children suggest that *some* left-handedness might be pathological, but some does not necessarily generalise to *all*. Further, left-handers among the learning disabled are more likely to have left-handed relatives than the right-handed disabled (Pipe, 1987).

Among the cerebral palsied, epileptic and the learning disabled, it is reasonable to suppose that distortions of the normal developmental path have influenced handedness in some cases. Children with hemiplegias of the right side must use the left-hand, and vice-versa. Thus it cannot be doubted that *some* left-handedness is associated with pathology. However, much of the literature on brain damage and handedness depends on the weaker but over-inclusive hypothesis that *all left-handedness depends on minor brain damage*. Is there support for the idea that minimal or subclinical brain damage can easily lead to changes of handedness? On the contrary, it appears that among people with known brain lesions, hand preferences were influenced only by specific lesions of the hand areas of the motor cortex (Milner, 1974). Peterson (1934) tested the readiness of rats to change paw preference and found no change except for highly specific lesions. Silva and Satz (1979) looked at human handedness in relation to abnormalities of the EEG. They found left-handers more frequent among people with left hemisphere lesions as expected, but also unexpectedly among people with bilateral lesions. That is, disruptions of cerebral growth other than specific lesions of the left hemisphere could lead to increased non-right-handedness. Among epileptics some but not all studies found more non-right-handers (review by Bingley, 1958). In the NCDS survey, there was no association between left-handedness and epilepsy (McManus, 1980b).

Satz (1972, 1973) performed a useful statistical "thought experiment" on the effects of changes of handedness due to pathology. If changes of handedness occur in either direction with equal frequency, the proportion of pathological cases among left-handers would be very much larger than among right-handers because of the smaller base rates of left- than right-handers in the population. This would be true whatever the exact mechanism (specific brain damage or more general jolting of the developmental process). This statistical fact has important consequences for the assessment of relationships between handedness and abilities. When groups of left- and right-handers are drawn from the general population, the proportion of "pathological" cases is higher among left- than right-handers. Relatively serious weaknesses in a few left-handers might give rise to significant differences between handedness groups, although the differences were not characteristic of "natural" left-handers. It was for this reason that individuals with slow peg moving times for either hand were excluded from my samples examined for abilities (in chapters 11–13).

The weakest and most pervasive version of the pathology hypothesis was that left-handedness is due to birth stress. Bakan (1971) reported that a higher proportion of left-handed male university students was born first or fourth plus than was born second or third. Although there was no difference for female students, Bakan suggested that left-handedness was due to stressful birth, presumed greater for first or fourth plus births. Hubbard (1971) described a larger student sample in which there was a mildly significant tendency in the opposite direction, more left-handers second- and third-born than first or fourth plus. In the same year, another student survey found no relationship between birth order and left-handedness (Gray, Hentschke, Isaac et al., 1971). These authors asked how many such findings would remain unpublished, and how the scientific world was to be kept informed of the weight of negative evidence. This query is especially apposite because a huge amount of journal space was devoted to the handedness and birth stress idea for a decade or more. The great majority of findings were negative, but any trends in the positive direction were given disproportionate attention. An especially powerful test of the birth order effect was made in Taiwan on 2101 elementary schoolchildren whose birth orders could be classified from one to nine. The mean laterality quotients of the 534 children who were first-born and 21 children who were ninth-born were identical, and there were no significant trends in the data (Teng, Lee, Yang et al., 1976). McManus (1981) analysed data for over 12,000 children in the British National Child Development Sample. There were no effects for birth order in children of either sex.

With regard to births classifiable as stressful, a prospective study of 1094 children born in Manchester in 1971 found almost entirely negative results for the many birth conditions examined (Smart, Jeffery and Richards, 1980). However, a high proportion of left-handers was found in two small groups of children, those delivered by breech, and those born to older mothers. It was these findings that were cited in the literature, while the negative results were ignored. In the NCDS survey, breech presentations were recorded for 82 males and 121 females, and in neither sex was the incidence of left-handedness elevated (McManus, 1981). Further, there were no significant effects for maternal or paternal age.

How did the birth stress theory account for the association of left-handedness in families? It was suggested, "Perhaps the familial tendency to left-handedness is mediated by a familial tendency to birth stress" (Bakan, Dibb and Reed, 1973, p. 365). This possibility was examined in my personally visited families of left-handed and right-handed parents. If left-handers are more likely to experience stress in giving birth, left-handed mothers should report more stressful births for their children than right-handed mothers. On the contrary, left-handed mothers reported stressful births for 23% of their children and right-handed mothers for 30% (Annett and Ockwell, 1980).

Aside from the weighty negative empirical findings, the hypothesis that atypical asymmetries are due to brain pathology is highly unlikely for several reasons. First, atypical brain laterality for speech was evident among young service men with dysphasias following war wounds, showing that there is natural variation for brain asymmetries in this particularly healthy section of the population (see chapter 4). Second, left-handedness occurs as a natural variant in man's primate cousins. The pathology hypothesis implies that natural primate variation for handedness was lost in the transition from hominoid (ape-like) to hominid (human-like) ancestors and then reintroduced in humans as "abnormal" variation. It is much simpler to assume continuity. Third, reports of birth stress are most common for first-borns, and yet first-borns have higher average IQs than later-born children (Bee, 1981). Finally, left-handers are often found among those with high achievements in the arts, music, sport and theatre (Barsley, 1966; see also chapter 12 above). The proposition that all these people suffered early brain damage, however minimal, is thoroughly implausible.

Stanley Coren (1992) adopted an implicit pathology hypothesis in his book, *The Left-hander Syndrome*, where he referred to non-right-handers as "alinormal". The main premise of his argument was that incidences of left-handedness are raised in many "at risk" groups, such as twins, epileptics and the learning disabled. Therefore, by implication, all left-handedness depends on similar (if unknown) risk factors. The idea that left-handers are more vulnerable than right-handers led him to suggest that they are more likely to have accidents and reduced life-expectancy. This idea generated considerable controversy, as considered in chapter 6.

Geschwind and Galaburda (1985a, 1985b, 1985c) referred to atypical asymmetries of hand and brain as "anomalous". A substantial proportion of the population must be "anomalous" on this model, because one-third of normal brains are atypical for PT (Geschwind and Levitsky, 1968), and one-third of people are not consistently right-handed (see chapter 2) in addition to others with atypical foot, eye and other preferences. The implication of the theory was that all of these atypical asymmetries require a "medical model" for their explanation. The three long papers of Geschwind and Galaburda cited above represent a massive and scholarly review of the possible causes of anomalous asymmetries. The RS theory was acknowledged (Geschwind and Galaburda, 1985a, pp. 446–447), but turned on its head, so to speak, by reversing the direction of causal influences. Whereas the RS theory proposed universal randomness plus a genetically variable agent for human directional asymmetries, "By contrast we postulate that in most humans there is an innate bias toward left-hemisphere dominance for both of these functions, and that certain influences during foetal life act to diminish this innate bias and thus to create random dominance. Like Corballis and Morgan, we believe in a 'left-shift' factor" (1985a, p. 447). This approach implies that left brain specialisation and right-handedness are normative for the human species, but that their expression is distorted by a multitude of non-genetic, accidental influences that increase randomness and so raise the proportion of atypical asymmetries. Geschwind and Galaburda sought examples of abnormal influences on handedness and cerebral dominance throughout the medical literature and found a multitude. The review was undertaken with the aim of explaining what for the RS theory are primarily accidental asymmetries. Some influences on asymmetry are systematic, as for sex and twinning, and some are abnormal, as for pathologies above and the hypothesised agnosic RS + gene. However, natural variation, accidental and genetic, must be distinguished from pathological variation before the causes of the latter can be distinguished.

Geschwind suggested a theory of the development of asymmetries that involved a complex of assumptions about how the species norm for left hemisphere dominance might be disturbed by influences associated with the male sex hormone, testosterone, giving increased risk of left-handedness, immune disorders and dyslexia. A review of studies following up the Geschwind theory found no substantial support (Bryden, McManus and Bulman-Fleming, 1994). Why was such massive effort unproductive? Because, in my view, it treated atypical asymmetry as pathological, not natural variation in the normal population.

GENETIC AND NON-GENETIC NATURAL VARIATION

Genetic theories of handedness imply that most left-handers occur as natural variants of *Homo sapiens*, even if a few originate pathologically. The first and predominant theory for most of the 20th century was that left-handedness is caused by a recessive gene (L) paired with a dominant gene for right-handedness (R) as outlined in chapter 1. The data did not fit the classic Mendelian pattern for a dominant-recessive pair of alleles, but various "fudge" factors, such as imperfect penetrance of left-handedness (even in LL genotypes) and partial expression in heterozygotes (RL genotypes) were proposed to account for the discrepancies. Trankell (1955) made nine estimates of the frequency of the L allele, based on three family types in three family studies available at that time. The estimates were remarkably consistent (39–44%) although frequencies of assessed left-handedness differed considerably between the studies. Trankell's estimates for the L allele agree very well with my estimate for the RS – allele(s) (43%) from dysphasia data. The problem with the recessive gene theory was that more than half of LL genotypes become right-handed, with equal probability in the different types of family. If imperfect penetrance were due to social pressures, surely the pressures to become right-handed would be smaller when parents were left-handed? The RS theory is consistent with Trankell's analysis for the L allele, except that the RS – allele is neutral for asymmetry and the RS + gene is not for handedness, but for left CD.

My first theory as to the genetics of handedness was a variant of the classic recessive allele theory, except that I suggested that heterozygotes might develop mixed-handedness (Annett, 1964). Annett, Lee and Ounsted (1961) had suggested that cerebral lateralisations could occur at random in mixed-handers. The 1964 genetic model suggested that people who carried both alleles (RL genotypes) could develop preferences for either hand and for either hemisphere. This was an important step on the way toward the RS theory because it supposed that most of the muddles in the literature about handedness and CD depended on a subgroup with random patterns of asymmetry. The RS theory goes much further because it proposes that random and independent asymmetries are a universal substrate on which a directional bias is superimposed. Before reaching this view, it was necessary to understand that the substrate itself is a continuous variable, and that discrete classifications depend on arbitrary cut-points, or thresholds of expression.

Characteristics like height, weight, and intelligence vary continuously in the population in Gaussian (normal) types of distribution. Such traits are likely to depend on the joint effects of many minor genes rather than a few major genes. Could the normal distribution of R–L hand skill asymmetry depend on many genes of small effect? Genetic models of polygenic inheritance assume that the relevant underlying variables are continuously distributed in the population and that classifications of diseases or other conditions depend on thresholds of expression (Carter, 1961; Falconer, 1965). This analysis fitted very well with my conclusion that handedness is a continuous variable, different incidences depending on arbitrary classifications. Different classifications merely implied different thresholds along a stable handedness continuum. My first reports of handedness in families calculated heritabilities, as for polygenic models (Annett, 1973a, 1978a). However, on finding that the hypothesis of single gene (RS +) could predict distributions in families precisely (Annett, 1978b), the vaguer polygenic hypothesis was redundant. It was important to ask, however, whether the polygenic model could be definitely *rejected*. Correlations were examined between first degree relatives in 63 personally visited families (Annett, 1978a, as described in chapter 5) and no convincing associations were found. The findings agreed with those for mice (Collins, 1969) that preferences are uncorrelated between relatives. The basic causes of handedness are non-genetic. This result was important for distinguishing the shape of the asymmetry distribution from its location. The normal distribution of asymmetry for handedness is accidental, congenital and non-genetic. It is the shift factor (RS) that is inherited, and genetically variable within humans but absent from great apes.

Handedness in families was examined by Risch and Pringle (1985), in the light of polygenic versus major gene models. Neither type of model could be ruled out but no specific version gave a particularly good fit. It is the predictive power of the RS single gene model that makes it worth attention (see chapters 5 and 7). If there were many genes of small effect determining human hand preferences, it would be surprising that none have been found in other species. It is plausible that one new laterality gene should have evolved in humans, but not several.

Chance as an agent of non-genetic natural variation

The foundation of the RS theory (1972) was the analysis represented by two normal distributions of R–L hand skill, one with mean at R = L and one with mean to the right of R = L (see Figure 3.7). The surprising implication was that there might be a factor that increased the probability of right-handedness but no comparable factor for left-handedness. Chance would be sufficient. This theoretical insight was followed up by a study of children in the families of L × L parents. Handedness distributions were consistent with the hypothesis of chance bias to either side (Annett, 1974). Layton (1976) independently developed the idea of chance determination of a lateral asymmetry. Layton studied a mutant strain of mice with a high prevalence of *situs inversus*. When the baby mice had been suckled, milk visible through the stomach wall showed that for 50% the stomach was on the left and 50% on the right. Layton hypothesised that the normal gene for visceral situs had lost its directional bias, and the mutant gene (the *iv* gene) gave random bias to either side. Since that time "chance postulates" have become commonplace in genetic theories of human laterality.

These theories look superficially similar, but there is a profound difference between the models of Annett and Layton that has been generally overlooked.

The key difference depends on the logic of "and" versus the logic of "or". The typical pattern of visceral asymmetry is found in all vertebrates and the relevant genes must be of great antiquity. The trait is well fixed because the mirror image pattern of situs is extremely rare, as discussed above. The direction of visceral situs is strongly determined such that all normally developing gene carriers show the typical pattern. Atypical situs is associated with a mutant gene, in the presence of which the direction of asymmetry is right or left, consistent with chance determination. Therefore, the mechanisms governing visceral situs can be described as showing clear directional asymmetry *or* chance. By contrast, the RS theory proposes that for handedness it is *chance that is the universal trait* that has been present for millions of years. It is common to all vertebrates and continues to affect the congenital growth of every individual. The directional bias to dextrality for handedness is specific to *Homo sapiens*, probably evolved within the last few million years, and is not even universal among modern humans. For handedness, the logic is "chance for everyone *and* dextral bias in some". The interesting question for humans is not the cause of handedness but the cause of the dextral bias.

The initial surmise (of Annett, 1972) that the cause of the displacement of the handedness distribution was a relative left hemisphere advantage was amply supported (see chapter 4). The discovery that RS could be due to a single gene (RS +) for left CD was the foundation of further developments of the theory. But how does this gene operate? In principle, such a gene could be universal such that everyone has left CD unless pathological influences distort the developmental path (as assumed by Geschwind and others, reviewed above). If there are natural, inherited differences between humans for CD, how could they arise? The simplest assumption was that atypical brain asymmetries arise by chance in the absence of the directional bias for left CD. For purposes of the RS genetic model (as set out in Figure 11.1), the RS + gene was assumed to induce left CD in all normal gene-carriers, and random CD in non-gene-carriers. Thus, the logic for the RS + gene, with respect to CD, is "directional bias or chance". It is like that of Layton for the *iv* gene with respect to CD but not with respect to handedness. This distinction is not made by other theories of handedness.

Are cerebral asymmetries likely to be discrete or continuous? Inspection of distributions of anatomical asymmetries suggests that they are continuous and normally distributed (e.g. findings for PT by Galaburda, Corsiglia, Rosen et al., 1987; Steinmetz, 1996). The specific physical basis of functional speech laterality is unknown at the time of writing. Analyses of functional laterality are mainly in terms of discrete classifications, dysphasias are present or absent, and lesions are right or left-sided. For this reason it was necessary to treat CD as a discrete variable. The BP + HA hypothesis demands, however, that the expression of the gene in terms of underlying mechanisms influencing CD, and their associated advantages and disadvantages for abilities are additive. Distributions of relative ability are probably continuous.

The extension of the RS theory to psychosis used the same chance hypothesis that is fundamental to all of the above analyses, but now chance asymmetries for a gene that has lost its directional coding. The logic for the *agnosic* gene is analogous to that for the *iv* gene. There is a directional gene that has lost its ability to code for left or right and therefore gives random bias to either side. The RS theory implies two patterns of cerebral symmetry, as represented in Figure 14.2. First, there is the natural symmetry of normal R − − genotypes when there are deficits to *neither* side. Second, there is the symmetry imposed by deficits to *both* sides in schizophrenics (50% of RS +a + genotypes). Both lack directional asymmetry, but the psychological consequences are likely to be very different. Crow, Crow, Done et al. (1998) found that children in the NCDS survey whose hand skills were similar between the sides tended to be poor for verbal and nonverbal intelligence tests, in comparison with children with definite asymmetries to left or right. The problems for ability might depend on what Crow called "hemispheric indecision". Such children may be more prevalent among those that subsequently develop psychosis. The R − − genotype is expected to have its own characteristic risks but also compensating strengths (see chapters 12 and 13). Random patterns of asymmetry give scope, however, for great variability in patterns of cerebral organisation, and hence considerable individual differences both in the normal R − − genotype, and in disordered genotypes (RS +a + and RS +a +a).

Variations on the theme of chance

With regard to chance postulates for handedness, theories other than the RS theory have adopted the Layton version, directional bias *or* chance. McManus (1979, 1985a) proposed that handedness is determined by a directional gene (D for dextrality) *or* a gene for chance (C for chance or fluctuating asymmetry). There are, in fact, several chance postulates in McManus's theory. First, there is a gene for chance that gives 50/50 right- versus left-handedness in CC genotypes. Second, half of DC heterozygotes express C by chance, half of these becoming left-handed (25% of DC left-handed). Third, when observed incidences differ from the "true" incidence of left-handedness, genotypes of right-handers are transferred to left-handers, or vice versa as needed, in proportion to their frequency. This is the same principle as an extra deal for a pack of cards. Further chance postulates were proposed to account for cerebral dominance, and for relationships between handedness and cerebral dominance. No direct links were made between asymmetries of hand and brain but there was a network of probabilities.

Left-handers are 7.75% of the population, made up of 1.2% CC and 6.55% DC genotypes, and all other incidences are erroneous (McManus, 1985a). However, this particular incidence is hardly ever observed so that fitting the model to data requires genotypes to be re-assigned to match the observed phenotypes. Because errors are likely to have random causes, the adjustment of genotype to phenotype follows the re-deal rule, as explained above. The most frequent genotype is DD, so shortfalls of left-handers are mainly made up by DD genotypes, 1.74% DD when 10% of the population are called left-handers, 5.61% DD for 15% left-handers, and 9.48% DD for 20% left-handers.

Tests of the model for a single generation *can never fail*, because there are no limitations on the relocation of genotypes between handedness types. Genetic predictions between generations do not fail when parental incidences of left-handedness are close to the supposed true value because there is plenty of scope to move the required genotypes to phenotypes in the filial generation. However, if parental incidences are high, as in the range of non-right-handedness, the majority of parents are of DD genotype for all family types. There are too few CC and DC genotypes to fit non-right-handers to a model designed for an incidence of left-handedness at 7.75%. Table 5.2 showed that the model could be fitted well enough when incidences were low but not when they were high. For this reason, the McManus model cannot predict non-right-handedness in families (Annett, 1996a) nor eye dominance in families (Annett, 1999a).

The application of the model to twins requires particular comment because McManus argued that the RS model was invalidated by its need for an "extra postulate", reduced expression in twins compared with the singleborn (see chapter 15). No study of twins in the literature recorded an incidence of left-handedness as low as 7.75%, the incidence postulated by McManus. An adjustment of genotype to phenotype has to be made for every sample. Because only one generation is involved, the extra deal cannot fail, and therefore the theory cannot be failed by twin data.

The original model did not provide for sex differences but McManus and Bryden (1992) introduced a new sex-linked gene to modify the expression of D. This idea was a major "extra postulate" for the theory. The revised model was said to improve on others in the literature, when considered against data for combined samples. However, the new proposal was not tested for fit to any specific data (in contrast to tests of the RS theory against all available data, separately and combined, in chapter 7 and Appendix VII).

It is common for the Annett and McManus models to be bracketed together as if doing a similar job in a similar way. Corballis (1997a) remarked that the two theories are virtually identical and McManus's terminology simpler! This view depends on a verbal gloss that equates the alleles D and C with RS + and RS –. This is not the case because D and C are for handedness, while RS + and RS – are for cerebral dominance. For the RS theory chance asymmetries are universal in every primate and perhaps all bilaterally symmetrical organisms while C, the gene for chance, is present in only a small proportion of humans. For the RS theory there is a continuum between strong right and strong left preferences, while for the McManus theory there are discrete types, right- and left-handers. A threshold approach was specifically rejected (McManus, 1985b) but it is fundamental to the RS theory. Thresholds allow phenotypes to be tied to genotypes at each level of incidence (see Appendices III–VI) so that the RS model is tested effectively for every data set. The McManus theory postulates distinct groups of right- versus left-handers but poor fits can be accommodated by the relocation of genotypes to phenotypes. The key difference for handedness is the distinction explained above between "directional asymmetry *or* chance" (the Layton type model adopted by McManus) and "universal chance plus dextral shift for some" (the RS model).

Klar (1996) proposed a genetic theory of handedness that is very like the RS theory but follows the logic of the Layton type model, a directional gene for right-handedness *or* a gene for chance. The latter gives precisely 50% left- and 50% right-handedness. Claims to fit this model to data depend entirely on the findings of Rife (1940). Rife happened to find about half (54.5%) left-handers in L × L families as would be predicted by a simple application of the Layton model to family handedness. Several tests of the model were proposed and met. However, the model is seriously restricted because it fits only one set of data, and without a threshold model or an extra deal rule it cannot be generalised. Klar argued that only Rife adopted the correct criterion, left preference for any one of 10 actions, that is, non-right-handedness. For students assessed in the 1930s who presumably learned to write around the time of WW1 the criterion gave an incidence of just under 9%. The gene and genotype frequencies deduced by Klar are almost identical to those deduced for the RS alleles (in chapter 5) because the former are based on 9% non-right-handers and the latter on 9% with right CD. However, Rife's criterion would not give 9% non-right-handers today. McGee and Cozad (1980) used Rife's tests and criterion and found some 24% non-right-handers. Table 7.2c showed that incidences varied between some 4% and 40% over studies. Klar ignored the problem of variable incidence. The solution of this problem, as described in chapters 2 and 3, was the foundation of the RS theory. As mentioned above, Trankell (1955) showed that Rife's data agreed very well with that of Chamberlain (1928) and of Ramaley (1913), when allowances were made for variable penetrance. There are regularities in the different sets of family data that cannot be glossed over with the claim that only Rife's data is worth attention. The genetic model proposed by Levy and Nagylaki (1972) also relied exclusively on Rife, and fitted no other data (Hudson, 1975).

Laland, Kumm, Van Horn et al. (1995, p. 441) proposed a theory of handedness as follows, "Variation in handedness among humans is generated by accidents of early development, which by chance give greater skill or strength to one side or the other. All our genes do is simply load the handedness die to favour the right." This, of course, is the foundation of the RS theory as argued in 1972 but Laland et al. were apparently unaware of this precedent. They proposed that the association of handedness in families is due to cultural inheritance. This implies that the probability of expressing left-hand preferences depends on exposure to left-handedness in the family. However, the findings for adoptive families (Carter-Saltzman, 1980), and for my L × L families with parents whose handedness was possibly pathological, contra-indicate a strong role for family experience. Cultural influences have an important role in the RS theory in moving thresholds of expression of left-handedness (from 1% for Japanese to 10% or more in our society). They also affect definitions of non-right-handedness (up to around 40%). These types of influence may vary to some extent within families, but the chief types of social sanction against left-handedness are likely to be common to families within a culture.

Yeo and Gangestad (1993) proposed a theory of handedness that shares certain features with the RS theory because it depends on a continuous normal distribution of asymmetry. They measured the continuum using the Annett peg moving task. However, instead of the RS assumption that the distribution is accidental and non-genetic, Yeo and Gangestad suggested that the distribution is the product of many genes of small effect. It is a polygenic theory, not of genes for handedness, but rather genes governing "developmental instability". A typical pattern of human asymmetry, for moderate left brain and right-hand bias, was taken to be the human species norm. Differences from the norm arise from distortions of early development that increase randomness in both leftward and rightward directions. This model resembles several others reviewed above in suggesting that there is a directional bias that is specific to humans but one that can be distorted by chance influences on development. In this theory, the chance element is hypothesised to depend on genetic homozygosity for genes that influence development. Whereas heterozygotes are suggested to be developmentally robust, protected from buffeting during foetal growth, homozygotes are vulnerable to distortions that send them off-course in either direction, toward strong right-handedness or toward left-handedness. Increased randomness is not due to genes for handedness or cerebral dominance as such, but due to combinations of the genes controlling development in general. This model predicts increased incidences of minor physical abnormalities (MPAs) at each end of the laterality continuum. MPAs are features like wide-spaced eyes, asymmetric ears and limbs of unequal size, that are thought to indicate disruptions of foetal growth.

With regard to handedness, the main prediction was that students at *both* ends of the laterality spectrum, right and left, would be more likely to have left-handed relatives than those in the centre. This finding was reported for a sample of students assessed for R–L hand skill. The proportion of left-handed parents, plotted over the R–L continuum of the students, showed a curvilinear regression. The proportion of non-right-handed parents increased slightly for students at the right of the continuum, as well as for students at the left. Inspection shows that the up-turn at the right was small and depended on very few students. Replication of the analysis in my samples found no tendencies for strong right-handers to have more left-handed relatives. They had *fewer*, as predicted by most genetic theories of handedness. Otherwise, the Yeo and Gangestad predictions for handedness in families remain unspecified and untested against the literature. With regard to MPAs at either end of the laterality continuum, the RS theory has no reason to doubt that extreme buffeting in foetal life, whether due to congenital accidents or developmental instability, could cause extreme asymmetries for handedness and other characteristics subject to developmental risk.

SUMMARY

This chapter reviews theories of handedness and draws comparisons between them and the RS theory. First considered are theories of right-handedness that regard left-handedness as due to pathology. This is the most prevalent but often implicit assumption in the literature. There is a long history of seeking causes for the dominant bias to the right-hand, physical, cerebral and social, without offering a systematic account of exceptions. The fact that exceptions are associated in families is attributed to social learning, or common liability to pathology.

Genetic theories endeavour to explain left-handedness as a natural phenomenon, due to genetic variation in the normal population. Early theories were dominated by the assumption of a gene for left-handedness. Single gene pair models did not fit the classic Mendelian pattern for dominant-recessive alleles, but superficially inconsistent studies (for incidence) were shown to be remarkably consistent by Trankell (1955), provided various levels of imperfect penetrance were invoked to allow more than half of recessive homozygotes to be right-handed. The RS theory reached a similar estimate of gene frequency to Trankell, but from data for dysphasia, not family handedness, for an allele neutral for laterality. My early model of the genetics of handedness (Annett, 1964) proposed variable expression in heterozygotes, an important step on the way to the RS hypothesis of universal randomness as a substrate for asymmetry phenomena. Multigene theories of handedness are implausible because they do not explain empirical data for R–L hand skill in families, and also for theoretical reasons.

All modern theories of handedness include chance postulates to account for left-handedness. An important distinction is made between models that invoke *directional asymmetry or chance* (the Layton model for an *iv* gene for *situs inversus*) and the RS model of *universal chance for all plus directional asymmetry for some*. The RS theory suggests that handedness is primarily due to chance while the influence of cerebral asymmetry on handedness is relatively weak. The RS + gene is "for" cerebral asymmetry, promoting left hemisphere specialisation. For CD, there is directional bias or chance, because RS – allele(s) are neutral for laterality. Similarly for the agnosic gene (RS +a), there is reversion to chance (a directional gene that loses its directional coding, like the *iv* gene).

Variations on the theme of directional bias or chance, as exemplified in the theories of McManus, Klar, Laland et al. and Yeo and Gangestad are outlined. None can account for the range of phenomena predicted by the RS theory. In spite of superficial appearances, the view that these theories closely resemble the RS theory is mistaken.

Conclusions

17 Summary
What, how and why?

When a detective reconstructs a crime or a palaeontologist makes a model of an extinct creature from a few fragments, there is an obligation to use all the evidence available but a need to go beyond that evidence. An attempt to see how the pieces fit together may lead to new insights, and show where further detail must be sought. The RS theory suggests that there is only one specific influence on human handedness, something that induces a cerebral asymmetry in favour of the left hemisphere during foetal growth. In order to isolate this one key feature, a great deal of ground must be cleared, and many overlain theoretical constructions removed. This chapter attempts to summarise and reconstruct by asking *what* are the facts about the RS theory, *how* do the proposed mechanisms (chance and RS +) operate, and finally *why*. The last question, the motivation for the crime, or the evolutionary pressures at work must go beyond the evidence to create a "just so" story for the evolution of human speech.

WHAT IS THE RS THEORY? SUMMARY PROPOSITIONS

This section summarises the facts, as deduced from the research that has been reviewed in this book. The facts that form the foundation of the RS theory can be represented as a series of levels, from behaviour to genetics, from the bottom to top of Figure 17.1.

1. Handedness is a continuous variable, ranging between strong left and strong right, with many mixtures of preference in between.
2. Levels of hand preference are associated with levels of relative hand skill that can be regarded as thresholds along an asymmetry continuum.
3. Relative hand skill (for actions not influenced by practice by one hand) is distributed in a unimodal normal curve.
4. The distribution of right, mixed and left preferences in humans and in some other species tend to be in binomial proportions (as expected for RR, RL and LL genotypes when mixed-handers are RL). The proportions are probably due to stable thresholds for levels of hand preference, such that

Level of analysis

Genetic
RS + gene   absent   present
genotypes   RS – –   RS + –, RS + +

Cerebral Asymmetry
Typical pattern   absent   present

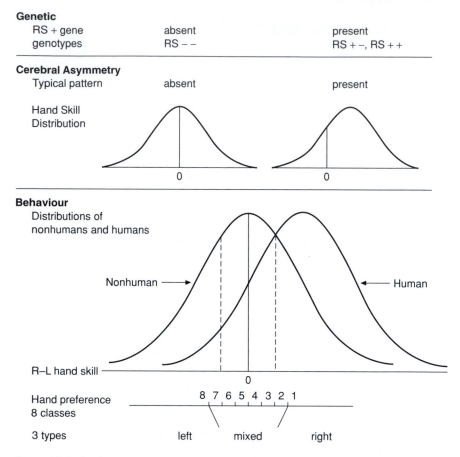

Hand Skill
Distribution

Behaviour
Distributions of
nonhumans and humans

Figure 17.1 A schematic representation of the development of the right shift theory,
from the analysis of hand preference (bottom) to RS + gene (top).

preferences tend to remain in binomial proportion when the normal curve
of asymmetry is displaced slightly to either side.

5. The co-ordination of hand preference and hand skill in humans, and the
percentage preferences of humans versus nonhumans (about 4, 32 and 66
for humans and 25, 50 and 25 for nonhumans, L, M and R respectively), are
consistent with normal curves with and without displacement to dextrality.
This allows us to distinguish the feature that is unique to humans, the shift
to the right.

6. Human laterality is of interest, not for handedness, but for the right shift
(RS) factor. What is this factor?

7. The RS factor is an asymmetry of the brain that gives a relative advantage to speech related areas of the left cerebral hemisphere compared with the right hemisphere. RS of the handedness distribution occurs because of incidental weakening of the left-hand.

8. The RS factor induces the left hemisphere to serve speech, in the course of normal development.

9. In the absence of the factor, left, right and bilateral speech lateralisations occur by chance. There may be many different combinations of lateralisation that arise by chance.

10. The frequency of right hemisphere speech can be deduced from population representative studies of dysphasia. Estimates from several sources agree that the frequency is just over 9% of the normal population.

11. Among people who lack the RS factor, handedness also depends on chance, chances independent of those for speech laterality. That is, there is no intrinsic connection between asymmetries for hand preference and cerebral speech.

12. Among people with atypical cerebral dominance, the frequency of right-handedness is greater than the frequency of left-handedness. Cultural pressures in Western societies are likely to make the proportion of left-handers for writing about 34% (about 2:1, right- to left-handers among right brained speakers). In other cultures the relative proportions might differ, but right-handers should always be more frequent than left-handers in cases of atypical brain laterality.

13. The RS factor could be due to a single gene (RS +), with alternate alleles at the same locus (RS −) neutral for laterality.

14. Because cerebral speech occurs by chance in RS − − genotypes, the gene frequencies can be inferred by estimating that the frequency of RS − − is twice the proportion of right hemisphere speakers. Twice 9.27% gives a population frequency of 0.1854 (as a proportion of 1), and the frequency of the RS − gene is the square root of this quantity (0.43). Hence, the frequency of RS + is estimated as 1 − 0.43 = 0.57.

15. The single gene hypothesis, with gene frequencies as just estimated, predicts the distribution of handedness in families. The threshold model for levels of hand preference allows predictions to be made at all observed levels of incidence from strict criteria (left-writing) to generous ones (non-right-handedness). It also predicts eye preference in families.

16. Family data that distinguishes the sex of parents and children is also predictable, provided assessments of handedness are by self-report in both generations. The predictions require the extent of RS to be greater for females than males, as expected if the RS + gene is expressed more strongly in females. The estimated differences are small, but confirmed by good matches between thresholds for paired samples of males and females (fathers and mothers, or brothers and sisters in the same study).

17. Studies collecting data by indirect report (typically students describing their parents' handedness) often give poor fits to the model. Superficial inspection

suggests that more left-handed children are born to left-handed mothers than to left-handed fathers. Deeper inspection reveals that some left-handed mothers were probably unreported by right-handed children. Re-assignment of right-handed children to left-handed mothers, increasing the incidence of the latter by only 1%, is sufficient to give good fits to the model.

18. Variable expression of the RS + gene between the sexes is probably due to relative maturity at birth, girls slightly more mature and more right shifted than boys. This principle is of great importance for understanding other groups that have reduced RS, including twins and low birthweight infants, who are likely to be less mature at birth.

19. The suggestion that the different shifts for twins and singletons represent a weakness of the RS model is mistaken. On the contrary, the hypothesis strengthened the model by leading to specific predictions that were later confirmed.

20. Relative hand skill remains constant with age (when relative hand skill is taken as a proportion of total skill in both hands, R–L%). This has been shown over most of the life-span in my samples, and over the school years in Guatemala. Relative asymmetry is probably a stable feature of human biology. Variable rates of preference between social groups can be regarded as due to experiential factors that influence the manifestation of hand preferences (threshold of expression) but not the underlying mapping between thresholds and genotypes.

21. The successful prediction of joint distributions of asymmetries (such as writing and throwing, hand and eye, planum temporale and handedness) depends on the stability of the mapping between incidences, thresholds and genotypes. The stability makes it possible to provide look-up tables that the reader may apply to new data (see Appendices III–VI).

22. The stability and consistency of the relationships demonstrated above imply that the genotype distribution on which they are founded merits serious attention. The genotypes suggest a genetic balanced polymorphism with heterozygote advantage.

23. The advantage of the RS + gene probably lies in the benefits it confers on speech learning by lateralising key features of the learning process to one hemisphere. Deaf-signers without speech also rely on the left hemisphere. This does not challenge the RS theory but rather demonstrates that the hemisphere asymmetry that normally induces the left side to serve speech, also induces that side to serve other types of early learning. That is, the effect of the gene on speech laterality must be distinguished from its mechanism.

24. The costs of the RS + gene probably induce some weakness of the right hemisphere whose precise nature cannot be clearly specified at present. The costs might be to spatial and mathematical reasoning, or perhaps to overall ability in physical and intellectual skills. It is also possible that the greatest cost of the RS + gene is a liability to mutate to a form that gives risk of psychosis.

25. The excess of left- and mixed-handers in certain talented groups (top sports-people, mathematicians, surgeons, artists and architects) is not due

to specific advantages for left-handers but rather to disadvantages to RS + + genotypes, such that the proportion of strong right-handers is reduced in these groups. The observed incidences (for example, about 15% for left-writing when the population incidence is 10%) are predicted if RS + + genotypes are missing from talented groups.

26. The costs for absence of the RS + gene (RS − − genotypes) lie in risks for speech acquisition and weak phonology. Problems are expected for some RS − − only, in whom chance patterns of asymmetry hinder learning processes. Such cases would include an excess of mixed- and left-handers. Controversies about handedness and early language learning difficulties, including dyslexia, are due to two important logical errors. The first error was to confuse evidence from the clinic (children selected for disorder and tested for handedness) with evidence from the classroom (children classified for handedness and tested for disorder). The RS model shows why only the former and not the latter should find effects for handedness. The second logical fallacy was to assume that *all* dyslexics (as opposed to *some* dyslexics) should have raised incidences of atypical laterality. The RS model led to the hypothesis that some dyslexics (probably those known as "surface" or "orthographic" types) are of RS + + genotype. These cases have weaknesses of word knowledge in the presence of good phonology. They are likely to include *fewer* mixed- and left-handers than the general population, not more as in RS − − genotypes.

27. The most serious cost of the RS + gene is that it might mutate to an agnosic form (RS +a) that has lost its directional coding. Whereas the normal gene says, in effect, "Impair one cerebral hemisphere, the right", the agnosic gene says, "Impair one hemisphere, side unspecified". When an agnosic gene is paired with a normal RS + gene (but not with an RS − gene), there will be impairment of both hemispheres in 50% of cases. If this is the cause of schizophrenia, then the RS model, as already developed on other evidence above, can account for the currently estimated risks to relatives.

28. The estimate of the frequency of the agnosic gene, sufficient to produce schizophrenia in about 1% of the population (given the parameters of the RS model above) leads to the deduction that the frequency of the homozygote (RS +a +a) will be 4 per 10,000. This is about the rate estimated for childhood autism. Certain other features of the RS model offer explanations for some puzzling features of autism. These ideas are recent, but deserve further exploration.

HOW DO CHANCE FOR HANDEDNESS AND A GENE FOR CEREBRAL DOMINANCE OPERATE?

The RS theory leads to a clear distinction between a universal substrate of lateral asymmetries that are due to chance, and a specific agent that induces hemisphere asymmetry in humans. The latter weights the chance throw but does not replace it. Handedness is distributed by chance in all bilaterally symmetrical creatures with potentially asymmetrical limb usage. Why is chance the substrate for every individual in many species?

When genetic instructions for the growth of a complex organism are translated into anatomy and physiology, there is scope for error. Any bilaterally symmetrical structure (model aeroplane or a large building) may depend on the same blueprint for both sides, but small differences could arise in the actual process of construction, leading to asymmetries of the finished product. An animal with an asymmetrical body will discover that one paw or other limb does what is wanted more quickly than its pair. The animal will come to prefer that paw when a choice is available. The asymmetry is accidental and physical but discovered in the course of use. The greater skill of one side implies no fundamental difference but merely that one side is found, through experience, to be more efficient for a specific activity. In so far as various activities depend on different parts of the body or on different levels of the nervous system, different sides may be preferred for different activities. Thus, one hand may be better for knapping a flint and the other side for throwing a missile. One side may better control the eye and the other the foot. Differences between the sides are discovered through experience and influenced by constraints of the physical and social environment (the design of tools and cultural expectations) but the preference is based on physical superiority of one side. In some cases the superiority will be so marked as to give the individual little choice as to the side to use, even if this requires resistance to external pressures. In the majority, the superiority will be so slight as to allow the individual to use either side, and conformity to the world bias (whether physical or social) will present no problem. Asymmetries of lateral skill arise as accidents in the growth of each individual in all complex animals that have choice in the use of limbs or sense organs. It is in this sense that it is argued that "chance" or "fluctuating asymmetry" is the universal basis of handedness in primates and other mammals, including human primates. The asymmetries arise independently for every individual, even in identical twins, so that RL twin pairs arise through congenital accidents in MZ as well as DZ pairs (or other siblings).

In the course of human evolution some small change occurred in the genome that weighted the chances in favour of right-handedness. Strong individual preferences for the left or the right-hand have been found in all primates studied, but none except man has been shown so far to differ from a racemic mixture of left and right, about 50% animals preferring each side. A change in a single allele at one locus would be sufficient to account for what I have called the RS + gene. The weighting may not be sufficient to countermand a strong accidental bias to the left. It is important to recognise that some left-handers carry the gene. Conversely, many right-handers (perhaps 12% of the population) are not gene-carriers. Humans not carrying the RS + gene develop all lateral asymmetries by chance alone, like other primates. The mechanism of the RS + gene is unknown at present, but it is inferred to weaken the right hemisphere's role in early learning, so that the infant is more likely to use the left side than the right, in early phases of speech and language learning.

The advantage of the gene that led to its selection in humans, was a benefit for speech learning. Learning is likely to be more efficient if input and output functions for the vocal tract and the ear are lateralised to one side. Exactly how this is achieved is unknown, but studies of left-hemisphere language through electrical stimulation mapping have found that phoneme discrimination and the control of mouth movements tend to depend on the same cortical areas (Ojemann and Mateer, 1979). If feedback information from the mouth and from the ear were received on opposite sides of the brain, learning would involve connections via the corpus callosum. This route would be longer and less efficient because the corpus callosum matures gradually over the early years. There is considerable variation between infants in the quantity of voice play during the first year. Ramsay (1980) found that infants who used left-hand reaching strategies were delayed in comparison with infants using right-hand strategies in producing combinations of phonemes in speech. When the coordination of information from mouth and ear is less than optimal, for whatever reason, the infant may be less interested in voice play. The exact nature of the difficulty experienced may differ according to accidental variations in cerebral organisation. There may be delay in learning to speak, or poor production of some speech sounds, or an inability to analyse the sound structure of some words when learning to read and write.

Children with gross defects of the speech apparatus learn to understand speech (Bishop and Robson, 1989a, 1989b; Lenneberg, 1962), indicating that overt production is not necessary for speech learning. The human instinct to acquire speech is a species universal that is more fundamental than the bias to the left hemisphere. It has its own genetic mechanisms (Bishop, North and Donlan, 1995; Fisher, Vargha-Khadem, Watkins et al., 1998; Gopnik and Crago, 1991) that are probably independent of the RS locus. The RS + gene is neither necessary nor sufficient for speech itself, because the gene is not present in nearly 20% of the population. However, although the RS + gene is not a prerequisite for speech, the promotion of left hemisphere lateralisation is likely to be an important aid to the efficiency of speech and language learning.

Research on the phonological loop that is hypothesised to function in short term or working memory gives some clues as to how speech and language learning might vary with the efficiency of an internal speech processing system (review by Baddeley, 1990). The phonological loop is suggested to include a phonological store that can retain speech items for a short time, and an articulatory rehearsal loop that may refresh the items and so aid their retention. The phonological loop does not appear to involve the external speech apparatus, but it is disturbed by overt articulation, as when participants in memory experiments are required to repeatedly say "the". It seems to act as an inner representation of speech input–output functions, that closely monitors ongoing events. The important point for the RS theory is that there are individual differences in the efficiency of the phonological loop. Children with less efficient systems are poorer at learning to read (Jorm, 1983) and slower to learn new words (Gathercole and Baddeley, 1990). It has been suggested that the phonological loop evolved as a language learning device (Baddeley, Gathercole and Papagno, 1998). The RS theory suggests that the efficiency of this device would be enhanced, by lateralising the components to one hemisphere. People with weak phonological memory are predicted to include more mixed- and left-handers than controls, as argued in chapter 13.

How would phonological processing be compromised in RS − − genotypes? Not all RS − − would be a risk. By chance, control could be well lateralised to one side, right or left in at least 50% of cases. Others also may develop reasonably effective systems for speech control. In some cases, however, chance arrangements would be less fortunate, perhaps because both hemispheres are involved in speech processing. This might place a greater load on speech production, storage and other functions than borne by the majority. This would not necessarily lead to overt difficulties, but there must be an increased *risk* of such problems. Patients with very limited short-term memories may function well on most cognitive tasks. Their special problems are revealed when the system is put under stress (Baddeley, 1990).

An advantage for some RS − − genotypes might be rapid recovery from speech disorders following head injuries. Rapid recoveries occurred following wounds to each side of the brain, but were more frequent for right lesion than left lesion cases. This suggests that both hemispheres may be involved in speech production in some RS − − genotypes, and that in the event of a unilateral brain lesion it is a relatively simple matter for the other hemisphere to take control. It must not be forgotten, however, that 40% of aphasics with right hemisphere lesions remained aphasic for years. In these cases, the right hemisphere must have served speech as fully as the left hemisphere in the majority of the population.

What processes lead to cerebral lateralisation? The mechanisms are almost certainly mediated through relative rates of growth. The differentiation of primitive gonads into testes and ovaries seems to be influenced by asymmetrical rates of growth on each side of the body, and these differ between birds and mammals (Mittwoch, 1973, 1977; Mittwoch and Mahadevaiah, 1980). Differential growth rates of the two sides of the brain appear to be significant for the anatomical and physiological bases of imprinting in birds and for the effects of sex hormones on brain development in mammals (Nordeen and Yahr, 1982). The chances that humans will develop epilepsy following early cerebral lesions to either side vary with age at the time of insult (Taylor, 1969). Studies of the relative growth of the two sides of the brain in foetal life have concluded that relative rates of growth differ at different stages of early development (Chi, Dooling and Gilles, 1977; Cunningham, 1902). However, it seems clear that some bias in favour of bringing the right-hand rather than the left-hand to the mouth is present from early foetal life, before the cerebral cortex is well defined (Hepper, Shahidullah and White, 1991).

The RS + gene probably introduces some slight modification of the primate pattern of cerebral maturation, a change that increases the probability that the left side will be at an optimal stage for learning during the first year of life when most babies establish their speech sound repertoire. The regulation of the growth processes through which these relative advantages and disadvantages are produced would vary with any factor that influenced growth. The maximum asymmetry in favour of the left hemisphere (for speech learning and for right-handedness) is expected in females who carry a double dose of the gene (RS + +). Lesser asymmetries are expected in those of other genotypes, in males, twins, and any whose developmental progress is delayed or distorted by extraneous factors. Thus, the incidence of right-handedness should be highest in early maturing girls and lowest in late maturing boys. The former should have well-developed verbal abilities, and relatively weaker nonverbal skills, while the latter should have the reverse pattern. Evidence for an advantage in verbal compared with spatial test scores in early developers and the reverse pattern in late developers has been reported (Waber, 1976).

People with sex chromosome anomalies have different patterns of relative ability for verbal and nonverbal skills. Turner's syndrome females who lack one X chromosome (45, X females) tend to have average verbal abilities but below average nonverbal, visuospatial abilities. Those with an extra X, whether XXY males or XXX females tend to have average nonverbal abilities but weaker verbal ones. These differences led Crow (1998) to suggest that a gene relevant for CD is located on the sex chromosomes, as considered further below. However, the critical variable for verbal and nonverbal abilities may be maturation rate. Netley and Rovet (1983) tentatively suggested that the pattern of findings would be consistent with the possibility that rapid development gives relative advantages to verbal skills and deficits for spatial skills, while late development gives the reverse pattern. Netley (1998) described support for this hypothesis. The RS theory expects early maturers to express the RS + gene more strongly than late maturers. Netley showed that the different patterns of ability associated with the sex chromosome aneuploidies are also associated with finger ridge counts, consistent with the idea that the critical variable for all of these differences is relative rate of growth in utero. The critical variable is unlikely to be testosterone because XXY males and XXX females resemble each other for weak verbal skills (Crow, 1995b).

The implications of the RS + gene for psychological processes can be regarded as trivial from several points of view. It assists, but is not a pre-requisite for speech and language growth, as explained above, However, in so far as the gene modulates the development of certain capacities, it may be relevant at each extreme of the normal range. Most children learn to speak, to read, to count, and to play games and perhaps musical instruments with varying levels of skill. Levels of achievement depend on a multitude of factors that are independent of the RS locus. However, the gene assists the development of language skills at the risk of some imbalance of cerebral function due to loss of right hemisphere capacity. Outstanding achievement in any area that requires maximum efficiency on *both* sides of the brain and body, (as in surgery, playing musical instruments, sports, spatial and mathematical reasoning) may be less likely in those of RS + + genotype.

It is important to recognise that handedness is not a *cause* of the language problems or the special skill. It would be clearly ridiculous to say, "This child is left-handed so s/he will be a late reader but an outstanding surgeon/musician/tennis player/mathematician." These outcomes depend on many special capacities and opportunities. It is possible, however, that some people who have strong talents in various directions are prevented from attaining the highest levels of achievement because the left side of the body (and the right hemisphere) cannot be controlled as efficiently as its owner could wish. For others, it is possible that the speech production mechanisms cannot be controlled as efficiently as desired. As reiterated several times above, classifying normal samples for handedness gives no clues as to levels of reading or other ability. Neither would such a classification give clues as to potential for football. Differences for handedness are weak correlates of differences associated with genotypes for the RS locus. But among children with serious delays in learning to read despite good intelligence and among children with outstanding gifts for football, mathematics or music (that is, children with the relevant genotypes) there will be small differences for handedness. Similarly, the sexes differ for effects associated with the RS + gene because gene expression varies with rate of maturation and females tend to mature earlier than males. But it would be as ridiculous to suppose that the gene is the *only* factor involved in sex differences in ability as it would be to suppose it is the only factor involved in musical or sports ability.

THE "WHY" QUESTION: "JUST SO" STORIES FOR HUMAN HANDEDNESS, SPEECH AND CEREBRAL DOMINANCE

If there is a single gene that distinguishes humans from apes for handedness and cerebral dominance it is interesting to speculate how and when this gene evolved. Such speculations amount to "Just so" stories, in the sense that they go well beyond the evidence that is likely to be testable. The idea that a single gene for cerebral dominance (CD) was a critical factor in human speciation was suggested by Crow (1998, 2000). These papers were published with several commentaries including Annett (1998b, 2000b). Crow's main suggestions were that modern *Homo sapiens* diverged from precursor hominids on account of a gene for CD that led to hemisphere specialisation as we see it today, and that this pattern of cerebral specialisation is the foundation of modern language and symbolic intelligence. Because there are sex differences for language skills, and because people with anomalies of the sex chromosomes tend to have weak verbal abilities compared with spatial abilities if they have an extra X (XXY males and XXX females) and the converse pattern of ability if they are missing an X (45, X females), Crow hypothesised that a gene for CD is located on the sex chromosomes. The gene was not expected to follow the usual pattern of sex linked inheritance because it is located in regions of the X and Y chromosomes that are homologous (have similar functions) but do not cross over during the formation of eggs and sperm. Similar genes on the different chromosomes carried by males and females would thus diverge over time. It is this divergence that Crow suggests is responsible for sex differences in relative cognitive abilities. A mutation of the gene for CD, or some abnormality of the associated mechanisms, was suggested to be responsible for schizophrenia.

An obligation to offer my own evolutionary scenario arises here because I agree with Crow's main conclusions with respect to schizophrenia, but not his further speculations as to evolutionary mechanisms. It was explained in chapter 14 that, on considering whether schizophrenia could arise from an anomaly of the RS + gene, I realised that an agnosic mutant could produce just the effects required. The two theories, Crow's for schizophrenia and mine for handedness and CD, meshed immediately. The RS genetic model could account for the inheritance of schizophrenia, without any modifications, apart from the introduction of the mutant form (RS +a). Thus I strongly support Crow's arguments that schizophrenia could be caused by an anomaly of the mechanisms of CD. What I do not support are Crow's further arguments about the evolution of CD. Why and how do our assumptions differ?

1. The RS + gene evolved to promote *speech, not language*. Hemiplegic children with equivalent physical impairments on either side had equivalent levels of verbal and nonverbal intelligence. The only difference was that children with left-sided brain lesions (right hemiplegia) had a history of speech disorders. This suggests that left CD aids the growth of speech, but it is not essential for language or intelligence. Left hemisphere lateralisation of speech is normally associated with left lateralisations for other aspects of language so that, by adulthood, most humans rely heavily on the left side for language functions. However, the typical pattern of CD is not the causal factor, but rather the result of an initial asymmetry for speech learning.

2. The RS + gene could not be critical for human speciation because nearly one in five modern humans do not carry the gene. The RS + gene remains unfixed, and genetically variable, in modern humans.

3. Did the gene originate with modern humans, some 100,000 years ago? Evidence from asymmetries in fossil skulls suggests that the modern pattern, greater left than right occipital width, and a tendency to greater right than left frontal width, has been present from the earliest skulls available, the australopithecines (Holloway, 1974; Holloway and LaCoste-Lareymondie, 1982). The number of skulls dating from before *Homo erectus* is small, but evidence is consistent over the whole fossil record, including Neanderthals (see review by Steele, 2000). The present pattern of cerebral asymmetries appears to have a very long evolutionary history. There were a few exceptions, as there are in modern humans, suggesting that a directional bias with individual variability, has been the pattern for Homo from the beginning. Whether similar asymmetries are present in higher apes (LeMay, Billig and Geschwind, 1982; Steele, 2000) remains debatable.

4. Sex differences arise, not because the RS + gene is located on the sex chromosomes but because the expression of the gene is modified by factors that influence growth and rate of early growth differs between the sexes. Netley's (1998) commentary on Crow (1998) strengthens the argument, that the critical factor is rate of growth. These observations concur with the conclusion that expression of the RS + gene also depends on rate of foetal growth, faster for females than males and faster for the singleborn than twins.

5. Sexual selection for language skills may well have been an important factor in human evolution, but this must be balanced with sexual selection for non-language skills, physical prowess and skills in manufacture. "Chatting up" and "sweet talk" are important but so are the attractions of the champion at arms or sport.

My evolutionary scenario suggests that the RS + gene evolved early in the divergence of hominids from the apes. It would have been helpful from the first stages of speech acquisition. An early start, together with the fact that it is not yet fixed in humans as a species, would imply it was always associated with risks. There was a balanced polymorphism from the beginning, balancing the advantages for speech against risks to nonverbal skills, and also the risks of mutation to an agnosic form. The most severe and prevalent patterns of modern psychosis might not have been evident at the beginning, because of short life expectancy and the more limited symbolic capacities being impaired. However, it is possible that risks of mental illness could have been present from the beginnings of human evolution.

The jump from "proto-language" (Bickerton, 1995), in chimpanzees using sign language for the deaf, and human children constructing their first phrases, to modern syntactic structures probably required many intervening phases of evolution. Human intelligence grows in every child through stages in which language and thought metamorphose from single words with meaning, through two and three word sentences, to the highest levels of symbolic logic. To say that modern man is capable of the highest levels of abstract symbolic intelligence (in logic and mathematics) does not imply that all of us can operate at that level, and certainly none of us do so all of the time. Similarly, our hominid ancestors would vary in the levels of speech and symbolic intelligence of which they were capable. The gradual pressures toward higher intelligence would raise the range of ability that humans might attain but this would be much more complex than envisaged by a single transition from proto-language to a modern syntax. The phases of human intellectual growth were delineated by Piaget (1950), and in many publications summarised in modern textbooks of child psychology. Evolutionary scenarios that neglect this gradual process, recapitulated in every child, neglect an opportunity to envisage stages of pre-operational thinking and then concrete operational thinking (perhaps in *Homo habilis* and *Homo erectus* respectively). Perhaps only modern humans attain the highest levels of abstract thinking, in higher mathematics and representational art, but as remarked above, how many of us do in fact operate at these levels? The evolution of modern language and intelligence has a long and gradual history. It is regarded as academically respectable to deny speech and language to all but the most modern humans. This conservative caution is not more defensible than the reverse assumption, that speech and language would take so long to evolve, and proceed through so many phases, that 5 million years was a very short period for such a tremendous evolutionary journey.

Why would a gene for speech lateralisation have been helpful from the start? Because speech is difficult. It is impossible for higher apes. The fact that human infants acquire the phonemes of their native language within the first year of life shows that there must be a strong instinctive component for speech learning in modern man. An aid to the acquisition process, lateralisation to the left hemisphere remains useful, because people lacking the RS + gene are at risk for poor phonology. Such a gene would have been useful from the beginning when the earliest attempts to produce speech sounds were being endowed with symbolic significance.

How would the transition from primate calls, grunts and pant-hoots to words with meaning be managed? Deacon (1997) pointed out that a key requirement for modern chimpanzees learning to use signs and tokens as words with meaning is a great deal of repetition. A young bonobo, Kanji, apparently learned incidentally during the training of his mother, but older chimpanzees took many trials. In our early ancestors, it is likely that a lot of repetition, probably linked with a rhythmic beat would be great aids in the process. Why do adolescents today enjoy listening and dancing to the same lyrics and simple tunes repeated *ad nauseam*? Because repetition was an important aid for the early growth of language and thought. This would be part of my evolutionary scenario for language learning.

What environmental pressures could drive the changes required at the earliest stages of divergence of humans from apes? If speech is so critical to human communication and if cerebral asymmetries were present in most early hominids, why not put the origins of speech with the origins of upright walking? I have always found the academically respectable scenario, the gradual drying of the climate and the spread of savannah, unconvincing. If other apes survived in the tropical forests, why not our hominoid ancestor? The aquatic ape theory of Sir Alister Hardy (Morgan, 1982) suggests that a group of apes was forced to adapt to a marine environment. It is possible that they were trapped on a tropical island, somewhere around the present highlands of Ethiopia, when the Atlantic ocean broke through the straits of Gibraltar about 5 million years ago, and flooded the Mediterranean sea and North Africa. Today there are vast salt deserts where great inland seas dried out. The aquatic ape theory does not require humans to have become sea creatures as fully adapted to a marine life as whales and dolphins. It requires only that they developed adaptations for wading and swimming as they searched for food on a sea-shore. The environment of human evolutionary adaptedness was almost certainly a stretch of water bordered by tropical vegetation. Think of any representation of a paradise island. It might have been an oasis in a desert, or a woodland lake in the savannah. It could also have been a sea-shore that must be explored for its resources, by creatures trapped in a familiar wooded environment, but one that could not sustain them without additional nutrition. Morgan makes the case that many human characteristics that we do not share with apes would be adaptations to water, the streamlining of the body and deposition of body fat, loss of hair except on the head, capacity to hold our breath, that would fit us for swimming. The latter would also be an important aid for speech production. But the adaptation to the sea-shore would simultaneously drive upright walking for wading in the shallows, freeing the hands to turn over pebbles, find molluscs, catch fish and so on.

Those that learned to find food in the sea, to wade and to swim would have advantages over those that remained tied to the former life in the forest. On the sea-shore communication by voice would be far more effective than any type of sign language that depended on visual contact. Think of Johnny Weismuller as Tarzan, with his feats of swimming, as well as his powerful call! Think also of modern media representations of long haired maidens rising from blue lagoons. On this scenario, the beginnings of vocal communication could have been contemporary with other early hominid features. That is my preferred view of the environment of early human adaptedness. These speculations are fanciful, of course, but far more appealing than the conventional story of gradual adaptation to the savannah, which to my mind gives no reason for the urgency, rapidity and great variety of early hominid forms. However, they have no direct relevance to the RS theory, except for underlining the fact that the development of speech as a medium of communication represented an enormous break between humans and other apes.

The idea that human physical and intellectual development is influenced by genetic variation will be resisted in many quarters. My hope is that the recognition that there are biologically based differences in children's approaches to similar learning situations and that these are part of *normal* variation will lead to useful analyses of the different ways in which children actually learn. Most children learn to read and to do basic arithmetic relatively easily. Some children may need to be taught fundamental skills, perhaps in phonological analysis or in spatial thinking, which come naturally to other children. If the bases of special problems can be discovered, it should be possible to devise teaching methods to circumvent them. To close our minds to the possibility that special needs arise naturally in the general population would be to neglect opportunities to compensate for them.

Appendices

I Notes on the assessment of preferences with an algorithm for subgroup handedness

THE ASSESSMENT OF HAND PREFERENCE

The Annett Hand Preference Questionnaire (AHPQ; see Figure 2.1) has been used to collect information by questionnaire and also as the basis for observational assessment. Questionnaire must be relied upon in some circumstances, but observation is likely to be more reliable. This is because people may differ between what they *say* and what they *do*. In my experience participants (Ps) often say they are fully right-handed but when persuaded to try the actions with tools provided, are often surprised to find they do some things the "left-handed way". This lack of personal awareness about everyday actions is the chief reason for using demonstration and observation when possible. In my observations of the hand preferences of students and children, materials such as playing cards, needle and thread, scissors, and toy hammer, as needed for each item of the AHPQ, were provided. If tools for demonstration are not available, Ps may be asked to mime the actions before responding.

When responses to all 12 items are available, subgroup handedness can be determined with the aid of the algorithm shown in Figure A.I.1.

ASSESSMENT OF EYE PREFERENCE

Eye preference was assessed with one or more of the following tasks.

a. Sighting a distant object through a hollow tube.
b. Sighting a distant line through a small hole in the centre of a cardboard held at arm's length by both hands. Each eye is covered in turn by the examiner (E) to discover which eye is viewing the line.
c. Sighting a near object, such as a pencil held at arm's length through the hole in cardboard held at half-arm's length. Cover each eye in turn as above.
d. Sighting a distant line through the hole in cardboard and bringing the board slowly toward the nose, keeping the line in view. The hole is brought to the eye in use.

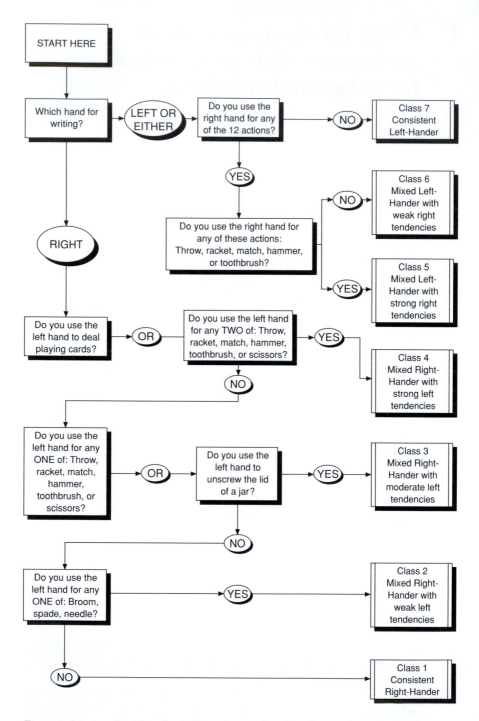

Figure A.I.1 An algorithm for finding subgroup hand preference from the AHPQ.

FOOT PREFERENCE

Ps were asked to kick a small ball, or to mime kicking, so as to score a goal in soccer.

For further information on the assessment of preferences see Annett (1992e).

II The peg moving task
Administration and norms

THE TASK

The peg moving task requires participants to move ten dowel pegs from one row of holes to another row. The dimensions of the board are shown in Figure A.II.1. The rows are 8 inches (20.32cm) apart (from centre to centre of the holes) and the holes are 1½ inch (3.8cm) apart (centre to centre). The holes are ½ inch (1.27cm) wide and ⅞ inch (2.2cm) deep. The original dowel pegs were ⅜ × 2 inches (0.9 × 8.1cm).

The board should be placed parallel to the edge of a flat surface of suitable height for the standing P. This might be a chair for a small child, or a workbench for a tall adult, but usually a normal table or desk.

INSTRUCTIONS FOR THE EXAMINER

The purpose is to discover how fast P can move the ten pegs in a perfect trial (without dropped pegs, or distractions). Certain rules must be observed.

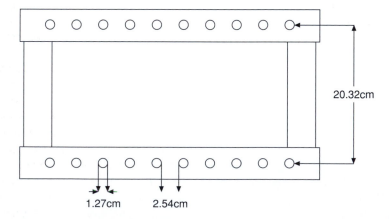

Figure A.II.1 Peg moving task dimensions.

- The participant/patient (P) should *stand*, facing the board on its longest dimension. The board should be placed so that the row of pegs is parallel to the edge or the table. If P must sit, the peg board should be placed on a straight, firm surface, placed so as to give the arm freedom of movement.
- A trial consists of a perfect run of ten peg placements, without dropping a peg or significant distraction. If any disruption occurs, the trial should be discarded and replaced.
- Pegs are moved one by one in sequence from the further to the nearer row.
- The right-hand works from right to left and the left-hand from left to right.
- Trials are made alternately (RLRLRL or LRLRLR) for three–five trials per hand. The starting hand may be chosen by P, or for research samples it may be appropriate to select the starting hand randomly.
- Time taken from P touching the first peg to releasing the last is measured by stopwatch to an accuracy of $^1/_{10}$s (or $^1/_{100}$s for a digital stopwatch).
- The examiner (E) should begin by demonstrating the task, moving the pegs as in a trial while saying "The task is to move the pegs from the top row to the bottom row like this, as fast as you can. It does not matter if you drop a peg. We will just start the trial again. The idea is to be as quick as you can, trying each hand in turn. Do not talk while moving the pegs because that slows you up."
- E then turns the board around for the start of the next trial. The accuracy of the timing of the start can be assured if E places a finger on top of the first peg while saying, "ready, steady, go", releasing the peg and starting the watch on "go".
- E should hold the board in place with one hand, taking care not to obstruct P's movement, to prevent the board moving during a trial.
- For all trials with an obvious fumble, poor start, dropped peg, talking or other distraction, discard and start again. The measure required is P's fastest accurate time.
- The time taken is given as E reads from the stopwatch, so that it becomes a game, with P trying to be faster next time. Encouragement should always be positive, e.g. "That was good, but see if you can be even faster."
- Small children sometimes bring both hands to the task, so it is useful to instruct them to put the "other" hand behind the back or into a pocket.

An example of the form used to record the information is given in Figure A.II.2. The *score* is the average time for five trials (or three for young children, as appropriate) taken by each hand. The aim is to find a reliable measure of P's movement time by each hand. If one trial is markedly slower than the others, it should be discarded, with the corresponding trial for the other hand removed also. This must be done only when one trial appears, in retrospect, to be in danger of seriously distorting the mean and never just to discard the slowest trial. Norms for performance in age groups are given in Table A.II.1.

Figure A.II.2 Annett peg board record form.

Table A.II.1 Norms for peg moving by each hand

Age (years.months)	Right-hand		Left-hand	
	Mean (s)	S.D.	Mean (s)	S.D.
< 3.9	24.3	4.5	26.3	5.0
3.9–4.2	21.7	3.6	23.4	4.2
4.3–4.8	19.1	2.7	20.6	3.5
4.9–5.2	17.2	2.4	18.6	2.7
5.3–5.8	15.7	1.7	17.0	2.3
5.9–6.5	14.4	1.5	15.6	1.9
6.6–7.5	12.8	1.3	13.9	1.8
7.6–8.5	11.9	1.1	12.9	1.6
8.6–9.5	10.9	1.1	11.8	1.4
9.6–10.5	10.4	1.1	11.3	1.3
10.6–11.5	10.0	1.0	10.9	1.2
11.6–12.5	9.7	1.0	10.5	1.1
12.6–13.5	9.6	1.0	10.3	1.1
13.6–14.5	9.3	0.9	10.0	1.1
14.6–15.5	9.2	0.9	9.9	1.1
15.6–16.5	9.1	0.9	9.8	1.0
16.6–17.5	9.0	0.8	9.7	1.0
17.6–18.5	8.9	0.8	9.6	1.0
18.6–19.5	8.9	0.8	9.6	1.0
19.6–24.11	8.8	0.9	9.5	1.0
25.0–29.11	8.8	0.9	9.5	1.0
30.0–34.11	8.9	0.9	9.6	1.1
35.0–39.11	9.0	0.9	9.7	1.1
40.0–44.11	9.2	0.9	9.9	1.1
45.0–49.11	9.4	1.0	10.2	1.2
50.0–54.11	9.6	1.0	10.4	1.2
55.0+	9.8	1.1	10.7	1.2

III Genotypes of left-handers (right-handers) per 1000 population for incidences from 1–40%, sexes combined

RS – –, RS + –, RS + + means at 0, 1.1z and 2.2z respectively

Genotype	RS – –	RS + –	RS + +	Total N
Frequency	185	490	325	1000
Percent				
1.0	9 (176)	1 (489)	0 (325)	10
2.0	16 (169)	3 (487)	0 (325)	20
3.0	24 (161)	6 (484)	0 (325)	30
4.0	30 (155)	9 (481)	0 (325)	40
5.0	37 (148)	13 (477)	0 (325)	50
6.0	43 (142)	16 (474)	1 (324)	60
7.0	49 (136)	20 (470)	1 (324)	70
8.0	54 (131)	25 (465)	1 (324)	80
9.0	60 (125)	29 (461)	1 (324)	90
10.0	65 (120)	34 (456)	1 (324)	100
11.0	70 (115)	38 (452)	2 (323)	110
12.0	74 (111)	43 (447)	2 (323)	120
13.0	79 (106)	48 (442)	3 (322)	130
14.0	83 (102)	54 (436)	3 (322)	140
15.0	87 (98)	59 (431)	4 (321)	150
16.0	91 (94)	65 (425)	4 (321)	160
17.0	95 (90)	70 (420)	5 (320)	170
18.0	99 (86)	76 (414)	6 (319)	180
19.0	102 (83)	82 (408)	6 (319)	190
20.0	106 (70)	87 (403)	7 (318)	200
21.0	109 (76)	93 (397)	8 (317)	210
22.0	112 (73)	99 (391)	9 (316)	220
23.0	115 (70)	105 (385)	10 (315)	230
24.0	118 (67)	111 (379)	11 (314)	240
25.0	121 (64)	118 (372)	11 (314)	250
26.0	124 (61)	124 (366)	13 (312)	260
27.0	126 (59)	130 (360)	14 (311)	270
28.0	129 (56)	136 (354)	15 (310)	280
29.0	131 (54)	143 (347)	16 (309)	290
30.0	134 (51)	149 (341)	17 (308)	300
31.0	136 (49)	156 (334)	19 (306)	310

Genotype	RS – –	RS + –	RS + +	Total N
32.0	138 (47)	162 (328)	20 (305)	320
33.0	140 (45)	168 (322)	22 (303)	330
34.0	142 (43)	175 (315)	23 (302)	340
35.0	144 (41)	181 (309)	25 (300)	350
36.0	146 (39)	188 (302)	26 (299)	360
37.0	148 (37)	194 (296)	28 (297)	370
38.0	149 (36)	201 (289)	30 (295)	380
39.0	151 (34)	207 (283)	32 (293)	390
40.0	153 (32)	214 (276)	33 (292)	400

IV Genotypes of left-handers per 1000 population for incidences 1–40%, sexes separately

RS – –, RS + –, RS + + genotype means are 0, 1.0z and 2.0z for males and 0, 1.2z and 2.4z for females respectively

Genotype	Males			Females		
	RS – –	RS + –	RS + +	R – –	RS + –	RS + +
Frequency	185	490	325	185	490	325
Percent						
1.0	8	2	0	9	1	0
2.0	16	4	0	17	3	0
3.0	23	7	0	25	5	0
4.0	29	11	0	32	8	0
5.0	35	15	0	39	11	0
6.0	40	19	1	45	15	0
7.0	46	23	1	52	18	0
8.0	51	28	1	57	22	1
9.0	56	32	2	63	26	1
10.0	61	37	2	68	31	1
11.0	65	42	3	74	35	1
12.0	70	47	3	78	40	2
13.0	74	52	4	83	45	2
14.0	78	57	5	88	50	2
15.0	82	63	5	92	55	3
16.0	86	68	6	96	61	3
17.0	90	73	7	100	67	3
18.0	93	79	8	104	72	4
19.0	97	85	8	107	78	5
20.0	100	91	9	111	84	5
21.0	103	97	10	114	90	6
22.0	106	102	11	117	96	7
23.0	109	108	12	121	102	7
24.0	112	114	14	123	109	8
25.0	115	120	15	126	115	9

Genotype	Males			Females		
	RS − −	RS + −	RS + +	R − −	RS + −	RS + +
26.0	118	126	16	129	121	10
27.0	120	133	17	131	128	11
28.0	123	138	19	134	134	12
29.0	125	145	20	136	141	13
30.0	128	151	21	139	147	14
31.0	130	157	23	141	154	15
32.0	132	163	25	143	161	16
33.0	134	169	27	145	167	17
34.0	136	178	28	147	174	19
35.0	138	182	30	149	181	20
36.0	140	188	32	151	187	22
37.0	142	194	34	153	194	23
38.0	144	200	36	154	201	25
39.0	146	207	37	156	207	27
40.0	147	213	40	157	214	28

V Thresholds of the R–L continuum measured from the mean of RS – –, showing the expected incidences of left-handed males and females, twin and singleton. Mean shifts are 1.0z, 2.0z for singleborn males, 1.2z, 2.4z for singleborn females, 0.67z, 1.33z for twin males, and 0.8z, 1.6z for twin females, for the RS + – and RS + + genotypes respectively

Threshold (z)	Singleton		Twin	
	Female	Male	Female	Male
−1.0	3.6	4.1	5.1	5.5
−0.9	4.3	4.9	5.8	6.7
−0.8	5.1	5.8	6.9	8.0
−0.7	5.9	6.8	8.1	9.4
−0.6	6.9	7.9	9.5	11.0
−0.5	8.0	9.2	11.0	12.9
−0.4	9.1	10.6	12.8	14.8
−0.3	10.5	12.2	14.7	17.0
−0.2	11.9	13.9	16.7	19.4
−0.1	13.5	15.7	19.0	22.0
0.0	15.2	17.8	21.5	25.0
0.1	17.0	19.9	24.0	27.8
0.2	18.9	22.3	26.8	30.5
0.3	21.3	24.7	29.5	34.0
0.4	23.2	27.3	32.8	37.5
0.5	25.6	30.1	36.0	41.0
0.6	28.0	32.9	39.0	44.5
0.7	30.6	35.9	42.5	48.0
0.8	33.2	38.9	46.0	51.5
0.9	36.0	42.1	49.5	55.0
1.0	38.8	45.2	52.5	58.5

VI Twins Genotypes of left-handers per 1000 population at incidences 10–45%:

RS + −, RS + + genotype means are 0.66z, 1.33z for males, 0.80z, 1.60z for females and 0.73z, 1.47z for sexes combined respectively

	Males			Females			Both sexes		
	RS − −	RS + −	RS + +	RS − −	RS + −	RS + +	RS − −	RS + −	RS + +
Frequency	185	490	325	185	490	325	185	490	325
Percent									
10.0	47	46	7	53	42	5	50	44	6
12.5	56	59	10	63	55	7	60	57	9
15.0	64	72	14	72	68	10	68	70	12
20.0	80	99	21	88	96	16	84	97	19
25.0	93	126	30	102	124	23	98	125	27
30.0	106	154	40	115	153	32	111	153	36
35.0	116	182	52	126	182	42	121	182	47
40.0	126	210	64	136	211	53	132	210	58
45.0	135	237	78	144	240	66	140	238	72

VII Studies of family handedness distinguishing the sex of parents and offspring grouped as follows

(a) Self-report in both generations and paternal incidences, (i) below and (ii) above 10%, (b) indirect report samples with paternal incidences, (i) below and (ii) above 7%

Parental incidence	Family			Sons					Daughters				
	N	% left	Father × mother	N	Obs. L	Exp. L	Chi-square Left	Right	N	Obs. L	Exp. L	Chi-square Left	Right
a. Self-report in both generations													
(i) <10%													
Annett (1978a)													
Father	1040	4.52	R × R	555	62	63.4	0.033	0.004	401	59	55.5	0.213	0.034
Mother	1040	3.56	R × L	17	4	3.3	0.132	0.032	20	3	4.9	0.732	0.237
Sons	597	12.06	L × R	25	6	4.7}	0.368	0.085	22	3	5.1}	0.884	0.269
Daughters	443	14.67	L × L	0	0	0}			0	0	0}		
Sum chi-sq.							0.655 d.f. 2					2.370 d.f. 2	
Ashton (1982)													
Father	1806	8.97	R × R	1210	191	183.1	0.343	0.061	1220	161	156.4	0.137	0.020
Mother	1806	7.64	R × L	88	17	21.8	1.043	0.343	118	29	26.5	0.240	0.069
Sons	1435	16.65	L × R	128	27	30.2	0.340	0.105	143	21	30.5	2.944	0.797
Daughters	1491	14.35	L × L	9	4	3.3	0.131	0.077	10	3	3.6	0.105	0.059
Sum chi-sq.							2.442 d.f. 3					4.371 d.f. 3	
Annett (1985a)													
Father	321	9.03	R × R	317	50	49.0	0.021	0.004	333	26	26.0	0.000	0.000
Mother	321	5.61	R × L	15	7	3.8	2.680	0.911	22	2	3.2	0.438	0.074
Sons	357	16.81	L × R	22	2	5.3}	1.829	0.628	33	6	4.5}	0.207	0.034
Daughters	390	8.72	L × L	3	1	1.1}			2	0	0.5}		
Sum chi-sq.							6.082* d.f. 2					0.754 d.f. 2	

(ii) >10%

McGee and Cozad (1980)

Father	616	R × R	19.64	489	112	113.4	0.017	0.005	570	99	99.6	0.003	0.001
Mother	616	R × L	16.72	91	38	31.9	1.187	0.639	123	35	35.4	0.005	0.002
Sons	737	L × R	27.27	130	39	43.5	0.471	0.237	131	38	35.8	0.133	0.050
Daughters	849	L × L	21.44	27	12	12.9	0.066	0.061	25	10	10.7	0.048	0.036
Sum chi-sq.							2.684 d.f. 3					0.278 d.f. 3	

Annett (1978a)

Father	1040	R × R	22.88	380	127	127.2	0.000	0.000	243	87	80.0	0.633	0.310
Mother	1040	R × L	24.52	95	49	44.5	0.451	0.397	84	40	40.3	0.003	0.002
Sons	597	L × R	39.53	83	35	37.7	0.193	0.161	79	29	36.6	1.589	1.374
Daughters	443	L × L	39.73	39	25	23.3	0.130	0.192	37	20	23.1	0.442	0.704
Sum chi-sq.							1.524 d.f. 3					5.038 d.f. 3	

Annett (1985a)

Father	321	R × R	25.23	204	68	67.3	0.007	0.003	229	61	54.8	0.698	0.220
Mother	321	R × L	26.17	74	30	34.2	0.525	0.452	69	22	25.6	0.512	0.302
Sons	357	L × R	39.50	57	28	25.5	0.239	0.194	62	22	22.1	0.000	0.000
Daughters	390	L × L	30.51	22	15	13.0	0.323	0.463	30	14	15.5	0.136	0.144
Sum chi-sq.							2.206 d.f. 3					2.012 d.f. 3	

b. Indirect report

(i) <7%

Chamberlain (1928)

Father	2177	R × R	4.18	4714	224	236.7	0.687	0.036	2511	84	88.6	0.244	0.009
Mother	2177	R × L	2.94	128	18	11.9	3.135	0.321	68	9	4.8 ⎱	3.766	0.284
Sons	5032	L × R	5.31	172	21	15.2 ⎱	2.656	0.279	96	5	6.4 ⎱	0.071	0.005
Daughters	2682	L × L	3.77	18	4	2.9 ⎰			7	3	0.9 ⎰		
Sum chi-sq.							7.115* d.f. 2					4.379 d.f. 2	

Parental incidence	Family			Sons			Chi-square		Daughters			Chi-square	
	N	% left	Father × mother	N	Obs. L	Exp. L	Left	Right	N	Obs. L	Exp. L	Left	Right
Annett (1985a)													
Father	745	4.56	R × R	1158	102	101.1	0.009	0.001	1104	72	83.2	1.503	0.122
Mother	745	2.95	R × L	31	5	4.8	0.009	0.002	42	9	6.0	1.541	0.255
Sons	1228	9.20	L × R	39	6	5.7	0.013	0.002	51	14	6.9	7.934	1.279
Daughters	1199	8.01	L × L	0	0	0			2	1	0.5		
Sum chi-sq.							0.036 d.f. 2					12.636* d.f. 2	
Annett (1973a)													
Father	3644	4.39	R × R	3853	402	412.2	0.251	0.030	3022	267	277.4	0.390	0.039
Mother	3644	3.71	R × L	163	43	30.1	5.506	1.248	125	39	21.2	15.025	3.063
Sons	4194	11.30	L × R	174	28	30.7	0.268	0.059	134	15	21.6	2.174	0.432
Daughters	3282	9.78	L × L	4	1	1.2			1	0	0.3		
Sum chi-sq.							7.362* d.f. 2					21.124* d.f. 2	
Rife (1940)													
Father	687	5.38	R × R	1189	105	106.0	0.010	0.001	804	46	56.0	1.801	0.135
Mother	687	5.09	R × L	39	6	6.1	0.001	0.000	36	10	4.7	5.933	0.894
Sons	1282	9.59	L × R	49	9	7.3	1.379	0.260	50	9	6.2	2.537	0.400
Daughters	896	7.59	L × L	5	3	1.3			6	3	1.4		
Sum chi-sq.							1.651 d.f. 2					11.698* d.f. 2	

Annett (1979)

Father	750	6.27	R × R	923	65	71.4	0.575	0.048	828	61	64.2	0.155	0.013
Mother	750	6.27	R × L	55	15	7.5	7.511	1.185	72	16	10.3	3.104	0.520
Sons	1041	8.45	L × R	61	8	7.9 }	0.018 }		57	5	7.8 }	1.301 }	0.212 }
Daughters	959	8.55	L × L	2	0	0.5	0.003		2	0	0.5		
Sum chi-sq.							9.334* d.f. 2					5.306 d.f. 2	

(ii) >7%
Annett (1979)

Father	818	9.53	R × R	352	61	63.1	0.071	0.015	340	44	46.1	0.098	0.015
Mother	818	6.36	R × L	21	7	6.0	0.153	0.062	27	11	6.4	3.329	1.032
Sons	414	19.56	L × R	39	12	10.7 }	0.191	0.075	35	6	7.8 }	0.782	0.237
Daughters	404	15.10	L × L	2	1	0.8			2	0	0.8		
Sum chi-sq.							0.567 d.f. 2					5.469 d.f. 2	

Spiegler and Yeni-Komshian (1983)

Father	1816	10.19	R × R	2629	372	359.7	0.423	0.067	2871	330	304.4	2.160	0.256
Mother	1816	8.20	R × L	223	49	50.4	0.038	0.011	229	42	43.3	0.042	0.010
Sons	3196	15.24	L × R	299	58	64.3	0.614	0.168	284	37	50.9	3.782	0.825
Daughters	3413	12.07	L × L	45	8	15.4	3.561	1.854	29	3	9.0	4.030	1.823
Sum chi-sq.							6.736 d.f. 3					12.930* d.f. 3	

Risch and Pringle (1985)

Father	1564	12.34	R × R	1727	208	200.2	0.306	0.040	1723	180	178.2	0.018	0.002
Mother	1564	7.29	R × L	134	31	26.2	0.879	0.213	147	32	27.3	0.820	0.187
Sons	2122	13.05	L × R	252	36	46.5 }	2.540	0.589	262	41	45.7 }	0.852	0.185
Daughters	2141	11.86	L × L	9	2	2.7			9	1	2.7		
Sum chi-sq.							4.568 d.f. 2					2.064 d.f. 2	

Note
*p < 0.05.

VIII An example of the genetic calculations for the dominant version of the RS model (see text)

Data of Chamberlain, 1928, as analysed by Annett, 1978b

(A) CALCULATE THE PROPORTIONS OF RIGHT- AND LEFT-HANDERS FOR EACH GENOTYPE IN THE TOTAL POPULATION OF PARENTS

Parental incidence = 0.0356

Population genotypes	Population frequency	Distance of threshold from the mean of each genotype	Dextral proportions under normal curves	Proportions of genotypes in the total population	
				Dextral	Sinistral
RS + +	0.3242	−2.844	0.9978	0.3235	0.0007
RS + −	0.4904	−2.844	0.9978	0.4893	0.0011
RS − −	0.1854	−0.907	0.8178	0.1516	0.0338
Total					0.0356

(B) CALCULATE THE GENOTYPES OF CHILDREN OF R × R, L × R AND L × L MATINGS

Parental genotypes	Filial genotypes		
	+ +	+ −	− −
Right × Right			
+ + × + +	0.104637		
+ + × + −	0.079140	0.079140	
+ + × − −		0.049046	
+ − × + +	0.079140	0.079140	
+ − × + −	0.059855	0.119710	0.059855
+ − × − −		0.037094	0.037094
− − × + +		0.049046	
− − × + −		0.037094	0.037094
− − × − −			0.022989
Total	0.322772	0.450270	0.157032	0.930074
Genotype proportions	0.347039	0.484123	0.168838
Left × Right			
+ + × + +	0.000234		
+ + × + −	0.000177	0.000177	
+ + × − −		0.000110	
+ − × + +	0.000177	0.000177	
+ − × + −	0.000134	0.000268	0.000134
+ − × − −		0.000083	0.000083
− − × + +		0.010927	
− − × + −		0.008264	0.008264
− − × − −			0.005122
Total	0.000721	0.020005	0.013603	0.034329 (× 2 for the total population including R × L matings)
Genotype proportions	0.0210137	0.582745	0.396243
Left × Left			
+ + × + +	0.00000052		
+ + × + −	0.00000039	0.00000039	
+ + × − −		0.00002442	
+ − × + +	0.00000039	0.00000039	
+ − × + −	0.00000030	0.00000060	0.00000030
+ − × − −		0.00001847	0.00001847
− − × + +		0.00002442	
− − × + −		0.00001847	0.00001847
− − × − −			0.00114108
Total	0.00000160	0.00008716	0.00117862	0.00126738
Genotype proportions	0.001262	0.068772	0.929966

(C) CALCULATE THE PROPORTIONS OF RIGHT- AND LEFT-HANDERS FOR EACH GENOTYPE IN THE FILIAL GENERATION

Filial incidence = 0.0477

Calculations are as in (a) when the threshold of left-handedness is at $-2.6455z$ for the RS + + and RS + – distributions and at $-0.7085s$ for the RS – – distribution. The proportions called sinistral are 0.00408 and 0.2394 respectively. The genotype frequencies deduced for each family type in (b) are multiplied by these proportions. For example, the proportion of left-handers in R × R families is calculated as follows:

$$
\begin{array}{llll}
\text{RS} + + & 0.347039 \times 0.00408 & = & 0.001416 \\
\text{RS} + - & 0.484123 \times 0.00408 & = & 0.001975 \\
\text{RS} - - & 0.168838 \times 0.2394 & = & 0.040420 \\
\hline
& & & 0.043811
\end{array}
$$

(D) COMPARE THE NUMBERS OF LEFT-HANDED CHILDREN EXPECTED IN EACH FAMILY TYPE WITH THE OBSERVED NUMBERS

	N children	Expected proportion sinistral	Expected number sinistral	Observed number sinistral	Chi-square
Right × Right	7225	0.0438	316.5	308	0.2302
Left × Right	464	0.0973	45.2	53	1.3617
Left × Left	25	0.2229	5.6	7	0.3655
Total					1.9574
					ns for 1 or 2 d.f.*

Note

*I have sought advice on the appropriate degrees of freedom but remain uncertain of the correct value. It is usual to deduct one degree of freedom if the gene frequencies were estimated from the data being fitted. Here, the gene frequencies were estimated from independent data.

References

Afzelius, B.A. (1976) A human syndrome caused by immotile cilia. *Science*, 193, 317–319.

Aggleton, J.P., Bland, J.M., Kentridge, R.W., & Neave, N.J. (1994) Handedness and longevity: Archival study of cricketers. *British Medical Journal*, 309, 1681–1684.

Aggleton, J.P., Kentridge, R.W., & Good, J.M.M. (1994) Handedness and musical ability: A study of professional orchestral players, composers and choir members. *Psychology of Music*, 22, 148–156.

Aggleton, J.P., Kentridge, R.W., & Neave, N.J. (1993) Evidence for longevity differences between left-handed and right-handed men: An archival study of cricketers. *Journal of Epidemiology and Community Health*, 47, 206–209.

Alexander, M.P., & Annett, M. (1996) Crossed aphasia and related anomalies of cerebral organization: Case reports and a genetic hypothesis. *Brain and Language*, 55, 213–239.

Alexander, M.P., Fischette, M.R., & Fischer, R.S. (1989) Crossed aphasia can be mirror image or anomalous. *Brain*, 112, 953–973.

Allard, F., & Scott, B.L. (1975) Burst cues, transitive cues and hemispheric specialization with real speech sounds. *Quarterly Journal of Experimental Psychology*, 27, 487–497.

Amunts, K., Jäncke, L., Mohlberg, H., Steinmetz, H., & Zilles, K. (2000) Interhemispheric asymmetry of the human motor cortex related to handedness and gender. *Neuropsychologia*, 38, 304–312.

Amunts, K., Schlaug, G., Jäncke, L., Steinmetz, H., Schleicher, A., Dabringhaus, A., & Zilles, K. (1997) Motor cortex and hand motor skills: Structural compliance in the human brain. *Human Brain Mapping*, 5, 206–215.

Amunts, K., Schlaug, G., Schleicher, A., Steinmetz, H., Dabringhaus, A., Roland, R.E., & Zilles, K. (1996) Asymmetry in the human motor cortex and handedness. *Neuroimage*, 4, 216–222.

Amunts, K., Schleicher, A., Burgel, U., Mohlberg, H., Uylings, H.B.M., & Zilles, K. (1999) Broca's region revisited: Cytoarchitecture and intersubject variability. *Journal of Comparative Neurology*, 412, 319–341.

Andrew, R.J. (1997) Left and right hemisphere memory traces: Their formation and fate. Evidence from events during memory formation in the chick. *Laterality*, 2, 179–198.

Annett, J., Annett, M., Hudson, P.T.W., & Turner, A. (1979) The control of movement in the preferred and non-preferred hands. *Quarterly Journal of Experimental Psychology*, 31, 641–652.

Annett, M. (1964) A model of the inheritance of handedness and cerebral dominance. *Nature, Lond.*, 204, 59–60.

Annett, M. (1967) The binomial distribution of right, mixed and left handedness. *Quarterly Journal of Experimental Psychology*, 19, 327–333.

Annett, M. (1970a) A classification of hand preference by association analysis. *British Journal of Psychology*, 61, 303–321.

Annett, M. (1970b) The growth of manual preference and speed. *British Journal of Psychology*, 61, 545–558.

Annett, M. (1970c) Handedness, cerebral dominance and the growth of intelligence. In D.J. Bakker & P. Satz (Eds.), *Specific Reading Disability: Advances in Theory and Method* (pp 61–79). Rotterdam: Rotterdam University Press.

Annett, M. (1972) The distribution of manual asymmetry. *British Journal of Psychology*, 63, 343–358.

Annett, M. (1973a) Handedness in families. *Annals of Human Genetics*, 37, 93–105.

Annett, M. (1973b) Laterality of childhood hemiplegia and the growth of speech and intelligence. *Cortex*, 9, 4–33.

Annett, M. (1974) Handedness in the children of two left-handed parents. *British Journal of Psychology*, 65, 129–131.

Annett, M. (1975) Hand preference and the laterality of cerebral speech. *Cortex*, 11, 305–328.

Annett, M. (1976) A coordination of hand preference and skill replicated. *British Journal of Psychology*, 67, 587–592.

Annett, M. (1978a) Genetic and nongenetic influences on handedness. *Behavior Genetics*, 8, 227–249.

Annett, M. (1978b) *A Single Gene Explanation of Right and Left Handedness and Brainedness*. Coventry: Lanchester Polytechnic.

Annett, M. (1978c) Throwing loaded and unloaded dice. *The Behavioral and Brain Sciences*, 2, 278–279.

Annett, M. (1979) Family handedness in three generations predicted by the right shift theory. *Annals of Human Genetics*, 42, 479–491.

Annett, M. (1982) Handedness. In J.G. Beaumont (Ed.), *Divided Visual Field Studies of Cerebral Organisation* (pp 195–215). London: Academic Press.

Annett, M. (1983a) Hand preference and skill in 115 children of two left-handed parents. *British Journal of Psychology*, 74, 17–32.

Annett, M. (1983b) Individual variation in directional bias in visual perception. *Perception*, 12, 71–84.

Annett, M. (1985a) *Left, Right, Hand and Brain: The Right Shift Theory*. London: Lawrence Erlbaum Associates Ltd.

Annett, M. (1985b) Which theory fails? A reply to McManus. *British Journal of Psychology*, 76, 17–29.

Annett, M. (1987a) La Latéralité manuelle des jumeaux: théorie due déplacement à droite. *Bulletin de Psychologie*, 40, 747–754. Reprinted as "Handedness in twins: The right shift theory". *Working paper number 22, National Child Development Study User Support Group*, March 1987.

Annett, M. (1987b) Handedness as chance or as species characteristic. *Behavioral and Brain Sciences*, 10, 263–264.

Annett, M. (1991a) Reading upside down and mirror text in groups differing for right minus left-hand skill. *European Journal of Cognitive Psychology*, 3, 363–377.

Annett, M. (1991b) Speech lateralisation and phonological skill. *Cortex*, 27, 583–593.

Annett, M. (1992a) Phonological processing and right minus left-hand skill. *The Quarterly Journal of Psychology*, 44A, 33–46.

Annett, M. (1992b) Parallels between asymmetries of *Planum Temporale* and of hand skill. *Neuropsychologia*, 30, 951–962.

Annett, M. (1992c) Spatial ability in subgroups of left- and right-handers. *British Journal of Psychology*, 83, 493–515.

Annett, M. (1992d) Five tests of hand skill. *Cortex*, 28, 583–600.

Annett, M. (1992e) Assessment of laterality. In J.R. Crawford, D.M. Parker, & W.W. McKinlay, (Eds.), *A Handbook of Neuropsychological Assessment* (pp 51–70). Hove, UK: Lawrence Erlbaum Associates Ltd.

Annett, M. (1993a) Handedness and educational success: The hypothesis of a genetic balanced polymorphism with heterozygote advantage for laterality and ability. *British Journal of Developmental Psychology*, 11, 359–370.

Annett, M. (1993b) The fallacy of the argument for reduced longevity in left-handers. *Perceptual and Motor Skills*, 76, 295–298.

Annett, M. (1993c) Rejoinder to "Annett's theory" by McManus, Shergill and Bryden (1993). *British Journal of Psychology*, 84, 539–544.

Annett, M. (1993d) The disadvantages of dextrality for intelligence—corrected findings. *British Journal of Psychology*, 84, 511–516.

Annett, M. (1994) Handedness as a continuous variable with dextral shift: Sex, generation and family handedness in subgroups of left- and right-handers. *Behavior Genetics*, 24, 51–63.

Annett, M. (1995a) The right shift theory of a genetic balanced polymorphism for cerebral dominance and cognitive processing. *Current Psychology of Cognition*, 14, 427–480.

Annett, M. (1996a) In defence of the right shift theory. *Perceptual and Motor Skills*, 82, 115–137.

Annett, M. (1996b) *Schizophrenia and autism considered as the products of an agnosic right shift gene*. Conference paper given at a Joint Meeting of the Association of European Psychiatrists and the Royal College of Psychiatrists, London, 9 July.

Annett, M. (1997a) Schizophrenia and autism considered as the products of an agnosic right shift gene. *Cognitive Neuropsychiatry*, 2, 195–240.

Annett, M. (1997b) Predictions for schizophrenia and autism from the right shift theory, fatal or fruitful? A rejoinder. *Cognitive Neuropsychiatry*, 2, 231–240.

Annett, M. (1998a) The stability of handedness. In J.K. Connolly (Ed.), *The Psychobiology of the Hand* (pp 63–76). London: MacKeith Press.

Annett, M. (1998b) Language, speech and cerebral dominance: Commentary on "The genetic origins of language" (Timothy J. Crow). *Current Psychology of Cognition*, 17, 1118–1125.

Annett, M. (1998c) Stories about hands, brain and minds. *Brain and Language*, 65, 356–358.

Annett, M. (1999a) Eye dominance in families predicted by the right shift theory. *Laterality*, 4, 167–172.

Annett, M. (1999b) Handedness and lexical skills in undergraduates. *Cortex*, 35, 357–372.

Annett, M. (1999c) Left-handedness as a function of sex, maternal versus paternal inheritance and report bias. *Behavior Genetics*, 29, 103–114.

Annett, M. (1999d) The theory of an agnosic right shift gene in schizophrenia and autism. *Schizophrenia Research*, 39, 177–182.

Annett, M. (2000a) Predicting combinations of left and right asymmetries, *Cortex*, 36, 485–505.

Annett, M. (2000b) No homo speciated on cerebral dominance: Commentary on Crow on language-sex-chromosome. *Psycholoquy*, Fri. Feb. 4.

Annett, M., & Alexander, M.P. (1996) Atypical cerebral dominance: Predictions and tests of the right shift theory. *Neuropsychologia*, 34, 1215–1227.

Annett, M., & Annett, J. (1979) Individual differences in right and left reaction time. *British Journal of Psychology*, 70, 393–404.

Annett, M., & Annett, J. (1991) Handedness for eating in gorillas. *Cortex*, 27, 269–275.

Annett, M., Eglinton, E., & Smythe, P. (1996) Types of dyslexia and the shift to dextrality. *Journal of Child Psychology and Psychiatry*, 37, 167–180.

Annett, M., Hudson, P.T.W., & Turner, A. (1974) The reliability of differences between the hands in motor skill. *Neuropsychologia*, 12, 527–531.

Annett, M., & Kilshaw, D. (1982) Mathematical ability and lateral asymmetry. *Cortex*, 18, 547–568.

Annett, M., & Kilshaw, D. (1983) Right- and left-hand skill II: Estimating the parameters of the distribution of L–R differences in males and females. *British Journal of Psychology*, 74, 269–283.

Annett, M., & Kilshaw, D. (1984) Lateral preference and skill in dyslexics: Implications of the right shift theory. *Journal of Child Psychology and Psychiatry*, 25, 357–377.

Annett, M., Lee, D., & Ounsted, C.O. (1961) Intellectual disabilities in relation to lateralised features of the EEG. In *Hemiplegic cerebral palsy in children and adults. Little Club Clinics in Developmental Medicine, No. 4*. London: Heinemann.

Annett, M., & Manning, M. (1989) The disadvantages of dextrality for intelligence. *British Journal of Psychology*, 80, 213–226 (see corrections, Annett, 1993d).

Annett, M., & Manning, M. (1990a) Reading and a balanced polymorphism for laterality and ability. *Journal of Child Psychology and Psychiatry*, 31, 511–529 (see "Corrigendum", Annett and Manning, 1994).

Annett, M., & Manning, M. (1990b) Arithmetic and laterality. *Neuropsychologia*, 28, 61–69.

Annett, M., & Manning, M. (1994) Corrigendum – Reading and a balanced polymorphism for laterality and ability. Journal of Child Psychology and Psychiatry, 31, 511–529. *Journal of Child Psychology and Psychiatry*, 35, 573–575.

Annett, M., & Ockwell, A. (1980) Birth order, birth stress and handedness. *Cortex*, 16, 181–188.

Annett, M., & Turner, A. (1974) Laterality and the growth of intellectual abilities. *British Journal of Educational Psychology*, 44, 37–46.

Ardila, A., Ardila, O., Bryden, M.P., Ostrosky, F., Rosselli, M., & Steenhuis, R. (1989) Effects of cultural background and education on handedness. *Neuropsychologia*, 27, 893–897.

Ashton, G.C. (1982) Handedness: An alternative hypothesis. *Behavior Genetics*, 12, 125–147.

Asperger, H. (1944) Die "Autistischen Psychopathen" im kindesalter. *Achiv fur Psychiatrie und Nervenkrankheiten*, 117, 76–136 (cited by Frith, 1991).

Azemar, G. (1993) Les gauchers en escrime: Données, statistique et interprétation. *Escrime Internationale*, 7, 15–19.

Azemar, G., Ripoll, H., Simonet, P., & Stein, J.F. (1983) Étude neuro-psychologique du comportement des gauchers en escrime. *Cinésiologie*, 22, 7–18.

Babcock, L.H., & Robison, R.A. (1989) Preferences of palaeozoic predators. *Nature*, 337, 695–696.

Baddeley, A., Gathercole, S., & Papagno, C. (1998) The phonological loop as a language learning device. *Psychological Review*, 105, 158–173.

Baddeley, A.D. (1990) *Human Memory: Theory and Practice*. London: Lawrence Erlbaum Associates Ltd.

Bailey, A., Le Couteur, A., Gottesman, I., Bolton, P., Simonoff, E., Yuzda, E., & Rutter, M. (1995) Autism as a strongly genetic disorder: Evidence from a British twin study. *Psychological Medicine*, 25, 63–77.

Bailey, A., Phillips, W., & Rutter, M. (1996) Autism: Towards an integration of clinical, genetic, neuropsychological and neurobiological perspectives. *Journal of Child Psychology and Psychiatry*, 37, 89–126.

Bakan, P. (1971) Handedness and birth order. *Nature, Lond.*, 229, 195.

Bakan, P., Dibb, G., & Reed, P. (1973) Handedness and birth stress. *Neuropsychologia*, 11, 363–366.

Baron, J., & Strawson, C. (1976) Use of orthographic and word-specific knowledge in reading words aloud. *Journal of Experimental Psychology: Human Perception and Performance*, 2, 386–393.

Barsley, M. (1966) *The Left-Handed Book: An Investigation into the Sinister History of Left-handedness*. London: Souvenir Press.

Bartley, A.J., Jones, D.W., Torrey, E.F., Zigun, J.R., & Weinberger, D.R. (1993) Sylvian fissure asymmetries in monozygotic twins: A test of laterality in schizophrenia. *Biological Psychiatry*, 34, 853–863.

Basser, L.S. (1962) Hemiplegia of early onset and the faculty of speech with special reference to the effects of hemispherectomy. *Brain*, 85, 427–460.

Beaton, A. (1979) Hemisphere function and dual task performance. *Neuropsychologia*, 17, 629–635.

Beaton, A. (1997) The relation of planum temporale asymmetry and morphology of the corpus callosum to handedness, gender and dyslexia: A review of the evidence. *Brain and Language*, 60, 255–322.

Beddington, R. (1996) Left, right, left . . . turn: News and views in developmental biology. *Nature*, 381, 116–117.

Bee, H. (1981) *The Developing Child* (3rd ed.). New York: Harper International.

Belin, P., Zilbovicius, M., Crozier, S., Thivard, L., & Fontaine, A. (1998) Lateralization of speech and auditory temporal processing. *Journal of Cognitive Neurosciences*, 10, 536–540.

Benbow, C.P. (1986) Physiological correlates of extreme intellectual precocity. *Neuropsychologia*, 24, 719–725.

Benton, A.L. (1962) Clinical symptomatology in right and left hemisphere lesions. In V.B. Mountcastle (Ed.), *Interhemispheric relations and cerebral dominance* (pp 253–263). Baltimore: Johns Hopkins Press.

Besner, D., Davies, J., & Daniels, S. (1981) Reading for meaning: The effects of concurrent articulation. *The Quarterly Journal of Experimental Psychology*, 33A, 415–437.

Bever, T.G., & Chiarello, R.J. (1974) Cerebral dominance in musicians and nonmusicians. *Science*, 185, 137–139.

Bickerton, D. (1995) *Language and Human Behavior*. Seattle: University of Washington Press.

Bingley, T. (1958) Mental symptoms in temporal lobe epilepsy and temporal lobe gliomas. *Acta Psychiatrica et Neurologica, Scandinavica*, Supplementum 120, 33.

Binkofski, F., Amunts, K., Stephan, K.M., Posse, S., Schormann, T., Freund, H.J., Zilles, K., & Seitz, R.J. (2000) Broca's region subserves imagery of motion: A combined cytoarchitectonic and fMRI study. *Human Brain Mapping*, 11, 273–285.

Bishop, D.V.M. (1989) Does hand proficiency determine hand preference? *British Journal of Psychology*, 80, 191–199.

Bishop, D.V.M. (1990a) *Handedness and Developmental Disorder*. Oxford: Blackwell.

Bishop, D.V.M. (1990b) Handedness, clumsiness and developmental language disorders. *Neuropsychologia*, 28, 681–690.

Bishop, D.V.M., North, T., & Donlan, C. (1995) Genetic basis for specific language impairment: Evidence from a twin study. *Developmental Medicine and Child Neurology*, 37, 56–71.

Bishop, D.V.M., & Robson, J. (1989a) Unimpaired short-term memory and rhyme judgement in congenitally speechless individuals: Implications for the notion of "articulatory coding". *The Quarterly Journal of Experimental Psychology*, 41A, 123–140.

Bishop, D.V.M., & Robson, J. (1989b) Accurate nonword spelling despite congenital inability to speak: Phoneme-grapheme conversion does not require subvocal articulation. *British Journal of Psychology*, 80, 1–13.

Blau, A. (1946) *The Master Hand. Research monograph, no. 5*. New York: American Orthopsychiatric Association.

Bock, G.R., & Marsh, J. (1991) *Biological Asymmetry and Handedness: CIBA foundation symposium 162*. Chichester: John Wiley.

Boder, E. (1973) Developmental dyslexia: A diagnostic approach based on three atypical reading-spelling patterns. *Developmental Medicine and Child Neurology*, 15, 663–687.

Boklage, C.E. (1977) Schizophrenia, brain asymmetry development and twinning: Cellular relationship with etiological and possibly prognostic implications. *Biological Psychiatry*, 12, 19–35.

Bolton, P., MacDonald, H., Pickles, A., Rios, P., Goode, S., Crowson, M., Bailey, A., & Rutter, M. (1994) A case-control family history study of autism. *Journal of Child Psychology and Psychiatry*, 35, 877–900.

Bourassa, D.C., McManus, I.C., & Bryden, M.P. (1996) Handedness and eye-dominance: A meta-analysis of their relationship. *Laterality*, 1, 5–34.

Bouterwek, E. (1938), cited by Zazzo, 1960.

Boycott, A.E., Diver, C., Garstang, S.L., & Turner, F.M. (1930) The inheritance of sinistrality in limnaea peregra. *Philosophical Transactions of the Royal Society of London*, B219, 51–131.

Brackenridge, C.J. (1981) Secular variation in handedness over 90 years. *Neuropsychologia*, 19, 459–462.

Bradley, L. (1984) *Assessing Reading Difficulties: A Diagnostic and Remedial Approach* (2nd ed.). London: MacMillan Education.

Bradshaw, J.L., & Rogers, L.J. (1993) *The Evolution of Lateral Asymmetries, Language, Tool Use and Intellect*. San Diego: Academic Press.

Brain, W.R. (1941) Visual disorientation with special reference to lesions of the right cerebral hemisphere. *Brain*, 64, 244–272.

Brain, W.R. (1945) Speech and handedness. *Lancet*, 249, 837–841.

Brazelton, T.B., Robey, J.S., & Collier, G.A. (1969) Infant development in the Zincanteco Indians of Southern Mexico. *Pediatrics*, 44, 274–290.

Briggs, G.G., & Nebes, R.D. (1975) Patterns of hand preference in a student population. *Cortex*, 11, 230–238.

Brinkman, J., & Kuypers, H.G.J.M. (1973) Cerebral control of contralateral and ipsilateral arm, hand and finger movements in the split-brain rhesus monkey. *Brain*, 96, 653–674.

Broadbent, D.E. (1956) Successive responses to simultaneous stimuli. *Quarterly Journal of Experimental Psychology*, 8, 145–152.

Broca, P. (1865) Sur le siège de la faculté du langage articulé. *Bulletin de la Société d'Anthropologie*, 6, 377–393.

Brooker, R.J., Lehman, R.A.W., Heimbuch, R.C., & Kidd, K.K. (1981) Hand usage in a colony of Bonnett monkeys (*Macaca radiata*). *Behavior Genetics*, 11, 49–56.

Brown, J.L. (1962) Differential hand usage in three year old children. *Journal of Genetic Psychology*, 100, 167–175.

Brown, R., Colter, N., Corsellis, J.A.N., Crow, T.J., Frith, C.D., Jagoe, R., Johnstone, E.C., & Marsh, L. (1986) Postmortem evidence of structural brain changes in schizophrenia. *Archives of General Psychiatry*, 43, 36–42.

Browne, T. (1981) *Pseudoxia Epidemica* (R. Robbins, Ed.). Oxford: Oxford University Press (originally published 1646).

Bryden, M.P. (1964) Tachistoscopic recognition and cerebral dominance. *Perceptual and Motor Skills*, 19, 686.

Bryden, M.P. (1977) Measuring handedness with questionnaires. *Neuropsychologia*, 15, 617–624.

Bryden, M.P. (1982) *Laterality: Functional Asymmetry in the Intact Brain*. New York: Academic Press.

Bryden, M.P., McManus, I.C., & Bulman-Fleming, M.B. (1994) Evaluating the empirical support for the Geschwind-Behan-Galaburda model of cerebral lateralization. *Brain and Cognition*, 26, 103–167.

Bullmore, E., Brammer, M., Harvey, I., Murray, R., & Ron, M. (1995) Cerebral hemispheric asymmetry revisited: Effects of handedness, gender, and schizophrenia measured by radius of gyration of magnetic resonance images. *Psychological Medicine*, 25, 349–363.

Burt, C. (1937) *The Backward Child*. London: University of London Press.

Byrne, B. (1974) Handedness and musical ability. *British Journal of Psychology*, 65, 279–281.

Byrne, R.W., & Byrne, J.M. (1991) Hand preferences in the skilled gathering tasks of mountain gorillas (Gorill g. berengei). *Cortex*, 27, 521–546.

Campbell, R., & Butterworth, B. (1985) Phonological dyslexia and dysgraphia in a highly literate subject: A developmental case with associated deficits of phonemic processing and awareness. *The Quarterly Journal of Experimental Psychology*, 37A, 435–475.

Cannon, M., Byrne, M., Cassidy, B., Larkin, C., Horgan, R., Sheppard, N.P., & O'Callaghan, E. (1995) Prevalence and correlates of mixed-handedness in schizophrenia. *Psychiatry Research*, 59, 119–125.

Capobianco, R.J. (1966) Ocular-manual laterality and reading in adolescent mental retardates. *American Journal of Mental Deficiency*, 70, 781–785.

Cardon, L.R., Smith, S.D., Fulker, D.W., Kimberling, W.J., Pennington, B.F., & DeFries, J.C. (1994) Quantitative trait locus for reading disability on chromosome 6. *Science*, 266, 276–279.

Carlier, M., Beau, J., Marchland, C., & Michel, F. (1994) Sibling resemblance in two manual laterality tasks. *Neuropsychologia*, 32, 741–746.

Carson, R.G., Chua, R., Elliott, D., & Goodman, D. (1990) The contribution of vision to asymmetries in manual aiming. *Neuropsychologia*, 28, 1215–1220.

Carter, C.O. (1961) Inheritance of congenital pyloric stenosis. *British Medical Bulletin*, 17, 251–253.

Carter, R.L., Hohenegger, M., & Satz, P. (1980) Handedness and aphasia: An inferential method for determining the mode of cerebral speech specialization. *Neuropsychologia*, 18, 569–574.

Carter-Saltzman, L. (1980). Biological and sociocultural effects on handedness: Comparison between biological and adoptive families. *Science*, 209, 1263–1265.

Carter-Saltzman, L., Scarr-Salapatek, S., Barker, W.B., & Katz, S. (1976) Left-handedness in twins: Incidence and patterns of performance in an adolescent sample. *Behavior Genetics*, 6, 189–203.

Casey, M.B. (1995) Empirical support for Annett's conception of heterozygote advantage. *Current Psychology of Cognition*, 14, 520–528.

Castles, A., & Coltheart, M. (1993) Varieties of developmental dyslexia. *Cognition*, 47, 149–180.

Cerone, L.J., & McKeever, W.F. (1999) Failure to support the right-shift theory's hypothesis of a "heterozygote advantage" for cognitive abilities. *British Journal of Psychology*, 90, 109–123.

Chamberlain, H.D. (1928) The inheritance of left handedness. *Journal of Heredity*, 19, 557–559.

Chapman, J.P., Chapman, L.J., & Allen, J.J. (1987) The measurement of foot preference. *Neuropsychologia*, 25, 579–584.

Cherry, E.C. (1953) Some experiments on the recognition of speech, with one and with two ears. *Journal of the Acoustical Society of America*, 25, 975–979.

Chesher, E.C. (1936) Some observations concerning the relation of handedness to the language mechanism. *Bulletin of the Neurological Institute of New York*, 4, 556–562.

Chi, J.G., Dooling, E.C., & Gilles, F.H. (1977) Gyral development of the human brain. *Annals of Neurology*, 1, 86–93.

Chiron, C., Leboyer, M., Leon, F., Jambaque, I., Nuttin, C., & Syrota, A. (1995) SPECT of the brain in childhood autism: Evidence for a lack of normal hemispheric asymmetry. *Developmental Medicine and Child Neurology*, 37, 849–860.

Chivers, D.J. (1974) *The Siamang in Malaya: A Field Study of a Primate in Tropical Rain Forest. Contributions of Primatology.* Basel: Karger.

Clapham, P.J., Leimkuhler, E., Gray, B.K., & Mattila, D.R. (1995) Do humpback whales exhibit lateralized behaviour? *Animal Behavior*, 50, 73–82.

Clark, M.M. (1957) *Left-handedness.* London: University of London Press.

Clark, M.M. (1970) *Reading Difficulties in Schools.* Harmondsworth, UK: Penguin.

Clark, W.E. Le Gros (1934) The asymmetry of the occipital region of the brain and skull. *Man*, 55, 35–37.

Cole, J. (1955) Paw preference in cats related to hand preference in animals and men. *Journal of Comparative and Physiological Psychology*, 48, 137–140.

Collins, R.L. (1969) On the inheritance of handedness: II. Selection for sinistrality in mice. *Journal of Heredity*, 60, 117–119.

Collins, R.L. (1970) The sound of one paw clapping: An inquiry into the origin of left handedness. In G. Lindzey & D.D. Thiessen (Eds.), *Contribution to Behavior-genetic Analysis—The Mouse as a Prototype* (pp 115–136). New York: Appleton.

Collins, R.L. (1975) When left-handed mice live in right-handed worlds. *Science*, 187, 181–184.

Collins, R.L. (1977) Toward an admissable genetic model for the inheritance of degree and direction of asymmetry. In S. Harnad, R.W. Doty, L. Goldstein, J. Jaynes, & G. Krauthamer (Eds.), *Lateralization in the Nervous System* (pp 137–150). New York: Academic Press.

Collins, R.L. (1985) On the inheritance of direction and degree of asymmetry. In S.D. Glick (Ed.), *Cerebral Lateralization in Nonhuman Species* (pp 41–71). New York: Academic Press.

Collins, R.L. (1991) Discussion: Genetics of handedness. In G.R. Bock & J. Marsh (Eds.), *Biological Asymmetry and Handedness. CIBA Foundation symposium 162* (pp 277–280). Chichester: John Wiley.

Coltheart, M. (1980) Deep dyslexia: A right hemisphere hypothesis. In M. Coltheart, K. Patterson, & J.C. Marshall (Eds.), *Deep Dyslexia* (pp 326–380). London: Routledge & Kegan Paul.

Coltheart, M. (1983) The right hemisphere and disorders of reading. In A.W. Young (Ed.), *Functions of the Right Cerebral Hemisphere* (pp 171–201). London: Academic Press.

Coltheart, M. (2000) Deep dyslexia is right hemisphere reading. *Brain and Language*, 71, 299–309.

Connolly, K., & Bishop, D.V.M. (1992) The measurement of handedness: A cross-cultural comparison of samples from England and Papua New Guinea. *Neuropsychologia*, 30, 13–26.

Conrad, K. (1949) Uber aphasische Sprachstorungen bei Hirnverletzten Linkshander. *Nervenarzt*, 20, 148–154.

Corballis, M.C. (1983) *Human Laterality*. New York: Academic Press.

Corballis, M.C. (1997a) The genetics and evolution of handedness. *Psychological Review*, 104, 714–727.

Corballis, M.C. (1997b) A house of cards? *Journal of Neuropsychiatry*, 2, 214–216.

Corballis, M.C., & Morgan, M.J. (1978) On the biological basis of human laterality: I. Evidence for maturational left-right gradient. *The Behavioral and Brain Sciences*, 1, 261–269.

Coren, S. (1992) *The Left-Hander Syndrome: The Causes and Consequences of Left-Handedness*. London: John Murray.

Coren, S., & Halpern, D.F. (1991) Left-handedness: A marker for decreased survival fitness. *Psychological Bulletin*, 109, 90–106.

Coren, S., & Porac, C. (1977) Fifty centuries of right handedness: The historical record. *Science*, 198, 631–632.

Coren, S., & Porac, C. (1980) Family patterns in four dimensions of lateral preference. *Behavior Genetics*, 10, 333–348.

Corina, D.P., McBurney, S.L., Dodrill, C., Hinshaw, K., Brinkley, J., & Ojemann, G. (1999) Functional roles of Broca's area and SMG: Evidence from cortical stimulation mapping in a deaf signer. *Neuroimage*, 10, 570–581.

Crabtree, T. (1976) Dyslexia goodbye. *New Society*, 1 January, 10–11.

Craig, J.D. (1980) A dichotic rhythm task: Advantage for the left-handed. *Cortex*, 16, 613–620.

Critchley, M. (1970) *Aphasiology and Other Aspects of Language*. London: Edward Arnold.

Crovitz, H.F. (1961) Differential acuity of two eyes and the problem of ocular dominance. *Science*, 134, 614.

Crovitz, H.F., & Zener, K.A. (1962) A group test for assessing hand and eye dominance. *American Journal of Psychology*, 75, 271–276.

Crow, T.J. (1984) A re-evaluation of the viral hypothesis: Is psychosis a result of retroviral integration at a site close to the cerebral dominance gene? *British Journal of Psychiatry*, 145, 243–253.

Crow, T.J. (1995a) A continuum of psychosis, one human gene and not much else – the case for homogeneity. *Schizophrenia Research*, 17, 135–145.

Crow, T.J. (1995b) The case for an X-Y homologous gene and the possible role of sexual selection in the evolution of language. *Current Psychology of Cognition*, 14, 775–781.

Crow, T.J. (1997a) Schizophrenia as a failure of hemispheric dominance for language. *Trends in Neurosciences*, 20, 339–343.

Crow, T.J. (1997b) Is schizophrenia the price that *Homo sapiens* pays for language? *Schizophrenia Research*, 28, 127–141.

Crow, T.J. (1998) Sexual selection, timing and the descent of man: A theory of the genetic origins of language. *Current Psychology of Cognition*, 17, 1079–1114.

Crow, T.J. (1999) The case for an Xq21.3/Yp homologous locus in the evolution of language and the origins of psychosis. *Acta Neuropsychiatrica*, 11, 54–56.

Crow, T.J. (2000) Did Homo sapiens speciate on the Y chromosome? *Psycholoquy*, 11.

Crow, T.J., Ball, J., Bloom, S.R., Brown, R., Bruton, C.J., Colter, N., Frith, C.D., Johnstone, E.C., Owens, D.G.C., & Roberts, G.W. (1989) Schizophrenia as an anomaly of development of cerebral asymmetry. *Archives of General Psychiatry*, 46, 1145–1150.

Crow, T.J., Crow, L.R., Done, D.J., & Leask, S. (1998) Relative hand skill predicts academic ability: Global deficits at the point of hemispheric indecision. *Neuropsychologia*, 36, 1275–1282.

Crow, T.J., & Done, D.J. (1995) Neurodevelopmental aspects of schizophrenia: The genetically determined trajectory of "hemispheric indecision". In N. Brunello, G. Racagni, S.Z. Langer, & J. Mendlewicz (Eds.), *Critical Issues in the Treatment of Schizophrenia. International Academy of Biomedical Drug Research, vol. 10* (pp 35–43). Basel: Karger.

Cruikshank, W.M., & Raus, G.M. (1955) *Cerebral Palsy: Its Individual and Community Problems*. Syracuse: Syracuse University Press.

Cunningham, D.J. (1902) Right-handedness and left-brainedness. *Journal of the Royal Anthropological Institute of Great Britain and Ireland*, 32, 273–296.

Cutting, J.C. (1994) Evidence for right hemisphere dysfunction in schizophrenia. In A.S. David & J.C. Cutting (Eds.), *The Neuropsychology of Schizophrenia* (pp. 231–242). Hove, UK: Lawrence Erlbaum Associates Ltd.

Dalby, J.T., Gibson, D., Grossi, V., & Schneider, R.D. (1980) Lateralized hand gesture during speech. *Journal of Motor Behavior*, 12, 292–297.

Dart, R.A. (1925) *Australopithecus africanus*: The man-ape of South Africa. *Nature, Lond.*, 115, 195–199.

Dart, R.A. (1949) The predatory implemental technique of Australopithecus. *American Journal of Physical Anthropology*, 7, 1–38.

Dassonville, P., Zhu, P., Uğurbil, K., Kim, S.G., & Ashe, J. (1997) Functional activation in motor cortex reflects the direction and degree of handedness. *Proceedings of the National Academcy of Sciences of the USA*, 94, 14015–14018.

David, A.S., & Cutting, J.C. (Eds.) (1994) *The Neuropsychology of Schizophrenia*. Hove, UK: Lawrence Erlbaum Associates Ltd.

Davis, A., & Annett, M. (1994) Handedness as a function of twinning, age and sex. *Cortex*, 30, 105–111.

Deacon, T. (1997) *The Symbolic Species*. London: Allen Lane.

Dechaume, M.P. (1957) *Contribution à l'étude de la dominance laterale chez les jumeaux*. Unpublished M.D. thesis, Paris (cited by Zazzo, 1960).

Dellatolas, G., Curt. F., Dargent-Paré, C., & de Agostini, M. (1998) Eye-dominance in children: A longitudinal study. *Behavior Genetics*, 28, 187–195.

Demarest, W.J. (1982) *Manual asymmetry in Guatemalan populations: A cross-cultural test of Annett's right shift theory*. Unpublished doctoral dissertation, University of Stanford.

Dennis, M., & Whitaker, H.A. (1977) Hemisphere equipotentiality and language acquisition. In S.J. Segalowitz & F.A. Gruber (Eds.), *Language development and neurological theory* (pp 93–106). New York: Academic Press.

Dennis, W. (1940) *The Hopi Child*. New York: Wiley.

Dennis, W. (1958) Early graphic evidence of dextrality in man. *Perceptual and Motor Skills*, 8, 147–149.

De Renzi, E. (1982) *Disorders of Space Exploration and Cognition*. Chichester, UK: John Wiley.

De Renzi, E. (1989) Apraxia. In F. Boller & J. Grafman (Eds.), *Handbook of Neuropsychology, vol. 2*. New York: Elsevier.

Deutsch, D. (1978) Pitch memory: An advantage for the left-handed. *Science*, 199, 559–560.

Deutsch, D. (1980) Handedness and memory for tonal pitch. In J. Herron (Ed.), *Neuropsychology of Left Handedness* (pp 263–271). New York: Academic Press.

De Vleeschouwer, K., Van Elsacker, L., & Verheyen, R.F. (1995) Effect of posture on hand preference during experimental food reaching in bonobos (*Pan paniscus*). *Journal of Comparative Psychology*, 109, 203–207.

Doupe, A.J., & Kuhl, P.K. (1999) Birdsong and human speech: Common theories and mechanisms. *Annual Review of Neuroscience*, 22, 567–631.

Dunn, L.M. (1959) *The Peabody Picture Vocabulary Test*. Minnesota: American Guidance Service Inc.

Edwards, S., & Beaton, A. (1996) Howzat?! Why is there an over-representation of left-handed bowlers in professional cricket in the UK? *Laterality*, 1, 45–50.

Efron, R. (1990) *The Decline and Fall of Hemispheric Specialization*. London: Lawrence Erlbaum Associates Ltd.

Eglinton, E., & Annett, M. (1994) Handedness and dyslexia: A meta-analysis. *Perceptual and Motor Skills*, 79, 1611–1616.

Elias, L.J., & Bryden, M.P. (1998) Footedness is a better predictor of language lateralization than handedness. *Laterality*, 3, 41–51.

Eling, P. (1984) Broca on the relation between handedness and cerebral speech dominance. *Brain and Language*, 22, 158–159.

Ellis, S.J., Ellis, P.J., & Marshall, E. (1988) Hand preference in a normal population. *Cortex*, 24, 157–163.

Elvevåg, B., & Weinberger, D.R. (1997) Schizophrenia and the right shift gene hypothesis: Some comments on the devil in the details. *Journal of Cognitive Neuropsychiatry*, 2, 221–225.

Ettlinger, G., & Moffett, A. (1964) Lateral preferences in the monkey. *Nature, Lond.*, 204, 606.

Fabbro, F., Brusaferro, A., & Bava, A. (1990) Opposite musical-manual interferences in young vs expert musicians. *Neuroreport*, 28, 871–877.

Fagot, J., & Vauclair, J. (1988) Handedness and bimanual coordination in the lowland gorilla. *Brain, Behaviour and Evolution*, 32, 89–95.

Falconer, D.S. (1965) The inheritance of liability to certain diseases, estimated from the incidence among relatives. *Annals of Human Genetics, London*, 29, 51–76.

Falkai, P., Bogerts, B., Schneider, T., Greve, B., Pfeiffer, U., Pilz, K., Gonsiorzcyk, C., Majtenyi, C., & Ovary, I. (1995) Disturbed planum temporale asymmetry in schizophrenia: A quantitative post-mortem study. *Schizophrenia Research*, 14, 161–176.

Falzi, G., Perrone, P., & Vignolo, L.A. (1982) Right left asymmetry in anterior speech region. *Archives of Neurology*, 39, 239–240.

Fennell, E., Satz, P., & Wise, R. (1967) Laterality differences in the perception of pressure. *Journal of Neurology, Neurosurgery and Psychiatry*, 30, 337–340.

Finch, G. (1941) Chimpanzee handedness. *Science*, 94, 117–118.

Fischer, R.S., Alexander, M.P., Gabriel, C., Gould, E., & Milione, J. (1991) Reversed lateralization of cognitive functions in right handers. *Brain*, 114, 245–261.

Fisher, S.E., Marlow, A.J., Lamb, J., Maestrini, E., Williams, D.F., Richardson, A.J., Weeks, D.E., Stein, J.F., & Monaco, A.P. (1999) A quantitative trait locus on chromosome 6p influences different aspects of developmental dyslexia. *American Journal of Human Genetics*, 64, 146–156.

Fisher, S.E., Vargha-Khadem, F., Watkins, K.E., Monaco, A.P., & Pembrey, E. (1998) Localisation of a gene implicated in a severe speech and language disorder. *Nature-Genetics*, 18, 168–170.

Fleminger, J.J., Dalton, R., & Standage, K.F. (1977) Age as a factor in the handedness of adults. *Neuropsychologia*, 15, 471–473.

Flynn, J.M., & Boder, E. (1991) Clinical and electrophysiological correlates of dysphonetic and dyseidetic dyslexia. In J.F. Stein (Ed.), *Vision and Visual Dyslexia, Vol. 13: Vision and Visual Dysfunction*. London: Macmillan.

Flynn, J.M., & Deering, W.M. (1989) Subtypes of dyslexia: Investigation of Boder's system using qualitative neurophysiology. *Developmental Medicine and Child Neurology*, 31, 215–223.

Fortey, R. (1998) *Life: An Unauthorised Biography*. London: HarperCollins. [Original work published 1997]

Foundas, A.L., Eure, K.F., Luevano, L.F., & Weinberger, D.R. (1998) MRI asymmetries of Broca's area: The pars triangularis and pars opercularis. *Brain and Language*, 64, 282–296.

Foundas, A.L., Falilhaber, J.R., Kulynych, J.J., Browning, C.A., & Weinberger, D.R. (1999) Hemispheric and sex linked differences in Sylvian fissure morphology: A quantitative approach using volumetric magnetic resonance imaging. *Neuropsychiatry, Neuropsychology and Behavioral Neurology*, 12, 1–10.

Foundas, A.L., Hong, K., Leonard, C.M., & Heilman, K.M. (1998) Hand preference and MRI asymmetries of the central sulcus. *Neuropsychiatry, Neuropsychology, and Behavioral Neurology*, 11, 65–71.

Fouts, R., & Mills, S. (1997) *Next of Kin: What My Conversations with Chimpanzees have Taught Me About Intelligence, Compassion and Being Human*. London: Michael Joseph.

Frackowiak, R.S.J. (1994) Functional mapping of verbal memory and language. *Trends in Neurosciences*, 17, 109–115.

Frackowiak, R.S.J. (1997) The cerebral basis of functional recovery. In R.S.J. Frackowiak, K.J. Friston, C.D. Frith, R.J. Dolan, & J.C. Mazziotta (Eds.), *Human Brain Function* (pp 275–299). New York: Academic Press.

Fried, I., Mateer, C., Ojemann, G., Wohns, R., & Fedio, P. (1982) Organization of visuospatial functions in human cortex: Evidence from electrical stimulation. *Brain*, 105, 349–371.

Friedman, H., & Davis, M. (1938) Left-handedness in parrots. *Auk*, 55, 478–480.

Frith, C.D. (1992) *The Cognitive Neuropsychology of Schizophrenia*. Hove, UK: Lawrence Erlbaum Associates Ltd.

Frith, C.D., & Frith, U. (1991) Elective affinities in schizophrenia and childhood autism. In P. Bebbington (Ed.), *Social Psychiatry: Theory, Methodology and Practice*. New Brunswick, NJ: Transactions Press.

Frith, U. (1989) *Autism: Explaining the Enigma*. Oxford: Blackwell.

Frith, U. (1991) *Autism and Asperger Syndrome*. Cambridge: Cambridge University Press.

Fudin, R., Renninger, L., Lembessis, E., & Hirshon, J. (1993) Sinistrality and reduced longevity: Reichlers' 1979 data on baseball players do not indicate a relationship. *Perceptual and Motor Skills*, 76, 171–182.

Fukuzako, H., Kodama, S., Fukuzako, T., Yanada, K, Hokazono, Y., Ueyama, K., Hashiguchi, K., Takenouchi, K., Takigawa, M., Takeuchi, K., & Manchanda, S. (1995)

Shortening of the hippocampal-formation in first episode schizophrenic patients. *Psychiatry and Clinical Neurosciences*, 49, 157–161.

Galaburda, A., Corsiglia, J., Rosen, G.D., & Sherman, G.F. (1987) *Planum temporale* asymmetry, reappraisal since Geschwind and Levitsky. *Neuropsychologia*, 25, 853–868.

Gallagher, H.L., Happé, F., Brunswick, N., Fletcher, P.C., Frith, U., & Frith, C.D. (2000) Reading the mind in cartoons and stories: An fMRI study of "theory of mind" in verbal and nonverbal tasks. *Neuropsychologia*, 38, 11–21.

Gannon, P.J., Holloway, R.L., Broadfield, D.C., & Braun, A.R. (1998) Asymmetry of chimpanzee planum temporale: Humanlike pattern of Wernicke's brain language area homolog. *Science*, 279, 220–222.

Gardner, M. (1967) *The ambidextrous universe*. London: Allen Lane.

Gathercole, S.E., & Baddeley, A.D. (1990) The role of phonological memory in vocabulary acquisition: A study of young children learning new names. *British Journal of Psychology*, 81, 439–454.

Gayan, J., Smith, S.D., Cherny, S.S., Cardon, L.R., Fulker, D.W., Brower, A.M., Olson, R.K., Pennington, B.F., & DeFries, J.C. (1999) Quantitative-trait locus for specific language and reading deficits on chromosome 6p. *American Journal of Human Genetics*, 64, 157–164.

Gazzaniga, M.S. (1995) Consciousness and the cerebral hemispheres. In M.S. Gazzaniga (Ed.). *The Cognitive Neurosciences* (pp 1391–1400). Cambridge, MA: MIT Bradford.

Geffen, G., & Caudrey, D. (1981) Reliability and validity of the dichotic monitoring test for language laterality. *Neuropsychologia*, 19, 413–423.

Geschwind, N. (1965) Disconnexian syndromes in animals and man. *Brain*, 88, 237–294 (Part I), 585–644 (Part II).

Geschwind, N., & Galaburda, A.M. (1985a) Cerebral lateralization. Biological mechanisms, associations and pathology I: A hypothesis and a program for research. *Archives of Neurology*, 42, 428–458.

Geschwind, N., & Galaburda, A.M. (1985b) Cerebral lateralization. Biological mechanisms, associations and pathology II: A hypothesis and a program for research. *Archives of Neurology*, 42, 521–552.

Geschwind, N., & Galaburda, A.M. (1985c) Cerebral lateralization. Biological mechanisms, associations and pathology III: A hypothesis and a program for research. *Archives of Neurology*, 42, 634–654.

Geschwind, N., & Levitsky, W. (1968) Human brain: Left right asymmetries in temporal speech region. *Science*, 161, 186–187.

Gesell, A., & Ames, L.B. (1947) The development of handedness. *Journal of Genetic Psychology*, 70, 155–176.

Ghent, L. (1961) Developmental changes in tactual thresholds on dominant and non-dominant sides. *Journal of Comparative and Physiological Psychology*, 54, 670–673.

Gibson, J.B. (1973) Intelligence and handedness. *Nature, Lond.*, 243, 482.

Gilbert, A.N., & Wysocki, C.J. (1992) Hand preference and age in the United States. *Neuropsychologia*, 30, 601–608.

Gillberg, C. (1991) Clinical and neurobiological aspects of Asperger syndrome in six family studies, In U. Frith (Ed.), *Autism and Asperger Syndrome* (pp 122–146). Cambridge: Cambridge University Press.

Gillberg, C., Gillberg, I.C., & Steffenburg, S. (1992) Siblings and parents of children with autism: A controlled population based study. *Developmental Medicine and Child Neurology*, 34, 389–398.

Gillies, S.M., MacSweeney, D.A., & Zangwill, O.L. (1960) A note on some unusual handedness patterns. *Quarterly Journal of Experimental Psychology*, 12, 113–116.

Gloning, K. (1977) Handedness and aphasia. *Neuropsychologia*, 15, 355–358.

Gloning, K., & Quatember, R. (1966) Statistical evidence of neuropsychological syndromes in left-handed and ambidextrous patients. *Cortex*, 2, 484–488.

Goodglass, H., & Quadfasel, F.A. (1954) Language laterality in left-handed aphasics. *Brain*, 77, 521–548.

Gopnik, M., & Crago, M.B. (1991) Familial aggregation of a developmental language disorder. *Cognition*, 29, 1–50.

Gordon, H. (1921) Left handedness, and mirror-writing, especially among defective children. *Brain*, 43, 313–368.

Gottesman, I.I. (1991) *Schizophrenia Genesis: The Origins of Madness*. New York: W.H. Freeman.

Gottesman, I.I., & Bertelsen, A. (1989) Confirming unexpressed genotype for schizophrenia. *Archives of General Psychiatry*, 46, 867–872.

Gottesman, I.I., & Shields, J. (1972) *Schizophrenia and Genetics: A Twin Study Vantage Point*. New York: Academic Press.

Goulandris, N.K., & Snowling, M. (1991) Visual memory deficits: A plausible cause of developmental dyslexia? Evidence from a single case study. *Cognitive Neuropsychology*, 8, 127–154.

Govind, C.K. (1989) Asymmetry of lobster claws. *American Scientist*, 77, 468–474.

Graves, R., Goodglass, H., & Landis, T. (1982) Mouth asymmetry during spontaneous speech. *Neuropsychologia*, 20, 371–381.

Gray, J.A., Feldon, J., Rawlins, J.N.P., Hemsley, D.R., & Smith, A.D. (1991) The neuropsychology of schizophrenia. *Behavioral and Brain Sciences*, 14, 1–84.

Gray, R., Hentschke, R., Isaac, S., Mead, R., Ozturk, A., Rieley, P. Smale, K., & Stern, R. (1971) Sampling variation of reported results. *Nature, Lond.*, 234, 230–231.

Green, M.F. (1997) What is atypical about atypical handedness in schizophrenia? *Cognitive Neuropsychiatry*, 2, 216–218.

Grigorenko, E.L., Wood, F.B., Meyer, M.S., Hart, L.A., Speed, W.C., Shuster, A., & Pauls, D.L. (1997) Susceptibility loci for distinct components of developmental dyslexia on chromosomes 6 and 15. *American Journal of Human Genetics*, 60, 27–39.

Gur, R.E. (1977) Motoric laterality imbalance in schizophrenia: A possible concomitant of left hemispheric dysfunction. *Archives of General Psychiatry*, 34, 33–37.

Haaland, K.Y., Harrington, D.L., & Knight, R.T. (2000) Neural representation of skilled movement. *Brain*, 123, 2306–2313.

Habib, M., Robichon, F., Levrier, O., Khahil, R., & Salamon, G. (1995) Diverging asymmetries of temporo-parietal cortical areas: A reappraisal of Geschwind/Galaburda theory. *Brain and Language*, 48, 238–258.

Hallgren, B. (1950) Specific dyslexia: A clinical and genetic study. *Acta Psychiatrica et Neurologica Scandinavia*, Suppl. 65, 1–287.

Halpern, D.F., & Coren, S. (1988) Do right-handers live longer? *Nature*, 333, 213.

Halpern, D.F., & Coren, S. (1990) Laterality and longevity: Is left-handedness associated with a younger age at death? In S. Coren (Ed.), *Left-handedness: Behavioral Implications and Anomalies* (pp 509–545). Amsterdam: North-Holland.

Hammil, D., & Irwin, O.C. (1966) IQ differences of right and left spastic hemiplegic children. *Perceptual and Motor Skills*, 22, 193–194.

Hanley, J.R., & Gard, F. (1995) A dissociation between developmental surface dyslexia and phonological dyslexia in two undergraduates. *Neuropsychologia*, 33, 909–914.

Hardyck, C., Goldman, R., & Petrinovich, L. (1975) Handedness and sex, race and age. *Human Biology*, 47, 369–375.

Harm, M.W., & Seidenberg, M.S. (1999) Phonology, reading acquisition and dyslexia: Insights from connectionist models. *Psychological Review*, 106, 491–528.

Harris, L.J. (1980a) Left handedness: Early theories, facts and fancies. In J. Herron (Ed.), *Neuropsychology of left handedness* (pp 3–78). New York: Academic Press.

Harris, L.J. (1980b) Which hand is the "eye" of the blind? A new look at an old question. In J. Herron (Ed.), *Neuropsychology of left handedness* (pp 303–329). New York: Academic Press.

Harris, L.J. (1989) Footedness in parrots: Three centuries of research, theory and mere surmise. *Canadian Journal of Psychology*, 43, 369–396.

Harris, L.J. (1991) Cerebral control for speech in right-handers and left-handers: An analysis of the views of Paul Broca, his contemporaries and his successors. *Brain and Language*, 40, 1–50.

Harshman, R.A., Hampson, E., & Berenbaum, S.A. (1983) Individual differences in cognitive abilities and brain organization, Part I: Sex and handedness differences in ability. *Canadian Journal of Psychology*, 37, 144–192.

Healey, J.M., Liederman, J., & Geschwind, N. (1986) Handedness is not a unidimensional trait. *Cortex*, 22, 33–53.

Hécaen, H. (1983) Acquired aphasia in children: Revisited. *Neuropsychologia*, 21, 581–587.

Hécaen, H., & Ajuriaguerra, J. (1964) *Left Handedness: Manual Superiority, and Cerebral Dominance*. New York: Grune & Stratton.

Hécaen, H., & Piercy, M. (1956) Paroxysmal dysphasia and the problem of cerebral dominance. *Journal of Neurology, Neurosurgery and Psychiatry*, 19, 194–201.

Hegstrom, R.A., & Kondepudi, D.K. (1990) The handedness of the universe. *Scientific American*, 262, January, 98–105.

Hellige, J.B. (1993) *Cerebral Hemisphere Asymmetry: Method, Theory and Application*. New York: Praeger.

Hepper, P.G., Shahidullah, S., & White, R. (1991) Handedness in the human fetus. *Neuropsychologia*, 29, 1107–1111.

Hicks, R.A., Johnson, C., Cuevas, T., Deharo, D., & Bautista, J. (1994) Do right-handers live longer? An updated assessment of the baseball player data. *Perceptual and Motor Skills*, 78, 1243–1247.

Hieronymous, A.N., Lindquist, E.F., & France, N. (1991) *Richmond Tests of Basic Skills*. Windsor: NFER-Nelson.

Hinshelwood, J. (1917) *Congenital Word-Blindness*. London: H.K. Lewis.

Hoadley, M.F., & Pearson, K. (1929) On measurement of the internal diameter of the skull in relation: 1. To the prediction of its capacity, II. To the "pre-eminence" of the left hemisphere. *Biometrika*, 21, 85–123.

Hochberg, F.H., & LeMay, M. (1975) Arteriographic correlates of handedness. *Neurology*, 25, 218–222.

Hoffman, R.E. (2001) Editorial: Language processing and hallucinated "voices": Insights from transcranial magnetic stimulation. *Cognitive Neuropsychiatry*, 6, 1–6.

Holloway, R.L. (1974) The casts of fossil hominid brains. *Scientific American*, 231(1), July, 106–115.

Holloway, R.L., & LaCoste-Lareymondie, M.C. de (1982) Brain endocast asymmetry in pongids and hominids: Some preliminary findings on the paleontology of cerebral dominance. *American Journal of Physical Anthropology*, 58, 101–110.

Hori, M. (1993) Frequency-dependent natural selection in the handedness of scale-eating cichlid fish. *Science*, 260, 216–219.

Horn, G., Rose, S.P.R., & Bateson, P.P.G. (1973) Monocular imprinting and regional incorporation of tritiated uracil into the brains of intact and "split-brain" chicks. *Brain Research*, 56, 227–237.

Hosokawa, S., Tsuji, S., Uozumi, T., Matsunaga, K., Toda, K., & Ota, S. (1996) Ipsilateral hemiplegia caused by right internal capsule and thalamic hemorrhage: Demonstration of predominant ipsilateral innervations of motor and sensory systems by MRI, MEP and SEP. *Neurology*, 46, 1146–1149.

Howlin, P., Mawhood, L., & Rutter, M. (2000) Autism and developmental receptive language disorder, a follow-up comparison in early adult life. II Social, behavioural and psychiatric outcomes. *Journal of Child Psychology and Psychiatry*, 41, 561–578.

Hubbard, J.L. (1971) Handedness not a function of birth order. *Nature*, 232, 276–277.

Hudson, P.T.W. (1975) The genetics of handedness – a reply to Levy and Nagylaki. *Neuropsychologia*, 13, 331–339.

Hugdahl, K. (1988) *Handbook of Dichotic Listening: Theory, Methods and Research.* Chichester: John Wiley.

Humphrey, M.E. (1951) Consistency of hand usage. *British Journal of Educational Psychology*, 21, 214–225.

Humphrey, M.E., & Zangwill, O.L. (1952) Dysphasia in left-handed patients with unilateral brain lesions. *Journal of Neurology, Neurosurgery and Psychiatry*, 15, 184–193.

Hyatt, B.A., & Yost, H.J. (1998) The left-right coordinator: The role of Vgl in organizing left-right axis formation. *Cell*, 93, 37–46.

Ingram, D. (1975) Motor asymmetries in young children. *Neuropsychologia*, 13, 95–102.

Ingram, T.T.S. (1959a) Specific developmental disorders of speech in childhood. *Brain*, 82, 450–467.

Ingram, T.T.S. (1959b) A description and classification of the common disorders of speech in children. *Archives of Disease in Childhood*, 34, 444–455.

Jablensky, A., Sartorius, N., Ernberg, G., Anker, M., Korten, A., Cooper, J.E., Day, R., & Bertelsen, A. (1992) Schizophrenia: Manifestations, incidence and course in different cultures. A World Health Organization ten country study. *Psychological Medicine*, Monograph Supplement, 20.

Jäncke, L., Schlaug, G., Huang, Y., & Steinmetz, H. (1994) Asymmetry of the planum parietale. *Neuroreport*, 5, 1161–1163.

Jantz, R.L., Fohl, F.H., & Zahler, J.W. (1979) Finger ridge-counts and handedness. *Human Biology*, 51, 91–99.

Johnson, D., & Myklebust, H. (1967) *Learning Disabilities: Educational Principles and Practices.* New York: Grune & Stratton.

Johnstone, E.C., Crow, T.J., Frith, C.D., Husband, J., & Kreel, L. (1976) Cerebral ventricular size and cognitive impairment in chronic schizophrenia. *Lancet*, 2, 924–926.

Johnstone, E.C., Owens, D.G.C., Crow, T.J., Frith, C.D., Alexandropolis, K., Bydder, G., & Colter, N. (1989) Temporal lobe structure as determined by nuclear magnetic resonance in schizophrenia and bipolar affective disorder. *Journal of Neurology, Neurosurgery and Psychiatry*, 52, 736–741.

Johnstone, J., Galin, D., & Herron, J. (1979) Choice of handedness measures in studies of hemisphere specialization. *International Journal of Neuroscience*, 9, 71–80.

Jones, P., Rodgers, B., Murray, R., & Marmot, M. (1994) Child developmental risk factors for adult schizophrenia in the British 1946 birth cohort. *Lancet*, 344, 1398–1402.

Jordan, H.E. (1911) The inheritance of left-handedness. *American Breeders Magazine*, 2, 19–29, 113–124.

Jordan, H.E. (1914) Hereditary left-handedness, with a note on twinning (Study I11). *Journal of Genetics*, 4, 67–81.

Jorde, L.B., Hasstedt, S.J., Ritvo, E.R., Mason-Brothers, A., Freeman, B.J., Pingree, C., McMahon, W.M., Peterson, B., Jenson, W.R., & Moll, A. (1991) Complex segregation analyses of autism. *American Journal of Human Genetics*, 49, 932–938.

Jorm, A.F. (1983) Specific reading retardation and working memory: A review. *British Journal of Psychology*, 74, 311–342.

Kanner, L. (1943) Autistic disturbances of affective contact. *Nervous Child*, 2, 217–250.

Kang, Y., & Harris, L.J. (1996) Accuracy of college students' reports of parental handedness. *Laterality*, 1, 269–279.

Karpinos, B.D., & Grossman, H.A. (1953) Prevalence of left-handedness among selective service registrants. *Human Biology*, 25, 36–49.

Keeley, L.H. (1977) The functions of paleolithic flint tools. *Scientific American*, 237(5), 108–126.

Kilshaw, D., & Annett, M. (1983) Right and left-hand skill I: Effects of age, sex and hand preference showing superior skill in left-handers. *British Journal of Psychology*, 74, 253–268.

Kim, S.-G., Ashe, J., Hendrich, K., Ellerman, J.M., Merkle, H., Uğurbil, K., & Georgopoulos, A.P. (1993) Functional magnetic resonance imaging of motor cortex: Hemispheric asymmetry and handedness. *Science*, 261, 615–617.

Kimura, D. (1961) Cerebral dominance and the perception of verbal stimuli. *Canadian Journal of Psychology*, 15, 166–171.

Kimura, D. (1964) Left-right differences in the perception of melodies. *Quarterly Journal of Experimental Psychology*, 16, 355–358.

Kimura, D. (1973a) Manual activity during speaking. I. Right handers. *Neuropsychologia*, 11, 45–50.

Kimura, D. (1973b) Manual activity during speaking. II. Left handers. *Neuropsychologia*, 11, 51–55.

Kimura, D. (1973c) The asymmetry of the human brain. *Scientific American*, 228, March, 70–78.

Kimura, D. (1977) Acquisition of a motor skill after left hemisphere damage. *Brain*, 100, 527–542.

Kimura, D. (1993) *Neuromotor Mechanisms in Human Communication*. Oxford: Oxford University Press.

Klar, A.J.S. (1996) A single locus, RGHT, specifies preference for hand utilization in humans. *Cold Spring Harbor Symposia on Quantitative Biology*, 61, 59–65.

Klicpera, C., & Gasteiger-Klicpera, B. (1994) Linkshandigeit und legasthenie: Kein beleg fur die rechtsverchiebungstheorie bei Wiener kindern, aber hinweise auf verzerrungen bei der auswahl von kindern fur fordermassnahmen. *Paediatrie und Paedologie*, 29, 11–15.

Knecht, S., Dräger, B., Deppe, M., Bobe, L., Lohmann, H., Flöel, A., Ringelstein, E.-B., & Henningsen, H., (2000) Handedness and hemispheric language dominance in healthy humans. *Brain*, 123, 2512–2518.

Knox, C., & Kimura, D. (1970) Cerebral processing of nonverbal sounds in boys and girls. *Neuropsychologia*, 8, 227–237.

Kocel, K.M. (1977) Cognitive abilities: Handedness, familial sinistrality and sex. *Annals of the New York Academy of Sciences*, 299, 233–243.

Kolb, B., & Milner, B. (1981) Performance of complex arm and facial movements after focal brain lesions. *Neuropsychologia*, 19, 491–503.

Kolb, B., & Whishaw, I.Q. (1996) *Fundamentals of human neuropsychology* (4th ed.). San Francisco: Freeman.

Kolvin, I. (1971) Studies in the childhood psychoses. I–VI. *British Journal of Psychiatry*, 118, 381–384, 385–395, 396–402, 403–406, 407–414, 415–419.

Komai, T., & Fukuoka, G. (1934) A study of the frequency of left-handedness and left-footedness among Japanese school children. *Human Biology*, 6, 33–42.

Kramer, M.A., Albrecht, S., & Miller, R.A. (1985) Higher frequency of left-breast cancer: A possible explanation. *Perceptual and Motor Skills*, 61, 583–588.

Kringlen, E., & Cramer, G. (1989) Offspring of monozygotic twins discordant for schizophrenia. *Archives of General Psychiatry*, 46, 873–877.

Kuhn, T.S. (1970) *The Structure of Scientific Revolutions* (2nd ed.). Chicago: University of Chicago Press.

Kurthen, M., Helmstaedter, C., Linke, D.B., Hufnagel, A., Elger, C.E., & Schramm, J. (1994) Quantitative and qualitative evaluation of patterns of cerebral language dominance. *Brain and Language*, 46, 536–564.

Lackner, J.R., & Teuber, H.L. (1973) Alterations in auditory fusion thresholds after cerebral injury in man. *Neuropsychologia*, 11, 409–415.

Laguitton, V., Demany, L., Semal, C., & Liégeois-Chavvel, C. (1998) Pitch perception: A difference between right- and left-handers. *Neuropsychologia*, 36, 201–207.

Lake, D.A., & Bryden, M.P. (1976) Handedness and sex differences in hemispheric asymmetry. *Brain and Language*, 3, 266–282.

Laland, K.N., Kumm, J., Van Horn, J.D., & Feldman, M.W. (1995) A gene-culture model of human handedness. *Behavior Genetics*, 25, 433–445.

Langdon, D., & Warrington, E.K. (2000) The role of the left hemisphere in verbal and spatial reasoning tasks. *Cortex*, 36, 691–702.

Layton, W.M., Jr. (1976) Random determination of a developmental process. *Journal of Heredity*, 67, 336–338.

Leask, S.J., & Crow, T.J. (1997) How far does the brain lateralize?: An unbiased method for determining the optimum degree of hemispheric specialization. *Neuropsychologia*, 35, 1381–1387.

Lehman, R.A.W. (1978) The handedness of rhesus monkeys. I. Distribution. *Neuropsychologia*, 16, 33–42.

Leiber, L., & Axelrod, S. (1981) Intra-familial learning is only a minor factor in manifest handedness. *Neuropsychologia*, 19, 273–288.

Leidy, L.E. (1990) Early age of menopause among left-handed women. *Obstetrics and Gynaecology*, 76, 1111–1114.

LeMay, M. (1977) Asymmetries of the skull and handedness: Phrenology revisited. *Journal of the Neurological Sciences*, 32, 243–253.

LeMay, M., Billig, M.S., & Geschwind, N. (1982) Asymmetries of the brains and skulls of nonhuman primates. In E. Armstrong & D. Falk (Eds.), *Primate Brain Evolution: Methods and Concepts* (pp 263–277). New York: Academic Press.

LeMay, M., & Culebras, A. (1972) Human brain morphologic differences in the hemispheres demonstrable by carotid angiography. *New England Journal of Medicine*, 287, 168–170.

Lenneberg, E.H. (1962) Understanding language without the ability to speak. *Journal of Abnormal and Social Psychology*, 65, 419–25.

Lenneberg, E.H. (1967) *Biological Foundations of Language*. New York: Wiley.

Levy, J. (1969) Possible basis for the evolution of lateral specialization of the human brain. *Nature, Lond.*, 224, 614–615.

Levy, J., & Nagylaki, T. (1972) A model for the genetics of handedness. *Genetics*, 72, 117–128.

Levy, J., Trevarthen, C., & Sperry, R.W. (1972) Perception of bilateral chimeric figures following hemispheric deconnexion. *Brain*, 95, 61–78.

Lewis, R.S., & Harris, L.J. (1990) Handedness, sex and spatial ability. In S. Coren (Ed.), *Left-handedness: Behavioral Implications and Anomalies* (pp 319–341). Amsterdam: North-Holland.

Liberman, A.M. (1989) Reading is hard just because listening is easy. In C. von Euler, I. Lundberg, & G. Lennerstrand (Eds.), *Brain and Reading* (pp 197–205). London: Macmillan.

Liberman, A.M., Cooper, F.S., Shankweiler, D.S., & Studdert-Kennedy, M. (1967) Perception of the speech code. *Psychological Review*, 74, 431–461.

Liberman, A.M., & Mattingley, E.G. (1985) The motor theory of speech perception revised. *Cognition*, 21, 1–36.

Liberman, I.Y. (1989) Phonology and beginning reading revisited. In C. von Euler, I. Lundberg, & G. Lennerstrand (Eds.), *Brain and Reading* (pp 207–220). London: Macmillan.

Lieberman, P. (1998) *Eve Spoke: Human Language and Human Evolution*. London: Picador.

Loberg, E.M., Hugdahl, K., & Green, M.F. (1999) Hemispheric asymmetry in schizophrenia: A "dual deficits" model. *Biological Psychiatry*, 45, 76–81.

Loehlin, J.C., & Nichols, R.C. (1976) *Heredity, Environment and Personality*. Austin, TX: University of Texas Press.

Loring, D.W., Meador, K.J., Lee, G.P., Murro, A.M., Smith, J.R., Flanigin, H.F., Gallagher, B.B., & King, D.W. (1990) Cerebral language lateralization: Evidence from intracarotid amobarbital testing. *Neuropsychologia*, 28, 831–838.

Luchins, D.J., Weinberger, D.R., & Wyatt, R.J. (1979) Schizophrenia: Evidence of a subgroup with reversed cerebral asymmetry. *Archives of General Psychiatry*, 36, 1309–1311.

Ludwig, M.E. (1939) Beitrag zur frage der bedeutung der unterwertigen hemisphare. *Zeistschrift Fuer die Gesamte Neurologie und Psychiatrie*, 164, 735–747.

Luria, A.R. (1970) *Traumatic Aphasia*. The Hague: Mouton (originally published 1947).

Mackintosh, N.J. (1998) *IQ and Human Intelligence*. Oxford: Oxford University Press.

MacNeilage, P.F., Studdert-Kennedy, M.G., & Lindblom, B. (1987) Primate handedness reconsidered. *Behavioral and Brian Sciences*, 10, 247–303.

Maier, M., Ron, M.A., Barker, G.J., & Tofts, P.S. (1995) Proton magnetic resonance spectroscopy: An *in vivo* method of estimating hippocampal neuronal depletion in schizophrenia. *Psychological Medicine*, 25, 1201–1209.

Manis, F.R., Seidenberg, M.S., Doi, L.M., McBride-Chang, C., & Petersen, A. (1996) On the basis of two subtypes of developmental dyslexia. *Cognition*, 58, 157–195.

Marchant, L.F., & McGrew, W.C. (1996) Laterality of limb function in wild chimpanzees of Gombe National Park: Comprehensive study of spontaneous activity. *Journal of Human Evolution*, 30, 427–443.

Marchant, L.F., McGrew, W.C., & Eibl-Eibesfeldt, I. (1995) Is human handedness universal? Ethological analyses from three traditional cultures. *Ethology*, 101, 239–258.

Marrion, L.V. (1986) Writing hand differences in Kwakiutls and Caucasians. *Perceptual and Motor Skills*, 62, 760–762.

Marshall, J.C., & Newcombe, F. (1973) Patterns of paralexia: A psycholinguistic approach. *Journal of Psycholinguistic Research*, 2, 175–199.

Mason, S. (1991) Origins of the handedness of biological molecules. In G.R. Bock & J. Marsh (Eds.), *Biological Asymmetry and Handedness* (pp 3–10). Chichester: John Wiley.

Mateer, C.A. (1983) Motor and perceptual functions of the left hemisphere and their interaction. In S.J. Segalowitz (Ed.), *Language Functions and Brain Organization* (pp 145–170). New York: Academic Press.

Mateer, C.A., & Dodrill, C.B. (1983) Neuropsychological and linguistic correlates of atypical language lateralisation: Evidence from sodium amytal studies. *Human Neurobiology*, 2, 135–142.

Mawhood, L., Howlin, P., & Rutter, M. (2000) Autism and developmental receptive language disorder – a comparative follow-up in early adult life: I. Cognitive and language outcomes. *Journal of Child Psychology and Psychiatry*, 41, 547–559.

Maynard-Smith, J., & Szathmáry, E. (1995) *The Major Transitions of Evolution*. Oxford: W.H. Freeman.

McCarthy, R.A., & Warrington, E.K. (1990) *Cognitive Neuropsychology: A Clinical Introduction*. London: Academic Press.

McGee, M.G., & Cozad, T. (1980) Population genetic analysis of human hand preference: Evidence for generation differences, familial resemblance and maternal effects. *Behavior Genetics*, 10, 263–275.

McGrew, W.C., & Marchant, L.F. (1997) On the other hand: Current issues in and meta-analysis of the behavioral laterality of hand function in nonhuman primates. *Yearbook of Physical Anthropology*, 40, 201–232.

McGuire, P.K., Syed, G.M.S., & Murray, R.M. (1993) Increased blood flow in Broca's area during auditory hallucinations in schizophrenia. *Lancet*, 342, 703–706.

McGuire, W.J., & McGuire, C.V. (1980) Salience of handedness in the spontaneous self-concept. *Perceptual and Motor Skills*, 50, 3–7.

McKeever, W.F., & Hunt, L.J. (1984) Failure to replicate the Scott et al. finding of reversed ear dominance in the native American Navajo. *Neuropsychologia*, 22, 539–541.

McManus, I.C. (1979) *Determinants of Laterality in Man*. Unpublished Ph.D. thesis. University of Cambridge.

McManus, I.C. (1980a) Handedness in twins: A critical review. *Neuropsychologia*, 18, 347–355.

McManus, I.C. (1980b) Left handedness and epilepsy. *Cortex*, 16, 487–491.

McManus, I.C. (1981) Handedness and birth stress. *Psychological Medicine*, 11, 485–496.

McManus, I.C. (1985a) Handedness, language dominance and aphasia: A genetic model. *Psychological Medicine*, Supplement 8.

McManus, I.C. (1985b) Right- and left-hand skill: Failure of the right shift model. *British Journal of Psychology*, 76, 1–16.

McManus, I.C. (1985c) On testing the right shift theory: A reply to Annett. *British Journal of Psychology*, 76, 31–34.

McManus, I.C. (1997) Autism and schizophrenia are not due to a single genetic locus. *Cognitive Neuropsychiatry*, 2, 226–230.

McManus, I.C., & Bryden, M.P. (1992) The genetics of handedness, cerebral dominance and lateralization. In I. Rapin & S.J. Segalowitz (Eds.), *Handbook of Neuropsychology, vol. 6: Child Neuropsychology* (pp 115–144). Amsterdam: Elsevier.

McManus, I.C., Murray, B., Doyle, K., & Baron-Cohen, S. (1992) Handedness in childhood autism shows a dissociation of skill and preference. *Cortex*, 28, 373–381.

McManus, I.C., Porac, C., Bryden, M.P., & Boucher, R. (1999) Eye-dominance, writing hand and throwing hand. *Laterality*, 4, 173–192.

McManus, I.C., Shergill, S., & Bryden, M.P. (1993) Annett's theory that individuals heterozygote for the right shift gene are intellectually advantaged: Theoretical and empirical problems. *British Journal of Psychology*, 84, 517–537.

McMeekan, E.R.L., & Lishman, W.A. (1975) Retest reliabilities and interrelationship of the Annett Hand Preference Questionnaire and the Edinburgh Handedness Inventory. *British Journal of Psychology*, 66, 53–60.

McRae, D.L., Branch, C.L., & Milner, B. (1968) The occipital horns and cerebral dominance. *Neurology*, 18, 95–98.

Meador, K.J., Loring, D.W., Lee, K., Hughes, M., Lee, G., Nichols, M., & Heilman, K. (1999) Cerebral lateralization: Relationship of language and ideomotor praxis. *Neurology*, 53, 2028–2031.

Mebert, C.J., & Michel, G.F. (1980) Handedness in artists. In J. Herron (Ed.), *Neuropsychology of Left-Handedness* (pp 273–280). New York: Academic Press.

Mehta, Z., Newcombe, F., & Damasio, H. (1987) A left hemisphere contribution to visuospatial processing. *Cortex*, 23, 447–461.

Meno, C., Saijoh, Y., Fujii, H., Ikeda, M., Yokoyama, T., Yokoyama, M., Toyoda, Y., & Hamada, H. (1996) Left-right asymmetric expression of the TGFß-family member *lefty* in mouse embryos. *Nature*, 381, 151–155.

Merrell, D.J. (1957) Dominance of eye and hand. *Human Biology*, 29, 314–328.

Michel, G.F. (1995) The handedness of Dr. Pangloss. *Current Psychology of Cognition*, 14, 575–580.

Milner, A.D. (1969) Distribution of hand preferences in monkeys. *Neuropsychologia*, 7, 375–377.

Milner, B. (1962) Laterality effects in audition. In V.B. Mountcastle (Ed.), *Interhemispheric Relations and Cerebral Dominance*. Baltimore: Johns Hopkins. Pp 177–195.

Milner, B. (1974) Hemispheric specialization: Scope and limits. In F.O. Schmitt & F.G. Worden (Eds.), *The Neurosciences: Third Study Program* (pp 75–89). Cambridge, MA: MIT Press.

Milner, B., & Taylor, L. (1972) Right hemisphere superiority in tactile pattern-recognition after cerebral commissurotomy: Evidence of nonverbal memory. *Neuropsychologia*, 10, 1–17.

Mishkin, M., & Forgays, D.G. (1952) Word recognition as a function of retinal locus. *Journal of Experimental Psychology*, 43, 43–48.

Mittler, P. (1971) *The Study of Twins*. Harmondsworth, UK: Penguin.

Mittwoch, U. (1973) *Genetics of Sex Differentiation*. New York: Academic Press.

Mittwoch, U. (1977) To be right is to be born male. *New Scientist*, 13 January, 74–76.

Mittwoch, U., & Mahadevaiah, S. (1980) Additional growth: A link between mammalian testes, avian ovaries, gonadal asymmetry in hermaphrodites and the expression of the H-Y antigen. *Growth*, 44, 287–300.

Money, J. (1972) Studies of the function of sighting dominance. *Quarterly Journal of Experimental Psychology*, 24, 454–464.

Morgan, E. (1982) *The Aquatic Ape*. New York: Stein & Day.

Morgan, M.J. (1977) Embryology and inheritance of asymmetry. In S. Harnad, R.W. Doty, L. Goldstein, J. Jaynes, & G. Krauthamer (Eds.), *Lateralization in the Nervous System* (pp 173–194). New York: Academic Press.

Morgan, M.J., & Corballis, M.C. (1978) On the biological basis of human laterality: II. The mechanism of inheritance. *The Behavioral and Brain Sciences*, 1, 270–277.

Morley, M.E. (1957) *The Development and Disorders of Speech in Childhood*. Edinburgh: E. & S. Livingstone.

Morrisby, J.R. (1955) *Differential Test Battery*. London: National Foundation for Educational Research.

Murray, R.M. (1994) Neurodevelopmental schizophrenia: The rediscovery of dementia praecox. *British Journal of Psychiatry*, 165, Suppl. 25, 6–12.

Murray, R.M. (1996) *Developmental insanity or dementia praecox: A new perspective on an old debate*. Paper given at a meeting of the British Association of Pharmacology, Schizophrenia: New Directions and Strategies in Schizophrenia Research – the Way Forward? University of Leicester, 2 April.

Naidoo, S. (1972) *Specific Dyslexia*. London: Pitman.

Natsopoulos, D., Kiosseoglou, G., Xeromeritou, A., & Alevriadou, A. (1998) Do the hands talk on the mind's behalf? Differences in language ability between left- and right-handed children. *Brain and Language*, 64, 182–214.

Neale, M.C. (1988) Handedness in a sample of volunteer twins. *Behavior Genetics*, 18, 69–79.

Ness, A.R. (1967) A measure of asymmetry of the skulls of odontocete whales. *Journal of Zoology*, 153, 209–221.

Netley, C. (1998) Sex chromosome aneuploidy and cognitive development. *Current Psychology of Cognition*, 17, 1190–1197.

Netley, C., & Rovet, J. (1983) Relationships among brain organization, maturation rate and the development of verbal and nonverbal ability. In S.J. Segalowitz (Ed.), *Language Functions and Brain Organization* (pp 245–266). New York: Academic Press.

Newcombe, F., & Ratcliff, G. (1973) Handedness, speech lateralization and ability. *Neuropsychologia*, 11, 399–407.

Newman, H.H., Freeman, F.N., & Holzinger, K.H. (1937) *Twins: A Study of Heredity and Environment*. Chicago: University of Chicago Press.

Nicholls, M.E.R. (1996) Temporal processing asymmetries between the cerebral hemispheres: Evidence and implications. *Laterality*, 1, 97–137.

Nopola-Hemmi, J., Taipale, M., Haltia, T., Lehesjoki, A.E., Voutilainen, A., & Kere, J. (2000) Two translocations of chromosome 15q associated with dyslexia. *Journal of Medical Genetics*, 37, 771–775.

Nordeen, E.J., & Yahr, P. (1982) Hemispheric asymmetries in the behavioral and hormonal effects of sexually differentiating mammalian brain. *Science*, 218, 391–393.

Nottebohm, F. (1970) Ontogeny of bird song. *Science*, 167, 950–956.

Nottebohm, F. (1977) Asymmetries in neural control of vocalization in the canary. In S. Harnad, R.W. Doty, L. Goldstein, J. Jaynes, & G. Krauthamer (Eds.), *Lateralization in the Nervous System* (pp 23–44). New York: Academic Press.

O'Boyle, M.W., & Benbow, C.P. (1990) Handedness and its relationship to ability and talent. In S. Coren (Ed.), *Left-handedness: Behavioural Implications and Anomalies* (pp 343–372). Amsterdam: North-Holland.

O'Callaghan, M.J., Burn, Y.R., Mohay, H.A., Rogers, Y., & Tudehope, D.I. (1993) The prevalence and origins of left-hand preference in high risk infants, and its implications for intellectual, motor and behavioral performance at four and six years. *Cortex*, 29, 617–627.

O'Callaghan, M.J., Tudehope, D.I., Dugdale, A.E., Mohay, H., Burns, Y., & Cook, F. (1987) Handedness in children with birthweight below 1000g. *Lancet*, 1, 1155.

Ojemann, G.A. (1983a) Brain organization for language from the perspective of electrical stimulation mapping. *The Behavioral and Brain Sciences*, 6, 189–206.

Ojemann, G.A. (1983b) The intrahemispheric organization of human language, derived with electrical stimulation techniques. *Trends in Neurosciences*, 6, 184–189.

Ojemann, G., & Mateer, C. (1979) Human language cortex: Localization of memory, syntax and sequential motor-phoneme identification systems. *Science*, 205, 1401–1403.

Oldfield, R.C. (1971) The assessment and analysis of handedness: The Edinburgh Inventory. *Neuropsychologia*, 9, 97–113.

Orlebeke, J.F., Knol, D.L., Koopmans, J.R., Boomsma, D.I., & Bleker, O.P. (1996) Left-handedness in twins – genes or environment. *Cortex*, 32, 479–490.

Orr, K.G.D., Cannon, M., Gilvarry, C.M., Jones, R.B., & Murray, R.M. (1999) Schizophrenia patients and their first-degree relatives show an excess of mixed-handedness. *Schizophrenia Research*, 39, 167–176.

Orton, S.T. (1925) "Word blindness" in school children. *Archives of Neurology and Psychiatry*, 14, 581–615.

Orton, S.T. (1937) *Reading, Writing and Speech Problems in Children: A Presentation of Certain Types of Disorders in the Development of Language*. London: Chapman & Hall.

Osmon, D.C., Panos, J., Kautz, P., & Gandhavadi, B. (1998) Crossed aphasia in a dextral: A test of the Alexander-Annett theory of anomalous organization of brain functions. *Brain and Language*, 63, 426–438.

Palmer, R.E., & Corballis, M.C. (1996) Predicting reading ability from handedness measures. *British Journal of Psychology*, 87, 609–620.

Papçun, G., Krashen, S., Terbeek, D., Remington, R., & Harshman, R. (1974) Is the left hemisphere specialized for speech, language and/or something else? *Journal of the Acoustic Society of America*, 55, 319–327.

Parsons, B.S. (1924) *Left-handedness*. New York: Macmillan.

Passingham, R.E. (1982) *The Human Primate*. San Francisco: W.H. Freeman.

Patterson, K., Vargha-Khadem, F., & Polkey, C.E. (1989) Reading with one hemisphere. *Brain*, 112, 39–63.

Paulesu, E., Frith, U., Snowling, M., Gallagher, A., Morton, J., Frackowiak, R.S.J., & Frith, C.D. (1996) Is developmental dyslexia a disconnection syndrome? Evidence from PET scanning. *Brain*, 119, 143–157.

Pedersen, P.M., Jorgensen, H.S., Nakayama, H., Raaschou, H.O., & Olsen, T.S. (1995) Aphasia in acute stroke: Incidence, determinants and recovery. *Annals of Neurology*, 38, 659–666.

Penfield, W., & Roberts, L. (1959) *Speech and Brain Mechanisms*. Princeton, NJ: Princeton University Press.

Perelle, I.B., & Ehrman, L. (1994) An international study of human handedness: The data. *Behavior Genetics*, 24, 217–227.

Perin, D. (1983) Phonemic segmentation and spelling. *British Journal of Psychology*, 74, 129–144.

Perlstein, M.A., & Hood, P.N. (1957) Infantile spastic hemiplegia: Intelligence and age of walking and talking. *American Journal of Mental Deficiency*, 61, 534–542.

Peters, M. (1990) Subclassification of non-pathological left-handers poses problems for theories of handedness. *Neuropsychologia*, 28, 279–289.

Peters, M., & Durding, B. (1978) Handedness measured by finger tapping: A continuous variable. *Canadian Journal of Psychology*, 32, 257–261.

Peterson, G.M. (1934) Mechanisms of handedness in the rat. *Comparative Psychology Monographs*, 46.

Petty, L.K., Ornitz, E.M., Michelman, J.D., & Zimmerman, E.G. (1984) Autistic children who became schizophrenic. *Archives of General Psychiatry*, 41, 129–135.

Piaget, J. (1950) *The Psychology of Intelligence*. London: Routledge & Kegan Paul.

Pipe, M.-E. (1987) Pathological left-handedness: Is it familial? *Neuropsychologia*, 25, 571–577.

Pipe, M.-E. (1990) Mental retardation and left-handedness: Evidence and theories. In S. Coren (Ed.), *Left-handedness: Behavioral Implications and Anomalies* (pp 293–318). Amsterdam: North-Holland.

Piven, J., Wzorek, M., Landa, R., Lainhart, J., Bolton, P., Chase, G.A., & Folstein, S. (1994) Personality characteristics of the parents of autistic individuals. *Psychological Medicine*, 24, 783–795.

Poizner, H., Bellugi, U., & Klima, E.S. (1989) Sign language aphasia. In F. Boller & J. Grafman (Eds.), *Handbook of Neuropsychology, Vol. 2* (pp 157–172). Amsterdam: Elsevier.

Policansky, D. (1982) The asymmetry of flounders. *Scientific American*, 246(5), 96–102.

Popper, K.R. (1963) *Conjectures and Refutations: The Growth of Scientific Knowledge*. London: Routledge & Kegan Paul.

Porac, C., & Coren, S. (1976) The dominant eye. *Psychological Bulletin*, 33, 880–897.

Porac, C., & Coren, S. (1979) A test of the validity of offsprings' report of parental handedness. *Perceptual and Motor Skills*, 49, 227–231.

Porac, C., & Coren, S. (1981) *Lateral Preferences and Human Behavior*. New York: Springer Verlag.

Porac, C., Coren, S., & Duncan, P. (1980) Life-span age trends in laterality. *Journal of Gerontology*, 35, 715–721.

Porac, C., Coren, S., Steiger, J.H., & Duncan, P. (1980) Human laterality: A multi-dimensional approach. *Canadian Journal of Psychology*, 34, 91–96.

Posner, M.I., & Raichle, M.E. (1994) *Images of Mind*. New York: Scientific American Library.

Previc, F.H. (1991) A general theory concerning the prenatal origins of cerebral lateralization in humans. *Psychological Review*, 98, 299–334.

Price, C.J. (1997) Functional anatomy of reading. In R.S.J. Frackowiak, K.J. Friston, C.D. Frith, R.J. Dolan, & J.C. Mazziotta (Eds.), *Human Brain Function* (pp 301–328). New York: Academic Press.

Price, C.J., Wise, R.J.S., Warburton, E.A., Moore, C.J., Howard, D., Patterson, K., Frackowiak, R.S.J., & Friston, K.J. (1996) Hearing and saying: The functional neuro-anatomy of auditory word processing. *Brain*, 119, 919–931.

Prior, M.R., & Bradshaw, J.L. (1979) Hemisphere functioning in autistic children. *Cortex*, 15, 73–81.

Provins, K.A. (1997) Handedness and speech: A critical reappraisal of the role of genetic and environmental factors in the cerebral lateralization of functions. *Psychological Review*, 104, 554–571.

Provins, K.A., & Glencross, D.J. (1968) Handwriting, typewriting and handedness. *Quarterly Journal of Experimental Psychology*, 20, 282–289.

Pujol, J., Delis, J., Losilla, J.M., & Capdevila, A. (1999) Cerebral lateralization of language in normal left-handed people studied by functional MRI. *Neurology*, 52, 1038–1043.

Ramaley, F. (1913) Inheritance of left-handedness. *The American Naturalist*, 47, 730–738.

Ramsay, D.S. (1980) Beginnings of bimanual handedness and speech in infants. *Infant Behavior and Development*, 3, 67–77.

Rasmussen, T., & Milner, B. (1975) Clinical and surgical studies of the cerebral speech areas in man. In K.J. Zulch, O. Creutzfeldt, & G.C. Galbraith (Eds.), *Otfrid Foerster Symposium on Cerebral Localization*. Berlin: Springer Verlag.

Rasmussen, T., & Milner, B. (1977) The role of early left brain injury in determining lateralization of cerebral speech functions. *Annals of the New York Academy of Sciences*, 299, 355–369.

Ratcliff, G., Dila, C., Taylor, L., & Milner, B. (1980) The morphological asymmetry of the hemispheres and cerebral dominance for speech: A possible relationship. *Brain and Language*, 11, 87–98.

Raven, J.C. (1958a) *Mill Hill Vocabulary Scale* (2nd ed.). London: H.K. Lewis.

Raven, J.C. (1958b) *Standard Progressive Matrices* (2nd ed.). London: H.K. Lewis.

Raven, J.C. (1963) *Guide to Using the Coloured Progressive Matrices*. London: H.K. Lewis.

Reed, J.C., & Reitan, R.M. (1969) Verbal and performance differences among brain-injured children with lateralized motor deficits. *Perceptual and Motor Skills*, 29, 747–752.

Reiss, M., & Reiss, G. (1997) Ocular dominance: Some family data. *Laterality*, 2, 7–15.

Resch, F., Haffner, J., Parzer, P., Pfueller, U., Strehlow, U., & Zermahn-Hartung, C. (1997) Testing the hypothesis of the relationships between laterality and ability according to Annett's right-shift theory: Findings in an epidemiological sample of young adults. *British Journal of Psychology*, 88, 621–635.

Rife, D.C. (1940) Handedness with special reference to twins. *Genetics*, 25, 178–186.

Rife, D.C. (1950) An application of gene frequency analysis to the interpretation of data from twins. *Human Biology*, 22, 136–145.

Rife, D.C. (1955) Hand prints and handedness. *American Journal of Human Genetics*, 7, 170–179.

Rife, D.C. (1978) Genes and melting pots. In R.T. Osborne, C.E. Noble, & N. Weyl (Eds.), *Human Variation: The Biopsychology of Age, Race and Sex* (pp 29–48). New York: Academic Press.

Risch, N., & Pringle, G. (1985) Segregation analysis of human hand preference. *Behavior Genetics*, 15, 385–400.

Ritvo, E.R., Freeman, B.J., Mason-Brothers, A., Mo, A., & Ritvo, A.M. (1985) Concordance for the syndrome of autism in 40 pairs of afflicted twins. *American Journal of Psychiatry*, 142, 74–77.

Ritvo, E.R., Ritvo, R., Freeman, B.J., & Mason-Brothers, A. (1994) Clinical characteristics of mild autism in adults. *Comparative Psychiatry*, 35, 149–156.

Ritvo, E.R., Spence, M.A., Freeman, B.J., Mason-Brothers, A., Mo, A., & Marazita, M.L. (1985) Evidence for autosomal recessive inheritance in 46 families with multiple incidences of autism. *American Journal of Psychiatry*, 142, 187–192.

Rizzolatti, G., & Arbib, M.A. (1998) Language within our grasp. *Trends in Neurosciences*, 21, 188–194.

Roberts, L. (1969) Aphasia, apraxia and agnosia in abnormal states of cerebral dominance. In P.J. Vinken & G.W. Bruyn (Eds.), *Handbook of Clinical Neurology, Vol. 4* (pp 312–326). Amsterdam: North-Holland.

Roberts, L.D. (1974) Intelligence and handedness. *Nature*, 252, 180.

Robins, A., Lippolis, G., Bisazza, A., Vallortigara, G., & Rogers, L.J. (1998) Lateralized agonistic responses and hindlimb use in toads. *Animal Behaviour*, 56, 875–881.

Rogers, L.J., & Kaplan, G., (1996) Hand preferences and other lateral biases in rehabilitated orang-utans, *Pongo pygmaeus pygmaeus*. *Animal Behaviour*, 51, 13–25.

Ross, G., Lipper, E., & Auld, P.A.M. (1992) Hand preference, prematurity and developmental outcome at school age. *Neuropsychologia*, 30, 483–494.

Rubens, A.B. (1977) Anatomical asymmetries of human cerebral cortex. In S. Harnad, R.W. Doty, L. Goldstein, J. Jaynes, & G. Krauthamer (Eds.), *Lateralization in the Nervous System* (pp 503–516). New York: Academic Press.

Russell, W.R., & Espir, M.L.E. (1961) *Traumatic Aphasia*. Oxford: Oxford University Press.

Rutter, M. (1991) Autism as a genetic disorder. In P. McGuffin & R. Murray (Eds.), *The New Genetics of Mental Illness* (pp 223–244). London: Butterworth-Heineman.

Rutter, M. (1996) *Genetics of autism: Clinical implications*. Plenary lecture at the Joint Congress of the Association of European Psychiatrists and the Royal College of Psychiatrists, London, 8 July.

Rutter, M., Tizard, J., & Whitmore, K. (1970) *Education, Health and Behaviour*. London: Longman.

Rutter, M., & Yule, W. (1975) The concept of specific reading retardation. *Journal of Child Psychology and Psychiatry*, 16, 181–197.

Salive, M.E., Guralnik, J.M., & Glynn, R.J. (1993) Left-handedness and mortality. *American Journal of Public Health*, 83, 265–267.

Satz, P. (1972) Pathological left-handedness: An explanatory model. *Cortex*, 8, 121–135.

Satz, P. (1973) Left-handedness and early brain insult: An explanation. *Neuropsychologia*, 11, 115–117.

Satz, P., Achenbach, K., & Fennell, E. (1967) Correlations between assessed manual laterality and predicted speech laterality in a normal population. *Neuropsychologia*, 5, 295–310.

Satz, P., & Fletcher, J.M. (1987) Left-handedness and dylsexia: An old myth revisited. *Journal of Paediatric Psychology*, 12, 291–298.

Schaller, G.B. (1963) *The Mountain Gorilla: Ecology and Behavior*. Chicago: Chicago University Press.

Schonell, F.J., & Schonell, F.E. (1952) *Diagnostic and Attainment Testing: Including a Manual of Tests, Their Nature, Use, Recording and Interpretation* (2nd ed.). Edinburgh, UK: Oliver & Boyd.

Schouten, M.E. (1980) The case against a speech mode of perception. *Acta Psychologica*, 44, 71–98.

Schulte-Körne, G., Grimm, T., Nothen, M.M., Muller-Myhsok, B., Cichon, S., Vogt, I.R., Propping, P., & Remschmidt, H. (1998) Evidence for linkage of spelling disability to chromosome 15. *American Journal of Human Genetics*, 63, 279–282.

Scott, S., Hynd, G.W., Hunt, L., & Weed, W. (1979) Cerebral speech lateralization in the native American Navajo. *Neuropsychologia*, 17, 89–92.

Segalowitz, S.J., & Bryden, M.P. (1983) Individual differences in hemispheric representation of language. In S.J. Segalowitz (Ed.), *Language Functions and Brain Organization* (pp 341–372). New York: Academic Press.

Seidenberg, M.S., & McClelland J.L. (1989) A distributed, developmental model of word recognition and naming. *Psychological Review*, 96, 447–452.

Seymour, P.H.K. (1986) *Cognitive Analysis of Dyslexia*. London: Routledge & Kegan Paul.

Sham, P. (1997) Schizophrenia, autism and agnosic right shift gene theory. *Cognitive Neuropsychiatry*, 2, 219–220.

Shankweiler, D., & Studdert-Kennedy, M. (1975) A continuum of lateralization for speech perception? *Brain and Language*, 2, 212–225.

Shaywitz, S.E., Shaywitz, B.A., Pugh, K.R., Fulbright, R.K., Constable, R.T., Mencl, W.E., Shankweiler, D.P., Liberman, A.M., Skudlarski, P., Fletcher, J.M., Katz, L., Marchione, K.E., Lacadie, C., Gatenby, C., & Gore, J.C. (1998) Functional disruption in the organization of the brain for reading in dyslexia. *Proceedings of the National Academy of Sciences of the USA*, 95, 2636–2641.

Silbersweig, D.A., Stern, E., Frith, C., Cahill, C., Holmes, A., Grootoonk, S., Seaward, J., McKenna, P., Chua, S.E., Schnorr, L., Jones, T., & Frackowiak, R.S.J. (1995) Functional neuroanatomy of hallucinations in schizophrenia. *Nature*, 378, 176–179.

Silva, D.A., & Satz, P. (1979) Pathological left-handedness: Evaluation of a model. *Brain and Language*, 7, 8–16.

Singh, L.-N., Higano, S., Takahashi, S., Kurihara, N., Futura, S., Tamura, H., Shimanuki, Y., Mugikura, S., Fujii, T., Yamadori, A., Sakamoto, M., & Yamada, S. (1998) Comparison of ipsilateral activation between right and left handers: A functional MR imaging study. *Neuroscience*, 9, 1861–1866.

Smart, J.L., Jeffery, C., & Richards, B. (1980) A retrospective study of the relationship between birth history and handedness at six years. *Early Human Development*, 4, 79–88.

Smythe, P.K. (2001) *Aspects of phonological processing in sub-groups of left and right handedness*. Unpublished Ph.D. thesis, University of Leicester.

Snowling, M.J. (1981) Phonemic deficits in developmental dyslexia. *Psychological Research*, 43, 219–234.

Soper, H.V., & Satz, P. (1984) Pathological left-handedness and ambiguous handedness: A new explanatory model. *Neuropsychologia*, 22, 511–515.

Sperry, R.W. (1974) Lateral specialization in the surgically separated hemispheres. In F.O. Schmidt & F.G. Worden (Eds.), *The Neurosciences: Third Study Program* (pp 5–19). Cambridge, MA: MIT Press.

Spiegler, B.J., & Yeni-Komshian, G.H. (1983) Incidences of left-handed writing in a college population with reference to family patterns of hand preference. *Neuropsychologia*, 21, 651–659.

Springer, S.P., & Deutsch, G. (1998) *Left Brain, Right Brain*. San Francisco: W.H. Freeman.

Springer, S., & Searleman, A. (1978) Laterality in twins: The relationship between handedness and hemispheric asymmetry for speech. *Behavior Genetics*, 8, 349–357.

Stanovich, K.E. (1994) Does dyslexia exist? *Journal of Child Psychology and Psychiatry*, 35, 579–595.

Steele, J. (2000) Handedness in past human populations: Skeletal markers. *Laterality*, 5, 193–220.

Steele, J., & Mays, S. (1995) Handedness and directional asymmetry in the long bones of the human upper limb. *International Journal of Osteoarchaeology*, 5, 39–49.

Steenhuis, R.E., & Bryden, M.P. (1989) Different dimensions of hand preference that relate to skilled and unskilled activities. *Cortex*, 25, 289–304.

Steffenburg, S., Gillberg, C., Hellgren, L., Andersson, L., Gillberg, I.C., Jakobsson, G., & Bohman, M. (1989) A twin study of autism in Denmark, Finland, Iceland, Norway and Sweden. *Journal of Child Psychology and Psychiatry*, 30, 405–416.

Stein, J.F., & McAnally, K. (1995) Auditory temporal processing in developmental dyslexics. *Irish Journal of Psychology*, 16, 220–228.

Stein, J., & Walsh, V. (1997) To see but not to read: The magnocellular theory of dyslexia. *Trends in Neurosciences*, 20, 147–152.

Steinmetz, H. (1996) Structure, function and cerebral asymmetry: In vivo morphometry for the Planum temporale. *Neuroscience and Biobehavioral Reviews*, 20, 587–591.

Steinmetz, H., Herzog, A., Schlaug, G., Huang, Y., & Jäncke, L. (1995) Brain asymmetry in monozygotic twins. *Cerebral Cortex*, 5, 296–300.

Steinmetz, H., Volkman. J., Jäncke, L., & Freund, H.-J. (1991) Anatomical left–right asymmetry of language related temporal cortex is different in left- and right-handers. *Annals of Neurology*, 29, 315–319.

Stevenson, J., Graham, P., Fredman, G., & McLoughlin, V. (1987) A twin study of genetic influence on reading and spelling disability. *Journal of Child Psychology and Psychiatry*, 28, 229–247.

Stocks, P. (1933) A biometric investigation of twins and their brothers and sisters. *Annals of Eugenics*, 5, 1–55.

Strauss, E., Gaddes, W.H., & Wada, J. (1987) Performance on a free-recall verbal dichotic listening task and cerebral dominance determined by the carotid amytal test. *Neuropsychologia*, 25, 747–753.

Strauss, E., & Wada, J. (1983) Lateral preferences and cerebral speech dominance. *Cortex*, 19, 165–177.

Studdert-Kennedy, M., & Shankweiler, D. (1970) Hemispheric specialization for speech perception. *Journal of the Acoustical Society of America*, 48, 579–594.

Subirana, A. (1958) The prognosis in aphasia in relation to cerebral dominance and handedness. *Brain*, 81, 415–425.

Suddath, R.L., Christison, G.W., Torrey, E.F., Casanova, M.F., & Weinberger, D.R. (1990) Anatomical abnormalities in the brains of monozygotic twins discordant for schizophrenia. *New England Journal of Medicine*, 322, 789–794.

Super, C.M. (1981) Cross-cultural research on infancy. In H.C. Triandis & A. Heron (Eds.), *Handbook of Cross-Cultural Psychology: Developmental Psychology, Vol. 4* (pp 17–53). Boston: Allyn & Bacon.

Supp, D.M., Potter, S.S., & Brueckner, M. (2000) Molecular motors: The driving force behind mammalian left–right development. *Trends in Cell Biology*, 10, 41–45.

Szatmari, P., MacLean, J.E., Jones, M.B., Bryson, S.E., Zwaigenbaum, L., Barolucci, G., Mahoney, W.J., & Tuff, L. (2000) The familial aggregation of the lesser variant in biological and nonbiological relatives of PDD probands: A family history study. *Journal of Child Psychology and Psychiatry*, 41, 579–586.

Tallal, P., Miller, S., & Fitch, R.H. (1995) Neurobiological basis of speech: A case for the pre-eminence of temporal processing. *Irish Journal of Psychology*, 16, 194–219.

Tan, U. (1990) The left brain determines the degree of left-handedness. *International Journal of Neuroscience*, 53, 75–85.

Tanaka, S., Kanzaki, R., Yoshibayashi, M., Kamiya, T., & Sugishita, M. (1999) Dichotic listening in patients with situs inversus: Brain asymmetry and situs asymmetry. *Neuropsychologia*, 37, 869–874.

Taniguchi, M., Yoshimine, T., Cheyne, D., Kato, A., Kihara, T., Ninomiya, H., Hirata, M., Hirabuki, N., Nakamura, H., & Hayakawa, T. (1998) Neuromagnetic fields preceding unilateral movements in dextrals and sinistrals. *Neuroreport*, 9, 1497–1502.

Tanner, J.M. (1978) *Foetus into Man*. London: Open Books.

Taylor, D.C. (1969) Differential rates of cerebral maturation between sexes and between hemispheres. *Lancet*, 19 July, 140–142.

Taylor, M.A., & Amir, N. (1995) Sinister psychotics – left-handedness in schizophrenia and affective disorder. *Journal of Nervous and Mental Disease*, 183, 3–9.

Temple, C.M. (1990) Academic disciplines, handedness and immune disorders. *Neuropsychologia*, 28, 303–308.

Teng, E.L., Lee, P.-H., Yang, K.-S., & Chang, P.C. (1976) Handedness in a Chinese population: Biological, social and pathological factors. *Science*, 193, 1148–1150.

Terrace, H.S., Petitto, L.A., Sanders, R.J., & Bever, T.G. (1979) Can an ape create a sentence? *Science*, 206, 891–902.

Thyss, J. (1946) *Étude bibliographique et critique du problème des gauchers*. Unpublished M.D. thesis, Paris (cited by Zazzo, 1960).

Torgerson, J. (1950) Situs inversus, asymmetry and twinning. *American Journal of Human Genetics*, 2, 361–370.

Torrey, E.F., Bowler, A.E., Taylor, E.H., & Gottesman, I.I. (1994) *Schizophrenia and Manic-Depressive Disorder: The Biological Roots of Mental Illness as Revealed by the Landmark Study of Identical Twins.* New York: Basic Books.

Toth, N. (1985) Archaeological evidence for preferential right-handedness in the lower and middle pleistocene and its possible implications. *Journal of Human Evolution*, 14, 607–614.

Trankell, A. (1955) Aspects of genetics in psychology. *American Journal of Human Genetics*, 7, 264–276.

Travis, L.E. (1959) *Handbook of Speech Pathology.* London: Peter Owen.

Tzourio, N., Nkanga-Ngila, B., & Mazoyer, B. (1998) Left planum temporale surface correlates with functional dominance during story listening. *Neuroreport*, 9, 829–833.

Vernberg, F.J., & Costlow, J.D. (1966) Handedness in fiddler crabs (Genus UCA). *Crustaceama*, 11, 61–64.

Vernon, M.D. (1957) *Backwardness in Reading.* Cambridge: Cambridge University Press.

Volate, D.R. (1984) Differential cerebral speech lateralization in Crow Indian and Anglo children. *Neuropsychologia*, 22, 487–494.

Volkman, J., Schnitzler, A., Witte, O.W., & Freund, H.J. (1998) Handedness and asymmetry of hand representation in human motor cortex. *Journal of Neurophysiology*, 79, 2149–2154.

Von Bonin, G. (1962) Anatomical asymmetries of the cerebral hemispheres. In V.B. Mountcastle (Ed.), *Interhemispheric Relations and Cerebral Dominance* (pp 1–6). Baltimore: Johns Hopkins University Press.

Waber, D.P. (1976) Sex differences in cognition: A function of maturation rates. *Science*, 192, 572–574.

Wada, J.A., Clarke, R., & Hamm, A. (1975) Cerebral hemispheric asymmetry in humans. *Archives of Neurology*, 32, 239–246.

Wade, D.T., Hewer, R.L., David, R.M., & Enderby, P.M. (1986) Aphasia after stroke: Natural history and associated deficits. *Journal of Neurology, Neurosurgery and Psychiatry*, 49, 11–16.

Wagner, R.K., & Torgersen, J.K. (1987) The nature of phonological processing and its causal role in the acquisition of reading skills. *Psychological Bulletin*, 101, 192–212.

Walls, G.L. (1951) A theory of ocular dominance. A.M.A. *Archives of Ophthalmology*, 45, 387–412.

Warren, J.M. (1953) Handedness in the rhesus monkey. *Science*, 118, 622–623.

Warren, J.M. (1977) Handedness and cerebral dominance in monkeys. In S. Harnad, R.W. Doty, L. Goldstein, J. Jaynes, & G. Krauthamer (Eds.), *Lateralization of the Nervous System* (pp 151–172). New York: Academic Press.

Warren, J.M., Ablanalp, J.M., & Warren, H.B. (1967) The development of handedness in cats and rhesus monkeys. In H.W. Stevenson, E.H. Hess, & H.L. Rheingold (Eds.), *Early Behavior: Comparative and Developmental Approaches.* New York: Wiley.

Warren, J.M., Cornwell, P.R., Webster, W.G., & Pubols, B.H. (1972) Unilateral cortical lesions and paw preferences in cats. *Journal of Comparative and Physiological Psychology*, 81, 410–422.

Warrington, E.K. (2000) The failure of language comprehension at sentence and phrasal levels in a patient who can speak normally. *Cortex*, 36, 435–444.

Warrington, E.K., & Taylor, A.M. (1973) Contribution of the right parietal lobe to object recognition. *Cortex*, 9, 152–164.

Weaver, R.F., & Hedrick, P.W. (1992) *Genetics* (2nd ed.). Dubuque, IA: W.C. Brown.

Weinberger, D.R. (1995) Schizophrenia: From neuropathology to neurodevelopment. *Lancet*, 346, 55–57.

Weinstein, S., & Sersen, E.A. (1961) Tactual sensitivity as a function of handedness and laterality. *Journal of Comparative and Physiological Psychology*, 54, 665–669.

Wexler, B.E., Giller, E.L., Jr., & Southwick, S. (1991) Cerebral laterality, symptoms and diagnoses in psychotic patients. *Biological Psychiatry*, 29, 103–116.

Wexler, B.E., & Halwes, T. (1983) Increasing the power of dichotic methods: The fused rhymed words test. *Neuropsychologia*, 21, 59–66.

White, K., & Ashton, R. (1976) Handedness assessment inventory. *Neuropsychologia*, 14, 261–264.

White, L.E., Lucas, G., Richards, A., & Purves, D. (1994) Cerebral asymmetry and handedness. *Nature*, 368, 197–198.

Whittington, J.E., & Richards, P.N. (1991) Mathematical ability and the right shift theory of handedness. *Neuropsychologia*, 29, 1075–1082.

Wilding, J. (1989) Developmental dyslexics do not fit in boxes: Evidence from the case studies. *European Journal of Cognitive Psychology*, 1, 105–127.

Williams, W.T., & Lambert, J.M. (1959) Multivariate methods in plant ecology: I. Association analysis in plant communities. *Journal of Ecology*, 47, 83–101.

Williams, W.T., & Lambert, J.M. (1960) Multivariate methods of plant ecology: II. The use of an electronic digital computer for association analysis. *Journal of Ecology*, 48, 689–710.

Williams, W.T., & Lambert J.M. (1961) Multivariate methods in plant ecology: III. Inverse association analysis. *Journal of Ecology*, 49, 717–729.

Willows, D.M., Kruk, R.S., & Corcos, E. (1993) *Visual Processes in Reading and Reading Disabilities*. Hillsdale, NJ: Lawrence Erlbaum Associates Inc.

Wilson, D. (1891) *Left-handedness*. London: Macmillan.

Wilson, J.R., De Fries, J.C., McClearn, G.E., Vandenberg, S.G., Johnson, R.C., & Rashad, M.D. (1975) Cognitive abilities: Use of family data as a control to assess sex and age differences in two ethnic groups. *International Journal of Aging and Human Development*, 6, 261–276.

Wilson, P.T., & Jones, H.E. (1932) Left-handedness in twins. *Genetics*, 17, 560–572.

Wing, L. (1981) Asperger syndrome: A clinical account. *Psychological Medicine*, 11, 115–129.

Wing, L. (1991) The relationship between Asperger's syndrome and Kanner's Autism. In U. Frith (Ed.), *Autism and Asperger Syndrome* (pp 93–121). Cambridge: Cambridge University Press.

Witelson, S.F. (1976) Sex and the single hemisphere: Specialization of the right hemisphere for spatial processing. *Science*, 193, 425–427.

Witelson, S.F. (1980) Neuroanatomical asymmetry in left-handers: A review and implications for functional asymmetry. In J. Herron (Ed.), *Neuropsychology of Left-handedness* (pp 79–113). New York: Academic Press.

Witelson, S.F., & Kigar, D.L. (1988) Asymmetry in brain functions follows asymmetry in anatomical form: Gross, microscopic, postmortem and imaging studies. In F. Boller & J. Grafam (Eds.), *Handbook of Neuropsychology, Vol. I* (pp 111–142). Amsterdam: Elsevier.

Witelson, S.F., & Kigar, D.L. (1992) Sylvian fissure morphology and asymmetry in men and women: Bilateral differences in relation to handedness in men. *Journal of Comparative Neurology*, 323, 326–340.

Witelson, S.F., Kigar, D.L., & Harvey, T. (1999) The exceptional brain of Albert Einstein. *Lancet*, 353, 2149–2153.

Witelson, S.F., & Pallie, W. (1973) Left hemisphere specialization for language in the newborn: Neuroanatomical evidence of asymmetry. *Brain*, 96, 641–646.

Wolff, S., & McGuire, R.J. (1995) Schizoid personality in girls: A follow-up study – what are the links with Asperger's syndrome. *Journal of Child Psychology and Psychiatry*, 36, 793–817.

Wolpert, L. (1991) *The Triumph of the Embryo*. Oxford: Oxford University Press.

Woo, T.L., & Pearson, K. (1927) Dextrality and sinistrality of hand and eye. *Biometrika*, 19, 165–199.

Wood, C.J., & Aggleton, J.P. (1989) Handedness and "fast ball" sports: Do left-handers have an innate advantage? *British Journal of Psychology*, 80, 227–240.

Wood, E.K. (1988) Less sinister statistics from baseball records. *Nature*, 335, 212.

Woodruff, P.W.R., McManus, I.C., & David, A.S. (1995) Meta-analysis of corpus-callosum size in schizophrenia. *Journal of Neurology, Neurosurgery and Psychiatry*, 58, 457–461.

Woolgar, J. (1997) *England's Test Cricketers 1877–1996*. London: Robert Hale.

Wright, I.C., McGuire, P.K., Poline, J.-B., Travere, J.M., Murray, R.M., Frith, C.D., Frackowiak, R.S.J., & Friston, K.J. (1995) A voxel-based method for the statistical analysis of gray and white matter density applied to schizophrenia. *Neuroimage*, 2, 244–252.

Yakovlev, P.I., & Lecours, A.R. (1967) The myelogenetic cycles of regional maturation of the brain. In A. Minkowski (Ed.), *Regional Development of the Brain in Early Life*. Oxford: Blackwell.

Yeo, R.A., & Gangestad, S.W. (1993) Developmental origins of variations in human hand preference. *Genetics*, 89, 281–296.

Yost, H.J. (1998) Left–right development from embryos to brains. *Developmental Genetics*, 23, 159–163.

Yousry, T.A., Schmid, U.D., Alkadhi, H., Schmidt, D., Peraud, A., Buettner, A., & Winkler, P. (1997) Localization of the motor hand area to a knob on the precentral gyrus. *Brain*, 120, 141–157.

Zaidel, E. (1978) Auditory language comprehension in the right hemisphere following cerebral commissurotomy and hemispherectomy: A comparison with child language and aphasia. In A. Caramazzo & E.B. Zurif (Eds.), *Language Acquisition and Language Breakdown* (pp 229–275). Baltimore, MD: Johns Hopkins University Press.

Zangwill, O.L. (1960) *Cerebral Dominance and its Relation to Psychological Function*. Edinburgh: Oliver & Boyd.

Zangwill, O.L. (1967) Speech and the minor hemisphere. *Acta Neurologica et Psychiatrica Belgica*, 67, 1013–1020.

Zatorre, R.J. (1989) Perceptual asymmetry in the dichotic fused words test and cerebral speech lateralization determined by the carotid sodium amytal test. *Neuropsychologia*, 27, 1207–1219.

Zazzo, R. (1960) *Les Jumeaux: Le Couple et la Personne*. Paris: Presses Universitaire de France.

Zilbovicius, M., Boddaert, M., Belin, P., Poline, J.B., Remy, P., Mangin, J.J., Thivard, L., Barthelemy, C., & Samson, Y. (2000) Temporal lobe dysfunction in childhood autism: A PET study. *American Journal of Psychiatry*, 157, 1988–1993.

Zilles, K., Dabringhaus, A., Geyer, S., Amunts, K., Qu, M., Schleicher, A., Gilissen, E., Schlaug, G., & Steinmetz, H. (1996) Structural asymmetries in the human forebrain and the forebrain of nonhuman primates and rats. *Neuroscience and Biobehavioral Reviews*, 20, 593–605.

Author index

Subject index